NEW BEGINNINGS

NEW BEGINNINGS

HOLOCAUST SURVIVORS IN BERGEN-BELSEN AND THE BRITISH ZONE IN GERMANY, 1945–1950

HAGIT LAVSKY

WAYNE STATE UNIVERSITY PRESS   DETROIT

Copyright © 2002 by Wayne State University Press,
Detroit, Michigan 48201. All rights are reserved.
No part of this book may be reproduced without formal permission.
Manufactured in the United States of America.
06 05 04 03 02   5 4 3 2 1

Library of Congress Cataloging-in-Publication Data

Lavsky, Hagit.
New beginnings : Holocaust survivors in Bergen-Belsen and
the British zone in Germany, 1945–1950 / Hagit Lavsky.
p. cm.
"Includes bibliographical references (p.) and index."
ISBN 0-8143-3009-6 (cloth : alk. paper)
1. Jews—Germany—History—1945–   2. Holocaust
survivors—Germany—Social conditions.   3. Holocaust
survivors—Germany—Politics and government.   I. Title.
DS135.G332 L37   2002
305.892'40435'09044—dc21
2001004775

Contents

Preface   9
Acknowledgments   13

Introduction   15
   The Occupation Administration   15
   Economic Conditions and Population Movements   16
   Occupation Policy and the Foundation of
      the Federal Republic   19
   Reparations, Restitution, and Indemnification   23

1. The Jewish Remnant in Germany   27
   Estimates for Jewish Survivors in Germany   27
   Demographic Profile of the Jewish Survivors in Germany   29
   Jewish Population Growth in Germany   32

2. The Liberation of Bergen-Belsen   37
   Bergen-Belsen as a Death Camp   37
   The Aftermath   41

3. The British Zone of Occupation   49
   Population, Economy, and Occupation Policy   49
   The British Policy Regarding the Jews   51
   The Jewish Population   55

4. Jewish Organizational Efforts in Bergen-Belsen   63
   Spontaneous Organization   63
   From Spontaneous Organizational Efforts
      to a National Struggle   70
   The Establishment of a United National Front   75

Contents

5. New Communities Rise from the Ashes   78
   The German Jewish Remnant in the British Zone   78
   Motives for the Reestablishment of German Jewish Communities   82
   Founders of the Jewish Communities   85
   The DP Communities   87
   Summary   90

6. The Jewish World Organizations and Jewish Emissaries   91
   British Jewry   92
   The Palestinian Zionist Role   101
   American Jewish Relief Agencies   106
   Summary   109

7. The Central Committee as an Instrument of Self-Government   110
   Goals and Infrastructure   110
   Economic Control   113
   Health Care   116
   Culture and Education   117
   Chief Rabbinate   117
   The Jewish Police: Self-Defense, Law, and Order   118
   Holocaust Commemoration   120
   The Struggle for Recognition   120

8. The Development of the Communities   124
   Statistical-Demographic Synopsis   124
   Immediate Needs   127
   Looking to the Future: Social and Cultural Roles   128
   The Beginnings of Regional Organizations   130
   Between Zionist Centralization and Independent Organizations   132
   The Fusion of the Work Association with the Central Committee   134
   From Zionist Centralization to German Jewish Separatism   137

Contents

9. **"*Unser Dirat Arai*": Society, Economy, and Culture in the Camps**   141
   - Temporary Dwelling in an Ex-Territory   141
   - Living Conditions   143
   - Occupational and Vocational Training   145
   - Forming Families   148
   - Communication and the Media   153
   - Arts and Leisure   157
   - The Role of Zionism, Tradition, and Politics in Sociocultural Life   161

10. **Looking to the Future: The Educational Program**   167
    - The Children   167
    - Challenge and Response: The Founding of Educational Institutions   168
    - Initiators and Teachers   170
    - Conditions and Constraints of Educational Activity   176
    - Ideology, Organization, and the Politics of Education   180
    - Jewish Education in the Communities   186

11. **Zionist Party Politics**   189
    - The Political Front   189
    - Cooperation and Solidarity with the *Yishuv*   196
    - Aliyah: The Focus of Zionist Activity   197
    - The Zionist Organization   199
    - The Shift from a Zionist to a General Nationalist Agenda   202

12. **End and New Beginnings**   204
    - Emigration and Aliyah   204
    - Closing the Bergen-Belsen DP Camp   210
    - Jews in Germany after Liquidation   212

    Conclusion: The *She'erit Hapletah* and Jewish Nationalism in the Post-Holocaust Era   215

   Notes   225
   Bibliography   277
   Index   295

PREFACE

This book concerns the initial rehabilitation of Jewish Holocaust survivors as reflected in the story of those who drifted to Germany between 1945 and 1950, either temporarily as displaced persons (DPs) in camps, or to settle as the founders of new Jewish communities. We shall explore the various ways in which Jewish survivors were involved, both passively and actively, in Jewish national discourse and struggle. In the history of the Jews in post-Holocaust Germany one may find the infrastructure for post-Holocaust Jewish identity laid, shaped by the interaction between Zionism, the Jewish Diaspora, and the *She'erit Hapletah*.

The contemporary history of the Jews in postwar Germany has engaged much research during the last two decades, and since the fall of the Berlin Wall, we have witnessed growing interest in this subject. The stimulus for current ongoing research originates from two perspectives. One perspective is the growing awareness of the importance of Holocaust survivors in shaping the collective memory of the Shoah. This awareness has produced many studies regarding the survivors as DPs and immigrants, not only in Israel and the U.S., where most of them went through a long process of absorption and rehabilitation, but also in Germany. These studies, many of which are in German, deal with a variety of factors: the policies of the Allies,[1] the activities of welfare agencies and emissaries,[2] the image of DPs as viewed through the eyes of the Germans,[3] the migration and absorption of Holocaust survivors,[4] and history of the Jewish DPs.[5]

Early studies conducted from this perspective were written from an external point of view rather than that of the Holocaust survivors themselves. These studies were conceived within the context of research on postwar policies and under the impact of an ever-growing sense of guilt and intensifying public discourse. The research focused primarily on political aspects and on the survivors' impact on politics and social developments, especially within the U.S., Israel, and Germany. Consequently, the DPs were treated mainly as an object of actions determined by other factors.[6] Recent developments in research have shifted interest toward a history of the survivors as such. This history is written not from an external vantage point, but with a view toward trying to understand the internal experience of the subjects.

Still, most of these studies hardly address the situation of the DPs outside the American zone in occupied Germany, despite acknowledging their importance.[7] Also, there is a dearth of case studies, despite their being essential for the understanding of internal sociocultural developments.

The other perspective concerns the history of the Jews who settled in Germany. As Sander L. Gilman states in his book *Jews in Today's German Culture*: "To be a Jew and to be a German after the *Shoah* was a heightened contradiction, but it was a lived, an experienced, contradiction. There were and are Jews in Germany and, indeed, there is an ever growing and expanding Jewish community."[8]

This indeed is a fact that until recently was neglected, if not denied, especially among scholars in Israel. The Zionist ban of 1950 on those Jews who decided to settle down in Germany instead of emigrating—even if not to Israel—echoed a general Jewish feeling that exists to this day. Moreover, there is almost a consensus among Jewish leaders that the Jews of postwar Germany have no common basis as a community. The term "German Jewry" has come to mean, exclusively, the Jews of Germany who escaped Hitler and continued to develop their German culture in other countries.

During the 1980s this attitude began to change. Indeed, a Jewish community had existed in Germany ever since 1945, but only recently has its expansion and growing presence in German culture, as well as in Jewish culture, drawn the attention of scholars to the phenomenon. This awareness has increased since the fall of the Berlin Wall and the encounter between writers and scholars from east and west. It seems that the unification gave rise to an evolving sense that there is a "new Germany" that is open and pluralistic, yet confident in its German culture. A fascination with what seems to be a burst of new Jewish vitality and culture has triggered efforts by German scholars to define anew a Jewish identity that fits into the general framework of German culture.

The widening interest in the Jewish presence in Germany has found expression by the growing number of Jewish periodicals, such as *Menora, Tribüne, Babylon, Nudnik, Semit-Times, Tachles*, and a vast amount of scholarly writing published in German journals. A whole range of scholarly institutions, museums, and publishing houses in Germany is nowadays dedicated to exploring the Jewish presence in Germany.

Already in 1986, a pioneering collection of articles was published by Micha Brumlik.[9] It contained, among other contributions, an attempt, by Monika Richarz, to sketch the history of Jews in both Germanys.[10] But it was Sander Gilman's abovementioned book that opened a new discourse in the English-speaking world.[11]

Focusing on the development of new Jewish life in Germany yielded mainly sociological and cultural studies concerned with the present situation. Some of them, as Gilman's, focus mainly on the issue of Jewish identity. Others try to explore the role and function of the Jewish presence in German society, politics, and culture as a whole.[12] Most are anchored in the social sciences rather than in historical analysis. These studies deal mainly with such issues as the "Jewish question" in Germany and Jewish-German or Israeli-German relations.[13] There are also local histories of various Jewish communities, almost all of which are published in German.[14]

In addition, there are numerous sociological studies, nearly all of which are based on interviews with first and second generation Jews.[15] A few of these studies provide some historical perspectives, notably those by Y. Michal Bodemann, Frank Stern, and Michael Brenner. Brenner has also produced an integrative history of the Jews in Germany, which discusses the situation of the DPs.[16] However, he treats the issues involved in a general manner.

The present study is meant to complement the available research in a few respects. First, it seeks to integrate the history of Holocaust survivors in Germany, DPs and German Jews alike. Second, it aims to illuminate their story as they experienced it and as they responded to objective reality. Third, this book concentrates on the case study of the British zone of occupied Germany, which has until now been neglected.

There are three reasons for this focus on the British Zone of Occupation in Germany. First, in that zone the occupying power was identical with the Mandatory Government in Palestine, the chief target of the Zionist struggle; second, Bergen-Belsen, the center of the British zone, was the largest camp in Germany; and third, the community organization in the British zone laid the basis for the overall organization of the Jews in Germany.

Preface

This study deals with the development of Jewish life in Germany in a comprehensive manner, examining all relevant components and factors, both separately and in combination: the outcome of the war; the policies of the Allies; economic, social, cultural, and political developments in West Germany; the involvement of world Jewish organizations and their policies concerning the survivors in general and those in Germany in particular; Zionist and Israeli policies and activities in regard to and on behalf of German Jewry; and the social-organizational structure developed by Jewish DPs. Political, social, cultural, and economic aspects of German-Jewish life are viewed as part of a multifaceted complex in which many factors come into play and have an impact on each other in the broad context of Germany, the Jewish world, Palestine-Israel, and the international arena.

Nevertheless, this is essentially a case study, limited to the organization and shaping of social-political life among the Jews in the British zone. A more general study would not have made it possible to penetrate into the daily life and varied perspectives of the people involved. As an individual case study, however, it bears its own characteristics. In many respects this study does not represent the whole picture. It is nevertheless my contention that the developments explored throughout this case study exemplify the basic situation of Holocaust survivors in occupied Germany. The view underlying this study is that the way in which the survivors responded to the situation in the British zone—despite all its special characteristics—can be regarded as typical for survivor's response to the post-Holocaust situation in general.

Acknowledgments

This study has been conducted under the auspices of the Samuel L. and Perry Haber Chair for Post-Holocaust Studies in the Avraham Harman Institute of Contemporary Jewry, The Hebrew University of Jerusalem. During the last decade I was fortunate to receive invaluable financial assistance from many institutions. St. Antony's College, Oxford, enabled me to use libraries and archives in England in 1991 as a Research Fellow. Research in Germany was made possible through grants of the Deutsche Akademische Austausch Dienst (DAAD) and the Ministry of Culture and Science of Lower Saxony. I am grateful to The Hebrew University and the Harman Institute of Contemporary Jewry for constant material assistance.

My research was conducted in many archives and libraries, and I wish to thank all the directors, librarians, and archivists of the following institutions for assistance and cooperation: the National and University Library, Jerusalem; the Yad Vashem archives and library, Jerusalem; the Central Zionist Archives, Jerusalem; the Central Archives for Jewish History, Jerusalem; Givat Joint Archives, Jerusalem; the Oral History Division at the Avraham Harman Institute of Contemporary Jewry, the Hebrew University of Jerusalem; the Wiener Library, Tel Aviv; the Bodleian Library, Oxford; the library of St. Antony's College, Oxford; Oxford Centre for Hebrew and Jewish Studies, Yarnton; the British Library, London; the Wiener Library, London; the Board of Deputies, London; the World Jewish Congress, London; the Hartley Library, University of Southampton; German Federal Archives Koblenz and Potsdam; the Zentralarchiv zur Erforschung der Geschichte der Juden in Deutschland, Heidelberg; Northrhine-Westfalia State-archives in Düsseldorf and in Münster; Lower Saxony State Archives, Hanover; Hamburg State Archives; the Jewish Community Archives, Hanover; the municipal archives of Bonn, Göttingen,

Acknowledgments

and Hanover; and the Niedersächsische Landeszentrale für politische Bildung, Hanover.

Many people have helped me in many ways during the research. My senior teachers and colleagues at the Harman Institute of Contemporary Jewry, The Hebrew University, Professor Yisrael Gutman and Prof. Jehuda Bauer, actually opened for me the field of Holocaust and Post-Holocaust Studies and were the first to encourage me to embark on the study of the British Zone. Ms. Perry Haber, the founder of the chair under which my research has been conducted, has always showed a great interest in my research. I would like to thank all those who gave oral testimonies in interviews or written ones in letters: Ms. Eugenie Brecher, Rabbi Prof. Mordechai Breuer, Ms. Sarah Eckstein-Grebenau, Mr. Ze'ev and Ms. Rachel Fishler, Mr. Helmut Fürst, Rabbi Avraham Greenbaum, Mr. Arieh Handler, Rabbi Leslie Hardman, Mr. Arieh and Ms. Sonia Havkin, Mr. Asher Leo Kempe, Mr. Michael Klodovsky, Mr. Yitzhak Kerbel, Ms. Hanna Landau, Mr. Shlomo and Ms. Paula Leshman, Rabbi Isaac Levy, Mr. Henry Lunzer, Mr. Shalom Maagan-Markovitz, Mr. Shmuel and Ms. Sarah Szmuelewicz, Prof. Jacob and Ms. Bertha Weingreen, Ms. Reuma Weizmann (Schwarz), and the late Mr. Norbert Wollheim.

Ms. Antje Naujoks, my research assistant and partner assisted me in many ways. Ms. Hannah Koevary conducted many of the interviews. Prof. Herbert Obenaus of Hanover University has been a partner in research of the Jews in Lower Saxony in the post-Holocaust period. Dr. Sybille Obenaus opened many windows to various aspects of Jewish life in Germany. Ms. Barbara Suchy of Düsseldorf, Dr. Hermann Simon of Berlin, and Dr. Michael Fürst of Hanover helped in many ways. My colleagues at the Institute of Contemporary Jewry, the publisher's readers for the manuscript, and Mr. Menachem Rosensaft in particular, gave many wise suggestions which helped me to improve the first draft.

I would like to thank Ms. Gila Brand and Dr. Moshe Goodman for editing and polishing my English writing. I would also like to thank the people at Wayne State University Press: the director, Mr. Arthur Evans; the project editor, Ms. Adela Garcia, who accompanied me with friendly efficiency through the process of publication; Mr. Jonathan Lawrence, copyeditor; and all those who worked with them to create a book out of a draft.

Last but not least—I wish to thank my husband and companion Natan, without whose constant encouragement and wise advice none of this would have happened.

Introduction

The Occupation Administration

In June 1945, following the end of the war in Europe on May 8, 1945, the Allies established the Allied Control Commission (ACC), which assumed control over Germany and divided it into four zones.[1] Berlin, taken by the Russian forces, became the seat of the ACC and was also divided among the four Allies. Assuming that a peace conference would follow soon after the end of the war in the Pacific, the Allies met in Potsdam from July 17 to August 2. The arrangements decided upon in Potsdam as temporary became permanent, however, due to rivalries that eventually led to the cold war.

The parties at the Potsdam conference agreed that all the areas captured by Hitler were to be returned to their former rulers. The provinces east of Oder-Neisse were returned to Poland, and northern Prussia would go back to the Soviet Union. The area defined as Occupied Germany was reduced by 25 percent, to 352,000 square kilometers, with a population prior to the expulsion of the Germans from the East of 60 million. This then was divided between the four powers, with northwest Germany placed under the British control. It included the future federal states of Schleswig-Holstein, Hamburg, Lower Saxony, and North Rhine–Westphalia, including the Ruhr region. This area was 97,000 square kilometers, with a population of 22.3 million. The American Zone in the south and the Soviet Zone in the east were 107,000 square kilometers each, with populations of only 14.3 million and 17.3 million, respectively. The French received a small area of 42,000 square kilometers with a population of 6 million including the Saar region on the southwest border.

Following the conference, the military coordinating body (Supreme Headquarters, Allied Expeditionary Force) was disbanded. The

Introduction

Allies established the Foreign Secretaries Council to coordinate policy in the various zones, and the Allied Control Council for Germany (CCG) as the supreme authority of the Allied government in Germany. The CCG was composed of four members representing the four powers, and it combined the duties of commanders in chief and military governors. The bulk of the work turned out, however, to be done at the next level below, that of the Coordination Committee. It was composed of the four deputy military governors, initially General Sir Brian Robertson, General Clay, General Sokolovsky, and General Költz. Below the Coordination Committee, the CCG was split into twelve directorates. Each of the four powers was broken down into divisions corresponding to the directorates.

For pragmatic reasons, the occupying powers tried at the outset to adjust themselves to the German administrative infrastructure. Therefore, many functions were quickly transmitted to local authorities, with supervision being retained by the occupying powers. This paved the way to the creation of the *Länder* (the regional states that would become the federal states), first in the Soviet Zone in July 1945 and then in the British Zone by the end of 1946. The Russians were also the first, in June 1945, to revive political parties, following the decision at Potsdam to encourage democratization. The Western Allies followed suit in August, but the zonal divisions complicated the process.

Economic Conditions and Population Movements

The destruction of Germany was almost total. Most of the large cities and industrial centers were completely ruined. The system of roads and railways system had collapsed, and hundred of thousands of civilians were without a roof above their head. Starvation, lack of basic necessities, and chaos reigned supreme. With German economy unable to provide even for minimal needs, the burden fell upon the occupying authorities, who found it difficult to cope with. The minimum nutrition ratio per capita set by the United Nations as sufficient for maintaining health and the ability to work was 2,500 calories per day. The authorities could allocate only 1,550 calories, and in practice even this could not be maintained.

People abroad, alarmed by what was occurring in Germany, started to send packages, and the package-sending enterprise developed into an organized system (Hoover packages). The lack of basic necessities combined with the availability of goods from abroad

Introduction

(from the United Nations Relief and Rehabilitation Administration [UNRRA] and military supplies to the soldiers) and agricultural products from German villages to create a huge black market based on barter. Cigarettes replaced money, and looting crops from villages became a common practice. Demoralization reigned, and people would not go to work, since barter and black-marketing provided much more than the limited rations allocated for working people.[2]

A major problem confronting the occupying authorities was the enormous postwar migration movement, which can be divided into three categories. The first category consisted of the 8 million forced laborers and prisoners of various nationalities who were liberated in Germany and Austria, 6 million of them in Germany alone. The first task was to facilitate their immediate repatriation to their home countries. UNRRA, founded in 1943 in anticipation of the liberation of Europe and the problem of refugees and DPs, was meant to give economic and social aid to countries that were under Nazi occupation and to help with repatriating the DPs. A distinction was introduced between "refugees" and "displaced persons." The former were defined as persons fleeing from their homelands without being able to return, and for their care an international organization, the Inter-Governmental Committee on Refugees (IGCR), had been founded before the war (following the Evian conference in 1938) to assist in migration and resettlement. The latter were defined as those uprooted by the war. They were considered the main postwar problem, encompassing the millions who had been deported by the Nazis to forced labor camps and concentration camps or who had fled their bombed hometowns. They were expected to return to their homelands, and thus the task of repatriation was the main task anticipated by UNRRA.

UNRRA began its work under the military administration, and millions of DPs were indeed repatriated within a few months, despite chaotic conditions and ruined roads and railroads. However, what was not expected was the fact that many of those defined as DPs refused to return to their homelands. With the end of the main repatriation movement in the summer of 1945, 2 million DPs still remained in the Western Zones of Occupation. These were Poles, Lithuanians, Russians, and Yugoslavs who were either afraid of being accused of collaboration with the Nazis or who preferred to escape the communist regimes or the economic situation in their home countries. By the beginning of December 1945, they numbered approximately 900,000 in western Germany.[3] This number was augmented by thousands of

Introduction

refugees fleeing from communist Eastern Europe, including many Jews driven away by anti-Semitic violence in Poland. Thus, by April 1947, after the eastern borders were closed by the Americans, the DP population still numbered about 650,000, including many Jews.[4]

In October 1945 UNRRA resumed the task of taking care of the DPs living in camps and assembly centers under the various military administrations. However, a little over a year later, in 1947, the UN recognized that the remaining DPs were in fact potential refugees, and the aim of repatriation or providing temporary care gave way to the mission of migration and resettlement. The International Refugee Organization (IRO) was then founded, replacing both UNRRA and IGCR.

A second category of the uprooted population was that of Germans who had fled their bombed homes. After the end of the war upon their return, they had to be provided with alternate housing and to be reunited with their families, which caused many problems for the occupying authorities. A calculation in October 1946 indicated that until then 1.9 million persons moved from the Soviet Zone to the west, and 557,000 moved in the opposite direction.

The third category was of Germans escaping the Red Army or deported from Eastern Europe immediately after the war. By the end of the war they numbered some 1.5 million in the American Zone. The Potsdam conference authorized the liberated eastern countries—Poland, Czechoslovakia, Hungary, Romania, and Yugoslavia—to expel the 9 to 10 million Germans back to Germany, and they arrived gradually within a few months.

The huge population movement created a threefold problem for the occupying powers. The first problem was the task of directing the movement, providing permanent housing, and thus ending the movement. The second problem was maintaining law and order while caring for the different populations of different status. With no clear future, the DP population threatened the public safety. The hungry and devastated German population, on the other hand, envied the DP population, which, cared for by UNRRA and Jewish welfare agencies, had all their needs provided for without having to work. Apart from the economic burden caused by the temporary population, this threatened morale and the rule of law. The third problem was the increase of the German population by 9 million people. In 1950, after completing the emigration or the resettlement of all the DPs and refugees, the British Zone was augmented by 4,940,000, while the American and French Zones together were increased by 4,100,000 inhabitants.[5]

Occupation Policy and the Foundation of the Federal Republic

Most scholars agree that despite the destruction of the German economy, the production potential of both agriculture and industry was not destroyed by the war. As for agriculture, even prior to the war the German economy depended on importing 20 percent of consumer goods, but on the other hand, the highly developed agricultural region in East Prussia served German needs adequately. Indeed, after the war Germany was denied the agricultural resources east of the Oder-Neisse Line, but in comparison with urban areas, the main agricultural regions in Germany were hardly touched by the bombings. As for industry, in the urban areas it was mainly buildings and roads that were destroyed. The industrial infrastructure was only partially damaged—10 percent of the metal industry, 10 to 15 percent of the chemical industry, and about 20 percent of the textile industry. Reconstruction of buildings and roads could have readily set industrial production in motion.

The Potsdam conference set the guidelines for the occupation: de-Nazification, demilitarization, democratization, deindustrialization, and decartelization (the Five D's). The last two principles followed the plan of Henry Morgenthau, Jr., the American finance minister in the former Roosevelt administration. Fraternization with Germans was also prohibited, and Nazi war criminals were to be brought before an international court of justice. Furthermore, reparations in kind were to be levied by the occupying powers. As the main agricultural potential was in the eastern part of Germany, while the main industrial areas were concentrated in the west (the Ruhr and Saar Valleys), the issues of coordinated policy and free exchange of goods between the four zones was essential. Therefore it was decided at the conference to treat Germany as one economic unit, with a coordination mechanism between the four zones.

Morgenthau's economic directives aimed at weakening the German industrial power and encouraging agricultural production. They included the prohibition of any war industry, the dismantling of plants with potential war production, and the supervision of the entire steel and chemical industry, foreign trade, and scientific research. Certain industrial branches were to be prohibited altogether, including benzene, synthetic rubber, and radioactive materials.

In March 1946 the Allies ruled that industrial production was to be limited to 50 percent of the 1938 level of production. The aim of establishing quotas was to eliminate the potential for war materials and to increase the productivity of agriculture to the degree that it would completely provide for domestic consumption. This would enable the industrial surplus to be used to pay the reparations that were being levied on Germany. At the same time, it was meant to dissolve cartels and trusts, especially in heavy industry, where most of the concerns had been supporters of Hitler.

However, Morgenthau's plan for a "Strong Europe—Weak Germany" prevented Germany's economic revival. There was a contradiction in the belief that agricultural production was an alternative to industrial production, since it was impossible to limit industry and at the same time to encourage agricultural production based on modern machinery. True, many of the big coal and steel plants, such as the Krupp plant, were not closed down but only expropriated. Nevertheless, during the process of deindustrialization the German economy lost 685 plants, valued at some $500 to $600 million. The value of industries transferred to the Allies as reparations is estimated at $1 billion. Hence, agricultural growth was limited and there was no industrial surplus to export in exchange for agricultural imports. Moreover, it soon became clear that rehabilitation of Europe was impossible without the German economy, with the Saar and Ruhr regions being sources of iron and coal for all of Europe. The need to reconsider the economic policy dictated by the Morgenthau plan was, however, only gradually accepted, since changing this plan would have meant forgoing the de-Nazification policy and the political weakening of Germany.

In May 1946 the Americans stopped dismantling heavy industry in their zone, but this was not enough, as the industrial focus was in the British Zone. Considering the extreme importance of the Ruhr industry, the British Control Commission authorities had the major responsibility. True, the British from the outset had their reservations toward the Morgenthau plan, and they did not consider the de-Nazification policy practical. They did, however, believe that Germany's military capacity should be destroyed, and they wished to strengthen cooperation between the Allies, including Soviet-Socialist Russia. Accordingly, for the sake of the new social order, the British Labor government conducted a nationalization scheme in order to put German industry under international supervision.

But the British would eventually have to relent, due to their economic dependence on the United States on the one hand and the growing tension between the United States and the USSR on the other. The economic situation in the British Zone was disastrous. England had to pay from its domestic budget some 70 percent of the living expenses in the British Zone, and the British government was thus compelled to introduce a restrictive domestic economic policy. This situation made England economically dependent on American support to maintain its zone. The Americans could sustain that burden only by a quick economic rehabilitation of Germany, which in their eyes could not be achieved by implementing the Morgenthau plan in the heart of German industry—the Ruhr region in the British Zone.

Thus, Britain relented and America declared in March 1947 what was to become known as the "Truman Doctrine" for the economic revival of Germany. It would be soon followed by the plan of Secretary of State George Marshall—the European Recovery Program—for a comprehensive scheme for Europe, including Germany. The American and British Zones united economically in "Bizonia" (a political union followed in the summer) and introduced a far-reaching lifting of the quotas policy. Despite Russian objections, the Marshall Plan was established by the Western Allies in March 1948. Eastern Europe and East Germany were excluded. Monetary reform—introducing the new German Mark—followed suit. At the same time, an agreement was signed between "The Six"—the Western Allies and the Benelux countries—on joint supervision of the Ruhr industries, to which the new German Federal Republic would be co-opted in November 1949. In May 1950, following an agreement with France regarding the Saar region, French foreign minister Robert Schumann declared the new common European supervision of the German coal and steel industries, known as the "Schumann Plan."

By April 1951 West Germany had received from the Marshall Plan matching investment funds of $2 billion. Together with monetary reform, the Marshall Plan quickly increased German domestic production. But due to population growth, the net per capita income growth—"the economic miracle"—began only in the early part of the 1950s. The main obstacle to German economic recovery is difficult to ascertain or define. Was it really due to occupation alone? And what was the breakthrough? Was it the change of policy, and if so, what was

Introduction

the decisive step? There is also disagreement regarding the causal connection between the economic issues and the political ties of the Allies. Did the former bring about the hostility, or vice versa? There is, however, no disagreement concerning the fact that the economic policy of the Western Allies was accompanied by Britain's growing dependence on the United States. This developed hand in hand with suspicion and enmity between East and West, which brought about the cold war and the formation of two Germanys.[6]

The foundation of Bizonia as an economic entity in the beginning of 1947, followed by its political unification in the following summer, was a decisive step toward independence. Frankfurt became the center of Bizonia, and its Executive Council included the heads of the states in the two zones and was placed under an Economic Council that represented the various states. With the transformation into a political unit, a new body—the Council of States—was founded to take part in economic legislation.

The decision of the London conference of March 1948 to implement the Marshall Plan on western Germany and to de facto annex the Saar region to France paved the way for the French Zone to join Bizonia, which became Trizonia. The Western Zones thus became an economic entity—the infrastructure for the state to come.

The last step was the Soviet blockade on Berlin following the monetary reform, which lasted from June 1948 until May 1949. The Soviet intention was to prevent the establishment of the Federal Republic by holding hostage Berlin, with its 2 million citizens. However, the United States succeeded in supplying Berlin through the airlift, and after eleven months the Russians once more permitted supplies to reach Berlin by road. But the blockade had convinced the Western Allies and the West German politicians that a united Germany was not to be established. The cold war was now a fact. Germany was divided and became the front line between the rival powers.

In September 1948 the West German leaders convened in Bonn in a constitutional assembly. In April 1949 Trizonia was declared a political entity, and the Allies transferred their powers to the assembly in Bonn. The German constitution was signed on May 8, 1949, and on May 23, following the end of the blockade, the Federal Republic of Germany (Bundesrepublik Deutschland), with Bonn as its capital, was declared.

In August 1949 the Christian Democrats, led by Konrad Adenauer, won the first federal elections. Theodore Heuss was elected

Introduction

president, and Adenauer became chancellor. Already in March 1949 the Soviets had declared the German Democratic Republic (Deutsche Demokratische Republik), but only in October 1949 was the state actually established, with East Berlin as its capital.

The Western Allies declared an end to the war status in Germany, lifted many sanctions (for example, the ban on building commercial ships), and replaced the military governors with high commissioners. The Federal Republic was invited to join international institutions and to become a member of the European Council. Nevertheless, the Allied military forces remained stationed in Germany, and the Allies retained the right of supervision on a broad range of issues, including foreign policy, reparations, restitution, and the DPs.

The last stage of complete independence was achieved in May 1952 with the signing of the agreement between the Western Allies and the Federal Republic to end the occupation of West Germany, with the exception of Berlin. The high commissioners also relinquished their authority, and the Federal Republic attained complete sovereignty. Immediately thereafter the Federal Republic joined the North Atlantic Treaty Organization.[7]

Reparations, Restitution, and Indemnification

A major concern of the Allies was the issue of reparations, which consisted of four distinct components[8]:

1. War reparations: payment levied on the defeated party—Germany—to be paid to the victorious party—the Allies—for losses sustained during the war. This issue was decided upon in Potsdam, but it was carried out by the Western Allies only partially in order to prevent the total collapse of the German economy.
2. Restitution of properties to their former legitimate and identified owners or heirs. As long as individuals were involved, this category presented no legal problem, but rather a practical problem, namely, of identification. This was particularly difficult regarding financial assets (bank deposits, shares, etc.), confiscation, and the return of properties to their legal owners. The occupation powers enforced restitution by law, as part of the de-Nazification policy. However, when property in question was communal property, questions arose concerning who were the legitimate heirs: the newly founded Jewish communities in Germany? Furthermore, what if

the prewar communities were not reestablished, as was often the case?
3. Indemnification for irretrievable property to individuals or communities.
4. Compensations for damages other than property, caused by the war and the Nazi regime.

The last two categories were the focus of discussions between the Allies. These were also the primary issues for the Jewish Agency (JA—the foremost institution of the World Zionist Organization and the Jewish community in Palestine) and the international Jewish organizations, such as the World Jewish Congress (WJC) and the American Jewish Joint Distribution Committee (JDC). Their relevance to the occupation policy in Germany was related partially to the DP problem and partially to the Jews who settled in Germany.

The concept that the Jewish people, as a nation among the nations, have the right to demand collective reparations had already been claimed by the Zionist leaders during the war. It became a main issue for the JA's postwar policy and was linked closely with its claim for an independent state and Jewish sovereignty in Palestine. In September 1945, Chaim Weizmann, president of the World Zionist Organization, presented the Jewish claims to the Allies:

1. That Jewish property in the occupied and neutral countries that has no surviving legitimate owners or heirs should be placed at the disposal of the national Jewish representatives to be used for the rehabilitation of the surviving victims. Part of these funds should be channeled to Palestine via the Jewish Agency to facilitate the resettlement of the survivors.
2. To include the Jewish people among the nations entitled to receive war reparations, for the development of the Jewish commonwealth in Palestine.
3. That funds thus placed at the disposal of the JA will be used to finance the settlement of 100,000 Jewish DPs in Palestine.

Britain refused to recognize the DPs as refugees eligible for resettlement and sought to solve the DP problem through UNRRA, whose mandate was repatriation. Facing the growing number of Jewish refugees and DPs, and the Jewish policy to connect this issue with the demand for sovereignty in Palestine, the British insisted on an

Introduction

exclusive repatriation policy. The Americans, on the other hand, encouraged a policy of resettlement. When the Allies convened in Paris in November–December 1945, the Jewish demands were only partially recognized. The conference also addressed the issue of compensation to victims of the Nazi persecution and decided to establish an international compensation fund for the rehabilitation of victims who were unable to return to their homelands. This definition included the refugees from Germany and Austria, either abroad or temporarily in Germany, aiming at emigration, and refugees from the Nazi-occupied countries who were unable to return. Most of the victims included in that ruling were Jews. Thus, although the Jewish people were not recognized as a nationality, the Allies practically recognized their responsibility to help the rehabilitation of the Jews.

In June 1946, the Five Powers Conference on Reparations for Non-Repatriable Victims of Nazism, representing the three Western allies, Czechoslovakia, and Yugoslavia, signed the agreement regarding the fund. They agreed to finance this fund through the gold found in Germany, $25 million raised from German property in neutral countries, and $25 million from heirless Jewish property. The project was not aimed at individual compensation but rather at welfare and rehabilitation for the general good. Since Jews constituted 95 percent of the potential benefactors, the Five Powers recognized the JDC and the JA as the organizations expected to submit rehabilitation projects to the fund. The JA and the JDC signed an agreement that permitted them to submit their projects jointly and to make the settlement of 100,000 DPs in Palestine a first priority. The projects were submitted by September 1946, but several years passed before they were put into effect. In the meantime, in 1947, the IRO replaced the UNRRA. Only after the Palestine issue was solved did the IRO, with the financing from the fund, help to transfer Jewish DPs and refugees to the newly established State of Israel (1948). The road toward a comprehensive agreement on compensation to the Jewish people was long, and the issue could be solved only a few years later, in 1953, between the new sovereign states, Israel and the Federal Republic of Germany.

As early as January 1943, the Allies had declared that any transfer of property by the Nazis and their Axis partners would be considered illegitimate, and that under the occupation the Allies would enforce legislation regarding restitution. Shortly after the establishment of the occupation administration, the Allies announced that whoever held property (land, buildings, and businesses) formerly owned by Jews or

Introduction

other victims of the Nazis should immediately report to the military government. The initial concept of declaring one law of restitution for all the zones of occupation was, however, not realized due to the growing discord between East and West.

The Americans took the lead in legislating restitution. In November 1947 they issued Regulation no. 59. This law addressed claims of two types: private property claimed by its original owners or heirs, and property that was not claimed by individuals, either because the owners or their heirs had not survived or could not validate their claims, or because the property in question had been communal. Concerning this second category, the law demanded the establishment of a special organization to replace the undefined or absentee successors, to whom the property would be transferred for the welfare and rehabilitation of the victims and the communities. This organization, the Jewish Restitution Successor Organization (JRSO), was founded in June 1948 and represented thirteen Jewish organizations, including the Jewish DPs and the representatives of the Jewish communities in the American Zone. JRSO was eligible for property claimed in the American Zone and Berlin. It was agreed, however, that allocation of the assets would not be confined to the American Zone exclusively, but, in accordance with emergency needs, either in Europe or in Israel (founded shortly before, in May 1948).

The French followed suit, but the British came forward with their legislation only in May 1949, and the Jewish successor organization for the British Zone—Jewish Trust Corporation—was founded even later, in 1950. The British legislation was delayed due to two policy principles: first, their insistence on leaving the main burden for the German government, and second, their refusal to distinguish between Jewish and non-Jewish victims. Be that as it may, in practice, during the period examined in this book, the legislation regarding restitution of heirless or communal property had marginal consequences for the communities and the German Jews in the American Zone, and none at all for the British Zone.[9]

As for the DPs, the matter of restitution did not apply to them. Moreover, under the *Wiedergutmachung* agreement of 1953 on indemnification, the Eastern European victims could not claim personal compensations. However, after the foundation of the *Länder* (federal states), even before the foundation of the Federal Republic, there was a beginning of legislation for compensation in the *Länder* level that affected some of the DPs.[10]

1

THE JEWISH REMNANT IN GERMANY

Estimates for Jewish Survivors in Germany

Among the 2 to 3 million survivors of the concentration camps in Germany and Austria, the Allies found a small number of Jews who had been transferred from camps in Poland just before the Nazis' final defeat. Not many survived the difficult trek that took place in the dead of winter, by foot or in vehicles not fit for human conveyance. But not for a moment did the Nazis suspend their horrific plans for the Jews of Europe. Even as the Red Army closed in on them, they did whatever they could to keep the destruction process going—with or without gas chambers.[1]

Only a rough estimate is possible regarding how many Jews were left on German soil when the Nazi death machine ground to a halt. Chaos reigned as masses of people took to the roads in the days leading up to the Nazis' final surrender on May 8, 1945, and thousands continued to die from starvation and disease even after the camps were liberated. Furthermore, when registration by the occupation authorities finally began, Jews were advised not to identify themselves as Jewish. Many survivors were understandably reluctant to reveal their Jewishness at this time, and they appeared in the listing by nationality only (a practice especially prevalent in the British Zone, as we shall see). It should also be remembered that the estimates cited on the following pages were reached shortly after the surrender or some time later, and may not be complete.

The earliest figures for the number of Jews on the European continent, and in Germany in particular, were calculated in June 1945, that is, four to six weeks after liberation. There were said to be 100,000 Jews in the American, British, and French Zones in Germany and Austria, and 80,000–90,000 in Germany alone. These estimates apply to camp survivors and German or Austrian Jews who survived in hiding, but not to areas conquered by the Russians.[2] Various researchers have offered assessments regarding the survivor population in Germany at the actual time of liberation, attempting to distinguish between those who came out of the concentration camps alive and those who managed to evade deportation altogether.

Concentration Camp Survivors

Estimates for the number of Jewish camp survivors in Germany and Austria range from 60,000 to 80,000, but the true figure was probably higher, as some of the estimates apply to the second half of 1945, after thousands more had died or been repatriated.[3] In his book on refugees in the post–World War II period, Jacques Vernant writes that out of a total of 90,000 DPs in Europe, 68,000 were in Germany, 12,000 in Austria, and 10,000 in Italy. In other words, only 13 percent of the survivors were found in Austria. Again, this estimate does not relate to liberation day but to the latter half of 1945. An entirely different set of figures is offered by Thomas Albrich, who studied the surviving remnant in Austria. On the basis of partial data from Austrian concentration camp lists, he places the number of Jewish survivors somewhere between 20,000 and 30,000 out of a total of 1.65 million DPs of different nationalities found in Austria on the day of liberation.[4]

    The discrepancy between Albrich and Vernant might be explained by the fact that in Austria in particular, the survivors dispersed extremely quickly. Immediately after the liberation, even before the war was officially over, refugees began fleeing in all directions. Albrich says that by the beginning of August 1945 there were no more than 7,000 Jewish survivors left in Austria.[5] Vernant's estimate is midway between Albrich's figure for the day of liberation and his figure for early August. If Albrich's average of 25,000 Jews in Austria on liberation day is subtracted from the maximum total of 80,000 for Germany and Austria, that leaves us with 55,000 Jewish survivors in Germany alone. These figures probably account for the thousands of Jews who left the country right away, but not necessarily those who died in the early weeks after liberation—all of which means that any such assessment must be treated with caution.[6]

Remnants of the German Jewish Community

The number of German Jewish survivors was very small. According to records from September 1944 of the Reichsvereinigung der Juden in Deutschland (National Association of the Jews in Germany, set up by the Nazi regime), a group of 15,000 Jews had not been expelled from the country because they were *Privilegierte* (privileged)—either "half-Jews" or married to Christians. Another 3,000 to 5,000 Jews had gone into hiding, which brings the number of Jews who survived outside the camps to 18,000 to 20,000.[7] Together with the 55,000 camp survivors, the total number of Jews in Germany after the war was 73,000 to 75,000.

But there were also German Jews who had been interned in camps outside Germany who returned there immediately upon liberation. About 5,000 Jews survived Theresienstadt. Some of them were taken to a special transit camp at Deggendorf, and others went back to their hometowns. Approximately 4,000 survivors from other camps and ghettos made their way home to Germany. All told, about 9,000 German Jews were liberated from camps in other countries and came back to Germany. Adding this number to those who were not deported to concentration camps brings us to 27,000–29,000, which, together with the 55,000 camp inmates liberated in Germany, comes to a grand total of 83,000 Jewish survivors.[8]

Demographic Profile of the Jewish Survivors in Germany

German Jews

The great majority of German Jews who survived were half-Jewish or converts to Christianity. Nearly one-quarter of the Jewish survivors—approximately 7,400 persons—were from Berlin, so statistics for this community are a useful indicator in this regard. The following calculations take into account a slightly higher figure—7,800—because this includes some 300 to 500 Berliners who "returned to faith"—that is, Jewish converts who reverted to Christianity during the Nazi era but returned to Judaism after the war.[9]

The largest group was composed of Jewish women married to "Aryan" men—the most protected category of Jews under the Nazi regime. Most of the children of such marriages were baptized in infancy, and the women did not usually rejoin the Jewish community after the war. There were 2,183 such women in Berlin, accounting for 28 percent of the survivors. The second group consisted of Jewish men married to "Aryan" women—*Privilegierte Mischehen* (privileged mixed marriages)—persecuted only toward the end of the Nazi regime. They numbered 1,964, or 25 percent of the survivors. The *Nichtprivilegierte Sternträger* (non-privileged Yellow Star bearers) were Jews with non-Jewish spouses who had no children, or whose children were grown up. Most of the Theresienstadt survivors belonged to this group. There were 1,791 Jews in this category, accounting for 23 percent of the survivors.

Aside from these intermarried couples, who made up 76 percent of the survivors, there were 1,416 Berlin Jews (18 percent) who hid during the war (*Untergrundler*), either with the help of non-Jewish relatives and friends or by using false papers. Only 62 members of the former Berlin community (less than 1 percent) survived the camps, and then there were 300 to 500 Jews who "returned to faith" (5 percent). More than 80 percent of the survivors were thus intermarried or Christians.

The age distribution of these survivors reflects the aging of the community, which was the pattern even before the Nazis came to power.[10] The trend became even more pronounced over time because the first to flee Germany were young people, and the children—the most vulnerable group—were virtually wiped out by the Nazis. Again, the Berlin community can serve as an example.

The largest group of Berlin survivors was made up of persons forty-five years of age and older. There were 4,473 people in this age group (57.3 percent). One-quarter of the survivors—1,118 persons—were over sixty. Those aged eighteen to forty-four—the most common age among Holocaust survivors, as we shall see later—were only the second-largest group in Berlin (33.7 percent). Fourteen- to seventeen-year-olds made up 2.5 percent, and children age thirteen and under made up 6.5 percent. Of the 506 children in this category, 144 were born after liberation. These statistics show that the average age of the surviving Berlin Jew was fifty-five.[11]

Another characteristic of the survivors was that many of them were highly educated free professionals, which was also typical of German Jewry as a whole before the Nazi period. In other ways, too, the educated and aging Berlin community was a reflection of German Jewry in the pre-Holocaust period. Assimilation had become so widespread that even before the war there had been predictions about a decline in the size of the Jewish community in Germany. These predictions came true, unfortunately, but for other reasons entirely. The bitter irony was that the assimilationist tendencies of the Jews—their relations with "Aryan" German spouses, neighbors, or friends—actually helped them to survive and awakened in them a sense of gratitude and obligation. Thus the desire of many survivors to remain in Germany—or, as in the case of German Jews interned elsewhere, to return to Germany—should come as no surprise. The age factor strengthened the desire to remain in Germany, although some of the German Jewish survivors did immigrate, mainly to the United States.[12]

Camp Survivors

When the liberators arrived, they found an assemblage of Jews from every country occupied by the Nazis. Although a precise breakdown is difficult to establish, we know that the original transports were chiefly from Poland and the Baltic countries, but subsequent arrivals were from other countries. The later they came, the greater the likelihood of having survived until liberation day. As many of the survivors were repatriated, however, the dominance of the Polish Jews became apparent. Those from France, Belgium, Holland, and other Western European countries headed home immediately.[13] The Hungarian, Czechoslovakian, and Romanian Jews were next in line.[14] Most of the remaining survivors were Polish Jews who refused to return to the graveyard of their people. Those who did go back to Poland did so mainly to search for relatives or retrieve property, but finding the country in ruins and still plagued by anti-Semitism, they soon retraced their steps to Germany (see below).

It is commonly assumed that more men survived than women, that the bulk of the survivors were young adults, and that the percentage of children and the elderly was negligible, and these assumptions are borne out by statistics from different sources. Of 24,334 DPs counted in Germany and Austria in July 1945, 53 percent (12,926) were men. Another source states that of 22,374 survivors, 67.4 percent (15,060) were between the ages of twenty-one and forty-five. A survey taken by the American Jewish Joint Distribution Committee in Bavaria at the beginning of 1946 reinforces these conclusions: the ratio of men to women was two to one, and 81 percent of the survivors were aged eighteen to thirty-nine.[15]

This demographic distribution was the direct result of Nazi policies. Children, the elderly, and the sick were systematically rounded up and sent to their deaths. Of the 1.35 million Jewish children in the countries of central and Eastern Europe conquered by the Nazis, only 150,000 survived the war.[16] Those who did were the more able-bodied, who were capable of doing forced labor, among them boys who managed to look older than their age. The percentage of men who survived was thus naturally greater than the percentage of women.[17]

Regarding the sociocultural profile of the camp survivors, the predominance of the middle classes seems quite clear. About 75 percent were members of the lower middle class—artisans, grocers, and small merchants.[18] This corresponds with the profile of Polish Jewry, which was uppermost in the DP camps. If not for the repatriation of Jews from Western European countries, the class structure might have been very different.

Some say that most of the survivors were secular Jews, and that the few religiously observant were affiliated with particularly militant ultra-Orthodox groups. These are subjective impressions, apparently based on the assumption that the great majority of Orthodox Jews in Poland had been murdered by the Nazis or escaped into Soviet Russia. If there were Orthodox survivors, they were Hungarian or Czechoslovakian Jews.[19]

Jewish Population Growth in Germany

Exodus from Eastern Europe

The Jewish remnant in Germany was soon joined by a great influx of Jewish refugees fleeing from Eastern Europe. This mass migration, known as the *Briha* (Hebrew for "escape" or "flight"), began in 1944 as Jewish partisans emerged who had gone underground or hidden in the forests during the war. Their destination was generally the Mediterranean coast, and eventually Palestine. What started out as a trickle developed in the course of 1945 into a deluge, as many other groups headed westward, assisted by the now multi-branched *Briha* organization: the 80,000 Jews who had remained in Poland at the end of the war; the 150,000 to 200,000 Jews who had returned to Poland in the wake of a repatriation agreement with the Soviet Union; and disillusioned survivors who had gone back to their liberated hometowns and changed their minds, heading once again for DP camps in Germany and Austria, or *Briha* points in Italy. These groups were joined in 1947 by refugees from Czechoslovakia, Hungary, and Romania.[20]

The Jews' chief motive for leaving Eastern Europe was anti-Semitism, of which the Kielce pogrom on July 4, 1946, was a particularly vicious example. During the first year after liberation there were close to a thousand victims of anti-Semitic violence in Poland.[21] But there were other motives, too. The war had left the countries of Eastern Europe in a state of economic collapse, and the Jews found themselves unable to retrieve property they had left behind. Furthermore, the political forecast was grim, which only strengthened the anti-Semitism that already abounded. All these factors convinced the Jews to leave their home countries and to rebuild their lives somewhere where they could be free—Palestine or the western democracies, preferably the United States. However, the road out of Europe was virtually blocked. In Palestine, the British Mandate adhered to the strict restrictions on Jewish immigration imposed by the White Paper of 1939, and after the war the monthly immigration quota was restricted to a temporary maximum of 1,500. The United States also had a rigid immigration policy that allowed in only a few thousand people per month at most. European refugees fleeing totalitarianism and communism were turned away in a similar fashion. Very few countries were willing to offer them a haven.

The only option was to join the DP population, which exerted pressure on the western governments, and especially the Mandatory authorities in Palestine. DP camps became the last resorts for those seeking a way out of Europe, and the population of these camps grew rapidly.[22] At the beginning of 1946 there were close to 70,000 DPs in Germany's three western zones and Berlin, not including 12,000 in Austria and 10,000 in Italy. By the end of the year, in the wake of the frantic exodus from Poland after the Kielce pogrom, the number rose to 230,000, with 180,000 DPs in Germany alone. The DP population in Germany reached a peak in the spring of 1947, after the arrival of refugees from Czechoslovakia, Hungary, and Romania. At that time there were about 190,000 DPs in western Germany (out of a total of 250,000 in Germany, Austria, and Italy). The figures began to drop only after the United Nations reached its decision on the partition of Palestine on November 29, 1947, which marked the onset of large-scale emigration.[23]

These figures do not include the considerable number of Jews who moved in and out between Austria, Germany, and Italy at some time after the war. Some 300,000 Jewish DPs and refugees are believed to have passed through Austria and/or Germany for longer or shorter periods of time.

The Jewish DPs in Germany: A Profile

Most of the DPs were Jews from Eastern Europe, but the new arrivals changed the demographic composition entirely. The original group of survivors, at the time of liberation, consisted exclusively of Jews who had experienced the concentration camps firsthand, with almost no children or elderly among them. By the end of 1946 nearly two-thirds of the DPs were refugees, many of them repatriates from the Soviet Union, which brought in married couples, children, and elderly. The large number of marriages was another factor. In the early months after the war, young survivors who had lost their families rushed to marry and establish new family units, which produced a baby boom a year later and filled the DP camps with children.[24]

When the war ended, the Jewish DPs continued to live behind barbed-wire fences. They found themselves packed into dozens of severely overcrowded labor or concentration camps, together with non-Jewish DPs. Sometimes camp survivors were housed together with their former guards and tormentors. They were treated in a humiliating manner and often victimized because of their Jewishness. Nutrition, sanitation, and living conditions were abominable. Two months after the war, they were still wearing their old concentration camp uniforms because no other clothing had been issued. No efforts were made to reunite families or to help survivors look for lost relatives, and the survivors could not do it themselves, since they could neither send nor receive mail.

Tens of thousands of DPs were interned in the large camps: Landsberg, Feldafing, and Föhrenwald in the American Zone, and Bergen-Belsen in the British Zone. Many others resided in smaller camps and in public or residential housing set up by the occupation authorities. DPs were not allowed to reside outside the camps or the "assembly centers" designated for them for fear that they would be too heavy a burden on the legal system and the German economy.

Responsibility for the DP population fell largely upon the military occupation authorities. Both the number of DPs and the length of time they remained in Germany far exceeded expectations. UNRRA did not have enough qualified personnel, and assembly centers designed to hold 2,000–3,000 people were forced to absorb more than 10,000. Although the Jews initially constituted only 10 to 20 percent of the DP population (later the proportions changed dramatically), they were the main problem because they had suffered most in the war and remained victims of anti-Semitism even afterward. Jews throughout the United States, Britain, and Palestine set up an outcry and lobbied their respective governments for more humane treatment.[25]

When the war ended, most of the Jewish DPs were in the British Zone in northern Germany. This soon changed, however, because the British would not admit Jewish refugees from the East. American policy was much more lenient.[26] In the summer of 1945, in the wake of harsh criticism from the American public, President Truman sent a special envoy, Earl G. Harrison, to inspect living conditions in the DP camps in the American Zone. Apart from Harrison's main recommendation—namely, to relieve the hardship by allowing the Jews to immigrate to Palestine, which had a political impact in the long run—conditions improved considerably after he submitted his report. Jewish DPs gained recognition as an ethnic group with special needs, and they were moved to separate camps where they enjoyed a greater degree of autonomy. Permission was granted to live outside the camps, German property was set aside for housing, and the large Jewish welfare agencies were allowed to expand their operations. A special adviser on Jewish affairs was appointed to the American military headquarters in Germany, and life in the camps became much more bearable.[27]

In the wake of David Ben-Gurion's visit to the camps in October 1945 as chairman of the Jewish Agency, the American occupation authorities were persuaded to steer the influx of Jewish refugees toward the American Zone and facilitate their absorption there. This was not the case in the British Zone, where the Jews did not enjoy any special privileges and the number of refugees was severely restricted. In December 1945, the British Zone was closed to newcomers altogether.

As a result, the proportion of Jews in the American Zone rose dramatically. By the end of 1945, 45,000 of the 70,000 Jewish DPs in Germany were living in the American Zone. A year later, the figure was 150,000 out of 180,000, and there was no change in this ratio until the liquidation of the camps in 1948–50.[28]

Emigration from Germany

Up until 1948, camp arrivals far outweighed departures, and illegal immigration to Palestine accounted for most of the exodus. Some 30,000 Jews from Austria and Germany found their way out of the country with the help of *Briha* activists (out of a total of 70,000 illegal immigrants leaving Europe for Palestine).[29]

The number of Jews immigrating to other countries was very small, as was the scope of legal immigration to Palestine. American restrictive immigration policy with respect to the DPs changed only slightly as a result of a Truman directive, under which about 28,000 Jewish DPs, of whom roughly 15,000 were from Germany, succeeded in entering the United States between May 1946 and June 1948, prior to the new Displaced Persons Act of 1948. During that time most of the immigrants from Germany who were admitted to the United States were Jews with German citizenship.[30]

Britain also admitted a small number of refugees, and the British Mandate issued approximately 6,000 immigration certificates to DPs in Germany between March 1947 and May 1948.[31] German Jewish emigration continued on a small scale, too.[32] All told, about 40,000 Jews left Germany before 1948, but the DP population was so large that this figure scarcely made a dent.

The situation changed radically after the establishment of the State of Israel and the implementation of new U.S. immigration laws shortly thereafter. The DP population in Germany shrank rapidly during the first half of 1948, and was already half the size—100,000 persons—by June. By the beginning of 1949 the number was down to 55,000, and by the end of the year only 27,000 "hard core" DPs were left in Germany. About one-third of the emigrants headed for the United States, but the other two-thirds settled in the new State of Israel, along with tens of thousands of Jews from all over Europe. Until 1950, the camps and assembly centers were liquidated one after another. Those DPs who remained in Germany joined the Jewish communities that began to rebuild themselves after the war, and the remainder gathered in Föhrenwald—the only camp that continued to function until 1956.[33]

2
THE LIBERATION OF BERGEN-BELSEN

British forces reached Bergen-Belsen on Sunday afternoon, April 15, 1945. At 3:07 P.M., the first tank rolled heavily over the camp's barbed-wire fence, advancing toward the German military base three kilometers away. By 3:30 P.M. the Germans had surrendered.

Bergen-Belsen, located near Hanover in Lower Saxony, was the second Nazi concentration camp in Germany to be liberated as World War II drew to an end. The first, Buchenwald, had been set free by American troops four days earlier. Gradually, over the next four weeks, all the other camps were taken over by the Allies, leading to the final Nazi defeat on May 8, 1945.

To the inmates of Bergen-Belsen, Captain Derrick Sington, commander of the psychological warfare unit, personified liberation. Minutes after the British entered the camp, it was his voice that boomed over the loudspeaker loud and clear: "*Ihr seid frei*"—"you are free!"[1] The *katzetniks* heard his call, but few could muster the strength to crawl out and greet him. For many, the liberators had arrived too late. Yet for these who did survive, the arrival of the British did not mean instant freedom. It was the start of another long period of incarceration on the accursed soil of Germany.

Bergen-Belsen as a Death Camp

Originally a prisoner-of-war facility, Bergen-Belsen was divided into two parts in April 1943.[2] Control of half the camp was transferred at this time into the hands of the WVHA (Wirtschafts-Verwaltungshauptamt), the SS economic-administrative authority in charge of all the concentration camps. As a detention camp (*Aufenthaltslager*), this part of Bergen-Belsen was to be used for Jews with dual and neutral citizenship (and eventually enemy citizens, too) who could be exchanged for Germans interned in enemy countries.

New Beginnings

Captain Derrick A. Sington, commander of the psychological warfare unit, entering Bergen-Belsen on April 15, 1945, voicing over the loudspeaker: "*Ihr seid frei*, you are free!" (Yad Vashem Photo-Archives [FA 179 4])

The bulk of these "exchange Jews" (*Austauschjuden*) were held in the "star camp" (*Sternlager*), so called because of the yellow Star of David they were forced to sew onto their clothes. Needless to say, the great majority of them were never used in any sort of exchange. Other camps were established as time went by: the "neutral camp" (*Neutralenlager*), the "special camp" (*Sonderlager*), and the "Hungarian camp" (*Ungarenlager*), set up in early July 1944. In March 1944, the other half of Bergen-Belsen, which was still a POW facility (*Häftlingslager*), was turned into a "convalescent camp" (*Erholungslager*), supposedly to care for those who arrived sick and debilitated. However, the journey itself was designed to weaken the evacuees. Many died en route or soon after their arrival. In January 1945 the "convalescent camp" was also taken over by the WVHA, and from then on it received transports of women evacuated from the camps in the East. In August a separate section, the "women's camp," was organized inside the "star camp" to accommodate women transferred from forced labor camps in Poland and Hungary. The first women's transport from Auschwitz arrived on August 23, 1944, and more women reached Bergen-Belsen in October and November as Auschwitz-Birkenau and other camps in the East were evacuated.

The Liberation of Bergen-Belsen

In the summer of 1944, conditions in Bergen-Belsen grew steadily worse. As Soviet troops advanced, transports from concentration camps in the East increased in frequency and size, with the large influx of women totally altering the demographic balance. These transports were to continue up to the very last minute. As many as 30,000 inmates of the Dora-Mittlebau camp and other camps in the Hanover vicinity arrived in the second week of April 1945.

From December 1944 to March 1945, some 40,000 to 50,000 persons were sent to Bergen-Belsen. However, the death toll on the way (as a result of the "death marches") and immediately after arrival was so great that the population of Bergen-Belsen did not actually increase. In all the confusion, it was hard to keep track of data. The Nazis, of course, destroyed as many records as they could before they surrendered, so that data from February 1945 onward are particularly scarce. Nevertheless, certain pertinent information has survived.

On March 1, 1945, for example, the population of Bergen-Belsen was 41,520. On March 15 the number was up to 45,117, but by March 31 it had dropped to 44,060 (including 2,800 exchange Jews in the "star camp," most of them ill), and by April 6, to 39,789. Tens of thousands died in the early months of 1945, and in March alone more than 18,000 died in Bergen-Belsen. Deaths from January until mid-April stood at about 35,000.

At the time of liberation, 60,000 persons were found in Bergen-Belsen. However, the majority of those from August 1944 had died or been killed in the interim, and less than half the population had been around prior to April 1945. As many as 30,000 had arrived in Bergen-Belsen just the week before. At the same time, three trainloads of exchange Jews (approximately 6,000 persons) had left the camp, presumably for Theresienstadt. The first train was stopped, bombarded, and finally liberated by American soldiers on April 13. The second was liberated by the Russians after two weeks on the road, and the third, carrying Hungarian Jews, was last seen near Berlin on April 17, but never heard of again.

The estimated number of those who perished in Bergen-Belsen prior to the liberation, not including those who died in transports to or from the camp, stands at about 37,000.[3] Most of these deaths occurred in the spring of 1945. The question is, why there were so many deaths when Belsen was not, in fact, an extermination camp? As Kolb explains, "Belsen was a camp where terror was boastfully and openly perpetrated. Here, masses of people were not sent to the gallows. Here, there were no gas chambers. Here, they died slowly, but surely. Starvation, the wanton neglect of hygienic conditions, contagion, terribly overcrowded barracks, brutality, the feeling of total degeneration—all these ensured that the needs of the crematoria would massively and steadily be filled."[4] At Bergen-Belsen, starvation and disease were both instruments of torture and angels of death. In late February 1945 a ration of two slices of bread and half a liter of watery soup with potatoes was distributed every day. In March the portions grew steadily smaller, and bread was scarce. In the final days before liberation there was no bread at all. Living conditions in the camp were shocking. The barracks consisted of four walls without windows or a decent roof. In the dead of winter, the inmates—sometimes as many as 1,500 in one barrack—slept huddled together on the floor.

Conditions were even more horrific in the quarter that served as an infirmary. Thousands of people were jammed into three huts with leaky roofs and very little in the way of medicines or medical equipment. Whatever cleaning was done resulted from the efforts of the inmate doctors. Hygiene was so bad as to be almost unspeakable. Of all the concentration camps, Bergen-Belsen was said to be the filthiest. In the spring of 1945, this "convalescent camp," accommodating 8,000 to 10,000 people, did not have a single toilet or water faucet. Inmates were forced to relieve themselves outside the barracks; some were too weak even for that. Drinking water was dispensed from a filthy container two or three hours a day. Washing was out of the question. In the days before liberation there was no water at all because the pump had been destroyed in a bombardment.

These catastrophic conditions led to the spread of infectious diseases that the weaker inmates were unable to withstand. Typhoid, known in Bergen-Belsen as *Lagerfieber* (camp fever), spread uncontrollably in the summer of 1944. Thousands of inmates contracted dysentery and other diseases of the digestive tract, from which many died. Tuberculosis was widespread, and a typhus epidemic broke out in early 1945. Every morning the barracks were littered with corpses that the inmates were physically incapable of removing themselves. Trucks arrived each day to transport bodies to the crematorium, but there were simply too many. By March the camp was strewn with piles of corpses in various stages of decomposition. In the days before the German surrender, prisoners were forced to dig huge pits and bury as many as they could, but even so, the SS could not hide the atrocities perpetrated in Belsen from the eyes of the British liberators.[5]

The Liberation of Bergen-Belsen

The liberation of Bergen-Belsen: Two women peeling potatoes while a third woman is lying exhausted nearby, and behind them a pile of unburied corpses (Yad Vashem Photo-Archives [FA 180 43]).

The Aftermath

The shock on the faces of the British troops upon entering Bergen-Belsen was documented by the journalists, news broadcasters, and press photographers who followed them into the camp, as well as the No. 5 Army Film and Photographic Unit. On April 19, the British papers splashed photographs and news reports of the horrors across their pages. The West already knew about the existence of extermination camps and the Nazi plans for getting rid of the Jews, but only with the liberation of the concentration camps was there a dawning realization in Britain of the magnitude of the catastrophe that had befallen European Jewry.[6]

New Beginnings

The British forces were not prepared for what they saw. Auschwitz, liberated by the Red Army in January 1945, was already infamous, but Bergen-Belsen, which began operating at a relatively late date, was not known as a death camp, and in fact became one only in the months before liberation. In the autumn of 1944, Royal Air Force aerial photographs of Bergen-Belsen were interpreted to be sections of the nearby military camp.[7] Moreover, while other camps had been evacuated and had ceased operating before the conquest, Belsen continued to function, with conditions there becoming even more horrendous in the final days. For those who marched through the gates on April 15, the shock was thus heightened by the fact that they beheld the atrocities of a "working" death camp.

The British reaction was commensurate with the greatness of that shock. Bergen-Belsen became the symbol of the satanic evil of the Nazi regime and figured highly in British anti-Nazi propaganda efforts in occupied Germany and on the home front. At the same time, a valiant attempt was made to save as many lives as possible and to rehabilitate the victims.[8]

Entering Bergen-Belsen, the British troops found two camps: the main camp (Camp One) and another camp (Camp Two), which was adjacent to the military camp, about a mile away. In Camp One there were 45,000 people, most of them barely alive, and some 10,000 corpses piled in the yards. The 15,000 inmates of Camp Two were in better shape, having only recently arrived at Belsen. Although many were starving or suffering from dysentery, they were strong enough to give their liberators a tumultuous reception, while those in Camp One could barely manage a weak cry. The military camp was large and modern, with public buildings, a fully equipped hospital, and a warehouse stocked with food.[9]

Liberation was scarcely felt on the day the British arrived, and the shooting and murders continued as if nothing had happened. As thousands of inmates lay in the barracks, too weak to move or to greet their saviors, others were gripped by an unbridled joy which, by nightfall, turned into rebellion. Over the next three days, dozens of starving prisoners were shot, mainly by the Hungarian soldiers who guarded the kitchen and manned the watchtowers under British supervision. Many *kapos* (KZ polizei—prisoners recruited to the concentration camp's police force to do the dirty jobs for the Nazis) were lynched during those first days.[10]

Upon their arrival, British forces cabled headquarters with an urgent request for food, water, and other assistance. The following morning, April 16, a tank arrived with the first shipment of supplies, but it did relatively little good. Unprepared for dealing with such an emergency, the British were unable to control the masses of starving people. That night and the following day the inmates, many of them recent arrivals, raided the kitchen and food stocks. A large number died through gorging, while many others succumbed because they were too weak to reach the food.

Another problem was the type of food. Army rations of canned meat and vegetables were not suitable for sick and starving people, many of whom were suffering from stomach ailments. It took the British two days to realize that the inmates required easily digested food such as rice, biscuits, and fresh milk, and more time passed before these items arrived. Thus thousands died in the first days after liberation because they could not get to the food, because they ate too much, or because they could not digest the food that was available.[11]

On April 17 the British began rehabilitation operations: burying the dead, cleaning and disinfecting the camp, administering medical treatment, and supplying food and water. The plan was to concentrate on Camp One, where the survivors were weakest and incapable of caring for themselves, and to liquidate it as soon as possible. In order to do so, Camp One inmates were gradually transferred to the military camp and Camp Two. In the military camp, now called Camp Three, special areas were designated for a hospital, children's houses, and a maternity ward.[12]

Food and Water Supply

The major problem was nourishing the starving inmates when at least a quarter of them could not care for themselves or digest what was given to them. As an emergency measure, medical personnel put together a concoction of dried milk, flour, sugar, salt, and water known as the "Bengal famine mixture," which had been successfully used on starving populations in India. This mixture was divided into portions believed to be medically appropriate. Forty tons of nonfat dried milk were airlifted from England for this purpose.[13] Nevertheless, unrelieved starvation continued to exact a heavy toll, even more so than gorging. The survivors complained that the portions were far too small, and some British accounts confirm this. Today, of course, it is hard to judge, but the fact is, Bergen-Belsen inmates were apportioned less than 1,000 calories a day. Until the third week in May, butter and margarine were in short supply, and staples such as dried eggs were largely unavailable.[14]

Another reason for the continued hunger was the difficulty in supplying food to those incapable of coming to the distribution points, especially during those first days when the number of helpless and incapacitated was so high. In addition, raids on the supply stations persisted, and it was difficult to keep inmates from devouring whatever food they could get their hands on before mealtimes.[15]

Survivors who went through remain haunted by the experience. They continue to be tortured by the memories of constant hunger and of friends and relatives dropping like flies for lack of nourishment, and continue to wonder whether the British really did as much as they could. Even now they have a gnawing suspicion that many of the thousands who died after the liberation could have been saved.[16]

Since the camp's water supply had been cut off about a week before liberation, water was initially brought in by convoys of water tankers. Later a pump was installed, and by April 19 emergency pipelines had been laid. A water disinfecting system, extremely important because corpses were occasionally found in the reservoir, was completed by April 29.[17]

Burying the Dead

According to official British estimates, the number of dead found in the camp at the time of the liberation was 10,000, with some 500 more dying each day. Mass burials began on April 17. SS personnel were forced to do the work as the survivors looked on with an understandable sense of revenge. The healthier survivors were encouraged to clean the barracks and remove the dead, and the Hungarian guards dug burial pits. No records were kept at this stage, and officiating at each mass burial were clergymen of different faiths. Signs were posted with the estimated number of victims and the date of burial. Only on April 24, after the matter of food and water had been tended to, did British military personnel begin to keep proper records. Eventually, individual burials were carried out, and an effort was made to mark the graves with identification numbers, nationality, and, if possible, the name of the deceased. It took the British until April 28 to bury the 10,000 bodies they found upon arrival. By the time Camp One was completely evacuated four weeks later, the number of dead was up to 23,000, reflecting the 13,000 additional deaths since the liberation.[18]

Medical Treatment and Sanitation

Of the 28,000 women in the camp when the British arrived, 21,000 required hospitalization. This was also true for 9,000 of the 12,000 men. Early screenings found 5,000 cases of famine oedema, 3,500 cases of typhus, 20,000 cases of dysentery and other stomach ailments, and 10,000 cases of tuberculosis. In all, there were at least 38,000 persons in urgent need of medical treatment. Obviously, it was impossible to treat so many at one time, and thousands died before reaching hospital. The first priority was the typhus epidemic, which was dealt with through lice sprays and quarantine. By April 18 some 500 typhus patients had been placed in a special ward set up in the SS camp pharmacy. Work was carried on around the clock to turn the military barracks into a hospital, which was ready for admissions on April 21. By April 30, 5,000 patients were transferred to the hospital, after being washed and disinfected. As many as 14,000 were being cared for by May 19.

Treating these patients was far from simple. Many were so weak that they responded badly to the treatment and died as a result. Large number of doctors and nurses fell ill, too.[19] All the while, British forces worked on establishing a sanitary infrastructure and embarked on a wide-scale disinfecting program, for without cleanliness there was no way to stop the spread of disease. Here, too, they encountered difficulty, since many of the survivors were initially unable, either emotionally or physically, to adhere to the most minimal standards of hygiene.[20]

Manpower and Supplies

At first, treatment was administered by medical units of the British army under the command of Brigadier H. L. Glyn Hughes, and the army's sanitation unit. A week later, a delegation of the British Red Cross and a twelve-person team of the Friends Relief Service (Quakers) led by Eryl Hall Williams arrived. On April 30, Dr. Meiklejohn of UNRRA brought over a group of ninety-seven medical students from London under the auspices of the Red Cross and the Order of St. John. These students were about to be sent to Holland but were diverted at the last moment to Belsen, where the situation was deemed more critical. They worked in the camp for a month. Units of the International Red Cross joined them, as did medical delegations from Switzerland and the Vatican. A reinforcement of 150 Belgian medical students arrived on May 26. As the weeks went by, more British medical units and an American field hospital unit were added. The strenuous tasks were carried out by 2,400 Hungarian soldiers. Nonetheless, because of the race against the clock and the shortage of professional staff, the British were forced to employ local Germans and POWs incarcerated in the nearby Celle camp, among them 40 doctors and 200 nurses. Even though the British supervised them closely, most of the patients were deathly afraid of them.[21]

In time, some of the more robust survivors were assigned light duties, among them six doctors. One of the most notable was Dr. Hadassa Bimko (later Rosensaft).[22] In their testimonies many survivors remember how healthy inmates devoted themselves to the care of sick and dying friends. When the time came for survivors to be transferred to the refurbished camp, the *Lagerschwester* (camp sisters), as they were called, volunteered to stay and help the dying. Military chaplains, including rabbis, also rendered important spiritual and physical succor.[23]

The liberation of Bergen-Belsen: Survivors in a barrack. (Yad Vashem Photo-Archives [1CO1]).

However, in facing the huge task of rehabilitating the survivors, a tremendous gap existed between needs and manpower. In a way, all the survivors were sick.[24] Hundreds of psychologists and social workers were needed, if only to help the survivors regain a sense of human dignity and self-respect. But such a staff was not available, of course, and many of those who lived through these times cannot forget their terrible sense of frustration.[25]

The same problem holds true with regard to vital equipment. Initial supplies came from British army emergency stores and then from German military warehouses, which were well stocked with food, electrical and technical equipment, beds, blankets, sheets, furniture, soap and disinfectants, clothing, and other items. There were Red Cross food parcels donated by Jewish organizations, which had been stolen by the Nazis, and contributions of food and medicine from British, Canadian, and American army units stationed in the area.[26] Another source was German civilian stocks. A quota was imposed on every man, woman, and child, first in Lüneburg (where British military headquarters were located), then in other areas of the British Zone. It brought in tens of thousands of blankets, bed linens, clothing, cleaning materials, food, and other supplies for the survivors of Bergen-Belsen and other camps.[27] The problem was that much of this equipment was not available during the first weeks after liberation, and there was not enough manpower to ensure its proper distribution, all of which might have saved lives.

The Liquidation of Bergen-Belsen

While these emergency measures were under way, the survivors were gradually transferred, in groups of 1,000, to the former military camp, now Camp Three. Beginning on April 24, the typhus-infested barracks of Bergen-Belsen were burned down, one by one. The transfer of inmates was completed on May 19. The evacuees, now housed in Camp Three according to nationality, totaled 27,000 persons. Approximately half that number were hospitalized. This was all that remained of the 60,000 survivors found in Bergen-Belsen on liberation day. Within these few weeks 13,000 had died and some 17,000 had repatriated.[28]

The death toll continued to mount after the transfer to the military camp, although the pace slowed somewhat. Those who arrived in Belsen several weeks after liberation were still horrified by what they saw—and this was after the British had worked frantically to improve the situation.[29] It was true that the liberated camp was packed with 60,000 sick and dying persons and that rescue activities were carried out while the war was still going on, with the British front only a few kilometers away. Nonetheless, the death rate was higher than one would have expected. During the first weeks, close to 500 people died every day, and a drop began to be felt only toward the end of April. In early May there were 200 deaths a day, going down to 50 by May 22 and 20 by June 20. From liberation day until June 20 an estimated 14,000 persons died, about 1,000 of them after the evacuation of Camp One.[30]

Despite these statistics, the emergency measures made a tremendous difference. Apathy no longer reigned. The survivors ceased to stare vacantly into space, and they stopped taking fright at the sight of every uniformed person who crossed their path. They began to take an interest in current events. Their sense of shame and modesty returned, and the women started paying attention to how they looked. Hope awakened within them, and they began thinking about the future. Just as quickly, however, there were survivors who sank into depression, for with this awakening came the inevitable confrontation with their terrible loss and the uncertainty that lay before them.[31]

On May 21, 1945, at 6:15 p.m., the last barracks of Camp One was set ablaze, and Colonel Bird, the camp commander, delivered a speech. All that was left was a sign at the entrance gate, bearing the following inscription in English and German:

> This is the site of the infamous Belsen Concentration Camp
> Liberated by the British on April 15, 1945
> Ten thousand unburied dead were found here
> Thirteen thousand more have since died
> All of them victims of the German New Order in Europe
> And an example of Nazi Kultur.[32]

Thus the Bergen-Belsen concentration camp was wiped off the face of the earth, with only the mass graves left behind as eternal testimony to the atrocities perpetrated there.

3

THE BRITISH ZONE OF OCCUPATION

Population, Economy, and Occupation Policy

In the face of the devastated German economy, the burden that fell upon the Allies was enormous, particularly in the British Zone. The region was poor in agricultural resources, and its industrial infrastructure had been largely destroyed in the war. These factors, together with the deindustrialization and demilitarization policies of the Allies, created a shortage of industrial merchandise that could be exchanged for food supplies. Even the most basic needs of the population, which was denser than in other parts of Germany, could not be met. The British Zone had a population of 21,936,500 by the end of 1946, which rose to 22,345,000 with the addition of 408,500 refugees and DPs. The British economy, which had itself suffered a severe setback during the war, was now being asked to shoulder responsibility for the survivors, too.

The DPs presented a special problem. In July 1945, after the bulk of the survivors had been repatriated, 2 million DPs remained in Germany; by the end of September, 650,000 remained in the British Zone alone. The figure dropped to 530,000 by the end of December, and then to 368,000 by summer, but there were still 264,000 DPs in the British Zone in February 1947. The military authorities thus faced an unforeseen challenge: establishing camps and assembly centers for DPs by nationality until a solution could be found. It was feared that allowing them to mingle with the German population would create an extra burden on the economy and a potential threat to law and order. No one was prepared for the possibility that hundreds of thousands of DPs would not be repatriated. The Western Allies could not force anyone to be repatriated, but the fact was there were very few alternatives.

The British military authorities found themselves saddled with an enormous problem for which they had no preparation or training whatsoever. Only in November 1945 was an agreement signed gradually transferring responsibility for the camps into UNRRA's hands.[1] It was no wonder, then, that the British, even more so than the Americans, looked for ways to lessen the burden posed by the DPs and the local German population.

The DPs were urged to return to their countries of origin, and severe restrictions were imposed on them in the hope of getting them to comply. As victims of the Nazis, the DPs were entitled to larger food rations and better treatment than the German population, but this was scarcely noticeable because the overall economic situation was so poor. A diet of 2,000 calories per day, with very little meat or dairy products, no fruits or vegetables, and scarcely any fat, would hardly suffice for people who had lived a normal life, let alone concentration and death camp survivors who had been starved, tortured, and weakened by malnutrition and disease for so many years, but even this ration was not implemented.

Worst of all, however, was being condemned to live in overcrowded barracks, with no privacy and under semi-military conditions that included being surrounded by a barbed-wire fence and denied freedom of movement to and from the camp. Many DPs naturally tried to settle outside the camps upon liberation, but the authorities were anxious to minimize this trend because it was perceived as placing too great a strain on the legal and economic system.[2]

The Germans were treated as enemies. Their food was strictly rationed, and only the barest essentials were provided—just enough to survive. Of course, there were also victims of the Nazis and former inmates of concentration camps among them, who were exempt from this harsh treatment, but it was more than half a year before special regulations were defined. "Zone Policy Instruction No. 20" was issued on December 4, 1945, and took several months to be implemented. This policy was basically a recommendation to the German authorities (who were considered responsible for all German citizens) that defined who was entitled to preferential treatment, that is, persons who had been persecuted or thrown into concentration camps by the Nazis on racial, religious, or political grounds. This was a very narrow definition, and victims had to prove that they had indeed been imprisoned for these reasons, participated in anti-Nazi activities, or collaborated with the Allies. Even if they did, however, there was little possibility of carrying out the order because better housing, food, clothing, and jobs were simply not available.[3]

The British Zone of Occupation

The Allies—and even more so, the British—faced the daunting task of solving the problems of many hundreds of thousands of DPs and outlining a plan for rebuilding Germany's ruined economy. In the midst of the chaos, the plight of the German Jews was not a top priority.

The British Policy Regarding the Jews

Of the 22,345,000 persons living in the British Zone at the end of 1946, some 18,800 were Jews—approximately .08 percent of the total population. Because the Jewish remnant was so small and the economic burden so heavy, the authorities were not as attentive as they might have been to the specifically Jewish aspects of the problem.

As for Jewish DPs, their starting point upon liberation was much lower than of the non-Jews. Most of the Jews had been in the death camps or taken part in "death marches," from which they emerged barely alive. The majority of the non-Jews had been in forced labor camps and were comparatively better off, physically and mentally. Thus the preferential treatment that was supposedly enjoyed by all DPs, which was not enough in any case, was even less adequate for the Jewish DPs.

For German Jews, the problem was compounded. Those who had been liberated from concentration camps were recognized as victims of the Nazis, but the liberated Jews, who were usually older and in worse health than their German counterparts, had no families to whom to return, no sources of income, and no social connections to assist them. In addition, there were some German Jews who had survived in their hometowns, without being deported. As such, they were not included in the "victims" category and were treated as ordinary Germans.[4]

The whole situation could have been changed after the initial chaos had died down and an official occupation policy was instituted, or as various issues were brought to the attention of the military government. Yet, because of the overall British approach to specifically Jewish problems, this was not the case.

From the very beginning, the British ignored the Jewishness of the victims of the Nazis. However horrific their testimonies in connection with Bergen-Belsen, they did not even bother to mention that most of the victims were Jews. This is astounding, indeed. Except for Sington's testimony, all public statements by liberators ignored the existence of Jewish prisoners and Jewish suffering. This includes Dr. W. R. F. Collis of the Red Cross, the medical student and volunteer

New Beginnings

G. Raperport, the official newspaper in the British Zone, the *British Zone Review*, and even documentary films shot in the first days after liberation, not to mention internal documents. Collis, for example, talks only about French prisoners awaiting repatriation, and Raperport makes not the slightest mention of Jews, even though he himself was probably Jewish, judging by his name.[5]

This was obviously a manifestation of some resentment toward Jews, despite the compassion the British felt for the victims of the Nazis as human beings. As a result, they adopted a policy whereby the Jews were treated just like all the others—in terms of their nationalities—and this was true even in respect to German Jews. According to British policy there were only two legitimate categories: enemy Germans and Nazi collaborators on the one hand, and victims of the Nazis and Allied collaborators on the other.

Since Jews were not a separate category, they did not enjoy any special status and were not entitled to better treatment by the authorities. For Jewish DPs this meant being pressured on the subject of repatriation. The majority of survivors from Eastern Europe refused to go back to their homelands and were placed in camps according to nationality—Polish, Ukrainian, and so on. Frequently this meant that Jews were forced to live alongside their former torturers and persecutors, under constant threat of attack.[6]

For the German Jews, the situation was even worse than for Jewish DPs. They had no special protection whatsoever. Soon after the war ended, the Allied authorities returned many civic and municipal responsibilities to the Germans. German Jews thus went back to being under the jurisdiction of German municipalities, like all other citizens. As we said before, concentration camps survivors were recognized as victims, but the degree of victimization was not considered greater in the case of Jews, and of course those who had been persecuted without being imprisoned or deported were not recognized at all.

Jews were thus treated as individuals—as DPs, German victims of the Nazis, or German citizens—rather than a group.[7] This attitude meant that the authorities turned a blind eye to the specific needs of the Jews as Jews, be it their individual physical needs or their spiritual need to be part of a community after losing their families and dear ones and being left alone in the world. This situation also made it difficult for any Jewish relief mission to operate, even after the military authorities and UNRRA permitted such groups to tend to the special needs of Jewish survivors.[8]

The British Zone of Occupation

At first there was no difference in this respect between British and American policy. However, the Americans, following the recommendations of Earl G. Harrison, introduced strict segregation between Jews and non-Jews. The DPs were placed in camps of their own, and German Jews had their status equated to that of DPs. The British, in contrast, stubbornly held to the principle of nonsegregation, only implementing reforms at the end of 1945—a process that took several months. They would not permit a separate Jewish welfare system or allow German Jews to benefit from such assistance. The appointment of special Jewish liaison officers and a Jewish adviser was delayed until the spring of 1946.[9]

Another important aspect of British policy was the attitude toward restitution of property and indemnification to the victims of Nazi persecution. This issue had already been raised in the fall of 1945 as part of the reparations claims submitted to the Allies by the Jewish Agency, the World Jewish Congress, and other Jewish organizations on behalf of the Jewish people. These claims became a matter for long and complicated political negotiations. In the meantime, however, there was identified Jewish property that had to be dealt with immediately, without waiting for a comprehensive solution. While the Americans enacted Military Rule No. 59 regulating restitution in their zone in November 1947, and the French authorities followed suit, the British refrained from addressing the matter altogether. Even when a restitution act was finally passed in May 1949, they blocked the way for the establishment of a Jewish successor organization that would manage heirless property, and the Jewish Trust Corporation came into being only in 1950. Again, they objected to distinguishing between Jews and non-Jews, and to any laws that granted the Jews preferential treatment. In the American Zone, Jewish individuals and new Jewish communities had recourse, at least in regard to restitution of property, to U.S. law or the Jewish Restitution Successor Organization, but the Jews in the British Zone had to apply either to the German municipal authorities (on communal property matters) or the German *Länder* (federal states) (for personal restitution). From 1949 the *Länder* handled indemnification and compensation in all zones, followed by the Federal Supplementary Law in 1953. Unsurprisingly, the first *Länder* to legislate in the sphere were in the American Zone, under American pressure.[10]

The official British explanation for this policy toward the Jews was that they did not practice racial discrimination like the Nazis. Preferential treatment, they held, would only arouse further anti-Semitism.

What was behind this pseudo-moralistic argument? Some historians believe that Great Britain's responsibilities in Palestine affected their approach, the fear being that Jewish national organizations would put pressure on the British authorities there to open the country to Jewish immigration.[11]

The British were generally strict about movement to and from their zone. As the flow of Jewish refugees from Eastern Europe accelerated, the British, unlike the Americans, tried to prevent illegal entry into territory under their aegis. On the one hand, they introduced an extensive intelligence system to nip such attempts in the bud even before refugees reached the borders; on the other hand, they supervised the DP population carefully in order to find illegals and throw them out. Not only were they concerned about the additional burden, but they were convinced that these refugees, most of whom were Jewish, were helping the Jewish DPs to organize, and that, together with the Zionist organizations, they would exert pressure on the British Mandatory authorities in Palestine.[12]

However, it was the British military officials in Germany who insisted on integration and keeping out refugees. Problems in Palestine were not their concern, but that of their superiors in London. Moreover, once the British Zone closed at the end of 1945, most of the potential pressure for aliyah (immigration to Palestine) came from the American Zone, where the policy was much more permissive. Hindering Jewish organization in the British Zone would not have had much impact, directly or through American intervention, on British Mandatory policy.

Indeed, there were other factors at work. Basically, the British were eager to lighten their burden and solve problems quickly. One scenario of which they were particularly afraid was large-scale immigration to England, which was then in the throes of a deep economic depression. To avoid this, they strove for rapid resettlement of the survivors in Europe, and in Germany in particular. Any special treatment or separate organization of the Jews would have been an obstacle to this process.[13]

Try as might one to find a rational—even innocent—explanation, the policies in the British Zone were really a continuation of deep-seated animosity toward the Jews. Despite the fact that the British had done more for the Jews than many other countries both before and during the war, latent anti-Semitism bubbled beneath the surface. Total disregard for the unique sufferings of the Jews under the Nazis

The British Zone of Occupation

Signs in the entrance of the DP camp Hohne (Belsen) (Yad Vashem Photo-Archives [1498/18])

was a subtle expression of their feelings, which had found expression in British war and immigration policy since the 1930s.[14] The policy toward the Jews in occupied Germany was just more of the same.

If the original intent of the British was to minimize the Jewish problem, they ended up doing the very opposite. The harsh living conditions and the perceived prejudice of the British authorities only fueled the Jewish national militants, both in the camps and in the cities of the British Zone.

The Jewish Population

Although it is difficult to determine the precise number of Jews in the British Zone, particularly in the first days after liberation, the assumption is that about half the surviving Jews in western Germany were gathered there. The figures range from 40,000 (before taking into account the high mortality rates and repatriation) and 20,000 (once the situation had stabilized). In any event, there were more Jews in the British Zone than in the American Zone at first, but the ratio soon changed with the influx of Jews from Eastern Europe to the

American Zone.[15] Survivors in the British Zone concentrated primarily in Bergen-Belsen—the largest of the concentration camps liberated in Germany, and subsequently the largest DP camp.

SURVIVORS OF BERGEN-BELSEN

When Bergen-Belsen was liberated on April 15, 1945, there were about 60,000 inmates, most of them sick and dying. This number declined drastically within the first few weeks. As many as 13,000 died and 17,000 were repatriated, leaving only 27,000 by the time the transfer to the adjacent military camp was completed on May 21. Of these, half urgently required hospitalization.[16]

Exactly how many Jews there were in this group is difficult to establish. Reading the many descriptions of the Bergen-Belsen concentration camp, the "Jewishness" of the camp is not entirely clear. No attempt, it seems, has been made to evaluate the percentage of Jews while Belsen was a concentration camp, and such an evaluation is indeed problematic. In the beginning the camp was obviously meant mainly for Jews, but over time many non-Jews were sent there. This ambiguity is increased by the testimony of outside observers who arrived after the liberation. The picture they painted was very much dependent upon whether they themselves were Jews or non-Jews, and even more so, whether or not they were British.

As a result, the ethnic-religious composition of the Belsen population at the end of the war has never been properly assessed. There is no question, however, that after its reorganization as a DP camp, Belsen was not only primarily Jewish but the very center of Jewish life in the British Zone.

As we have said, Bergen-Belsen was initially a detention camp for exchange Jews. When a section of the camp was turned into a "convalescent camp" in March 1944, however, the situation changed. No data exist for most of the transports after that date. The majority of these newcomers died, and records were wantonly destroyed just before the camp was turned over to the British. Nevertheless, when the "convalescent camp" first opened, before the camps in the East were evacuated, the Jews were apparently a minority in Bergen-Belsen. We know, for instance, that of the 612,000 people transported to Germany in August 1944, only 60,000 were Jews from the Łódź ghetto and 90,000 were Hungarian Jews. In other words, Jews made up less than

25 percent of these transports. A document from January 10, 1945, that lists prisoners in Bergen-Belsen by nationality indicates that only 342 of the 1,823 "convalescent camp" inmates were Jewish.[17]

At the beginning of 1945, after large transports of women arrived from Auschwitz-Birkenau and other concentration camps in the East, the ratio changed drastically. Most of these women, especially those who arrived between the beginning of December 1944 and the beginning of March 1945, were Jews. The transports of men were more heterogeneous, but since the proportion of women was now greater, the proportion of Jews rose also.[18]

The claim that the Jews were the dominant element in Bergen-Belsen is strengthened by Eberhard Kolb's study, especially the last chapter, where he metes out the blame for the Bergen-Belsen atrocities—first and foremost, the murder of Jews. In particular, he singles out Josef Kramer, the last commandant, whose brutality toward the Jews persisted even after Himmler explicitly ordered that the killing be stopped.[19]

After the liberation of Bergen-Belsen, Jewish army chaplains and official reports testify to mass burial ceremonies officiated by chaplains of different faiths. The implication is that non-Jewish victims were also being buried at this time, although no one knows how many.[20]

Captain Sington estimates that Camp One held 25,000 women, among them 18,000 Jews, accounting for over 70 percent of the total. He offers no estimate for the men of Camp One, of whom there were about 15,000, or for the population of Camp Two. We know that women constituted the majority of the prisoners in the last days, and that the proportion of Jews was particularly high. Yet Sington's report on the establishment of Belsen's international committee on April 20, which lists the names of all the members, mentions only three Jews.[21]

Other testimony corroborates the fact that Jews were in the majority. Rabbi Isaac Levy's letter of April 26 to the *Jewish Chronicle* states that there were 25,000 Jews in Camp Two.[22] If we combine Levy's figures for Camp Two about two weeks after the liberation with those of Sington, which relate only to the women of Camp One, Jewish inmates account for more than half the population prior to the commencement of repatriation.

Evidence supporting this conclusion may be found in the testimony of Rabbi Hardman, who relates that when he arrived from Holland the day after liberation, his colleagues in Celle were in a somber mood. "Keep a stiff upper lip, Padre," a colonel told him, "we have just been into Belsen concentration camp and it's horrible. But you have got to go there. You'll find a lot of your people."[23] Rabbi Hardman's claim that Jews came up to him wherever he went might also bear out the presence of a great many Jews, but it is possible that he was approached by Jewish inmates when they saw the Jewish chaplain's insignia on his uniform.

That the Jews constituted the camp's salient element a short while after the liberation is reflected in Sington's description of the various cultural activities he helped to organize after Belsen was turned into a DP camp. Cabaret performances began on May 24, and a library was already functioning before that. Although these and other cultural activities were meant for all the inmates, not just the Jews, most those involved in setting them up and running them were Jews. Sington, unlike other British officials, does not hide this.[24] When Camp Three, the DP camp, came into being, the dominance of the Jews increased even more.[25]

Jews in Bergen-Belsen as a DP Camp

The one factor that determined the Jewishness of Bergen-Belsen more than any other was undoubtedly the repatriation process—the return of survivors to their homelands—which began immediately after the war and was encouraged by the Allies. Repatriation commenced in May, beginning with the French, Dutch, and Belgian survivors, and continued throughout the summer. Czechs and Slovaks also left Belsen at that time. On May 8, 1,000 Czechs were transferred to a temporary camp in Celle, and a convoy of children led by Dr. Collis left for Czechoslovakia in July. Yugoslavs were repatriated in early August, and Hungarians and Romanians in September. Those who remained were mainly Poles. By May 21, when Camp One was evacuated, more than 17,000 people had gone home.[26]

Thus the proportion of Jews was even greater in the beginning of June, although their overall number declined. One reason for the decrease is that some of the repatriates to France, Holland, and Belgium were Jewish.[27] Secondly, some of the Polish Jews left Belsen, voluntarily or otherwise, in the wake of the authorities' attempts to expedite their transfer to Poland. In May 1945 about 1,100 Polish Jews were moved to Celle for this purpose but adamantly refused to return to Poland, preferring to remain stateless and to be sent instead to the stateless persons' camp in Lingen, on the Dutch border.[28] They were later followed by another 3,000 Jews.[29] The evacuation of the sick was a third factor. On June 19 a group of about 400 sick patients left Bergen-Belsen for Lübeck, en route to Sweden. The Swedish government had offered refuge to 7,000 ailing survivors for a period of six months, and in July more than 6,000 were transferred, the great majority of them Jews.[30] Finally, some 14,000 persons died, and again the vast majority were Jews.[31] Despite the fact that the total Jewish population was thus down to 12,000 by the beginning of June, the percentage of Jews in Bergen-Belsen rose to about two-thirds of the overall population, which was approximately 18,000.[32]

To summarize, the British found some 30,000 Jews in Bergen-Belsen when they set the camp free, which was about half the camp's population, and that number was reduced by the time two months had passed. Deaths were the primary reason for this. If we assume that most of the 14,000 who died until mid-June were Jews, 10,000 seems to be a reasonable, albeit low, estimate for Jewish deaths during the first weeks of liberation. Then there was the transfer of 4,000 Jews to Celle and Lingen, and the repatriates, who numbered no more than 4,000 in May. Obviously, all these figures and estimates must be viewed with caution. Let us remember that months passed before lists of survivors were compiled, and the first book of names put together by the Central Jewish Committee came out only in September 1945. No records were kept of those interred in mass graves, although this was done in other liberated camps, such as Buchenwald.[33] Furthermore, the situation was chaotic and people were constantly on the move. Just as there was both forced and voluntary movement out of Belsen, there was also movement into Belsen: Jews from other liberated camps converged there, and some of those returned who had been transferred out. By late summer, the proportion of Jews in Belsen was even higher. Nevertheless, it seems clear that the Jewish element was dominant even during the first six weeks, from the time of liberation until the liquidation of Camp One and the reorganization of the military camp (Camp Three) as a camp for DPs.

After those first six weeks, Bergen-Belsen's Jewish population remained relatively stable because the British refused to admit refugees from the East. This numerical stability also affected the camp's socio-demographic character, which was unique from the outset. Because the Belsen concentration camp served as a "waiting" camp for exchange Jews, there were relatively many children there, some accompanied by a parent, others alone. Transports from death and forced labor camps that arrived up until the very last moment also contributed to the population's makeup, which was not typical of the surviving remnant. There was an exceptionally high ratio of women, and a large number of children—nearly 500—who were either survivors of Belsen or transferred just before liberation from Buchenwald and Theresienstadt.[34]

In Bergen-Belsen, as in other camps in Germany, Polish Jews were the most numerous. There was also a large group of Hungarian Jews—about 3,000—who had survived Auschwitz and constituted at least one-quarter of the camp's Jewish population. Most of the Hungarian Jews were Orthodox, and together with the Polish Hasidim, they formed a strong Orthodox core. Many of the Polish Hasidim were taken to Celle in the hope of persuading them to return to Poland, but some eventually went back to Belsen and others stayed on in Celle, establishing a community there.[35]

Along with a small number of refugees who managed to infiltrate Bergen-Belsen despite British policy, this population mix produced a healthy socio-demographic profile. Stability did not imply stagnation. Most of the survivors were young men and women who had lost all their relatives, and hence the drive to reestablish family units was very strong. Many marriages took place during the first months after liberation, sometimes as many as six or seven a day, followed by a baby boom. By the beginning of 1948, 1,000 babies were born in Belsen, and by the time the camp was liquidated in September 1950 there were 1,000 more.[36]

Distribution of Jews in the British Zone

When the war ended, close to half of the Jewish survivors in western Germany were to be found in the British Zone. This is because Bergen-Belsen was the chief holding ground for prisoners transferred from the East, and also because there were many forced labor camps in the vicinity that supplied the Nazis with workers for the ammunition industry. The percentage of Jews in these camps was quite large, especially in Hanover and, to a lesser extent, in Neuengamme (Hamburg); unfortunately, we have no reliable estimate for how many of them survived.[37]

The bulk of the Jews—12,000 out of 20,000—were in the Belsen camp. The rest were scattered among other camps in the British Zone: Celle, Diepholz, Kaunitz, Lingen, Lübeck, Lüneburg, and Neustadt.

There were also small clusters of Jews in Brunswick, Cologne, Düsseldorf, Hamburg, Hanover, and Kiel. Some were living inside the cities and others in camps on their outskirts, as in Celle, Hanover, and Kiel.

It is virtually impossible to estimate the number of Jews living outside Belsen immediately after the liberation. The earliest figures at our disposal are from the summer and autumn of 1945, and they tend to be incomplete. Moreover, with all the migration from place to place in these early days, much of the information is contradictory. It is believed, for example, that there were 2,000 Jews in Celle, 600 in Lüneburg, and 1,000 in Neustadt.[38] When it comes to Lübeck, one source says there were 800 Jews, going down to 400, and another source says there were only 100–200.[39] For Hamburg the figures range from 1,600 German Jews at liberation to 650, later joined by 500 survivors from Theresienstadt and other camps.[40] Between 200 and 300 Jews are said to have returned to Düsseldorf, 300 to Bonn, and 500 to Cologne.[41]

By the beginning of 1946 there were roughly 16,000 Jews in the British Zone, with 9,000 in Bergen-Belsen. At the same time, there were 8,500 Jews living in the cities outside the camps (1,500 in the British sector of Berlin). Hamburg had a Jewish population of 800; Cologne, 700; Düsseldorf and Celle, 400 each; Lübeck, Gelsenkirchen, and Lüneburg, 300 each; and Brunswick, 150.

German Jews accounted for only half the Jewish population in the cities. There were 4,000 German Jews and 3,750 Polish Jews. The rest were mainly Hungarian and Romanian. Some 10,000 half-Jews were also affiliated with the Jewish communities.[42]

Within the British Zone, there were forty-five DP camps. Twenty-one of them were very small, with fewer than 10 DPs each. Others were somewhat larger: fourteen camps held up to 50 persons, four camps up to 200, and three camps held 350 to 800 each. Bergen-Belsen, as noted, was the largest, with 9,000 DPs.[43]

By the end of 1946 there were still about 16,000 Jews in the British Zone, among them 6,300 city dwellers. The Jewish DP population at this time was around 12,500, with 11,400 of them in Bergen-Belsen. A large number of these—5,000–6,000—were German Jews.[44] During 1947 these figures dropped even further as the British restricted and then prohibited the entry of refugees, at the same time encouraging immigration to the United States and, later, to Palestine.[45]

To conclude, compared with their counterparts in the American Zone, the Jewish population in the British Zone was small and quite stable from the end of 1945 onward. The percentage of city dwellers was high, and many were German Jews. The group that stood out, however, was that of the DPs, concentrated almost entirely in Bergen-Belsen—by far the largest camp in Germany (almost twice the size of Landsberg, the largest camp in the American Zone). Thus it is not surprising that Bergen-Belsen soon became the social, organizational, and political center of the survivors.

4

JEWISH ORGANIZATIONAL EFFORTS IN BERGEN-BELSEN

Spontaneous Organization

The survivors in Bergen-Belsen were quick to organize. As soon as the camp was liberated they established a fifteen-member multinational committee, only three of whose members were Jews.[1] No one expected this committee to last long. It was believed that the camp would soon be liquidated through repatriation or emigration, and indeed, the three Jewish members—French, Dutch, and Hungarian—soon returned to their home countries. During these early days, however, a framework for Jewish self-government was also evolving. The survivors in Camp Two, who had arrived only recently and were in better shape than those in Camp One, began to organize. Three blocks of survivors elected committees, and on April 25 a joint committee was formed consisting of representatives of all three. The main purpose was liaison with the British authorities. The elected chairman was a Dutch Jew who was soon repatriated to Holland. He was replaced by a Czech Jew who went back to Czechoslovakia. Finally, Josef (Yossele) Rosensaft, chairman of one of the block committees, became head of the committee, despite the fact that he could not speak English.[2]

This is how Rosensaft himself described his election twenty years later:

> On April 16th or 17th people gathered. . . . There were a few candidates. . . . The *Katzetniks*—the people of Bedzin—who knew me very well and were the most robust among us, suggested me as a candidate. But there was also another incident that was very significant in those days. The food was distributed by the *Blockälteste* and there was one of them—not so righteous but not a beast either—who was asked to change his way of doling out the soup. If he mixed it, the soup would be thicker for all. The man responded by striking the complainer on

the head with the ladle. I grabbed the ladle out of his hand, sent him to join the queue, and began doling out the soup myself, making an effort to treat everybody equally. This in itself, along with the support of the Bedzin survivors, was enough to make me chairman of the committee.[3]

Thus Bergen-Belsen already had a functioning Jewish committee within two weeks of liberation.[4]

Much can be learned about the character of this organization from the survivors who helped to establish it and the people they elected as their leaders. By sheer luck, nearly half of the survivors arrived just a few days before liberation. Therefore, despite the horrible conditions prevailing in the camp, most of them were still in reasonable physical shape, and many were young. In a letter to the *Jewish Chronicle*, the Jewish army chaplain, Rabbi Levy, draws an admiring portrait of them ten days after the Nazi defeat:

> But in the midst of all this horror . . . would that I could find another word . . . life goes on and a spirit and a determination to live have kindled a new fire amongst the younger victims. The Hebrew tongue is heard within this camp. Hebrew songs are being sung. The young Zionists of Poland and Hungary and Czechoslovakia have fought throughout their suffering to maintain their balance and have survived. Shall I ever forget . . . those meetings within the huts when we sat and talked and sang Hebrew songs? Will the world believe that such a spirit of obstinacy and tenacity is possible? Two days ago I met a group of young Zionists from Poland. They were living in one of the filthiest of the blocks but their own corner was spotless. Upon the departure of the S. S. they have found a few beds and cupboards and tablecloths and the other meagre necessities for a decent existence. . . . Here the voice of Palestine is heard and the yearning is intense. They speak Hebrew and talk of their future in Palestine. I joined them one evening and we sat and talked and sang songs. They asked for news of the *Yishuv* [the Jewish community in Palestine] and its progress, of the effects of the war upon the kibbutzim. Of how they yearn for their true freedom. We talked to a late hour and then we stood and sang *Hatikvah* [the Jewish national anthem]. "*Od lo avedah tikvateinu*" ["Our hope is not lost yet"]. Those words had a new meaning when we sat in such surroundings. And can I forget the meeting yesterday with over 2,000 men in Camp Two—the first visit they had received from a Jew from the outside world? By chance I saw one of their band waiting outside Camp No. 1. He had come to ascertain whether the mother and sister of one of his comrades were still alive. Thank God, they were and we could bring

greetings from one half of the family to the other. Five years absence had separated them and now they are both in Belsen. Upon his left arm was a blue and white armlet bearing the words "*Segan hablock*" [assistant block manager]. His comrade had a similar armlet bearing the word "*Mitbach*" [kitchen]. I learned from them that there were many Jewish men in the other camp and arranged with them for a meeting. It was an unforgettable experience. Haggard men, old and young massed in the square between the blocks and I stood upon a table and talked to them. They thirstily waited for news of the day when they would be free completely and be permitted to leave the camp. Would to Heaven that I could have told them. Who knows when that day will come. The youths, numbering some 300, paraded specially for me and marched to the meeting, each one bearing a blue and white *Magen David* [Shield of David] on his cap and the national flag fluttering before the parade. Could I resist the temptation to stand at the salute in greeting this young army of stalwarts and survivors? Speeches were delivered in Hebrew and Yiddish. For the first time I had met the last remaining traces of Polish Jewry in Germany. Hebrew was everywhere to be seen and heard. The self-appointed committee of "*Block-Leiters*" [block managers] called me to conference. The door of their room bore a Hebrew inscription.[5]

David Kudish and Captain Deutsch, both members of the Jewish Brigade, were also deeply impressed by the Zionist spirit demonstrated by the survivors. Kudish wrote:

At this moment of writing I'm near a place called Celle, northeast of Hanover. In this place I have met about 1,100 Jews, all Polish Jews who have been brought there from Belsen and various camps; they are there ostensibly for the purpose of being sent back to Poland. I don't think I need tell you that for all of them there is only one land to go to and that is *Eretz Yisrael*. Not only do they say they don't want to go, but that they won't go back. I don't think there is one who has not lost most of his family. Most of them are the only survivors of whole families. . . . Hardly any children are left. . . . What remains are old men before their time, among whom are a few *chalutzim* [pioneers] from *Hashomer* and *Gordonia* [Zionist youth movements]. . . . If you could have seen with what joy they grabbed the paper on which was printed the first Hebrew words they had seen in so many years, how they sang Yiddish and Hebrew songs . . . poems of Bialik which were at that moment so dear to them. When I go there, immediately they all come round to say *Shalom Aleichem* [Hebrew greeting], . . . while the *chalutzim* look into my hands to see if I have an *iton* [newspaper], . . . anything in Hebrew, anything from

Eretz, and how inadequate I feel myself, not to be able to do more than the nothing I am only able to do.[6]

Captain Deutsch claimed to have spoken more Hebrew during his two weeks in Bergen-Belsen than he had in the two previous years.[7]

Back in the Polish and Lithuanian shtetels (small towns), these young people apparently belonged to Zionist youth movements and were preparing for a life of pioneering in Palestine. They could speak Hebrew and had known Hebrew songs from their childhood. The spirited group had a significant impact on the mood in the camp. First of all, they were quite numerous. Second, they were physically and mentally strong, which is probably why they survived in the first place. If anyone could organize the survivors, broken and exhausted by their ordeal, they could. Moreover, these young people had something to offer. They had a real goal. They were full of hope, and their strong Zionist belief and enthusiasm transmitted itself to others. Their personal fate became inextricably linked to the fate of their own people, leading to a spontaneous decision not to return to Eastern Europe. Even before the survivors had recovered sufficiently to decide what to do next—to search for relatives, to try and build something out of the ruins, to think about the future—these young Zionists served as a compass and a guide.

The Provisional Committee, led by Rosensaft, functioned until the first Congress of the *She'erit Hapletah* (the surviving remnant) met in Bergen-Belsen in September 1945. Committee members came and went, and the names are not consistent in all the sources, but certain figures do stand out.[8] One, of course, was Yossele Rosensaft (1911–75), the chairman. Rosensaft was born in Bedzin, Poland, the son of Gur Hasidim (the followers of the Rabbi of Gur, an extreme hasidic trend). He rebelled against his strict religious home and became a Zionist, joining the left-wing Poale Zion movement. Rosensaft's leadership qualities were already evident prior to the war, particularly during the Nazi occupation. In June 1943 he and his family were rounded up in Ghetto Bedzin. On the way to Auschwitz he managed to jump off the train and returned to the ghetto. He was caught again and again, managing to escape several times. In April 1944 he was deported to Auschwitz, transferred to another camp, and then sent to Dora-Mittelbau. He ended up at Bergen-Belsen in the large transport that arrived two weeks before liberation.

Full of vigor and fiercely dedicated to his goal, Rosensaft had a special talent for identifying problems and improvising solutions. He was not a member of the elite or the intelligentsia but was a genuine representative of the Polish Jewish masses. He spoke their language and understood their needs and wishes. Rosensaft was endowed with natural wisdom and a keen sense of justice. He was generous, spontaneous, and open with people and possessed a fine sense of humor. On the other hand, he was a determined man who wanted things done his way and would take vigorous action to ensure that they were. Although he knew only Yiddish, he would take on anyone—generals, politicians, and intellectuals, Jewish or non-Jewish. His self-confident, lively approach worked like a charm. Even when people criticized his autocratic manner, it was hard not to succumb to the man's charisma.

Rosensaft emerged from the trauma of the Holocaust stronger in body and mind than most of his comrades. His life experiences and resistant nature helped him to become a master problem solver. He remained at Bergen-Belsen and served as chairman of the Central Committee of the British Zone until its final days, in the summer of 1950. In 1957, after having settled with his family in Switzerland, he immigrated to the United States. Throughout his life, however, he maintained a firm commitment to Israel, fostering ties and participating in business and public affairs.[9]

Israel Moshe Olevsky (1916–66), born in Osienciny, Poland, was an Orthodox rabbi and a member of the strictly Orthodox non-Zionist Agudath Israel movement. He, too, moved from one concentration camp to another before reaching Bergen-Belsen, where he was reunited with his elder brother, Rafael. After liberation, he settled in the nearby town of Celle (to which about 1,000 Belsen survivors were transferred by the British), dedicating himself to religious affairs and education. A founding member and leader of the Hasidic community established in Celle by the Polish Jewish DPs, Olevsky represented this community in the Provisional Committee and later in the Central Committee of the British Zone. In Celle he married a fellow survivor (his first wife had perished in the Holocaust), and in 1950 they immigrated to the United States. Like Rosensaft, he maintained warm connections with Israel, and was buried in Jerusalem.[10]

Rafael Gershon Olevsky (1914–81), the elder brother of Israel Moshe, a teacher and journalist, had been a member of the General Zionist Party in Poland and active in Keren Kayemet Le'israel (Jewish National Fund) before being deported to the camps. In Bergen-Belsen he met his brother, the only other family member to have survived.

New Beginnings

After being elected head of his block, Olevsky became a member of the Provisional Committee, and then president of the committee in Celle, where he was transferred for a short while. He was also a cofounder and editor of *Unzer Sztyme* (Our Voice), the first publication of *She'erit Hapletah*. When the Central Committee was formed, he became one of the three leaders of its Culture Department and Historical Committee and helped to organize illegal immigration to Palestine. In Bergen-Belsen he married a survivor, and his eldest daughter was born there. In 1949 Olevsky moved to Israel, where he was among the founders of a Bergen-Belsen survivors' organization—Irgun She'erit Hapletah Mehaezor Habriti (Bergen-Belsen)—of which he was chairman for many years.[11]

Dr. Hadassa Bimko (1910–97), from Sosnowiec, Poland, was a dentist who studied medicine in Nancy. She was also at home in Hebrew culture and an ardent Zionist. She was deported to Auschwitz, and then to Belsen, where she arrived on November 23, 1944, and made a name for herself in caring for the children during the horrors of Belsen in its worst times, before and after liberation. She then headed a team of survivor-doctors who actively assisted the British in their rescue efforts, and soon became the head of the Health Department of the Jewish Central Committee, where she continued to care particularly for the children. Broad-minded, educated, and proficient in many languages, Bimko was a key witness in the Lüneburg trials (British military tribunal on Bergen-Belsen crimes), which opened in September 1945. Bimko married Yossele Rosensaft, and their only son, Menachem, was born in Belsen. After settling in the United States with her family, she became active in commemorating the Holocaust and was one of the founding members of the United States Holocaust Memorial Museum in Washington, D.C.[12]

Rabbi Dr. Hermann (Zvi) Helfgott (Asaria) was born in 1913 in Beodra, Banat, to a hasidic family. He studied rabbinical studies and philosophy in Sarajewo, Wienna and Budapest and served in the Yugoslavian army as an army chaplain-officer. In 1941 he was captured by the Germans. Liberated by the British near Celle, he arrived at Belsen on April 30, 1945, and immediately assumed the role of army chaplain, doing whatever he could to ease the suffering and promote the rehabilitation of the survivors. Shortly afterward the Yugoslavian Anti-Fascist Committee in Germany asked him to serve as liaison officer in the repatriation of Yugoslavian nationals, and he joined the Jewish Provisional Committee.

Helfgott was essentially a middleman. He was a survivor of the war, not of the concentration camps; he was neither a liberator nor a foreign emissary, although he functioned like one; and he felt a spiritual affinity with the Eastern European survivors, although he was at home in the German Jewish culture. As a rabbinical authority, he enjoyed wide acceptance and was soon appointed chief rabbi for the British Zone. When Israel's War of Independence broke out, Helfgott made aliyah and joined the Israeli army. Later he returned to Germany to serve as the rabbi of Cologne and Hanover for a number of years. Helfgott is the author of many books on the history of German Jewry and on the post-Holocaust period.[13]

Norbert Wollheim (1913–98), born in Berlin, was active in Jewish community affairs. When the Nazis came to power, he helped to organize the transfer of Jewish children and youth to England. During the war he was a forced laborer at Auschwitz-Birkenau, working at the I. G. Farben factory. His wife and son perished, but Wollheim survived. Liberated near Lübeck, he was soon recognized by his fellow survivors as a natural leader. In June, upon hearing about the Jewish organizational efforts in Bergen-Belsen, he was eager to take part. There were no communication or transportation services in the civil sector until about six months after liberation, and he had to be very skillful and enterprising to get around, but Wollheim managed to reach Belsen and join the Provisional Committee, although he continued to reside in Lübeck. With his knowledge of German and English, he became Rosensaft's righthand man in handling liaisons between Bergen-Belsen and the outside world. When the Central Committee of the British Zone was founded in September 1945, Wollheim was appointed deputy chairman and head of its Department for Community Affairs. In 1951, after remarrying and establishing a new family, he immigrated to New York and became an accountant. Wollheim maintained an ongoing interest in Jewish affairs and Israel and helped to organize projects commemorating the Holocaust.[14]

Paul Pinhas Trepman (1916–87) was a teacher and a member of the Zionist Revisionist movement in Warsaw. After spending most of the war in the Polish underground, he ended up in Bergen-Belsen and was set free by the British. Trepman was among those who were temporarily transferred to Celle. There he helped to publish *Unzer Sztyme* and establish a Jewish school, in which he taught. Aside from serving on the Central Committee as one of the three heads of its Culture Department, Trepman was an active member of the Revisionist Betar movement in the British Zone. Eventually he immigrated to Canada and became the director of the Jewish library in Montreal.[15]

Berl (Dov Bernhard) Laufer, from Chrzanów, Poland, had been a leader of Gordonia, the Labor Zionist youth movement, before being deported to Auschwitz, where most of his family perished. Naturally drawn to public activity, he headed the committee of survivors transferred to Celle and then became secretary of the Central Committee elected in September 1945. Laufer was one of the organizers of Noham (Noar Halutzi Meuhad), a pioneer youth movement established in Germany. After his immigration to Canada he worked tirelessly to commemorate the Holocaust, and Bergen-Belsen in particular.[16]

David Rosenthal (born 1919) was a Yiddish author and Labor Zionist from Warsaw who also survived Auschwitz. Together with Trepman and Olevsky, he helped to publish *Unzer Sztyme*, and he served with them as cultural director of the Central Committee. Rosenthal immigrated to the United States and settled in Philadelphia.[17]

In short, the Provisional Committee constituted an extremely diverse group. Many of the members were former intellectuals, representing a wide range of political beliefs and degrees of religious observance. Most had been active in communal affairs before the war, and quite a few had been Zionists, but none had actually been a leader in the past and few had known each other previously.[18]

The organization of Jewish DPs in Bergen-Belsen was thus a spontaneous phenomenon that gave birth to a new set of leaders with no legacy of former leadership but with a common spiritual and ideological background. These were not people resting on their laurels or pressured into becoming leaders by any outside force, but individuals who stood out in the first days after liberation because they were able to respond constructively to the situation at hand. The emergence of the Bergen-Belsen leadership was a product of the indefatigable spirit of a large group of survivors who were able to set the tone right from the beginning. When freedom did not come immediately, they were bitterly disappointed, but adversity, it turns out, only strengthened their resolve and lent greater force to their national aspirations.

From Spontaneous Organizational Efforts to a National Struggle

> The freedom they have now is bitter. Bitter disillusion came in the wake of liberation. They live in ex-German barracks in which the

Russians had been. The place was in the filthiest condition . . . [and] are terribly overcrowded. . . .

This week-end they were told that they had to come to a decision. . . . Their choice was either to retain Polish citizenship and return to Poland or else to renounce Polish citizenship and become "Stateless." Nobody wanted to go back to Poland, and yet they didn't want to remain "Stateless," they were afraid of being "Stateless. . . ."

Yesterday, when I saw them, they told me that a Polish officer had informed them at Bergen that they had no need to renounce Polish citizenship, but can state thus: that they are still Polish citizens, but want to go to *Eretz Yisrael* and not to Poland. I think they are taking this step. . . . Myself I am somewhat suspicious of this. . . .

Some of them rather than be "Stateless," would go back to Poland, *if they would be sure of being allowed to emigrate to Palestine.*[19]

The disappointment the DPs felt after liberation was a main factor in turning their spontaneous organizational attempts into a solid national framework. The Provisional Committee represented a broad cross section of the DP population, but in the face of harsh conditions and hostility toward Jewish cohesiveness, embracing Zionism provided a strong focal point around which the survivors could rally. The early elected Jewish leadership thus became a cornerstone for national unification that encompassed all the Jews in the British Zone.

Soon after its election, the Provisional Committee set to work to construct a framework and define its goals. On July 8, 1945, a conference was held in Bergen-Belsen and attended by fifty-four representatives of the camps in the British and American Zones, as well as representatives of the American Jewish Joint Distribution Committee (JDC) and the British Jewish Relief Unit (JRU). The purpose of this conference was "to discuss the present and the future of the Jewish people in the camps."[20] A committee was elected at this forum to represent the Jewish DPs in contacts with the military authorities, the Allies, and the United Nations, and to pose three demands: unrestricted emigration for those who refused to be repatriated; the provision of necessary infrastructure for cultural, educational, and vocational centers in the camps that would operate until emigration became possible; and recognition of the committee as the authorized representative of all Jews in the American and British Zones.

Eight days later, on July 16, 1945, a second convention took place, this time of British Zone representatives only, but including representatives of the Jewish communities outside the camps. By this time the

The First Congress of the *She'erit Hapletah*, September 1945: the cover of the protocol of the proceedings of the congress, issued by the Central Committee (private collection)

Jewish Organizational Efforts

Provisional Committee established in Bergen-Belsen seems to have extended its authority over the whole of the British Zone. At this forum, a subcommittee was elected to prepare for a general Jewish congress in Germany, and the forthcoming Zionist Congress was also discussed (the Twenty-second Zionist Congress was not scheduled to take place before December 1946; the convention participants may have had in mind a meeting of Zionist officials in London in August 1945).[21]

These conventions were not really about Zionism. The goal was to organize a united front against the strict rules laid down by the British, to improve living conditions in the camp, and to speed up the liberation process. However, in the time between these gatherings and the next convention in September, the Zionist spirit seems to have strengthened and become much more intense. This occurred for a variety of reasons, both positive and negative. One of the leading positive factors was the cultural and educational activity of the Provisional Committee, which was clearly Zionist in orientation and did wonders for the overall mood. A school and a kindergarten were already operating in Bergen-Belsen and Celle by June. The teacher in Celle was Paul Trepman, and in Belsen, too, the teaching staff came from among the survivors. The entire curriculum was in Hebrew, and Land of Israel studies were a major component.[22]

July 20 brought the appearance of the first issue of *Unzer Sztyme*, one of the first Yiddish newsletters to be published in post-Holocaust Germany.[23] Behind it stood three Provisional Committee members—David Rosenthal, Paul Trepman, and Rafael Olevsky—who had long dreamed of putting out a Jewish newspaper but were prevented from doing so by a British ban on such activity in the camps. After all three were transferred to Celle, they were finally able to realize this dream. Due to British restrictions and the lack of equipment, the first issues were handwritten and mimeographed, and rather than coming out twice a week as planned, a whole month passed before the next issue appeared. Nevertheless, *Unzer Sztyme* carried a vibrant Zionist message that spread throughout the British Zone.

Around this time, the first soldiers of the Jewish Brigade appeared in the British Zone.[24] Their immediate involvement in Jewish cultural activity, schools, and pioneer training programs strengthened the Zionist fervor that had already taken root. These soldiers constituted practically the only contact with the Jewish world outside Germany, which made them particularly influential, and increased the survivors' desire for a connection with Zionism and *Eretz Yisrael*.[25]

British Jews sent in by the JRU also bolstered the Zionist spirit. The JRU was not a Zionist entity, but most of its workers held Zionist beliefs and belonged to Zionist organizations. The same held true for the military chaplains who came to Belsen. A point worth remembering is that as the horrific outcome of the Holocaust came to light and the Jewish world embarked on a mission to rehabilitate the surviving remnant—the *She'erit Hapletah*—pro-Zionist consensus emerged that had not existed before. In 1943, presidential elections for the Board of Deputies of British Jews were fought on Zionist versus non-Zionist lines and won by a prominent Zionist—Professor Selig Brodetsky, a member of the World Zionist Executive. The strictly Orthodox Agudath Israel movement also began to reevaluate its anti-Zionist thinking, and at the convention of its British branch in May 1945 it declared the rehabilitation of Holocaust survivors and resettlement in Palestine mutually dependent. One of the heads of the Central British Fund, which organized and financed the Jewish Committee for Relief Abroad toward the end of the war, was the well-known Zionist Norman Bentwich. The chief rabbi of Great Britain, Joseph Hertz, who set up the Chief Rabbi's Religious Emergency Council for European Jews, was a long-standing Zionist, too.[26]

Aside from these positive reasons for embracing Zionism, there was also an element of defiance. The intransigence of the British liberators on many issues and the harsh living conditions to which the Jews were subjected in the British Zone—and this included rescue teams from abroad as well as survivors—created a wall of resistance that helped to reinforce the Jewish national struggle. Whereas welfare workers from America and Britain continued to arrive, emissaries from Palestine were barred from the British Zone, and despite a concerted diplomatic effort by the Jewish organizations in Britain and the World Jewish Congress (WJC) to bring about a change in the British policy, no changes were made. The British insisted on nonseparation of the Jews in the camps and prevented affirmative actions on behalf of the Jews in the cities. This hindered improvement of living conditions, work of Jewish missions from abroad, the appointment of Jewish liaison officers, and so forth. In consequence, relief efforts specifically earmarked for Jewish welfare were severely restricted.[27]

The British also disrupted Jewish attempts to organize. All requests for a general Jewish congress were turned down, no separate Jewish representational bodies were recognized, and no delegations were allowed to visit Bergen-Belsen from other parts of Germany or abroad. The attitude of the British is perhaps best exemplified by their refusal to use the name "Bergen-Belsen," even though the DP camp was only a short distance from the liquidated death camp. In all British documents it is referred to as the "Hohne camp," Hohne being another small town nearby.[28]

Through their actions, the British liberators thus defeated their own purpose. Their anti-Jewish policies created a broad Jewish front inside and outside Germany aimed at the achievement of immediate Jewish national goals. From here, the move to long-range national goals was only a matter of time.

The Establishment of a United National Front

On July 25, 1945, a general assembly was held in Munich to address issues of concern to both the American and British Zones. In practice, it was run by the leaders of the American Zone alone and failed to establish a united organization for the whole of Germany. However, now that a separate framework had been created for the American Zone, the leaders of Bergen-Belsen realized they would have to be more forceful in convening a congress for the British Zone.[29] Without applying to the authorities, the congress was scheduled for September 1945 in a deliberate attempt to circumvent the British prohibition on delegates from abroad. The idea was to take advantage of the many Jewish leaders and journalists allowed into Germany as participants or observers at the Lüneburg trials, about to open on September 17.

The congress took place as planned on September 25–27, without obtaining British permission. A total of 210 delegates, representing a population of 40,000 Jews from forty-two camps and communities, convened at Bergen-Belsen. Theoretically, various zones of occupation were participating, but this time the American Zone (Bavaria) was absent and the congress was run by the leaders of the British Zone. Representatives of many Jewish organizations were present, too, mostly from Great Britain: Selig Brodetsky, president of the Board of Deputies and a member of the Zionist Executive; Samuel Sidney Silverman, a member of the British Parliament and chairman of the WJC in Britain; journalist Alexander L. Easterman, head of the WJC political department; representatives of the JDC (Jacob L. Trobe) and JRU (Leonard Cohen); a delegation of Jewish Brigade soldiers lead by Meir Grabovsky-Argov, a member of the Zionist Actions Committee; British officers devoted to the Jewish cause, such as Brigadier Glyn Hughes and Jewish army chaplains; and a large number of journalists, including Norman Lurie, the war correspondent attached to the Jewish Brigade.

The Bergen-Belsen congress convened under the Zionist flag, which had already been adopted as the Jewish flag throughout the post-Holocaust Jewish world. The congress was also united in its call to "Open the Gates of Palestine"—the slogan that appeared in Hebrew, Yiddish, and English on the front page of the congressional protocol. The congress began with the singing of *Hatikvah* (the Jewish national anthem) and a march to the mass graves led by a group of young survivors in blue and white uniforms, waving blue and white banners. In the unveiling of the memorial to the dead, Rosensaft said a few words that expressed the solemnity of the occasion: "Standing over this grave, we swear by all that is holy to devote our lives, saved purely by chance, to our people and our one and only homeland—*Eretz Yisrael*."

The main speakers—Rosensaft and Wollheim on behalf of the survivors, and Brodetsky and Silverman on behalf of world Jewry—were united in their demand to solve the Jewish DP problem through resettlement in *Eretz Yisrael*—the sole solution, from their point of view. The many others who took part in the congressional debates, representing a wide spectrum of political beliefs, followed suit. In his concluding remarks, Brodetsky put into words what everyone was feeling:

> I came here with a sense of anxicty. I have no right to talk to you as a peer to his peers. You are the heroes. There is no Jew in the world who can say to himself that he has done everything he could do to help you. I was afraid even to laugh in your presence. But, confronting your laughter—I begin to smile. I will convey your greetings to the Jews abroad . . . and tell the world what is happening here. . . . I came here not only to see you but to plead for your assistance in the struggle for *Eretz Yisrael*. Your congress has inspired me, and created a sense of hope. I shall return to Britain with your songs on my lips and your spirit in my heart. When next we meet let it be in *Eretz Yisrael*.

Rosensaft ended with a similar hope: "We are now entering an era in which we must fight for our rights. We have been slaves, but now we are free, the children of a free nation. . . . May we be blessed to convene our next congress in *Eretz Yisrael*."[30]

The Bergen-Belsen congress, which started out as a general assembly of the *She'erit Hapletah*, focused, in the end, on the British Zone alone, laying the foundations for a more solid organizational structure. A seventeen-person Central Committee was elected, representing the entire region, with its headquarters in Bergen-Belsen. Yossele Rosensaft was elected chairman, and Norbert Wollheim was chosen as his deputy and the representative of the communities. Berl Dov Laufer was appointed organizational secretary; Hadassa Bimko, head of the Health Department; Olevsky, Trepman, and Rosenthal, heads of the Culture Department and editors of *Unzer Sztyme;* and Sami Feder, founder of the KZ Yiddish theater "Kazet Theater" ("Kazet," pronounced "Katzet," stands for the two letters KZ, the German abbreviation for "Konzentrationslager"=Concentration camp), that gave its premiere at the congress, theater director. Rabbi Israel Moshe Olevsky represented the Orthodox sector, and Rabbi Zvi Helfgott was the authority on rabbinical issues. Shmuel Weintraub of Hapo'el Hamizrahi (the religious Zionists) and Karl Katz of the Bremen community took charge of the Economic Department, which handled the allocation of food, clothing, and housing.[31]

The congress in September 1945 thus gave birth to an active national organization that appeared as a united front demanding free immigration to Palestine. This demand could not surprise on the background described above, and especially following Earl G. Harrison's recommendation that the Jewish DP problem be solved through immigration to Palestine. At this time, however, this demand did not aim at a Jewish state, which was not even on the political agenda of the World Zionist Organization.[32] The DPs became increasingly militant as time went on, resorting to demonstrations, strikes, and even violence. When David Ben-Gurion, head of the Jewish Agency, arrived at the end of October 1945 he found a cohesive and determined Jewish entity, ready to join the Zionist struggle for immigration to Palestine.[33]

5

NEW COMMUNITIES RISE FROM THE ASHES

The German Jewish Remnant in the British Zone

Before the Nazis came to power, close to 560,000 Jews lived in Germany. By 1939 some 322,000 had emigrated, and in 1941, when emigration ground to a halt, the Jewish population was down to 150,000. Most were eventually deported and perished in the camps. The number of German Jewish survivors on German soil at the time of liberation was probably 18,000 to 20,000. Adding to that number were some 9,000 survivors of the concentration camps, mainly Theresienstadt, who returned to their hometowns.[1] We shall turn our attention to the most important communities in the British Zone, examining the fate of the surviving German Jews who would rebuild these communities after the war.

COLOGNE

The Jewish community in Cologne had been the fifth largest in Germany. In 1925 it was home to 16,000 Jews, and the Nazi census in 1933 found 14,800 *Glaubensjuden* (practicing "full" Jews in Nazi terminology) and about 5,700 *Rassejuden* (Jews by race). Nazi persecution was particularly harsh in Cologne, and it began before the boycott of April 1933. Many local Germans took an active part in the November 1938 pogroms. In the course of the 1930s the Jewish population diminished rapidly through death, suicide, and emigration. In the census of 1938 there were 8,406 Jews, of whom 431 were *Rassejuden* and 1,541 *Mischlinge 1. Grades* (first-degree mixed Jews, according to Nazi racial terminology, i.e., persons with one Jewish parent). After October 1941, emigration was halted and deportations began. By then there were only 6,277 Jews left in Cologne, with another 1,400 in the surrounding area. Most were transferred to barracks at Fort V in Müngersdorf. The transports were mainly to Łódź, Theresienstadt, Riga, and Minsk, and many of the deportees ended up in extermination camps. By the end of 1943, Cologne was almost without Jews. The deportation of half-Jews and Jewish spouses began after July 7, 1944. Nazi persecution in Cologne claimed the lives of some 11,000 Jews, including 95 percent of those deported to Theresienstadt. Very few of the deportees survived.

When the Americans took over Cologne on April 21, 1945, after a fierce battle, they discovered 40–50 Jews who had survived in hiding or with the help of non-Jews.[2] Soon after liberation, about 100 survivors returned from Theresienstadt and another 400 from other concentration camps. At the beginning of 1946 the community numbered 700, more than half of them married to non-Jews. Camp survivors made up the bulk of the population.[3]

Düsseldorf

Düsseldorf, the principal city of North Rhine–Westphalia, had a population of about half a million before the war, including a sizable Jewish community. In 1925 there were 5,130 Jews, and according to the Nazi census of 1933 there were another 3,000 who did not hold official membership in the community. After the Nazis came to power the number declined through emigration, but by 1938 there were still about 3,500 Jews in Düsseldorf. The Kristallnacht pogrom, which began on November 9, 1938, in the wake of the assassination of Ernst vom Rath, the German secretary of the German embassy in Paris, was particularly calamitous for Düsseldorf because this was vom Rath's hometown. The rate of emigration accelerated, and by May 17, 1939, only 1,831 *Glaubensjuden* remained, and these were confined to designated houses. From October 1941, Jews from the Düsseldorf district (including Wuppertal, München-Gladbach, Duisburg, Oberhausen, and Krefeld) were deported to the ghettos of Łódź, Minsk, and Riga, and later to Lublin and Theresienstadt.

By June 1943 only a few Jews remained, most of them through the help of Christian relatives, friends, or neighbors; all lived in mixed marriages or had been born into mixed families. They spent their days in forced labor, cleaning streets and removing debris. In September 1944 this group was sent to a forced labor camp near Hanover, and from there to Theresienstadt in February 1945, where over 2,200 of the deportees perished.

New Beginnings

Located in the heart of the Ruhr industrial region, Düsseldorf was surrounded during the war by six forced labor camps. Jews were incarcerated there, too, but no figures are available.

When American troops entered the bombarded city on April 17, 1945, there were only 57 surviving Jews.[4] They were soon joined by a small band of Jews from the forced labor camps and a few returnees from Holland (Düsseldorf is near the Dutch-German border). With the addition of 200 concentration camp survivors, the Jewish population rose to 400 by January 1946. Nearly 75 percent were married to non-Jews.[5]

HAMBURG

In the pre-Nazi era, Hamburg boasted the fourth-largest Jewish community in Germany. In the general census of June 1933, Hamburg Jews numbered 16,885, comprising 1.5 percent of the total population. In the nearby communities of Altona and Wandsbeck there were 2,000 and 200 Jews, respectively.

By the time the Nazis came to power, the number of Jews was considerably lower. Many had emigrated, but there were also hundreds of suicides and Nazi murders. By 1939 the Jewish population had been reduced by half. Of the 8,000 Jews who remained, many were elderly. Between 1933 and 1941 an estimated 9,000–10,000 Jews left greater Hamburg. Deportations to Łódź, Minsk, and Riga began in October 1941, and somewhat later to Auschwitz and Theresienstadt. The last transport departed on February 14, 1945. Most of the Hamburg deportees—approximately 7,800 persons—perished in the camps.[6]

There were many concentration camps in and around Hamburg. Neuengamme, one of the most infamous, operated as an extension of Sachsenhausen beginning in 1938. From 1940 on it supplied slave laborers for the war industry. Some 13,000 Jews were held at Neuengamme before being deported to death camps. In the spring of 1944, Jewish prisoners from Auschwitz and other death camps were transferred to Neuengamme and its subsidiary camps of Neugraben am Falkenbergsweg and Sasel. Included in the transport were 1,000 women from Czechoslovakia, Holland, and Germany, many of whom died from tuberculosis. Others were killed when the British bombed the camp.

Just before the fall of the city, the Nazis evacuated the male inmates of Neuengamme to the prisoner-of-war camp Sandbostel; the women were sent to Bergen-Belsen. Nine thousand prisoners were boarded on three ships in the port of Lübeck. When they reached Neustadt on May 1945, two of the ships were bombed by the British, who were deliberately misinformed by the Nazis, and the vessels sank with all their passengers. Some 7,000 prisoners drowned in the disaster, many of them Jews.[7]

When Hamburg surrendered on May 3, 1945, after heavy bombardment, the liberators found 638 Jews in the city—352 women and 286 men—all married to non-Jews. Between May and August 1945, 500 survivors of the last transport to Theresienstadt arrived, and gradually the German Jewish population grew to 1,330–1,400. More than half of the survivors were over fifty years of age, and many of them were gravely sick.[8]

Hanover

Hanover, the most important city in Lower Saxony, approximately equal in size to Düsseldorf, had a population of 423,000 in 1925, including 5,500 Jews. Jewish emigration, which began shortly after the Nazis came to power, was counterbalanced by an influx of Jews from small towns and villages, as the big city offered more opportunities to hide. By 1938 some 2,200 Jews had left Hanover and environs (including Schleswig-Holstein). The Nazis deported 1,000 Polish Jews who had been living in the city (among them the parents of Herschel Grynzpan, who took revenge by shooting the secretary of the German embassy in Paris, Ernst vom Rath—the event that served the Nazis as an excuse for the Kristallnacht pogrom). But even after the pogrom, emigration from Hanover did not reach the proportions of the Jewish exodus from other German cities.

The 2,271 Jews remaining in Hanover on May 1939 were confined to *Judenhäuser* (Jews' houses). From December 1941 to February 1945, a total of 2,400 Jews were rounded up and taken to Riga, Warsaw, Auschwitz, and Theresienstadt. Hanover's 175 *Privilegierte Mischehen* (privileged mixed couples with children) were exempt from living in the ghetto or deportation, except for Jewish husbands. All the men were, however, taken to forced labor camps.[9]

Hanover was a center for such camps, which served the local ammunition industry. When the war ended there were 40,000 forced laborers in the Hanover region and six concentration camps with about

6,000 prisoners, many of them Jews. In two of the camps Jews were in the majority: in Ahlem, a former Jewish gardening school, there were some 1,000 Polish Jews from the Łódź ghetto, and in KZ (Konzentrationslager [concentration camp]) Mühlenberg there were several hundred Jewish prisoners who had been transported from Auschwitz at the beginning of 1945. In the last weeks before the German surrender, many of them took part in the death marches to Bergen-Belsen and Neuengamme. When the city surrendered on April 10, 1945, a total of 1,200 Jewish survivors were found in the concentration camps in Hanover.[10]

In the city itself, American troops found 20–30 Jews with non-Jewish spouses and approximately 100 half-Jews. They were soon joined by 120–180 Jews who survived the last transport to Theresienstadt, in February 1945. Thus, the German Jewish population of Hanover was now about 250, most of them returnees from the camps.[11]

Motives for the Reestablishment of German Jewish Communities

The tiny German Jewish remnant in the cities, as well as a large percentage of those who lived through the camps and returned home, owed their survival, as we have seen, to being married to non-Jews or converting to Christianity. Privileged to some degree, they were either deported at a later stage of the war or not deported at all, some hiding with the help of non-Jewish relatives or friends, and others able to secure false papers.[12] Most were highly assimilated members of German society and on the verge of abandoning Judaism before the Nazis came to power. They were older people, many of them educated free professionals or former businessmen.

Having tenuous ties to the Jewish community was not unique to this group. In fact, many of those who lived in Germany before the war were acculturated, integrated, or assimilated Jews. However, both the emigrants and those who remained in Germany began to realize that their self-image as Germans was an illusion, and they sought to identify themselves as Jews once again. Those who were younger and in good health managed to leave Germany before it was too late, but they left their elderly parents behind. Others sent their children abroad but were not able to join them.[13] Opportunities to emigrate decreased in tragic disproportion to the growing desire to escape, which reached a peak in 1938 and 1939. Those who remained were mostly older people whose health declined rapidly during war. That any of them managed to survive the concentration camps was mainly due to their being deported to Theresienstadt very late in the war and then liberated before the Nazis managed to transfer them to Auschwitz.[14]

In the postwar period a number of German Jewish survivors immigrated, mainly to the United States, but also to Palestine, where they had relatives who had left before the catastrophe.[15] The majority, however, resettled in Germany, some without renewing their connection to Judaism, others as founders of Jewish communities.

The establishment of the new communities took place in the early weeks after liberation, in the midst of great chaos, as solutions were sought for the DPs in general and the Jewish DPs in particular. Economic hardship was very great in the British Zone.[16] In the pandemonium, the plight of the German Jews was all but forgotten. Matters might have improved when the chaos was brought under control and an official occupation policy was decided upon, yet this was not the case because the British refused to see the Jews as a separate category.[17] In consequence, the German Jews found themselves in even worse straits than the Jewish DPs, who did enjoy a certain measure of special protection as DPs. Soon after the war, the Allies returned many civic responsibilities to the Germans. German Jews, who were considered German citizens rather than DPs, thus came under the jurisdiction of various German municipalities. Furthermore, only those who had been deported to concentration camps or to ghettos in the East, or who had been forced into *Judenhäuser* in Germany, were treated as victims of the Nazis. This despite the fact that all the surviving Jews, even those who had managed to escape deportation or arrest, had suffered during the war, living in hiding and constant fear. When liberation came at last, they, too, were malnourished, depressed, and in urgent need of medical attention and special care.

Why did these people resettle in Germany? They could have declared unwillingness to return to the land of their persecutors and received DP status. Some did choose this option and were sent to Deggendorf, a DP camp in the American Zone. Many, however, were old and exhausted. They did not have the strength to go on wandering, to be holed up in camps, and to start new lives in foreign countries. All they wanted was to live the rest of their tortured lives in peace. Some felt a sense of loyalty to those who had rescued them—the Christian spouses and friends who had taken risks for their sake.

New Beginnings

Whatever reasons these German Jews had for returning, the cities to which they returned were demolished—especially Hamburg and Cologne—and the economy lay in ruins. Hospitalization, medical care, and housing were their most urgent needs. Their homes were either destroyed by bombing or occupied by others. They had neither property nor income. Most were reluctant to work for German employers. Very few free professionals could rebuild their careers, and businesses could not open their doors without receiving the permission of the authorities or purchasing stock. Some of the survivors did have somebody waiting for them—a non-Jewish partner or friend to whom they owed their lives—but most had no one. Their families had perished, and if they had relatives abroad who had managed to emigrate in time, they had lost contact. Food, clothing, and coal were in short supply, and transportation and communication facilities were almost nonexistent. On the verge of physical and mental breakdown, the survivors were desperate. What gave them the strength to survive somehow was hope for the future. Now, upon their return, they faced a grim reality, and their last shreds of hope were rapidly disappearing.

The liberators, as we have seen, basically ignored them, and the same was true in the Jewish world. Everyone was so busy with the survivors of the concentration camps that no one actually thought about the special problems of the German Jewish remnant. The first Jewish emissaries to reach Germany, who were late in arriving due to various obstacles, were overwhelmed with work in the DP camps.[18]

Without an anchor in the world and with bleak prospects for the future, the German Jews realized that there was no one to turn to apart from themselves. The only solution, they decided, was to organize. Joining associations for victims of the Nazis was not deemed sufficient, and in any case, many German Jews did not qualify for membership because they had not been in the camps. Moreover, their needs were not only physical, but spiritual as well. They longed for Jewish companionship and renewed contact with long-forgotten Jewish traditions. These Jews, who had given up much of their Jewishness before the war, only to be treated as pariahs under the Nazis, now sought a positive, honorable, and fully Jewish life as an expression of gratitude for having been saved.

The desire to organize as a Jewish community was not shared by all the survivors. Many preferred to reintegrate into German society, already being very far from Judaism and any Jewish connection. Some had returned to Germany only temporarily, planning to join family abroad. On the other hand, there were quite a few non-Jewish spouses who identified with their Jewish partners and cast their fate with the Jews during the Nazi era. These people were now eager to belong to a Jewish community. For some, there were also material incentives for joining the Jewish community: special assistance could be obtained through various overseas welfare agencies, both Jewish and non-Jewish. Such people were called *Paketjuden* (package Jews). This was not, however, a widespread phenomenon.[19]

Founders of the Jewish Communities

All the postwar communities were founded by former members of the German Jewish community who made it through the war—as members of the privileged class, in hiding, or as concentration camp survivors. Most were intermarried. On April 29, 1945, Jewish survivors in Cologne—among them Fritz Loewenstein, son of the former Jewish community chairman—met in the synagogue and established a Jewish community board of seven persons. All of them, including the chairman, Hermann Bramson, had survived in the underground—*Untergrundler*. As hundreds of Jews returned from the camps, the community expanded and more people sought to become involved. A new board was elected on November 22, 1945, and Dr. Herbert Lewin, former chief physician of the Jewish hospital, was voted chairman. Toward the end of 1946, when Lewin opened a women's clinic, he was replaced by Moritz Goldschmidt, a Jew from Essen.[20]

Düsseldorf's fifty-seven remaining Jews met as soon as the war was over and elected three veteran residents to head the community. The first was Dr. Rudolf Braunschweig, whom the Nazis had appointed Jewish chairman of the region (*Gau*). He had fled to Vienna in early 1943, but was captured and deported to Auschwitz. After the liberation he returned to Germany. The second was Hamburg-born Philipp Auerbach, who was also deported to Auschwitz after being arrested by the Gestapo in Belgium. He was liberated by the Americans at Buchenwald. In September 1946, after spending several months in Düsseldorf, Auerbach moved to Munich, where he became Staatskommissar für die Opfer des Faschismus (State Commissioner for the Victims of Fascism). His career ended with his being brought to trial on charges of bribery and corruption. He committed suicide in 1952. The third nominee was Julius Dreifuss, who survived the war in hiding outside Düsseldorf. Dreifuss's wife, Meta, a convert to Judaism, was active in Jewish education and cultural affairs. In 1946 he was appointed chairman of both the Düsseldorf Jewish community and of the land organization of all the Jewish communities of North Rhine–Westphalia.[21]

The reorganization of the Jewish community in Hamburg was more complex. The first body to be established was the Aid Committee for the Jews and Half-Jews of Hamburg, headed by a Hamburg attorney, Max Heinemann, and Dr. Ludwig Loeffler, a survivor of the camps. Heinemann had been authorized to oversee the community property by Dr. Max Plaut, the former chairman, who escaped deportation and went to Palestine in 1944, and a Hamburg banker, Max Warburg, a former member of the Reichsvertretung who settled in the United States. Two other organizations active immediately after the war were the Notgemeinschaft der durch die Nürenberger Gesetze Betroffenen (Association of Victims of the Nuremberg Laws) and Die aus Theresienstadt (Those from Theresienstadt), formed a little later by the survivors of Theresienstadt.

The Jewish community of Hamburg was formally established only on September 18, 1945. A five-member board was elected, including Max Heinemann and Ludwig Loeffler, with Harry Goldstein as chairman. Apart from Loeffler, all were married to non-Jews and had survived the war in Hamburg. The community statutes were issued at the beginning of October.[22]

In Hanover, as in Hamburg, a formal leadership body was preceded by the establishment of a spontaneous organizational framework: an aid committee formed a few days after liberation to assist returnees from the concentration camps, and a separate body was organized by survivors of the labor camps. These organizations continued to operate until 1955, although most of the DPs were gone by then.[23] In August 1945 an official Jewish community board was elected, composed of Norbert Prager (a Polish Jew who had been living in Germany since before the Nazi period), Adolf Nussbaum, and Alfred Jonas, all of whom had survived in Hanover.[24]

Most of these community leaders were relatively young. Hermann Bramson of Cologne was forty years old, and his colleague, Dr. Herbert Lewin, was forty-six. Ludwig Loeffler of Hamburg and Philipp Auerbach of Düsseldorf were both thirty-nine, and Julius Dreifuss of Düsseldorf and Moritz Goldschmidt of Cologne were also under fifty. There were, of course, exceptions: Hamburg's Harry Goldstein was sixty-five. They were thus energetic and motivated enough to take upon themselves the weighty task of helping others. Most of them survived the war in their hometowns or returned to them afterward, continuing to serve the Jewish community for the rest of their lives, like Prager in Hanover and Dreifuss in Düsseldorf. Only a few emigrated, as in the case of Heinemann, who left Hamburg for the United States at the end of 1946 in order to join a son who was serving in the American army.[25]

The DP Communities

As we have seen, there were two groups of Jews who settled in the cities—German Jews and DPs.[26] Most of the DPs who took up residence in the cities did so for practical reasons and did not mean to stay there permanently. In Hamburg, for example, there were a few hundred DPs (estimates range from 300 to 800 because people were constantly moving in and out of the city) who had formerly been interned in DP camps in the vicinity. In an effort to get out of Germany, they were seeking a chance to board any ship leaving the port. Others hoped to find better housing, food, and clothing than were available in the camps.[27] In Hanover, a large number of labor camp survivors—approximately 1,200 persons—took over several buildings around the city and founded their own organization, although this conflicted with the interest of the rest of the newly founded Jewish community. This separation existed until 1955, at which time the *Gemeinde* (the Jewish community board) and the DP's Jewish Committee merged and formed a united community framework.[28] In other cases, the DPs were the founders of postwar Jewish communities, as in Brunswick, Celle, and Lübeck.

Brunswick

Before the war, Brunswick (Braunschweig) boasted the second important Jewish community in Lower Saxony, after Hanover. There were 1,750 Jews living there in 1925, but by 1933 only 680 were left, as the city was a Nazi stronghold. In 1939 the number was down to 180, and any remaining Jews were deported between 1942 and 1945.[29] No Jews were left when the Allies arrived, but about 30 deportees, most of them married to non-Jews, returned to Brunswick after the liberation. Some of the 600 DPs scattered in small pockets in and around the city were Jews, but because they were dispersed, organization was difficult.

New Beginnings

Karl Mosberg, one of the few German Jews in Brunswick, did most of the work, drawing up lists and basically getting the community together. After spending the last four months of the war in Theresienstadt, Mosberg returned to Brunswick to join his wife, who was never deported. He became a mediator between the scattered survivors and the welfare agencies who, with the help of the British authorities, found a substitute for the destroyed synagogue and began restoring the Jewish cemetery.

Before the *Gemeinde* was organized, the welfare office in Brunswick was basically run by the survivors, both German Jews and DPs. In the beginning of September 1945, the office was moved from the *Rathaus* (the municipality) to the *Gemeindehaus* (the Jewish community center), formerly the home of the local rabbi. This move was not only a material improvement but a shift away from dependence on the welfare office and an opportunity to run an independent community center. Its activities were much the same as those that concerned all German Jewish communities: consecration of a new synagogue in the *Gemeindehaus* to replace the old synagogue that had been destroyed (an air-raid shelter now stood on its place); searching for Jewish communal property; maintaining the two old Jewish cemeteries; organizing social and educational activities; offering legal advice and information; distributing donations from overseas; and caring for the DPs who wandered through the town in search of relatives. All of this work was carried out by members of the community, most of them DPs. The legal adviser, for example, was a Polish Jewish DP who had been a lawyer before the war. This organization was the sole authority in matters concerning the Jews in Brunswick, and all welfare work was conducted under its auspices. The only difference between the Brunswick community, composed mainly of DPs, and other German Jewish communities was that most of its members were expected to emigrate. The infrastructure for Jewish life that was laid down, however, would later serve as a solid basis for the German Jews who remained.[30]

Celle

Celle, a small town not far from Hanover with a population of 28,000, was home to only 60 Jews in 1933. This number dropped by one-half as members of the community emigrated or moved to the big cities. The last three families in Celle occupied the synagogue building until being deported in the beginning of 1943. Only one survivor returned to Celle.[31]

Celle was the biggest community in postwar Germany that was organized exclusively by DPs. Some 2,000 survivors, mainly Polish Jews, were transferred from Bergen-Belsen to a DP camp in Celle in a British effort to alleviate the overcrowding in Belsen and encourage repatriation to Poland. The authorities warned the survivors that they would be declared stateless if they refused to go back to Poland, but they chose to give up their Polish citizenship and remain in Celle. Under the leadership of Rabbi Israel Moshe Olevsky,[32] they applied to the municipal authorities in June 1945 and won formal recognition as a Jewish community. This allowed them to reclaim community property: a row of buildings on Im Kreise Street, the old synagogue (which was not burned down on Kristallnacht in November 1938 because it was adjacent to a leather factory), and the cemetery. In September 1945 the British decided to transfer the DPs back to Belsen. While the majority did return, a group of 600 decided to stay behind even, if this meant losing their status as DPs and the special privileges that went with it. These Jews preferred to lead a quasi-normal independent life rather than go back to the camps. In March 1946, 450 Jewish DPs were registered as residents of the town. Under Olevsky, the lifestyle became distinctly Hasidic.

This unique Hasidic community was liquidated in 1950, when the DPs emigrated en masse (Olevsky settled in the United States). The synagogue stayed open for several years, serving a tiny group of Jews who remained, but it closed in 1962.[33]

Lübeck

Lübeck was the largest of several small communities in the province of Schleswig-Holstein. In 1925, 629 Jews were living in Lübeck, but only 250 were left by 1937. Deportations—first to Riga, then to Theresienstadt—began in December 1941. Only one woman survived.[34] A group of 100–200 Jews liberated from concentration camps in the region found their way to Lübeck after the war, along with 600 other Jewish survivors. About 400 were repatriated to Czechoslovakia. Many of the remaining 400, some living in town and others in the camps outside it, were Hungarian or Greek Jews.[35]

The founder of the Jewish community, Norbert Wollheim, was not a DP but rather a German Jew.[36] Wollheim, thirty-two, a native of

Berlin, was liberated by the Americans near Lübeck, where he had just escaped from a death march. In Lübeck he obtained permission to use the old synagogue building, which was still standing, although it had been seized by the authorities and ransacked. He also participated in the establishment of the Central Committee in Bergen-Belsen. Wollheim remained in Lübeck until his immigration to the United States in 1951, combining efforts to improve the lot of Jewish survivors in the British Zone with chairmanship of the Lübeck community. As a result, this community very much depended on aid extended by relief agents, especially Rabbi Munk of the Chief Rabbi's Religious Emergency Council and Rabbi Greenbaum of the Jewish Relief Unit.[37]

Summary

By the beginning of 1946, a whole network of Jewish communities existed in the British Zone. Some were founded by German Jews, such as Cologne and Hamburg, with 700–800 members; Düsseldorf, with 400 members; and Hanover, with 250 members. Then there were DP communities such as Brunswick, Celle, Lübeck, and Lüneburg with a membership of 300–500 or less. Many small clusters of Jews, usually a combination of German Jews and DPs, could also be found in the British Zone. All these communities soon began to organize on a regional basis.[38]

6

THE JEWISH WORLD ORGANIZATIONS AND JEWISH EMISSARIES

Besides the United Nations Relief and Rehabilitation Administration (UNRRA), founded by the Allies to provide economic and social aid to war survivors, Jewish organizations were also active in this sphere, setting up new rescue and welfare institutions or revamping old ones. The American Jewish Joint Distribution Committee (JDC), founded in 1914 and instrumental in saving many Jewish lives during World War II, worked nonstop after the war to alleviate the hardships of Jewish DPs and to help Jewish communities in Europe get back on their feet. In Great Britain the Jewish community established the Jewish Committee for Relief Abroad (JCRA) and the Chief Rabbi's Religious Emergency Council (CRREC). Many other organizations—some veteran institutions like the Organization for Rehabilitation and Training (ORT), the Jewish child care agency Oeuvre Secours pour Enfants Juifs (OSE), and the Hebrew Immigrant Aid Society (HIAS), and some newly founded, like the Jewish Agency's Welfare Mission—became involved later on. However, it would be some time before these institutions were allowed to send their workers into occupied Germany. One explanation for this delay is the military authorities' resistance to outside interventions. UNRRA, the largest civilian authority in Germany and Austria, was supposed to run the camps and supplement the basic food and clothing supplies provided by the army. However, due to complaints about the inefficiency of this organization, the army was not inclined to let civilians get in the way or to permit a slew of small voluntary agencies to run the show.[1] On the other hand, this does not explain why non-Jewish civilian groups like the Quakers—organizers of the Friends Relief Service—were allowed into Bergen-Belsen long before Jewish civilians.[2]

When the camp was liberated, the first Jews from the outside world were soldiers and officers of the British army. These were followed by members of the Jewish Brigade and only later by welfare emissaries. The task at hand was gargantuan by any standard, and it was made all the more difficult by the delay. "Rehabilitation work under present circumstances is impossible," wrote Jane Leverson, who reached Bergen-Belsen with the Friends Relief Service team in June 1945. She cited the president of the DP committee as saying, "We want homes, and to be able to *live*, as people, once again."[3] At the end of November she emphasized the survivors' desperate need for "security—security and affection. They need to live a normal life, among normal people. This can never be achieved for the majority of them, in Occupied Germany. Some may be saved if they can get into a friendly, normal environment soon. Some, but not all, but all should have the opportunity."[4]

The absence of any formal Jewish delegation for weeks and months after liberation added to the survivors' deep sense of bitterness. They felt abandoned by their own people. Once the emissaries did arrive, however—primarily from Great Britain, Palestine, and the United States—they fulfilled an important function: helping the survivors to help themselves.

British Jewry

Army Chaplains and the Chief Rabbi's Religious Emergency Council

Rabbi Isaac Levy of London and Rabbi Leslie Hardman of Leeds were British army chaplains. Hardman arrived at Belsen with the liberating forces and stayed there as a de facto welfare officer. He was followed by Levy, a senior Jewish chaplain with the Twenty-first Army Group, and other officers and rabbis in uniform. Others were the liberated Yugoslav officer Rabbi Hermann Zvi Helfgott (Asaria), who reached Belsen about two weeks after liberation, and Rabbi Goldfinger (Ben Jeshaya) of the French army.[5]

The army permitted these rabbis to overstep their formal duties as military chaplains and extend aid to the Jewish survivors, first alone and then in collaboration with the emergency crews. The most immediate task was identifying the Jewish dead and preparing them for burial according to Jewish law. This was a particularly difficult undertaking during the first few weeks, when thousands of corpses were buried in mass graves; individual burial became possible only later on. At the same time, a tremendous effort was made to locate relatives, both inside and outside the camp. The survivors were obsessed with finding family—signifying their will to live—and the chaplains did their utmost to assist, utilizing contacts in Germany and abroad and sending out letters via military post (in contravention of army orders).

In their fight against despair and apathy, the rabbis found that religious ceremonies did much to encourage the survivors and improve the general mood. Organizing Friday night meals, welcoming the Sabbath with kiddush and candles, singing traditional songs and prayers, and handing out wedding bands to young married women (not knowing yet if they were widows)—such activities brought some comfort to the survivors.[6]

Struggling under this unforeseen burden, the chaplains appealed to British Jewry to send material assistance and manpower without delay. The military authorities, which distinguished between groups of survivors on the basis of citizenship and religion alone, did allow rabbis to enter the British Zone. During the first week of May, a few more rabbis arrived: Munk, Vilensky, and Baumgarten, sent by the CRREC and the JCRA under UNRRA auspices, and military chaplains Greenbaum, Richards, and Elton. Some of them were posted to Belsen, and others to Celle, Brunswick, and Hamburg.[7] The rabbis were thus not only religious functionaries but also rescuers in the broad sense, providing crucial moral support in the early days when conditions were at their worst, but also strengthening the hand of German Jews seeking to build new communities—Greenbaum and Munk in Hamburg and Celle, Goldfinger in Brunswick, and so on.[8]

The original goal of the CRREC (founded by Chief Rabbi Joseph Herman Hertz in 1938 as the Chief Rabbi's Religious Emergency Fund for German and Austrian Jewry) was to save children and to bring rabbis from central Europe, finding positions for them in England. It was headed by Hertz's son-in-law, Rabbi Solomon Schonfeld of the Adath Yisrael synagogue in London, then president of the Union of Orthodox Hebrew Congregations in England. After the war, the CRREC devoted itself to rehabilitating Jewish communal life in Europe, distributing religious articles, organizing "Mobile Synagogue Ambulances" (synagogues on wheels), and providing rabbinical guidance to the communities.[9]

Emissaries of the CRREC gained entry to Bergen-Belsen before the JCRA because it was a religious association, and religion was the only sphere in which the British recognized any special Jewish needs. In effect, the rabbis dispatched by the CRREC were relief workers, not

An open-air prayer service in the Freedom Square, conducted by military chaplains (Yad Vashem Photo-Archives [FA 185 154])

just clergymen. Most of them were more than willing to embark on this humanitarian mission, but their dual role sometimes caused problems. Supplies sent by the CRREC were often earmarked for religious survivors only, and certain rabbis clung to the notion that they were merely religious functionaries, ignoring other pressing needs. In distributing religious articles, some rabbis gave priority to one group over another.[10] In order to prevent such mismanagement and regulate liaison with the British authorities, the JCRA reached an agreement with the CRREC whereby the rabbis would operate under JCRA supervision. If possible, the rabbis would concentrate on religious matters, but in places where they worked alone they would coordinate all relief activities.[11] The CRREC and the JCRA functioned quite well together, despite occasional personal grievances and misunderstandings.[12]

The Jewish Relief Unit

After the chaplains, the next to arrive in the British Zone were the workers of the British Jewish Relief Unit (JRU), organized by the

JCRA. This committee was founded in 1943 by the Joint Foreign Committee of the Board of Deputies of British Jews (BD) and the Anglo-Jewish Association (AJA), and it operated under the auspices and financial responsibility of the Central British Fund (CBF). The Central British Fund for German Jewry was founded in 1933 to assist Jews persecuted by the Nazis. Its Jewish Refugee Committee helped settle German Jews who fled to England and also sponsored settlement projects in Palestine.

The JRU was the JCRA's operational arm in Europe. Its activities were coordinated with the army and UNRRA. The chairmen were Dr. Redcliffe Nathan Salaman, a British scientist deeply involved in Jewish community and Zionist affairs, and Leonard Cohen of Manchester. Professor Norman Bentwich, attorney general in Palestine during the 1920s, thereafter professor at the Hebrew University of Jerusalem, and then director of the League of Nations Commission of Jewish Refugees from Germany, was vice-chairman.[13]

Unlike the JDC, the JCRA was a young institution with no experience in overseas relief operations and only a small professional staff. Its main resource was human capital—young, spirited volunteers full of enthusiasm but in need of training. Throughout 1943, as the magnitude of the task at hand was beginning to unfold, the JCRA devoted itself to organizing and manpower training.[14] When the war ended and it became clear that JCRA emissaries were most needed in Germany, and especially in the British Zone, the British barred their entry for nearly two months. Whatever relief work was done was carried out by the Jewish chaplains and a Jewish social worker, Jane Leverson, who officially arrived as part of the Quaker team—the Friends Relief Service. As Leverson later explained:

> When I was accepted by the Friends Relief Service as a relief worker, the Jewish Committee for Relief Abroad, to whom I was well-known, arranged that I could wear their badge (a bronze shield of David) and represent them if I was working in an area where there were Jews and they did not have their own representative. Accordingly, whilst I was carrying out the clothing distribution at Belsen, the Jewish Army Chaplain of the 8th Corps (the Rev. Leslie Hardman) who was working at Camp 1, heard of me and asked if I could join him since I was the only Jewish civilian relief worker in Belsen.[15]

Turned away by the British authorities in early May, the JRU team, composed of twelve men and women, went to Holland and

Belgium. Finally, in the wake of unrelenting pressure by the JCRA and Jewish army chaplains (Rabbi Brodie in London and Rabbi Levy in Belsen), the group, which had gone to Holland, was allowed to cross the border into Germany. They reached Diepholz, a transit camp, on June 21. Heading the team was Shalom Markovitz, a leader of Bahad (acronym for the Zionist youth movement Brith Halutzim Datiyim, or Association of Religious Pioneers). Among its members were two sisters, Erica and Judith Lunzer, of Bahad in London, and Bertha Weingreen, a professional relief worker whose husband, a Hebrew professor at Trinity College, Dublin, later joined the team to supervise educational activities. Soon afterward a second team arrived, led by Lady Rose Henriques, head of the JCRA's German Department, and was posted at Celle, twelve miles outside Bergen-Belsen. In August 1945 the team from Holland was finally admitted to Belsen, and another group, led by Jack Brass of Habonim (Labor Zionists), followed shortly afterward. The upshot was that the JRU began working in Belsen only four months after liberation, by which time even the soldiers of the Jewish Brigade had been toiling there for at least a month.[16] Initially, the JRU worked under the auspices of the Red Cross, but when UNRRA took over in November 1945 the JRU also came under its jurisdiction.[17]

As time passed, the presence of the JRU grew stronger. By April 1946 there were sixty-eight JRU workers in Germany (out of a total of seventy-nine JRU relief workers), and by summer the figure was up to ninety-two. Some were sent to the American Zone and others to Berlin.[18]

The volunteers represented a broad spectrum of English Jews. Some were born in England, but many were recent immigrants, among them a high percentage of German Jews. Some were religious or even ultra-Orthodox. A large percentage were Zionists—members of Hehalutz, Hashomer Hatza'ir, and Habonim, or Bahad Poel Mizrahi (Religious Zionists)—encouraged to take part in the relief and rehabilitation mission by their movements. Most were young and single, but there were also a number of older married persons, such as Bertha Weingreen and Shalom Markovitz, who were moved by a deep sense of duty and prepared to go off to Germany even if it meant being separated from their families.[19] As we have said, there were also quite a few rabbis, sent by the CRREC under a special agreement with JCRA.[20] Volunteers usually signed up for at least a year, but many of them—the Lunzer sisters, Bertha Weingreen, and Hanna

Bernhard-Rath, for example—stayed much longer, totally immersed in their work.[21]

The JRU enjoyed very limited funding, receiving most of its supplies from the JDC, which encountered no end of problems in organizing and shipping essential provisions from America.[22] Restrictions imposed by the British also impeded the JRU's ability to substantially improve living conditions. Thus most of its energies were devoted to emotional and spiritual rehabilitation, with an emphasis on the future. In practice, this meant organizing cultural and educational programs, vocational training, and child care in Bergen-Belsen and DP centers such as Diepholz.[23]

The JRU was also involved in medical and health care. Its workers held key positions in the Glyn Hughes Hospital (named after the British officer who organized rescue operations in Bergen-Belsen upon liberation). With the financial backing and encouragement of the CBF and the JDC, the JRU established the Bad Harzburg convalescent home, which took in sick and elderly German Jews and organized the transport of tuberculosis patients to Merano (Italy) and Switzerland for recovery. Another project organized in the British Zone was a hostel in the countryside of Lüneburg for Jewish children from Berlin.[24]

Community work was a major component of the JRU's activity. JRU volunteers, especially the rabbis, played a dominant role in reviving Jewish religious, cultural, and social life in Germany. Reverends Greenbaum, Goldfinger, and Carlebach served as regional representatives in Hamburg, Brunswick, and Bremen and supervised Jewish communal affairs in the many small communities that had sprung up outside Belsen.[25] The JRU was also helpful in contact with the British and German authorities, particularly in the matter of restitution and indemnification. One person who had a major impact in this sphere was Henryk Van Dam, who served as the German Jews' legal adviser.[26] One of the highlights of the JRU's activity was the visit of Rabbi Leo Baeck for the High Holidays during 1948.[27] Rabbi Baeck, who had been the leader of German Jewry under the Nazi regime, had survived Theresienstadt and settled in London. His visit was accepted by the German Jewish survivors as recognition and approval of the continuity of Jewish existence in post-Holocaust Germany.

The JCRA was a natural candidate to work with German Jews, due to its experience with the Committee for Jews in Germany since 1933 and the fact that many JRU volunteers were of German origin and spoke German fluently.[28] Some of the volunteers, such as van Dam and

E. G. Lowenthal, JRU's field director for Germany, eventually settled in Germany and went on to become important figures in the German Jewish community.[29]

The work of the JRU in Germany was founded on a sincere desire to rekindle life and hope for the Jewish survivors. All sectors of British Jewry joined in, and the survivors themselves actively cooperated. However, beyond the problems with certain rabbis, the lack of financial resources, and the British policy constraints, the road was not always a smooth one. The JRU never took a clear political stance, trying to maintain a united front between Zionists and non-Zionists, secular and ultra-Orthodox. This required compromise and concession, which sometimes led to friction and disagreement. Many volunteers were fervent Zionists, and they cooperated with the Zionist emissaries in organizing illegal aliyah. The JCRA believed that such activities endangered its fragile relationship with the British authorities, and it dismissed any JRU worker suspected of involvement. There was also friction between the JRU and Yossele Rosensaft, who favored a militant Zionist approach.[30]

Moreover, the JCRA was special in that it did not repudiate the legitimacy of Jewish life in Germany and was instrumental in helping to rebuild the community. Yet alleviating the hardship of the DPs and the refugees was the main task at hand, and immigration to Palestine seemed to be the right answer. By the summer of 1950, in the wake of the establishment of the State of Israel and the onset of mass emigration, the JCRA closed down its offices in Europe and many of the staff members themselves left for Israel.

British Jewish Political Intervention

As soon as the hostilities ended, and before the welfare agencies were admitted into Germany, several British Jewish organizations sprang into action. The two most important bodies in this sphere were the British section of the World Jewish Congress (WJC) and the Board of Deputies of British Jews (BD, mainly through its Committee for the Jews in Germany), who waged a political struggle on behalf of the survivors, demanding that Jewish delegations be allowed to enter the camps and form a firsthand impression of what was needed. Their goals were to organize relief activities, improve living conditions, convince the military authorities to appoint a Jewish adviser, and above all to change the British attitude with respect to segregation and special treatment of the Jews.[31]

Despite the involvement of a number of prominent British Jews—Lady Eva Reading, president of the British section of the WJC; Sydney S. Silverman, chairman of the WJC and a member of British Parliament; Selig Brodetsky, a distinguished mathematician and expert in aerodynamics, as well as chairman of the BD and a member of the World Zionist Executive; and journalist Alexander L. Easterman, director of the WJC's political department—no headway was made at first, even after changes began to be implemented in the Americans Zone in the wake of the Harrison report.[32] The Jewish leaders did not give up, however, and they intensified their efforts after attending the congress in Bergen-Belsen in September 1945. Slowly, their pressure bore fruit. The British introduced segregationist policy in the camps, arranged for preferential treatment of German Jews, and allowed a Jewish adviser to be appointed.[33] This, however, was not achieved until the JDC and the BD sent a commission to the British Zone in March 1946 to survey the conditions of the Jews. It was this commission's report that finally broke down British resistance.[34]

The Jewish adviser was Colonel Robert Solomon, who held the post from the spring of 1946 until his untimely death in the spring of 1948. His main task was to bring special Jewish needs to the attention of the British military authorities and to smooth as much as possible the complicated relationship between the Jews and the British.[35] It is due to his initiatives that the British embarked on the "Grand National" operation of legal aliyah from the British Zone in 1947, which enabled six thousand DPs to make their way to Palestine.[36] Solomon also contributed greatly to the cooperation between the British military authorities and the JRU within their effort to relieve the hardship of the German Jews and allow them to organize. Even after Solomon's entry into the arena, the BD and the WJC kept up their political activity on behalf of the survivors, supporting and supplementing Solomon's activity.[37]

The efforts of the British Jews on behalf of the survivors were characterized throughout by a deep sense of affinity. The survivors looked upon them as true partners. Proximity to Germany enabled frequent visits and telephone calls, which led to the development of personal relationships. This close connection was exemplified by Noah Barou, the general secretary of the WJC, who came to Belsen so often that he was treated by the survivors as one of their own. All Rosensaft had to do was pick up the phone to London, knowing that Barou had an intimate understanding of the circumstances in Germany and was personally invested in the survivors' welfare. In July 1947 the survivors' organization in the British Zone applied to join the WJC, and it was accepted as an equal member.[38]

The Jewish adviser, Robert Solomon, did not settle in Germany, but traveled back and forth. In consequence, he remained in the job for the whole period—in contrast to the high turnover rate among the American Jewish advisers.[39] Later, when the British relaxed their restrictions on travel, Rosensaft and Wollheim made frequent trips to London to take part in British-Jewish negotiations on behalf of the Central Committee.[40] On the whole, the JRU's workers stayed in Germany for longer periods than the workers of the JDC because it was easier for them to go home for a vacation and then come back refreshed.[41]

Another characteristic of the British Jews who came to Belsen was their Zionist fervor, which began to grow during the war and became stronger in reaction to the British Mandate in Palestine and the plight of the survivors. Even to non-Zionists, it was obvious that these factors were interrelated. Brodetsky, chairman of the BD since 1943, was—as already noted—a member of the World Zionist Executive. Rabbi Joseph Hertz was a longtime Zionist supporter. Norman Bentwich, one of the heads of the JCRA, was a Zionist and spent many years in Palestine as attorney general to the Mandatory administration in the 1920s and as a professor at the Hebrew University from 1932 to 1951. Lady Eva Reading, daughter of the pro-Zionist Sir Alfred Mond (Lord Melchett), was herself a staunch Zionist. Noah Barou was a Poalei Zion leader, and the Jewish adviser, Robert Solomon, had formerly been the chairman of the Jewish National Fund in Britain. Many of the JRU workers in Germany belonged to Zionist youth movements.

This pro-Zionist stance was not only a personal matter. The WJC was a Zionist-oriented organization from its inception in 1936. The CBF was deeply involved in building up the Jewish settlement in Palestine through its projects to help rescue German Jews. Even institutions that had been far from, or even opposed to, Zionism before the war changed their approach afterward. The change in the BD's approach to Zionism began with Brodetsky's election in 1943, and the favor for Zionism grew steadily stronger, especially after its delegates attended the congress of the *She'erit Hapletah* in Belsen in September 1945.[42] For Agudath Israel the turning point came in May 1945, when it joined world Jewry in demanding that the British open the gates of Palestine.[43]

The Zionist inclination must not, though, be overestimated. The BD, CBF, and JCRA were non-Zionist in principle. They were prepared to lend a hand to the Jewish national struggle as a humanitarian effort, but they were law-abiding British citizens and would do nothing to compromise that. The JCRA, for instance, saw nothing wrong with resettling Jews in Germany—the bane of Zionists—and did all it could to further this goal.[44] The JCRA was a British agency in every respect. Unlawful or anti-British activities were out of the question, and pursuing such activity was suspended.[45] Efforts to reorganize Jewish life in Germany also had to conform to British policy considerations and British interests.[46]

The warm relationship that developed between British Jewry and the survivors, a pro-Zionist outlook, and British loyalty created the basis for a serious rehabilitation effort in the British Zone in Germany, allowing the British Jews to fill a special role, beyond that of the JDC or the Jewish Agency. Moreover, the combination of personal commitment, pro-Zionism, and neutrality served as a firm basis for cooperation with the Jewish Agency, the JDC, and the Central Committee of the British Zone.

The Palestinian Zionist Role

The Jewish Brigade

Established by the British War Cabinet in September 1944 in compliance with demands for a military corps under Jewish insignia, the Jewish Brigade, consisting of Palestinian Jews, took part in the British invasion of Italy. Together with Jewish soldiers of other units, the Jewish Brigade soldiers established in October 1944 the Merkaz Lagola (Center for the Diaspora), a committee that had no official status but went on to play a key role in aiding concentration camp survivors and paving the way for mass immigration to Palestine.

At the end of May 1945, when the Jewish Brigade moved up to Tarvisio in northern Italy, four adventurous soldiers crossed the border into Austria and returned with the news that they had found Jewish survivors in the camps there. More soldiers went to find survivors in Austria and Romania. At this point, however, they channeled their efforts into smuggling Jews into Italy and from there to Palestine in the framework of the *Briha*, an illegal flight and immigration enterprise organized by the Mosad Le-Aliyah Bet (or "Mosad") of the Haganah underground defense organization of the *Yishuv*. The Mosad sent a delegation of Jewish soldiers into Austria and Germany, ostensibly looking for relatives. The delegation, headed by Aharon Hoter-Yishai, left Tarvisio on June 20 and reached Munich on June 22. In this way, contact was established with the American Zone.

Aside from their assistance in the *Briha* and illegal immigration operations, the Jewish Brigade soldiers provided the survivors with clothing, food, gasoline, and other items—either from their own rations or stolen from army supplies. By the time the brigade was moved to Antwerp at the end of July 1945, the soldiers perceived locating survivors and extending aid as their main goal.[47]

Jewish soldiers were already present in the British Zone in May 1945,[48] but the first members of the Jewish Brigade arrived in July 1945. By early 1946 there was a total of sixteen, six of them active in Bergen-Belsen.[49] The Palestinian soldiers had neither money nor political influence to offer, but they did provide moral support. Dressed in uniforms emblazoned with the Jewish star, they were a tangible symbol of *Eretz Yisrael* and Jewish national pride. They saw themselves and were viewed by those around them as emissaries of the Jewish *Yishuv* in Palestine, although they were not officially recognized as such and received no real support from the *Yishuv* until the arrival of the Jewish Agency's rescue teams at the end of the year.[50]

The soldiers devoted their energy to educational activities, *hachsharah* (pioneer training), youth programs, and survivor organization, thus strengthening Zionist enthusiasm. From the July conference to the congress in September 1945, members of the Jewish Brigade were not so much initiators as supportive, encouraging onlookers.[51] One of the brigade's most important achievements in the realm of education was the opening in December 1945 of a Hebrew high school—the joint initiative of Belsen survivor Helen Wrubel and David Littman, a brigade soldier.[52]

In all its activity, the Jewish Brigade saw before it the twin goals of rehabilitation and aliyah. The road to rehabilitation lay in strengthening bonds with *Eretz Yisrael* and preparing the survivors for their ultimate renaissance in the national homeland. A distinction, however, must be made between the brigade soldiers and the Palestinian emissaries who arrived at the end of the year. Unlike these emissaries, who represented political parties, youth movements, and kibbutz movements, the Jewish Brigade soldiers avoided any party politics. This

Jewish World Organizations

Soldiers of the Jewish Brigade with Dr. Hadassa Bimko (Rosensaft), head of the Health Department (Yad Vashem Photo-Archives [FA 185 161])

nonpartisan approach added to the esteem in which the brigade was held by the survivors, who perceived it as the only true representative of the *Yishuv*.[53]

The official mission from Palestine reached Bergen-Belsen in December 1945, and the Jewish Brigade was liquidated not long afterward, in May 1946. Some of the soldiers remained in Germany, however, and continued to work with the survivors.[54]

The Palestine Mission (Welfare Groups)

Toward the end of the war, the Jewish *Yishuv* in Palestine, like Jews the world over, geared up for rescue operations and welfare work in Europe. Following the establishment of UNRRA in late 1943, the Jewish Agency and Vaad Leumi (National Council) founded the Council for Welfare Groups for the Diaspora, headed by Dr. Nissan Katznelson. In April 1945, after lengthy negotiations with the military authorities and UNRRA, the council dispatched its first rescue team to Greece.

Direct contact with central Europe and Jewish camp survivors was still a long way off, despite the fact that the situation in the DP camps and the urgent need for help had been communicated through the Jewish Brigade soldiers, who had reached Germany in July. Eliyahu Dobkin of the Jewish Agency Executive had also visited the camps in the American Zone, in July, and secured UNRRA's consent for a thirty-six-person task force from Palestine, but the military authorities refused to allow such bodies into the country until September 1945, and even then there was no way of transporting them from Palestine to Europe.

David Ben-Gurion, chairman of the Jewish Agency, visited the camps in Germany at the end of October 1945 and succeeded in convincing General Eisenhower to send planes to Palestine specifically for this purpose. The first plane arrived in Palestine within a month, and left for Germany on December 8 with the first team. The group of twenty, headed by Haim Hoffmann (Yahil), reached the camps on December 11, seven month after liberation.[55] The British Zone had to wait even longer. The first Jewish Agency emissary, Kurt Lewin, arrived in Belsen in March 1946, almost a year after liberation.[56]

By May 1946 there were ten emissaries in the British Zone: the head of the team, two who worked as teachers at the children's home in Blankenese, four in Bergen-Belsen, one in Hanover, one in Ahlem, and one in Neustadt. The number of emissaries from Palestine and the jobs they did changed very little over the coming months, in contrast to the growing number of emissaries to the American Zone. In Germany as a whole the emissaries numbered 152 by the second half of 1947.[57]

The Palestine emissaries were delegates of various political parties and kibbutz movements. They saw themselves as representing both the Jewish *Yishuv* and their movements, and their ultimate goal was to prepare the survivors for life in Palestine. Physical conditions in the camps had already improved by the time they arrived, and the work of the Jewish welfare agencies was already in full swing. The Palestinian emissaries thus concentrated not on welfare, but rather on Zionist education, pioneer training, political activism, and aliyah. These activities were pursued along party lines, with the emissaries trying to recruit people to their respective parties, in contrast to the nonpartisan approach of the Jewish Brigade soldiers before them. Only the teachers delegation, which reached Germany in the summer of 1947, took a neutral stance.[58] In general, however, Palestine emissaries represented

David Ben-Gurion (in black overcoat), chairman of the Jewish Agency, with a group of Bergen-Belsen leaders including Yossele Rosensaft (third from left) (October 1945) (Yad Vashem Photo-Archives [FA 185 176])

the entire political spectrum from left to right and from Orthodox Poalei Agudath Israel (PAI) to underground Irgun.

The emissaries in the British Zone were also members of different political movements. However, they were an exception in that they did not allow their political views to affect their work. Kurt Lewin, the head of the mission, was a member of Kibbutz Kfar Hamakkabi (affiliated with HaKibbutz Hame'uhad—the United Kibbutz movement), but he refrained from party politics. Mordechai Breuer, sent to Germany by the PAI in May 1946, and Menahem Ehrlich, an emissary of the Mizrahi movement, taught together at the Hebrew high school as well as in religious study frameworks. Tsemah Tsamriyon, a former Jewish Brigade soldier, was a Revisionist, but he worked hand in hand with all the others. Zionism was the common goal, and political interests were laid aside to achieve it—even if this meant drawing fire from their own political parties.[59]

New Beginnings

The relatively minor role played by the Palestine emissaries in the British Zone was shaped by several factors. For one, Bergen-Belsen and the British Zone as a whole were already organized along clear Zionist lines before their arrival. There was an active Histadrut Zionit Ahidah (United Zionist Organization) in the zone, which served as a cooperative framework for all sectors of the Jewish population, and the JRU—the chief source of outside aid—was also very pro-Zionist. Moreover, the bulk of the survivors were in the American Zone, which resulted in the British Zone's being lower on the Palestine emissaries' scale of priorities.[60] Thus they were not "trailblazers" but rather pursued their work within the general framework of cooperation and unity that existed in the British Zone.

American Jewish Relief Agencies

In America there were several Jewish overseas relief agencies already active well before the war. Those that sent teams to the British Zone were the American Jewish Joint Distribution Committee (JDC), the Hebrew Immigrant Aid Society (HIAS), and the Organization for Rehabilitation and Training (ORT). Pride of place, however, goes to the JDC, from which both HIAS and ORT received much of their funding.[61]

THE AMERICAN JEWISH JOINT DISTRIBUTION COMMITTEE

The JDC, established in America in 1914 to extend aid to persecuted Jews and to resettle Jewish refugees, was initially headed by members of German Jewish upper class. Over time, Eastern European Jews—Orthodox Jews, liberal socialists, and Zionists—rose to positions of prominence, and second-generation Eastern Europeans also filled the most important professional and managerial roles.

Among the German Jewish leaders was Edward Warburg, the son of JDC founder Felix M. Warburg, who resigned his chairmanship to join the American army but resumed his position after demobilization. Properties belonging to the Warburg family in Hamburg, which was in the British Zone, were turned into Jewish welfare institutions: the Warburg estate at Bad Harzburg became a convalescent home, and the estate at Blankenese became a children's home.

From 1940 the chairman of the JDC's European Executive in Paris was Dr. Joseph J. Schwartz, whose name was to become virtually synonymous with the JDC. Schwartz's deputy, Moses W. Beckelman, and the directors for Germany, Herbert Katzki, Jacob L. Trobe, and Samuel L. Haber, also played key roles in the committee's relief work in Germany.

From 1939, the JDC's chief fund-raising instrument in the United States was the United Jewish Appeal. Contributions had been rising steadily, but after the war they shot up dramatically. Between 1945 and 1948 the JDC raised a total of $194,332,033, of which $20,628,500 (about 11 percent) was spent on relief efforts in Germany and Austria.

In addition, the JDC mobilized hundreds of American Jewish field-workers for its operations in Europe, the Middle East, and Shanghai, the main centers of Jewish refugees. With salaries very low, the incentive was usually idealism or adventure-seeking, but because families were often left behind, few were willing to stay for more than short shifts. This rapid turnover was the great bane of the JDC's overseas operations because as soon as workers gained enough experience to be useful, they left.

Another feature of JDC relief works in Europe was organizing shipments of food, clothing, medical supplies, and other items. A volunteer organization called Supplies for Overseas Survivors (SOS), which began putting together clothing shipments in early 1946, was harshly criticized for sending worn, inappropriate garments that only undermined the self-esteem of the survivors. SOS took these comments to heart and organized its shipments more carefully later on, transferring some 26 million pounds of good-quality provisions by the time it ceased operations in April 1949: 14 million pounds of food, and the rest clothing, medical supplies, and so on.[62]

Due to the military authorities' reluctance to admit civilians into Germany, the JDC arrived in the camps quite late. The first JDC relief team entered Buchenwald in June 1945, and it was not until August 4 that another team—carrying no supplies—was allowed into Munich. Another small team reached Bergen-Belsen in early July, also empty-handed. There was little it could do beyond helping the survivors to organize and to attend the survivors' July conference.[63]

JDC involvement in the British Zone was most extensive in Bergen-Belsen. The team that arrived in July was headed by Maurice Eigen, who got along well with Yossele Rosensaft but at first had little to offer aside from organizing a mail service that was grudgingly tolerated by the British authorities. In October 1945, when the first JDC shipment came in, the authorities would not allow Eigen to distribute these supplies to Jews only, in keeping with their policy of not recognizing the Jews as a separate group.

Eigen left in November 1945 and was replaced by David B. Wodlinger, who tried to compile a list of all Belsen camp inmates. He found this to be an impossible task because Rosensaft, in an effort to obtain extra rations from the British, did not erase the names of inmates who had left the camp or died. Wodlinger complained about the shoddy quality and insufficient quantity of the clothing shipped to Germany by the JDC, but he lauded the shipments of food, especially to the small German Jewish communities-in-the-making, which helped to keep them going. Wodlinger's successor, Samuel J. Dallob, a Canadian, remained in Bergen-Belsen almost until its liquidation.

The JDC ran educational programs and counseling services in the British Zone—not only in Belsen, but also in some of the smaller camps and the German Jewish communities. From October 1945, shipments of goods were handed over to Rosensaft and the Central Committee for distribution.[64] These shipments were often delayed, however, causing severe shortages that were felt most of all in the British Zone, where the special needs of the Jews were not recognized and UNRRA supplies were particularly inadequate because German Jews were not listed as entitled to UNRRA support. The obstacles placed in the way of the Jewish welfare enterprise led the JDC to appoint a joint committee of inquiry in collaboration with the JCRA. The joint team was headed by Harry Viteles of the JDC and Alexander Brotman of the BD. The committee compiled a detailed report and a series of recommendations that were submitted to the British authorities and apparently made enough of an impact to change their minds. For the first time, the British agreed to the appointment of a Jewish adviser and the establishment of segregated Jewish camps, among other concessions.[65]

JDC operations in the British Zone were sponsored by an American Jewish organization, but very few Americans were actually involved. Most of the field-workers were Jews from Canada, England, or other countries, in addition to a large number of DPs. Nevertheless, the unsympathetic attitude of the military authorities lent an American Jewish presence in the British Zone special significance. The JDC was highly respected by all the Jewish organizations active in the British Zone, and by the Central Committee in particular.[66] However, there was also much disagreement between the Central Committee and the JDC in matters of exercising authority.[67]

Although the quantity of goods shipped to the British Zone by the JDC was quite large and the scope of the JDC's activity extensive, there is no question that the JRU and British Jewry constituted a far more dominant presence, thanks to the political advantages and geographical proximity they enjoyed.[68]

Summary

The Jewish organizational work in post-Holocaust Germany was marked by cooperation between Zionists and non-Zionists—a dramatic shift in the Jewish world as it confronted the horrors of the Holocaust and the magnitude of the DP problem. This cooperation was especially pronounced in the British Zone, at a time when the British adopted a hard-line policy with respect to the Jews in Germany and Palestine alike. On the one hand, the aim was to achieve segregation and introduce a separate apparatus for Jewish relief work through diplomatic channels, meanwhile carrying on as best as possible under the constraints of British policy. On the other hand, a concerted effort was made to implement what seemed at the time (and as the Harrison report manifested, not only to Jews) to be the one feasible solution to the Jewish problem: opening the gates of Palestine. This cooperative effort was presided over by the JRU, by far the largest agency at work in the British Zone, and enhanced by the existence of a strong Central Committee that genuinely represented all the zone's Jews in a show of Jewish unity distinctly pro-Zionist in character.[69]

7

THE CENTRAL COMMITTEE AS AN INSTRUMENT OF SELF-GOVERNMENT

Goals and Infrastructure

One of the outcomes of the First Congress of the *She'erit Hapletah*, which convened on September 25–27, 1945, was the election of a Central Committee (CC) to oversee Jewish affairs in the British Zone. Josef Rosensaft (Belsen) was elected chairman; Norbert Wollheim (Lübeck), vice-chairman; Berl Laufer (Belsen), general secretary; Dr. Hadassa Bimko (Belsen), head of the Health Department; Karl Katz (Bremen) and Samuel Weintraub (Belsen), heads of the Economic Department; Rabbi Dr. Zvi Helfgott (Belsen), head of the Rabbinical Department; David Rosenthal (Belsen), Paul Trepman (Belsen), and Rafael Olevsky (Belsen), heads of the Cultural Department and editors of the official organ *Unzer Sztyme*; and Sami Feder (Belsen), director of the theater. Other members were M. B. Gutman (Belsen), Rabbi Israel Moshe Olevsky (Celle), and S. Rosendorn (Neustadt).[1] The CC was made up almost entirely of inmates from Bergen-Belsen, and at first it served both the British Zone as a whole and the Belsen camp. In March 1947, however, a few months before the Second Congress of the *She'erit Hapletah*, a special committee was set up just to deal with Belsen.[2]

Although representatives of Belsen were in the majority and Belsen was by far the largest center of Jewish population in the British Zone, the purpose—albeit unspoken—of the CC was to represent all the Jews in the zone, regardless of political, social, or cultural divisions.[3] Representatives of every party were thus included, from Zionist-leftists (Rosensaft) and Orthodox Zionists (Weintraub) to Revisionists (Trepman), ultra-Orthodox Agudists (I. M. Olevsky), and modern Orthodox (Helfgott). Other camps and communities also enjoyed representation: Rosendorn of Neustadt, and Olevsky of Celle represented the

The Central Committee and Self-Government

DP centers outside of Belsen, and German Jewish communities were represented by Wollheim of Lübeck and Katz of Bremen.

The CC was basically a highly centralized organization. Against the backdrop of harsh conditions, British hostility toward Jewish cohesiveness, frequent anti-Semitic outbursts by the Germans and the non-Jewish DPs, scarce welfare resources, and the prospect of a long struggle for freedom, an authoritarian, all-embracing framework was regarded as the only solution. The CC set out to be the sole governing body of the Jews in the British Zone, responsible for both internal affairs and liaison with world Jewish organizations and the British authorities.[4] To achieve this goal, it embarked upon a broad range of semigovernmental activities: partnership with world Jewish organizations, political activism, and diplomatic efforts on behalf of the survivors.

Yossele Rosensaft (right), Chairman of the Central Committee, with Noah Barou, delegate of the World Jewish Congress (Yad Vashem Photo-Archives [177FO6])

Norbert Wollheim, Vice-Chairman of the Central Committee and head of the Communities Department (Yad Vashem Photo-Archives [156BO5])

The following event may serve as an illustration for the CC's ambition. A scheme to send Jewish orphans from the concentration camps to England in the summer of 1945, conceived by the British Jewish institutions and approved by the British authorities, was fiercely opposed by the Central Committee, claiming responsibility for "their" children. British Jewish leaders tried to persuade the heads of the CC to allow the children's transfer to England on the ground that this was only a temporary solution and that eventually they all would be taken to Palestine. Even the Zionist Youth Aliyah emissary in Paris, Georg Landauer, was a partner to these efforts. The DP leaders, however, were not convinced. While there were some children from the British Zone among those sent to England in October 1945, most waited for the special certificates that enabled them to reach Palestine. A group of the children of Belsen—numbering approximately 100—went indeed to Palestine, escorted by Dr. Hadassa Bimko on behalf of the CC, as part of a group of 1,000 youngsters for whom special certificates were procured in April 1946.[5]

In its bid to become the exclusive instrument of Jewish national self-government, the CC worked on several fronts. It battled against the "divide and rule" policy of the British and against the German authorities' efforts to hinder its involvement, but also against excessive intervention on the part of world Jewish organizations. The CC claimed that it understood the needs and wishes of the survivors better than those on the outside did, and that having control over supplies and sharing in the management of welfare and rehabilitation projects was crucial. Internally, a centralized apparatus was deemed essential for preserving unity and equality and for ensuring that protégés of certain organizations were not singled out for preferential treatment. With the economic conditions being what they were and the flourishing black market, centralization also prevented the misappropriation of supplies and profiteering and kept up moral standards.

In seeking to become the main governing and representative body, the CC went through various phases of development and suffered a number of setbacks, especially during its first years of existence. From September 1945 until the Second Congress of the *She'erit Hapletah* was convened in the British Zone in July 1947, the committee underwent many changes in composition, authority, and functioning. By the eve of the Second Congress, however, it was well on its way to reaching its goal.

Economic Control

The first step to becoming a dominant governing body was to gain control of all incoming supplies and to oversee their allocation and use. This was the rationale behind the establishment of the Economic Department, which was responsible for handling shipments of food, clothing, and equipment for private or public use. An agreement was reached with the JDC whereby all supplies were delivered to the central storehouse in Belsen and then distributed throughout the zone.[6] This arrangement, however, was difficult to carry out because of transportation problems, the fact that there were separate rules for DPs and German Jews, and rivalry between the JDC, JRU, and CRREC.

The Central Committee's chief rival was a group of 1,500 Orthodox Jews affiliated with Agudath Israel, most of them Hungarians, who made up a large percentage of the Belsen population. The bone of contention was the religious supplies shipped to Germany by the CRREC, which were being distributed only to those who were Orthodox. Rosensaft and the emissaries of the JRU bitterly complained: the food products were vital to all, and even non-Orthodox Jews wanted a share of the religious articles.[7] Rosensaft also protested that religious needs were given precedence over other essential needs—for example, the construction of a ritual bath (*mikve*) at the expense of firewood despite the harsh winter conditions and the severe shortage of coal for heating.[8]

The Orthodox Hungarian Jews, on the other hand, claimed that the CC was neglecting their needs and accused the JRU of putting the Zionist DPs before all others. The response was just the opposite of what was intended by centralizing the allocation and distribution of supplies: the Hungarian Orthodox of Belsen broke away from the CC and established a separate *Kehillah* (religious community)—Adath She'erit Yisrael.[9]

This group was supported to some degree by the CRREC (Rabbi Schonfeld, the head of CRREC, was himself an Agudist) on the grounds that its interests were not represented in the CC. Since they could not use the regular, nonkosher food supplied by the welfare organizations, these survivors were felt to be in worse straits than other DPs.[10] Although it was true that they were not represented in the CC, the Orthodox Hungarians were not the only Orthodox group in the British Zone. There was a large community of Polish Hasidim in Celle whose spiritual leader, Rabbi Israel Moshe Olevsky, also represented them in the CC, and in Belsen itself there was a group of Orthodox Zionists, Hamizrahi, with a delegate in the CC (Samuel Weintraub).[11]

In the end, CRREC support of the *Kehillah* was affected by a dispute between the CRREC and the JCRA, whose field director in 1946 was Henry Lunzer, a strong supporter of the CC. Moreover, many of the rabbis acting on behalf of the CRREC—in particular, Rabbi Greenbaum and Rabbi Munk—were highly critical of Adath She'erith Yisrael's Rabbi Meisels, whom they accused of being motivated by political interests. The JCRA, as we have seen, insisted on complete cooperation between the JRU and the CRREC.[12] Thus, despite the CRREC's recognition of the *Kehillah* as a separate organization, CRREC shipments were not sent directly to the *Kehillah* but channeled through Lunzer.[13]

In order to resolve the conflict, the CRREC tried to persuade the *Kehillah* to become the spokesman for all Orthodox groups. In this way, it would enjoy both representation in the CC and the continued assistance of the CRREC. This could be achieved only if the CC was willing to make concessions and allow decisions regarding the allocation of supplies to remain in JRU and CRREC hands.[14] An arrangement with the JCRA was worked out in November 1946, and in January 1947, Adath She'erith Yisrael and Hamizrahi signed an agreement that formed the basis for an Orthodox union and cooperation with the CC.[15]

From the point of view of the CC, however, this arrangement was unsatisfactory because it left some control in the hands of the JRU and the CRREC. As Wollheim put it, the CC welcomed assistance meant to promote independent activity and development, but aid from organizations outside Germany made no sense unless it enjoyed the CC's full consent and was based on shared responsibility.[16] The CC was upset at what it perceived as a challenge to its authority, whereas it was accused by others of arrogance and antireligious behavior. The result was serious friction, which was finally resolved in early 1947 when the CC was officially recognized as a full partner. In theory, the JCRA agreed to consult it on all matters. In practice, however, the JRU shipped supplies directly to various institutions and emissaries, and the CC was informed rather than consulted.[17]

The dispute with the Orthodox was not the only one. The CC also fought with the JDC, its main supplier. At a certain point, the JDC, disturbed by reports of poor management, decided to set up a distribution center in Bremen, outside Bergen-Belsen. Even then the CC insisted on having a representative there, Karl Katz.[18] Rosensaft was adamant about being a partner in all JDC decisions regarding allocation of supplies, and he does seem to have achieved a kind of shared responsibility in that field.[19] The CC also demanded control over supplies to the Jewish communities in the British Zone, and a special center—a *Wirtschaftsamt* (Economic Department)—was established in August 1946 to assume responsibility for this task.[20]

By the time the Second Congress of the *She'erit Hapletah* was held in July 1947, a kind of compromise had been achieved: the CC was not the supreme authority, but it was recognized by all participants as sharing responsibility with the welfare organizations. The CC no longer had an economic department at its Belsen headquarters,[21] but the Wirtschaftsamt was a sign of its importance in the German Jewish arena.[22] Without having absolute power or independent financial resources, the CC managed to gain a foothold in almost every sphere of Jewish life in the British Zone.

Health Care

The Health Department of the CC, the framework for which had been established by the Provisional Committee, supervised health care throughout the British Zone. It controlled all medical institutions in the zone with the goal of monitoring the general state of health of all Jews. The institutions themselves were funded by the JDC and JRU, but due to the shortage of professional manpower the CC was unable to achieve all it set out to do, namely, to provide a full range of medical and psychological services by Jews and for Jews. In Belsen, where the CC enjoyed a large measure of control, it made a point of bringing in only Jewish doctors and health workers. In the course of time this policy was adopted with respect to the Glyn Hughes Hospital, a medical facility established immediately after liberation on the grounds of the military camp (Hohne), which became the Bergen-Belsen DP camp. Hadassa Bimko, head of the CC Health Department, was already the chief professional link with the British when the rescue operation, headed by Brigadier Glyn Hughes, sprang into action, and it was Bimko who became administrative director of the hospital named for him. By August 1946 the hospital admitted only Jews, and by the end of 1947 it was open to Jewish patients from all over the British Zone.[23]

Other Jewish facilities included Blankenese, a convalescent home for children in Hamburg, established at Bimko's initiative; a religious children's home in Lüneburg that accepted children mainly from Orthodox families; an orphanage in Belsen; and the Bad Harzburg convalescent home, which opened at the beginning of 1947 under the joint auspices of the JDC, the JRU, and the CC (this facility catered primarily to the German Jewish community). Another project organized by the CC was screening for tuberculosis. Jews from all over the British Zone were examined and treated, and arrangements were made for their follow-up care at sanatoria in Switzerland and Italy. After years of neglect and malnutrition, dental treatment was also a pressing need. Bimko had been a dentist before the war and was thus particularly qualified to take charge in this field. A clinic was established, and a dental lab specializing in prosthetics was opened by the Organization for Rehabilitation and Training (ORT).

In all that concerned health care, specifically the care of children, the CC was thus a dominant force. Hadassa Bimko devoted herself to the cause, to the point of personally escorting the transports of children to Palestine in 1946.[24]

Culture and Education

As we have seen, the Provisional Committee which preceded the CC was the initiator of major cultural-educational enterprises: a Yiddish newspaper, the first Jewish school, and a Yiddish theater. The Cultural Department of the CC continued these projects and developed many others as well. The department organized holiday celebrations, for example on Purim and Passover, Sabbath gatherings, a library, and most importantly, schools and adult education programs. Even when the CC was not the actual founder, as in the case of the Beth Jacob Talmud Torah and the ORT vocational school, it supervised these institutions, as attested to by its signature on official certificates and its request for periodic reports.[25]

Chief Rabbinate

The goal of the CC Rabbinical Department was to serve as the chief rabbinate of the British Zone and to resolve matters of halakah (Jewish law) in both the camps and the communities. Rabbi Helfgott, the head of the department, was not formally recognized at first by the CRREC emissaries or the British. In the case of the CRREC, objections to Helfgott were clearly linked to its Agudath Israel orientation and support of a separate Orthodox *Kehillah*, while Helfgott was a modern Orthodox Zionist and represented a less rigid approach to religious practice and law. It would only agree to a rabbinate council of rabbis from among the inmates and rabbis affiliated with the CRREC. Rabbi Helfgott did not enjoy official status, but in practice he was in charge of the Belsen camp and was considered a supreme halakic authority in the British Zone, and it was Helfgott whom the rabbis of Celle and Hanover consulted.[26] The British authorities granted Rabbi Helfgott recognition as the chief rabbi of the British Zone only in July 1947, on the eve of the Second Congress of the *She'erit Hapletah*, when their resistance to the CC began to soften, but the rabbinate was active long before this.[27]

A major concern was issuing death certificates to survivors who had lost a spouse in the war and verifying the validity of conversions in cases of mixed marriages between Germans and Jews. From the beginning of 1946, the CC Rabbinical Department became the sole authority in the sphere of marriage licensing and weddings. In certain communities it oversaw kosher slaughter (which was prohibited in Belsen), the construction of ritual baths (in Belsen and in Celle), and circumcisions.[28]

On the eve of the Second Congress, certain major obstacles were removed that allowed the work of the department to move into high gear. An agreement was reached between Agudath Israel and Hamizrahi, the *Kehillah* became the spokesman of all Orthodox groups, and a separate committee was elected for the Belsen camp in which the Agudists, who were not members of the CC, were also represented. This gave the department leeway to enforce religious rules in the camp and also opened the way for CRREC recognition.[29] Then, around this same time came British recognition—the last hurdle in the acceptance of the CC Rabbinical Department as Belsen's chief rabbinate.

Now it was free to work toward the general implementation of Jewish law in public life. The CC called upon residents of Belsen to observe the Sabbath and prohibited the use of vehicles in and around the camp. The Rabbinical Department became the exclusive authority in all matters of halakah, supervising the work of rabbis, ritual slaughterers, and circumcisors and issuing rulings on questions pertaining to Jewishness, qualifications for serving on committees, and other matters. By the time the Second Congress convened in July 1947, the rabbinate was in a position to submit proposals that were then accepted at the congress as resolutions, attesting to the growing power of what had become the chief rabbinate of the British Zone.[30]

The Jewish Police: Self-Defense, Law, and Order

The motives for establishing a police force came from different directions. First there was self-defense: anti-Semitic attacks by Polish, Ukrainian, and Lithuanian DPs were not uncommon, and calling in a Jewish force rather than a German one was much preferred. At the same time, there was a flourishing black market in the camp, which led to inequality and generally lowered moral standards. The British military authorities had declared an all-out war on the black market, so again, the only way to keep out external intervention was to have Jews do the policing. In addition, a Jewish police force was a source of Jewish pride and self-esteem.

The demand for a Jewish police first arose after the camp's Beth-Midrash (Jewish study house) was attacked by Polish hooligans on the seventh day of Hanukkah in December 1945. The camp already had its own police force, but it was made up of Poles, in keeping with the predominant nationality in the camp (Polish Jews and non-Jews were all the same as far as the British were concerned). In any case, the response of the camp police to this attack on a Jewish institution was deemed "shameful" by CC secretary Dov Laufer. After staging a demonstration, the residents got together and established a Jewish police force. It was composed of a group of former partisans, under the leadership of Sydney Kahan of the JRU and a soldier of the Jewish Brigade. At the beginning of 1946, Simcha Winnik of Belsen assumed command of the force, and the CC appointed Szmayahu Bloch as chief inspector.[31]

At first, the Jewish police were unarmed and lacked basic equipment and uniforms. Uniforms were provided through the help of the JDC and the JRU, but the British objected to the carrying of weapons. This posed a particular problem in the first half of 1946, when the force's main task was to safeguard Jews against the abuse of the armed Polish police, who not only failed to protect them against attacks by Polish DPs but took an active part in the violence. Demands to supply the Jewish police with arms and to integrate them with the Jewish Brigade were thus raised time and again.[32]

Another major challenge to the Jewish police was the black market, the existence of which was a natural consequence of the economic circumstances. Many DPs—not only Jews—were tempted to peddle basic commodities on the black market. This was one of the main fronts on which the CC did battle, convinced that it was detrimental to the Jewish cohesiveness and unity so important for a national struggle. The Jewish police devoted much energy to the task, but the obstacles were numerous. Many of the Jews involved in these shady dealings were respected members of the community, and reacted badly to the intrusion into their affairs of a Jewish police, associated in their minds with the Gestapo and collaboration with the enemy. On the other hand, the British authorities insisted on being the sole authority in this sphere, imposing curfews and conducting raids as if the Jewish force were nonexistent.[33]

The situation changed dramatically in June 1946, when the Polish DPs were evacuated and Belsen finally became an entirely Jewish camp. Under the command of David Kalnitsky, more policemen joined the force and its sphere of responsibility broadened, even including such aspects as sanitation.[34]

The Jewish police were assisted in their struggle for law and order by a Jewish court, inaugurated in the spring of 1946 under the auspices of the CC. Just how effective this court was remains unclear.[35] The jurisdiction of the police force was limited, however, to Belsen itself, which means that it was powerless to stop racketeering and vice in other camps. Neustadt, for example, was a notorious hotbed of illicit trade, gambling, and prostitution.[36]

Holocaust Commemoration

Commemorating the Holocaust was another sphere in which the CC was active. A historical committee was established to record eyewitness accounts for preservation at the YIVO archives;[37] groups of survivors were encouraged and organized to testify at the tribunals of Nazi war criminals;[38] a service was set up to help survivors search for relatives;[39] and a legal department was established to offer advice in matters of restitution and indemnification.[40] As Harry Viteles of the JDC commission put it: "The CC was not only concerned with welfare but with every phase of Jewish life."[41]

Special emphasis was placed on commemorating Liberation Day—April 15. The first anniversary of this event (which occurred during Passover) was a grandiose affair that involved consecrating the Jewish monument erected by the CC, as well as a large parade and mass demonstration. The purpose of the event went beyond commemoration, though. More than anything, the aim was political: a call to free the Holocaust survivors from their continued bondage. The CC and the British further clashed on the erection of a memorial in Belsen, which the British insisted must be of an international character. Indeed, the issue of commemoration was an integral part of the CC's struggle for recognition, and was in itself a cornerstone of the Jewish national struggle.[42]

The Struggle for Recognition

Among the survivors, the CC enjoyed wide acceptance—except, as we have said, among the ultra-Orthodox. The authority of the CC extended throughout the British Zone, with special emphasis on cooperation between the Belsen camp and the Jewish communities.[43] The cooperation was initially based on the close working relationship

Jewish police soldiers guarding the Jewish Memorial on the Liberation Day ceremony, April 15 (1947?) (Yad Vashem Photo-Archives [FA 186 258])

between the chairman and vice-chairman—Rosensaft and Wollheim. The circulars of the CC and its departments were always directed to all committees and Jewish communities in the British Zone. *Unzer Sztyme* reported on affairs in all the communities, and the work of the Health, Rabbinical, and Economic Departments took these different populations into account. Together, Rosensaft and Wollheim dedicated themselves to creating a united framework catering to the needs of both the DPs and the German Jews.[44]

All of this contributed to the CC's struggle for the recognition of the Jews as a national entity. Once the CC was accepted as the national leader by all the Jews of the British Zone, half the battle was won. Recognition by world Jewish organizations had been forthcoming from the outset: Rosensaft and his colleagues were considered—and behaved like—political leaders, and participated in Jewish diplomacy on behalf of the *She'erit Hapletah* as equal partners. In the World Jewish Congress forum this was particularly true. The JCRA and JDC were

New Beginnings

The Second Congress of the Liberated Jews in the British Zone, Bad Harzburg, July 1947 (Yad Vashem Photo-Archives [FA 186 288])

more hesitant in granting Rosensaft full partnership, as manifested in the dispute over distribution of supplies, but even these organizations saw the CC as a sort "German Board of Jewish Deputies" and fought for its recognition.[45]

Enjoying the support of the world organizations, Rosensaft and Wollheim not only corresponded directly with British, German, and UNRRA officials and met with them occasionally, but frequently traveled overseas to participate in diplomatic efforts, conventions, and consultations with world Jewish leaders.[46] Eventually, the CC even became part of the WJC.[47] From the summer of 1947 it officially represented the interests of the British Zone's Jews in the WJC, and in July 1948 it sent delegates to the WJC's second plenary assembly in Montreux.[48]

Rosensaft appealed directly to world Jewish leaders as an authentic representative of the Yiddish-speaking masses in Germany. Wollheim was more of a diplomat, with the requisite background

The Central Committee and Self-Government

and command of languages (German and English). In goals and devotion to the cause, however, there was no difference between them. In negotiating with British and American Jewish leaders, they stood on principle and refused to even consider separating the DPs and German Jews. Wollheim displayed stubbornness in the extreme. When the British Jewish leadership, and particularly the Jewish adviser, Solomon, adopted a compromising stance on this matter in talks with the British, Wollheim vehemently objected. At one point, when Solomon threatened to resign in protest and the British gave in and accepted his demand for recognizing the organization of German Jews, Wollheim still refused to accept anything less than united DP–Jewish German representation.[49] Wollheim even turned down the WJC's invitation to join its ranks as a representative of the German Jews, as well as an invitation to participate in a United Jewish Appeal rally.[50]

At the Second Congress in July 1947, Wollheim had his way. An administrative system was constructed that accentuated the unity of Belsen and the Jewish communities.[51] The Second Congress, preceded by the establishment of the Belsen Committee, was the climax of this long struggle. The Belsen Committee was proof that all parties recognized the CC and that the British, too, were beginning to soften.[52]

The Central Committee's battle for recognition and the British refusal to comply were clearly linked to the Zionist struggle against Mandatory rule in Palestine. Not long after the Second Congress, when the UN voted in favor of the partition of Palestine, the British no longer stood in the CC's way and the CC stopped insisting on unified leadership. In fact, the DPs and German Jewish communities chose separate paths, the DP leadership promoting emigration and liquidating the camps, and the Jewish community leadership supporting continued life in Germany.[53]

8

THE DEVELOPMENT OF THE COMMUNITIES

Statistical-Demographic Synopsis

Between 1946 and 1949 the Jewish communities in the British Zone went through a process of consolidating their population. On the one hand, most of those who planned to emigrate did so by the end of 1949. On the other hand, some of the Eastern European Jews who had left the camps and preferred to stay in Germany joined the communities. Interestingly enough, these in- and outflows were quite moderate and almost offset each other, as is shown by Table 1.

Alongside the numerical stability of the population, the communities' social character saw very little change. Most of them were still dominated by the German Jewish establishment who had founded them and which still composed the majority of the membership. By the end of 1949 most of the members lived in intermarriage. The average age was high, and the percentage of elderly women was great. The number of children grew slowly, and most of the communities suffered from the burden of numerous old, sick, and unemployed members. By the end of 1949 the percentage of employed males in the main cities ranged from 40 percent in Cologne to 66 percent in Kiel, and was somewhat above 50 percent in Hamburg, Hanover, and Düsseldorf.[1]

One of the main problems immediately encountered by the communities was establishing the prerequisites for membership. As previously noted, a great number of Jews did not wish to join a community at first but preferred to resettle and integrate in Germany as German citizens. But before long, many of them—in particular, those who first sought to solve their problems as victims of the Nazis by joining one or another general organization, such as the Vereinigung der Verfolgten des Naziregimes (Association of Those Persecuted by the Nazi Regime [VVN]) and the Vereinigung der von Nürnberger

Development of Communities

Table 1: Demographic Profile of the Jewish Communities in the British Zone

	Number of Members		Percent Adults / Age		Percent Adult / Sex		Number of Children	Percent Origin	
(1)	(2)	(3)	(4)	(5)	(6)	(7)	(8)	(9)	(10)
	1946	1949	18–55	55+	M	F	0–18	Ger.	Mix.
Hamburg	1,300	1,246	60	35	—	—	5	70	70
Lower Saxony									
Hanover	300	260	75	20	48	52	21	100	60
Brunswick	254	—	—	—	49	51	28	—	—
Göttingen	32	—	—	—	56	44	4	—	—
Oldenburg	45	42	—	most	—	—	—	100	—
Osnabrück	79	73	—	38	—	—	—	78	—
North Rhine									
Düsseldorf	1,250	1,050	67	29	—	—	—	80	75
Cologne	539	680	66	26	—	—	—	77	55
Bonn	100	85	—	—	—	—	—	—	90
Duisburg	44	—	—	—	24	76	5	most	—
Essen	144	—	—	most	43	57	20	86	92
Krefeld	75	95	—	—	—	—	—	—	—
München-Gladbach	72	67	—	—	—	—	—	—	—
Oberhausen	38	—	—	—	34	66	9	—	100
Westphalia									
Dortmund	189	—	—	80	—	—	8	—	—
Bilefeld	72	74	—	many	—	—	2	—	—
Detmold	47	49	—	—	—	—	2	some	most
Gelsenkirchen	70	—	—	—	—	—	4	—	—
Herford	47	38	—	—	—	—	1	—	—
Münster	64	60	—	most	—	most	5	most	—
Recklinghausen	119	21	—	—	61	39	1	—	—
Schleswig Holstein									
Kiel	150	60	70	13	40	60	17	58	70
Amrum	43	—	—	—	—	—	—	most	—
Eckernförde	14	10	—	—	—	—	—	50	—
Eutin	13	12	—	—	—	—	—	—	—
Felsenburf	19	21	—	—	—	—	—	—	—
Friedrichstadt		12	—	—	—	—	—	—	—
Lübeck	100	—	—	—	—	—	—	few	—
Neumünster	7	—	—	—	—	—	—	—	—
Rendsburg	7	—	—	—	—	—	—	—	—

Note to table 1: This table is calculated on the basis of numerous reports of various types, made by the JRU, JDC, British authorities, and German authorities, and a full list of them is beyond the needs of this book. As various reports indicate different categories of the data, the data here were chosen and calculated according to the following parameters:

For all the columns, the report of September 1949, submitted to the conference on the "Future of the Jews in Germany," held in Heidelberg [mimeograph, GJA], were preferred. These data relate to the main communities: Cologne, Düesseldorf, Hamburg, Hanover, and Kiel.

Column (1) is divided by *Länder*, and the main community (the capital) in each is shown by bold letters. It does not include communities composed exclusively of DPs, and includes only a sample of the many scattered small communities.

Column (2): data for 1946 when available. As data often contradict each other (given for different points of time), those which were most frequent were chosen.

Column (3): data were taken of the latest available date in 1949.

Column (5): in some cases the data refer to the age above 50 years.

Column (6) and (7): percentage only for the numbers given for males and females, which often do not add up to the total numbers given in either columns (2) and (3).

Column (9) refers to the percentage of those of German origin and/or those who lived in Germany before 1933.

Column (10) refers to the percentage of intermarriages with German spouses, calculated for the married adults only, including widows and widowers but not bachelors.

Gesetzen Betroffenen (Association of Those Affected by the Nuremberg Laws)—finally approached the Jewish communities with the aim of becoming members. This phenomenon was accompanied by the Jewish communities' continuous efforts to prevent persons from belonging to more than one organization and possibly receiving double welfare care.[2]

Moreover, most of the founders of the communities were married to non-Jews who had remained loyal to their Jewish partners throughout the horrors of the Nazi persecution and now wished to join the Jewish community. The question of the status of non-Jews was one of the main problems facing the communities and the Jewish organizations with respect to their relations with and attitude toward the German Jewish community at large. This aspect of the problem created tensions in the communities and had to be resolved, usually according to halakah. In Cologne from the start, and in Hamburg a year later, membership was restricted to Jews by religion or by origin who had not converted to Christianity. This meant that membership became, in most cases, an individual rather than a family matter. In other communities the problem continued to be a matter of debate for years, sometimes concerning the qualification of the heads of the community and sometimes as a matter of conflict with the rabbinate. The solution had to comply with the formal drafting of the communities' statutes and the acquiring of their official status.[3] The development and the process of consolidation of the Jewish communities in the British Zone must be understood against this backdrop.

Immediate Needs

As we have noted, all the Jewish communities were established in response to the urgent needs of the survivors, and accordingly, their activities focused on these requirements. The first needs to be addressed were basic ones: reclamation of communal property; care of the lonely, elderly, and sick members; and advising members on matters such as reclaiming expropriated property or preparing for emigration. Some of these functions were carried out independently by the communities through direct negotiations with local municipal authorities—for example, to obtain temporary accommodations, homes, and hospital care for the elderly. In Cologne, the community reclaimed the synagogue and the Israelitische Asyl (Jewish Shelter) and turned both into temporary shelters.[4] In Hamburg, the Aid Committee (the predecessor of the formal community) secured the only two buildings of the prewar community's property that had not been destroyed in the bombing: the Invalids' and Old People's Home, and the synagogue that had survived the 1938 pogrom.[5] In many communities, however, the communal property had been destroyed or expropriated. In Düsseldorf the community center was in ruins, as was the situation in Essen and München-Gladbach. The silver belonging to the Hamburg Hebrew Congregation had been deposited in the Altona museum, and only some of it was returned to the community on loan, as an advance payment for future restitution. The matter of restitution of communal and private property of German Jews was complicated and far from being resolved, especially in the British Zone. The individual communities—with no legal status as heirs of the prewar communities or as the exclusive representatives of the Jewish people—could not solve this problem. The issues of legal status and restitution were closely interrelated and would become (as examined later in this chapter) the central role in the struggle to establish an overall organization representing the common interests of the communities.[6] In cases of advising individuals in matters of emigration and/or securing the return of private property, the JRU representatives, working hand in hand with the communities, were of great service.[7]

In the case of welfare projects, the communities filled an essential role, serving as a link, both between municipal or provincial German welfare authorities and the needy individuals, and between the Jewish welfare organization and the community members. The communities demanded that they alone be considered the exclusive responsible authority through which the welfare care was allotted and allocated. Occasionally there were competitive actions by some interest groups (such as the VVN), but on the whole, in these matters the communities received the full support of all the welfare authorities—British, German, and Jewish. All of them accepted that centralization of allotments and allocations was basically in their best interest, and here was a factor for the construction of central organizations on the basis of the *Land* or even beyond that.[8]

Looking to the Future: Social and Cultural Roles

Another crucial role of the communities was spiritual welfare, a need reflected by the desire to establish the communities anew—a sort of *Ja-sagen zum Judentum* (saying yes to Judaism). A synagogue was the first and most natural place for the scattered Jewish survivors to meet, and services were held in the first days after liberation. Responding to the initiatives of the communities, the JRU emissaries and the rabbis sent by the CRREC played a decisive role in this area by reorganizing Jewish religious, cultural, and social life and by supplying prayer books and other materials. They guided and organized services, weddings, and even circumcisions—the latter being rare in the early period. The events at Hamburg were quite symbolic: on August 7, 1945, there was a ceremony of the first circumcision in Hamburg for many years. The boy's parents had been the last Jewish couple to marry in April 1943 in Hamburg. A month later they were deported to Theresienstadt. On August 12, a few days after the circumcision, the first wedding since 1943 was celebrated. The bridegroom was a Jew from Germany, and the bride was a Polish DP.[9]

In most newly established communities, the first concern was obtaining a place for worship. This involved either restoring the old synagogue (if it still existed) or receiving a suitable building to hold services in and to serve as a community center. Indeed, in religious and cultural matters the communities depended heavily on the work of the English rabbis and the JRU workers, who continued to serve the communities for many years. Religious services were entirely dependent on the availability of rabbis, who had to travel from one community to the next (in many communities, services were held only occasionally). There was also the problem of those who wished to fulfill their religious feelings in different ritual patterns. This was practically impossible, both because of the lack of premises for different synagogues in the same community and because of the limited availability of rabbis and cantors of various religious attitudes. For many years the communities—even the larger ones—depended on rabbis and cantors visiting from abroad. The smaller communities could not afford their own kosher butchers, ritual baths, and so forth, and depended on regional arrangements. These difficulties, again, were matters to be solved, at least partially, on the basis of some kind of umbrella organization.[10]

The support from abroad in spiritual matters was not confined to religious matters. One of the main contributions of the emissaries was to organize social, cultural, and educational activities, for which the communities' leaders lacked both the mental and the psychological skills and energy. Many of the community leaders were not inclined to spirituality, and all their efforts were naturally aimed at meeting urgent material needs. The emissaries in many ways filled this gap, indeed feeling that here was their main vocation. They used the synagogues as cultural and social centers for organizing lectures and a variety of sociocultural events, particularly the holidays, such as Hanukkah and Purim. They organized Hebrew and English lessons, arranged for donations of books from abroad, and established libraries in many communities.[11]

The chief concern of the communities was education. The fact that there was only a limited number of children and youngsters magnified the problem, since teachers from abroad could not organize special Jewish schools for so few children. As a result, these few children went to German schools and received their Jewish education elsewhere, generally through some type of informal education. This function, too, could not be fulfilled by the communities individually. Understanding this, the Central Committee of the British Zone made efforts to include the communities in its activities, particularly by helping with the organization of youth groups. This aid was, however, granted along strict Zionist lines, whose raison d'être was the liquidation—rather than the consolidation—of Jewish communities in Germany.[12]

Another matter that occupied the communities from the start was the restoration of cemeteries, which served both spiritual and practical needs. There was a desire to show identification with the former community by restoring a sense of continuity and tradition, by preserving the testimony of the great past. This meant fulfilling a duty to the dead and commemorating the catastrophe that had befallen the Jewish people at large, and German Jewry in particular. This was, in fact, one of the justifications for resettling in Germany. In Hamburg this was particularly evident. A survivor provided information that enabled the community to locate and retrieve many religious items that had been buried in the cemetery in order to preserve them from the Nazis. There was also, of course, an immediate need for cemeteries, for death took a high toll on the old and sick.[13]

Encounters with anti-Semitism, which was manifested mainly in the desecration of Jewish cemeteries, put an extra weight on the role of the Jewish communities vis-à-vis the German authorities, demanding protection and financing for the restoration of the cemeteries.[14]

The Beginnings of Regional Organizations

The Jewish communities had their own specific needs apart from those they had in common with the DPs. For the same reasons that German Jews organized their own local communities, they eventually decided to create regional organizations. The first to be established in Germany was the Landesverband (Land Association [LV]) of North Rhine region, which was initiated by Philipp Auerbach of Düsseldorf. This regional organization also sought to represent the communities in Westphalia, which shortly afterward officially organized as a separate LV, although they were actually subordinate to the LV of North Rhine. This was due, first, to the prestige and authority of Auerbach, who was in charge of the Jewish welfare in the region's welfare committee, and second, to demographic reality, since in Westphalia there were only small communities, with a small number of German Jews.

The organization represented about 1,700 Jews in North Rhine, most of them German Jews, and about 700 Jews in Westphalia, the majority of them living in Kaunitz as DPs. The most important communities that belonged to the organization were Cologne, with 600 members, Düsseldorf, with 200 members, and Essen, with 130 members. Other communities were Bonn, Krefeld, and Wuppertal, with 70 to 80 members each, and smaller communities, such as

Aachen, München-Gladbach, and Duisburg. Auerbach, Julius Meier from Cologne, and Alfred Löwenthal from Aachen were the chairmen. Düsseldorf was the "capital" due to its being Auerbach's hometown and the seat of the welfare offices for the British Zone. The LV nevertheless was considered a branch affiliated with the CC, which had been previously established. At the opening meeting, Wollheim represented the CC, Lunzer the JRU, Wodlinger the JDC, and Rabbi Munk the CRREC.[15]

The targets of the organization were many. First, it aimed at negotiating the restitution of the communities' property. Second, it was to centralize the material support received from Jewish organizations abroad and to supervise its allocation. Third, it would negotiate with the various German communal and regional authorities and organizations in order to supplement the welfare allotments, and would receive the needed authorizations for opening shops, firms, and the like. Another important goal was to create an educational system and vocational training parallel to that which already existed in Bergen-Belsen but unavailable to the many Jews scattered outside the camp. There was also responsibility to look after the religious needs of the various communities, to provide personnel, to take care of cemeteries, and similar concerns.[16] All these goals could be dealt with more efficiently through an organization designed to act on behalf of the communities, which the CC, due to lack of funds, could not. On the other hand, it was important to be affiliated with the CC in order to have its support.

At this time there were already two main attitudes toward an overall community organization. On the one hand was the stance of Norbert Wollheim, who did not foresee any future for Jews in Germany and regarded the LV as a tool for a transitional period until mass emigration would end Jewish life in Germany. On the other hand there was Auerbach, who believed in a future for Jews in Germany and hoped that the LV would become a tool in establishing this future. Ultimately, the difference between these two concepts was in the sphere of political strategy. Wollheim strove to achieve the cooperation of the world Jewish organizations, chiefly of the Jewish Agency and the Palestine Jewish leaders. For Auerbach, the chief partners for the LV political activity were the British and German authorities, on whom the well-being of the Jews in Germany depended. Basically, it was the disagreement between a Zionist and a non-Zionist, though both sides were ready to compromise. Wollheim did not neglect those Jews who would not be

New Beginnings

able to leave Germany, and Auerbach recognized the importance of the Zionist goal as a focus for Jewish solidarity.[17]

The process of organizing the Jewish communities in the British Zone, which began with the establishment of the LV, reflected the shift from one attitude to another. At first the Zionist view was accepted, which stressed centralization under the auspices of the CC. Then the non-Zionist attitude approach ruled, which meant the separation between the CC and the communities.

Shortly after the establishment of the LV of North Rhine and Westphalia, another LV was established—that of Schleswig-Holstein, with its center in Kiel.[18] In Lower Saxony, however, no organization was founded, even after the unification in 1946 of the three provinces (Hanover, Brunswick, and Oldenburg) to become a *Land*. The Hanover Jewish community, with its 250 members, was actually the only significant German Jewish community in this region; the others—Brunswick and Celle—were DP communities under the auspices of Bergen-Belsen. The other minor mixed communities (Göttingen and Osnabrück, for example) were dependent on Hanover.[19]

Between Zionist Centralization and Independent Organizations

Before long, further steps were taken to organize all the communities in the British Zone under the auspices of the Central Committee. In a meeting on May 9, 1946, in Bremen in the presence of representatives of the CC and the welfare organizations, the *Arbeitsgemeinschaft* (Work Association) for the British Zone was founded, chaired by Wollheim and Karl Katz of the Bremen community, and without the participation of Auerbach and the LV of North Rhine and Westphalia.[20] Auerbach tried to establish an alternative organization with its seat in Düsseldorf, but before long, at a meeting in Bergen-Belsen on June 25, 1946, the two organizations established a joint committee—the *Zonenausschuss* (Zone Committee)—under the leadership of Auerbach but with full subordination to the CC.[21]

In August 1946 Auerbach was nominated as *Staatskommissar* (state commissioner) in Bavaria and moved to Munich, and Julius Dreifuss—the chairman of the Düsseldorf community—was elected also chairman of the Zone Committee. In October 1946, at his initiative, the joint committee finalized merger between the two organizations and became the Rat der Jüdischen Gemeinden der britischen Zone (Council of the

Jewish Communities in the British Zone). The council was now headed by Wollheim, with its center in Lübeck.[22]

In the meantime a similar initiative was in process in the American Zone. There, Hans Lamm, who represented the American-Jewish Conference, established in March 1946 the *Interessenvertretung* (Interests-Representation of the Jewish Communities, abbreviated herein as I-RJC) in Stuttgart, the seat of the German *Länderrat* (Lands' Council). The aim of this organization was to deal with the issue of restitution, indemnification, and compensation (*Wiedergutmachung*) on behalf of all the Jewish communities in Germany; in this organization, Auerbach represented the British Zone.[23]

The I-RJC did not, however, succeed in maintaining contacts with the other zones of occupation, mainly the British, and in addition failed to gain the trust of the leaders there. Thus, a year after its foundation, a competing initiative took place, led by Wollheim, with the full support of two representatives of the JRU: E. G. Lowenthal, who was responsible for the whole British Zone, and Hendrik van Dam, who was nominated by JRU as the legal counselor of the Jewish communities there. By the end of March 1947 a meeting of Jewish lawyers convened in Detmold, and shortly thereafter, in April 20, a general conference was called at Eilshausen (the seat of the JRU headquarters), in which all zones of occupation and Berlin were represented. Here, with the Jewish Agency representative in the I-RJC, Meinhold Nussbaum, but without any other representative of the I-RJC present, it was agreed upon to establish a Work Association to deal with all issues concerning the Jewish communities of Germany. Unlike the case of the I-RJC, here the issue of compensation was only one—and not the most important—point on the agenda. More important were the issues of the legal status of the communities, welfare, education, and cultural activity, which were placed on the top of the agenda.[24]

In early June 1947, in Frankfurt, the Arbeitsgemeinschaft der jüdischen Gemeinden Deutschlands (Work Association of the Jewish Communities of Germany)—representing also the Soviet Zone and Berlin—was established, and here too, Wollheim represented the British Zone in the executive.[25] The main goal of the new organization was, as already mentioned, to deal with the future of the Jews in Germany and to establish the legal basis for their communities. This, of course, included the issue of restitution and the status of the communities. While the I-RJC and Auerbach, personally, strove to gain the status of representing the Jewish people in general, the world Jewish organizations did not accept this. From their perspective, the communities in Germany could at most constitute a local representation in the negotiations, without other status of representing the Jewish case in general. The new organization therefore served the interests of all those who objected to Auerbach's claim of representing—through the I-RJC—the Jewish claims of compensation. Wollheim, as a German Jew and a Zionist at one and the same time, personified the opposition to Auerbach's pretension, and was thus the main force behind the founding of the new organization.

One must bear in mind, however, that all these arguments were latent. On the surface, pro-Zionism was the bon ton; everyone supported Zionist demands and to some extent doubted the possibility of a Jewish future in Germany. Publicly, Auerbach saw in the Jewish future in Germany a mission of being both judge and prosecutor on behalf of the Jewish people, while Wollheim regarded this phase as necessary but transitional and unwanted.[26]

The Fusion of the Work Association with the Central Committee

Now that an umbrella organization of the Jewish communities in Germany was founded to attend to their interests, Wollheim felt free to further the aim of unifying the Council of the Jewish Communities and the CC in the British Zone by establishing a new organization to replace them. His plan of a single organization for the sake of unity—which was discussed early in June 1947—was not welcomed, however, by either Colonel Solomon, the Jewish adviser, or by the JRU heads, Norman Bentwich and Lady Rose Henriques, who insisted on the necessity of maintaining the current situation: on the one hand, separate organizations to care for the varying interests of the DPs and communities, and on the other, full cooperation in matters concerning the Jewish people as a whole.

Interestingly enough, full support was given to Wollheim by none other than Karl Marx. Marx was the founder and editor of the *Jüdisches Gemeindeblatt für die Nord-Rheinprovinz und Westfalen*, the first and only newspaper published in German in the British Zone. Its first issue as a biweekly appeared on April 15, 1946, the anniversary of Belsen's liberation. A few months later, in November 1946, its subtitle was changed to *für die britische Zone*, and by September 1948 it appeared as a weekly. Finally, in April 1949, it was published as the *Allgemeine*

Wochenzeitung der Juden in Deutschland, the central organ for German Jewry.[27] Marx was considered the genuine representative of German Jews and communal interests. Nevertheless, he supported Wollheim's strategy: "This fusion might become an historical turning point. It is such because it is an external manifestation toward the whole world, that the lesson of the former years has driven us to fuse into a united movement, to ignore all party, political and ideological differences, being conscious of our obligation to fight together for our future, for the future of our children and their children, for the recognition of our national identity."[28]

The will to pursue the unification of the Jews in Germany was manifested in another step, the foundation of the chief rabbinate of the British Zone under the leadership of Rabbi Zvi Asaria-Helfgott, who was a member of the CC and the director of its Rabbinical Department. Alongside this another decision was made: the Council of the Jewish Communities officially elected Hendrik van Dam of the JRU as its legal adviser.[29] For van Dam this was a decisive personal step from representing an external welfare organization to a career in the German Jewish community. A few years later he would become the general secretary of the Central Council of the Jews in Germany.

Indeed, it must be emphasized that Marx and the community leaders had their own reasons to support Wollheim. They understood that unity was important for the future of the Jews in Germany. For them unity meant recognition by world Jewry of the legitimacy of Jewish existence in Germany and the integration of the German Jewish community with world Jewry. For Wollheim, however, the aim was "Zionization" of the Jewish communities in Germany.

The process of unification under Zionist auspices reached its climax at the Second Congress of the Liberated Jews in the British Zone, which convened in Bergen-Belsen and Bad Harzburg in July 1947. This congress enclosed a circle that had opened two years earlier at the first congress. Then, in September 1945, shortly after liberation, the foundations were laid for cooperation between the communities and the DPs to establish a united Jewish front against British policy which did not recognize Jews as Jews. Now, two years later, three issues had to be confronted. First, the British continued their opposition to any inclusive but separate Jewish organization. Second, the interests of the communities suffered under the existing system by which they were represented, as a separate organization, under the auspices of the CC, since this enabled the British to insist on their principle that the communities should be integrated into the general German communal system and were not of concern to the British. Third, the need for world Jewish organizations to intervene on behalf of German Jewish interests could not be satisfied without the linkage between these interests and the interests of world Jewry. World Jewry, which was now, in its post-Holocaust era, clearly painted with national and pro-Zionist colors, placed aliyah and the claims for restitution as national Jewish matters of immediate priority.

The Second Congress was marked by anti-British protest. The British, who opposed its very convening, refused any assistance and refrained from participation or presentation. The German authorities also did not want to be involved. On the other hand, the Jewish Agency, the World Jewish Congress, the JDC, and the JRU were heavily represented. German Jewish leaders from the American Zone also participated. The congress elected a new Central Committee and an executive of thirteen members: seven representatives of Bergen-Belsen and six representatives of the communities. Besides this executive there was a larger council with thirty-five members, of whom nineteen represented the camps and sixteen the communities.

The congress also discussed and accepted resolutions concerning purely communal matters such as the chief rabbinate, community membership requirements, and requirements for elected communal functions. In the latter case it was decided that a Jew married to a non-Jew, with only a few exceptions, would not be eligible for communal leadership. In the British Zone, however, there were many special cases among the existing leadership, so this rendered the resolution into a theoretical declaration that could not be implemented. Last but not least, at this congress the CC was recognized as an affiliate of the WJC.[30]

In his speech, Wollheim expressed his interpretation of the congress's decisions:

> What is our status in Germany and in the world? In Germany we feel the tension East-West, the Iron Curtain. Political position of France and Britain. Neo-Fascism in Germany: our distrust is justified.... What is going to happen, if the Occupation Forces will be withdrawn? Consequently we must liquidate not necessarily tomorrow, because here we do not live in security.... However, by gradually leaving Germany we do not want to forfeit our rights to fight for our claims here, in particular for the aged people, who have to remain and to die in Germany. Moreover, the IRO [International Refugee

Organization] Charta embraces also German Jews (in addition to DPs). Hopes that UNO [United Nations Organization] report on Palestine will be accepted. We have to work in still closer contact with the World Jewish Congress and the Jewish Agency. We expect liaison and advice from the Jewish Adviser. We shall fight for the economic existence of the Jews in towns until such time as they can emigrate and for the training of the DPs for their future in Palestine.[31]

What at that time seemed to be the climax in fulfilling the goal of fusion was, however, marking its end.

From Zionist Centralization to German Jewish Separatism

As illustrated by the movement of a pendulum, the success of one trend to fulfill its goal of unification in its extreme form challenged the other side, the opposing trend. The Zionist struggle for aliyah against the British immigration policy in Palestine intensified, while other issues concerning the welfare of the survivors, and especially the Jews in the towns, were virtually neglected. This order of priorities was exemplified by the *Exodus* affair, which took place during the Second Congress and continued thereafter.[32]

The Jewish (Zionist)-British conflict during this period went through great strategic changes on both fronts. Prior to the Second Congress, and mainly afterward, the British began to relent regarding their strict policy against Jewish national representation of German Jews. They began to understand that their flat refusal to any general national Jewish organization badly affected Jewish moderate leaders. Colonel Solomon, the Jewish adviser, threatened to resign, together with Brodetsky from the BD and Silverman and Barou from the WJC. Solomon demanded recognition of the organization of German Jews as a separate organization under the chairmanship of Norbert Wollheim. At the same time, he and other English Jewish leaders tried to convince Wollheim and his colleagues to forgo complete fusion with the CC, since the British would never accept this. On the other hand, Solomon claimed that the matter of the CC as the sole representative of Bergen-Belsen could be resolved.[33]

It seems that the readiness of the British (though reluctantly) to soften their former position against the Jews in Germany was related to developments concerning Palestine. On November 29 the UN General Assembly voted in favor of the partition of Palestine, creating an Arab-Palestinian state and a Jewish state. Shortly thereafter, the

British began to prepare for their withdrawal from the country. Soon the gates of Palestine were to open; an independent State of Israel was to be declared, with aliyah for all to become a reality. The aliyah from the British Zone in Germany was already accelerated due to operation "Grand National"—the aliyah of DPs that had been initiated by Solomon in the spring of 1947.[34]

The first sign of the new phase in British-Jewish relations in Germany was Wollheim's readiness to recognize the fact that the fusion of German Jewish affairs with DP affairs was in fact against the interests of the general representation of German Jewish communities through the Work Association. Immediately after the Second Congress, in August 1947, the Rat der Gemeinden beim Zentralkomitee der befreiten Juden der britischen Zone Deutschlands (Council of Communities at the Central Committee of the Liberated Jews in the British Zone of Germany) was revived.[35]

The *Exodus* affair, around which German Jews and DPs presented a united front,[36] delayed the separation of the two organizations. However, during the summer months of 1948 the process of separation was resumed and gained momentum through the WJC convention in Montreux, Switzerland, in July 1948, which dealt with restitution and the need to represent Jewish claims in Germany. At this conference the status of the Jewish communities in Germany was hotly debated, and the need for organizing the communities as an interest group was actually placed in the forefront. The London executive of the WJC, and its leader Noah Barou, strongly supported the case of the Jewish communities in Germany, which served to encourage them to renew their initiative for a separate organization.[37]

Another factor was the emigration of DPs to the newly declared State of Israel. From May 1948 until June 1949, 57,000 DPs emigrated from Germany to Israel, and 13,000 more went to the United States.[38] The camps in Germany were closed down one after another, and the CC itself began to decline. The Zionist struggle, which until then had been the driving force for cooperation with the CC, was no longer relevant, and thus the communities distanced themselves from the CC, turning to follow their own interests concerning their future in Germany and, accordingly, to organize themselves.[39]

In the meantime, from October 1947, the general German Jewish Work Association embarked on a series of decisions regarding their future in Germany. This included establishing the *Wohlfahrtsstelle* (welfare station) in Frankfurt and struggling against anti-Semitism. However, concerning the most troubling issue, restitution, there was no progress, since the organization in the British Zone, with its Zionist ties, refused to act. Following the conference on the Jewish future in Germany, which took place in September 1949 in Heidelberg, it became clear that an all-inclusive representation of Jewish interests in Germany was needed and that the inclusion of the British Zone's Jewish communities was essential.[40]

Shortly before that, in March 1949, the British authorities had at last recognized the organization of the Jewish communities under Wollheim's leadership. This recognition came as a result of the British accepting that the issue of Jewish existence in Germany and the status of the communities were no longer a matter for the British authorities but for the newly established Federal Republic and its states. The first step in this direction had already been taken in Hamburg, where in December 1948 a law was adopted recognizing the Jewish community as a *Körperschaft des öffentlichen Rechts* (association by public law), which had been its status before the Nazi era.[41]

In May 1949, at a meeting of the Council of Communities with the CC executive, the closing of the CC and the gradual separation of the Council of Communities was decided upon. Both representatives of the JRU—van Dam and Heymann (who had replaced Lowenthal)—strongly encouraged this decision and offered their services to the Council of Communities.[42] On the other hand, the Jewish Agency resisted any step taken toward the Jewish future in Germany and declared its intention to close its offices in Germany.[43]

In September 1949, a convention of all the Jewish communities in the British Zone was held in Hamburg. This convention was the last event organized under the auspices of the CC, and the line delineating the division between the concept of a Jewish future in Germany and the Zionist view was clearly marked. Wollheim attempted—in vain—to persuade his audience to subordinate the Jewish community in Germany to the world Jewish representation as a matter of common interest: "You have to recognize the arguments of the external organizations. The heirless property is no doubt a general Jewish matter.... Our interests are recognized abroad. There is a great mistrust out there regarding everything German. It is believed that Jewish life in Germany is *contradicto in adjecto*. The former Jewish-German prestige, as much as it had not been destroyed, exists solely in the emigration."[44]

Restitution and reparation were indeed the central issues causing the final separation from the CC on the one hand and leading toward an independent German Jewish organization on the other.

Before long, in December 1949, separation from the CC was accomplished: the Council of Communities became independent and reorganized as the Verband der Jüdischen Gemeinden Nordwestdeutschland (Association of the Jewish Communities of North-West Germany), which in its turn led to the establishment, by the end of 1950, of the Central Council of the Jews in Germany.[45]

9

"Unser Dirat Arai": Society, Economy, and Culture in the Camps

Temporary Dwelling in an Ex-Territory

"*Unzer Dirat Arai*" (Our temporary dwelling)—this how the survivors defined their situation.[1] Many sources indicate that life in Bergen-Belsen had much in common with that in an ordinary Jewish community, particularly after Belsen became an exclusively Jewish camp. Other sources seem to emphasize the unique abnormal conditions under which Jews tried to make life as normal as possible. Actually, these different sources are not contradictory, but rather complement each other. They differ concerning the time to which they refer and on their point of view.

As for the time, there was a difference between the first period after liberation, which lasted for more than a year, and the second period, which started in late 1946. The first period was marked by harsh supply conditions and a rigid British policy that prevented extensive Jewish welfare and placed many constraints on earmarked Jewish activity. This period ended gradually during the spring and summer of 1946, and from then on there was much more room for Jewish-organized public activities.[2] Nevertheless, examined objectively, the situation was abnormal, even after the change. Each camp was an ex-territorial entity, separated from German civilian population, dependent on the British and UNRRA administration on the one hand and on Jewish welfare on the other.

Relations with the German population surrounding the camp were nonexistent or negative. The German authorities had no contact with the camps, and once when the British authorities tried to involve them—in connection to the campaign against black-marketing—they encountered stiff Jewish resistance. Jews objected to any interference by the German civil authorities, even in matters that were under their control.³ Jewish camp inmates could encounter Germans on two levels only. The first was the numerous anti-Semitic attacks on Jewish cemeteries and synagogues occurring outside the camps, but raising Jewish fears and responses within the camps nonetheless. Between January and June 1947 eight cemeteries were desecrated, and the statistics for the year mention twenty-six such incidents.⁴ The second level was dictated by economic needs. Jews in the camp would, as much as they could, profit from their interactions with Germans—mostly through trade and barter in the black market, and sometimes through hiring Germans as servants.⁵

Anti-Semitic attacks by non-Germans, mainly Poles and Lithuanians, presented a major problem within the camps as well. Jews suffered constantly from violence in Belsen and other camps having a significant Jewish presence.⁶ There were also many complaints against British soldiers, either for ignoring German or Polish anti-Semitism or even for introducing anti-Semitic propaganda and collaborating with the German police in connection with efforts to eliminate the black market.⁷ The evacuation of the Poles from Belsen in the summer of 1946 considerably improved relations between the Jewish inmates and the British.⁸

Objectively, however, the constraints of camp life and the sense of a transitional situation lasted for years and did not offer any hope for the immediate future. This could not be changed without some opportunities for emigration. Moreover, despite improvements in some areas, economic constraints persisted. During the harsh winter of 1946–47 (temperatures fell to -20°C—35°C) there were shortages of food, clothing, and heating, which reminded the inmates of the previous winter, shortly after liberation.⁹ Hence the sources focusing on this objective situation are justified in their negative view of life in the camps.

On the other hand, after life became normalized (in the narrow sense that normalcy may be applied to camp life), people resumed many of the activities that are found in a vibrant Jewish community. In this chapter we shall try to reconstruct the many aspects of daily life in the camp in order to understand what it was like for Jewish men, women, and children to live for years in these transitional conditions. This study will focus upon Bergen-Belsen in the period that may be considered most stabilized, starting in the spring and summer of 1946 and ending with the beginning of mass emigration toward the end of 1948.

Society, Economy, and Culture

Living Conditions

ACCOMMODATION

Officially, there were three areas in the camp. One, called the "American Zone," consisted largely of those internees who had been liberated in Belsen and had managed to accumulate some possessions. The other two areas were populated by newcomers.[10] Most of the people—some 8,000 out of 10,000–11,000, lived in barracks. Usually the barracks was two stories high, and each floor had a long corridor with ten rooms, a kitchen, and a bathroom. In the "Families' barracks" each family had a room. In the other barracks, each room was occupied by three to six persons. Some of the blocks were defined as kibbutzim—occupied by members of youth groups according to their political affiliations, running a communal life in the barracks. Many blocks were much too crowded, some were composed of large halls that did not offer any privacy, and others were lacking windows. By April 1946 there were still shortages of beds, mattresses, blankets, and linen.[11]

Of course, problems arose from the conditions of living with limited private space, since this forced a mix of private and public arenas (cooking, laundry, washing in common spaces) and resulted in filth and unattended garbage. One learns about these problems through the various notices and regulations distributed by the camp committee or by the camp Jewish police. It was forbidden, for example, to put garbage in the corridors, to use the corridors for cooking, or to throw garbage out of the windows.[12] Living in barracks hindered the process of rehabilitation, of regaining the sense of responsibility for cleanliness, for the well-being of others.[13] Indeed, living conditions improved during the summer of 1946 (married couples and singles no longer lived together in the same room, soap and detergents were provided, and so forth). However, the basic condition of living in barracks—sleeping, eating, and dressing in a single room while cooking and washing in a common kitchen and bathrooms—did not change, and people lived in this manner for many more years.

However, over the course of time many people managed to make their rooms resemble a normal flat by adding furniture and dishes, acquiring electrical equipment for light, heating, and cooking, and decorating with curtains and other materials, either self-made or bought or exchanged for other commodities (as we shall note later when dealing with economics and occupation). The use of electrical equipment even reached the point that the camp police distributed orders to reduce electrical usage because the camp's electrical system was overloaded.[14]

An upper class developed that consisted mainly of those who managed to build up an extensive legitimate and black market trade. Some of them even bought cars and traveled for business. These people usually did not live in the barracks but managed to acquire a house or flat in the vicinity of Belsen. Some of the leaders also belonged to the upper class. Rosensaft and his family lived in a flat in Belsen, Olevsky had a house and a car in Celle, Wollheim lived in a house in Lübeck with his family, and Rabbi Meisels had an official car with driver at his disposal, but these were exceptions. Many ordinary people, though not becoming rich, managed to improve their living conditions and accumulate property for their current use or for their entrepreneurial endeavors (as will be seen later in this chapter) as well as for their future.[15]

Food and Other Supplies

Shortages of food persisted for many months, causing a strike in October 1945.[16] The daily ration of 2,000 calories per capita for DPs in the camps was never fully enforced and, of course, it did not imply what the composition or the quality of the food to be distributed would be. There was a constant lack of fat and proteins, fresh vegetables, fruits, and milk, even after the first year. Cooked food was supplied by central kitchens and distributed through canteens. Each canteen served some one thousand people, so no one could expect subtle flavors or a varied menu. Many—survivors and social workers alike—complained that even the minimum that could have been done with the poor food rations was not done (either for lack of expert cooks, cooking equipment, or spices). Thus, most people would prefer to get—according to their ration card—uncooked food and to cook it either in their room or in the common kitchen.[17]

The rations were composed of the UNRRA supplies plus the JDC supplements, some of which were allocated specifically for the sick, laborers, pregnant women, nursing mothers, and children. A major supplementary source was the CRREC, which was meant to provide items for the needs of religious people, such as kosher food. These organized collective supplies were supplemented with packages sent to individuals. Some of these packages were sent by relatives or friends abroad;

others came through an organized adoption project, in which organizations, communities, and individuals in England "adopted" communities, organizations, and individuals among the survivors by regularly sending them packages. These packages included a variety of goods, from food, clothing, and cigarettes to cosmetics, hygienic supplies, stationary and writing materials, sewing materials, and toys.[18]

These packages became the backbone of the camp economy, one of the various ways developed to replace supplies that were lacking. One method was the use of the large quantities of cigarettes, coffee, or cocoa, which replaced money and were used for barter. Another method was the use of falsifying statistics and identity cards. Many people owned more than one ration card, due to an extensive issuing of cards in the names of people who had died or left the camp. These cards were nicknamed in Yiddish *"Toyten-cards"* or *"Toyten indexes"*—dead people's cards or indexes—and their missing holders were called *"Malochim"*—angels. Parts of the rations—especially cigarettes, as previously mentioned—were used for exchange for food or goods, either with people in the camp, with Allied soldiers, or with the German population nearby. In this way the camp inmates also gradually accumulated many other needed commodities, such as clothing, furniture, kitchen utensils, and electrical equipment. These items were also used for acquiring equipment and machines, or even farm animals such as cows and poultry, for starting a business.[19]

Occupational and Vocational Training

Theoretically, there was every motive for people to live idly. The camp was separated from the German economy and dependent on British and Jewish welfare. There were many constraints on gainful employment, such as the lack of raw materials and the refusal to work with or for Germans on the one hand, and, on the other, no real incentive to work for a living, since basic needs were met through welfare. This counterproductive framework was one of the prime concerns among the welfare personnel. They often expressed their fear that idleness could become the nurturing ground for black-marketing and crime and prevent the success of rehabilitation programs.

Since the DPs received food and no money, black-marketing and barter was the only way they could get what they needed in the German market. The Germans, on the other hand, were interested in supplementing, through the black market, the meager rations allocated to them by the authorities. No wonder, then, that selling and buying in the black market was part and parcel of daily life for many camp inmates, and that for some it became an expanding business. These few became well-known merchants, commuting constantly between Belsen and Hanover and making Belsen their main base.[20]

Thus, Belsen attracted the attention of the British military authorities, and raids upon Belsen took place. The Central Committee and the Jewish police in the camp made the black market their main target, trying to minimize it and to prevent the need for British authorities to intervene.[21] However, the main strategy for minimizing the expanding black market and its corruptive effect was the constant effort to create alternative and productive ways of earning a livelihood. Indeed, against the initial, quite pessimistic expectations, and due to many initiatives both by the welfare organizations and individual camp inmates, a camp economy was developed that was not entirely based on the black market.

Vocational training was initiated by the camp organizations, the JRU, the JA, and the ORT, and was financed mainly by the JDC. In Belsen, various courses in different trades, such as automobile mechanics, auto driving, sewing and dressmaking, electromechanics, and carpentry, were started. These sporadic courses run by the camp inmates developed into a full-time vocational school that was taken over by the ORT, with Jack Weingreen of the JRU as the headmaster. During its first year of operation this school trained some 900 students, each for a period of six months, and by the end of 1946 there were at one time some 400 participants. Some of the teachers also came from among the camp inmates.[22] The main focus for vocational training was the programs developed for the needs of the camp inmates. In the Glyn Hughes Hospital, nurses were systematically trained under the supervision of the matron, Eva Minden (Kahn) of the JRU.[23] For manufacturing false teeth, a laboratory was opened through the initiative of the dentist Dr. Hadassa Bimko Rosensaft, herself a survivor. This provided new teeth for the hundreds of survivors whose teeth had deteriorated through the long years of neglect and malnutrition.[24] Some of the vocational school workshops, such as the workshop for repairing and manufacturing shoes, also served the needs of the camp population. The various kibbutzim also initiated workshops for training and for producing supplies. They, together with the Jewish Agency, also developed a program to train agriculturists. The UNRRA authorities allocated local farms for this program and so supported this enterprise.[25]

Students of ORT vocational school's laboratory for manufacturing false teeth (Yad Vashem Photo-Archives [168FO5])

Vocational training for Belsen's inmates was not confined to Belsen. Ahlem, a former Jewish gardening school near Hanover (used as a Gestapo prison during the war), was leased to the ORT in May 1946. The JRU and the JDC also supported an agricultural school for kibbutz members there.[26] Neustadt-Holstein also became a center for vocational training—mainly maritime training—by the ORT, using the ex-Nazi naval school and facilities located there. The school opened in May 1947 and provided accommodation and services—including a nursery—for 120 students from Belsen, men and women, in addition to some 60 students from Neustadt and the vicinity.[27] A vocational school functioned in Hanover as well, offering courses in machine tooling, mechanics, electronics, and dressmaking, and maintaining workshops for dressmaking and corsetmaking, puppets, and toys. In addition, there were training programs in many other locations. By early 1948 there were some 2,000 ORT students in the British Zone.[28]

The courses and centers not only prepared people for the future, but also provided them with a job to earn a living, either by paying students during their studies or by marketing their products in the camp or to the British. After students received their diplomas, the ORT also helped them to obtain tools and machinery to establish their own workshops.[29] Thus they could support themselves and also save for a future after emigration.

However, vocational training was only one of the many ways in which camp inmates earned their living. Many people offered their skills or were employed by UNRRA and the Jewish welfare services: teachers, nurses, policemen, clerks, locksmiths, technicians, shoemakers, bakers, and others. They were paid by extra rations which they could use in exchange for other commodities.[30] Those who had prior experience in various trades were able to offer their services locally or to open workshops and shops of various types in the camp. These shops were called "canteens," and on walking through the streets in Belsen (or for that matter, reading the advertisements in *Unzer Sztyme*) one could find hairdressing services being offered for men and women, dry cleaning, shoe repairs, printing, and chauffeuring. These small businesses were the natural response to a growing demand that increased in quantity and diversification among the camp inmates, along with the process of establishing families and settling down.[31]

Forming Families

The most significant factor in establishing a feeling of normality in the camps was the forming of new families. As already indicated, many of the survivors were young men and women between twenty and thirty who found themselves alone, their entire families—parents, spouses, children, brothers and sisters—murdered by the Nazis. Only a few were lucky enough to find some survivors. After liberation, many were too ill and apathetic, or haunted by the drive to search and find their beloved ones. Indeed, there were some stories that seem miraculous of husbands and wives or mothers and children finding each other by sheer accident.[32] The desire to find relatives was stronger than any fear of disillusionment. The organized search for relatives developed from the initial spontaneous initiatives of the survivors (assisted by the Allied Jewish chaplains) to an organized system run by the JDC and the JA that embraced the whole Diaspora and continued to function for many years. Sometimes it was only after many years that people would find their lost ones in an unexpected corner of the world.[33]

However, the drive to regain a sense of living quickly overcame these obstacles of poor health, uncertainty concerning the fate of relatives, and loneliness. The natural way to fight despair, to make the grim present appear somewhat brighter, and to face an unclear future was to find love and friendship. Living together in the barracks meant that there was constant contact between people and an ongoing opportunity to approach each other on a personal level. Young widowers met widows and shared their grief, grievances, and fears. Psychologically it was easier for a woman who had lost her husband and children to find an open ear and heart in a man who had suffered the same tragedy. They could understand each other more readily than could an outsider from the world at large. They did not have to talk too much concerning the dark side in their recent past lives. They also shared a sense of pragmatism and skepticism which meant that they did not expect to find eternal love in a new marriage. The drive for forming couples was also motivated by the yearning to find some privacy within the camp, since only a family could eventually obtain a room for itself. In this respect, the kibbutzim constituted a kind of substitute for families, securing their own barracks and pursuing their lives in a family mode. Thus, forming couples very quickly led to marriages as a road to rehabilitation and normalization within that very abnormal environment.

Much attention was paid to weddings, and very often they were the main agenda in the social life of the camp. During the first year after liberation there were numerous weddings, not uncommonly six or more in a single day, even fifty in a week. During 1946 there were 1,070 weddings.[34] But statistics, as impressive as they may appear, do not convey the atmosphere surrounding the weddings. To get married had many bright, as well as sad, aspects, reflecting the essence of being a survivor in a DP camp. First, there was a question of halakah (Jewish law). Most couples decided to be married in a Jewish wedding ceremony. It was not just a question of being religious. Even for the secular, it meant forming a new link with the past, overcoming the disaster and continuing the family chain, being Jewish, and keeping and manifesting the Jewish tradition.[35] In order to have a *huppah* (Jewish wedding ceremony) one would need to obtain a rabbinical license to marry, certifying that one is free to marry. Thus, entering a new marriage meant admitting to the fact that there was no hope of finding the lost spouse. Despite this, some couples were troubled with uncertainty regarding their lost ones, an uncertainty that could haunt them for years.[36]

Preparing a wedding involved many social and economic initiatives. How was one to prepare a proper bridal gown? Young brides and their friends exercised their imagination and ability to turn old clothes, obtained from the JDC, into an elegant dress. How would the wedding be announced? Here was an incentive for printers and artists to produce announcements in the papers and on the walls and to distribute invitations. How would the ceremony and the reception be arranged? Here was an opportunity to designate rooms for celebrations and parties, to decorate them and maintain them as such, to transform the rations into cuisine catering, and to form music and drama groups to perform on that joyous occasion.

The invitations and the descriptions of individual weddings often, however, reflect the dark side of the event. Many invitations are signed by the bride and bridegroom, with no father or mother inviting guests to their children's wedding. Sometime the name of a single relative—an uncle or a cousin—appears, further emphasizing the tragedy behind the scenes. The ceremony itself was painful. The mention of loved ones who were absent sadly demonstrated the dark holes in the circle of family and friends. Most if not all of the camp leaders—Rosensaft, Bimko, Wollheim, Trepman, Laufer, and the Olevsky brothers—married survivors. Many of those interviewed for this study were survivors who married in the camp and shared with us their experiences. Many others married emissaries, such as Rabbi Avraham Greenbaum, who came to work in the camps.[37]

With the weddings, new families were formed and babies were born. In the spring of 1946 it was anticipated that by the end of the year nearly 1,000 babies would be born in the British Zone, with nearly 200 in Belsen alone. As more people fleeing from Eastern Europe arrived in the British Zone, the number of families, many of them with young children, grew and also contributed to the growing rate of pregnancies and births. By the end of 1946 the composition of Belsen's population had already changed: 1.7 percent were infants up to two years old. The birthrate grew constantly, and in Belsen's hospital alone 555 births were registered in 1946. Between October 1946 and July 1947, 650 babies were born in the British Zone, some 400 in Belsen alone. By 1948 the one thousandth Jewish baby was born in Belsen. For early 1948 the statistics number 1,278 children up to the age of three, with 934 in Belsen alone.[38]

The growing number of pregnant women and babies posed a huge challenge. As women survivors became pregnant before gaining their full strength and health, the task of rehabilitation was confronted by the constant shortage of proper nutrition. For the pregnant women it sometimes meant even deterioration of their well-being. Moreover,

Society, Economy, and Culture

First wedding at Belsen, soon after liberation (June 1945) (Yad Vashem Photo-Archives [FA 185 156])

babies born to undernourished mothers were in jeopardy for their healthy development. In addition, undernourished mothers found it difficult to breast-feed their babies. This was further compounded by the shortages of baby food. Combined with the problems of health and nutrition was the difficulty of baby care in general. Most of the new mothers did not have guidance from mothers, grandmothers, experienced sisters, or aunts who in former times would have surrounded the young mother before and after birth. Most of the mothers also lacked training in the basic rules of child care, hygiene, and cooking.

Thus, as the growing number of pregnancies and babies presented the welfare workers with a serious burden, mother and child care became a major focus of concern. Growing families and improvement of health contradicted each other. Due to the numerous pregnancies, births, and infants and the growing number of elderly people who arrived as refugees from Eastern Europe, looking after the sick and the children became a central occupation for the welfare agencies. The number of children sent to Sweden, Switzerland, and Italy

New Beginnings

Celebration the birth of the thousandth baby born in the camp, January 1948 (Yad Vashem Photo-Archives [3979/1])

and those hospitalized for short periods in convalescent homes in the British Zone constantly grew.

To be sure, despite the efforts invested in improving health, nutrition, and conditions for child care, camp life in itself prevented complete normalization. Even in its later phase, and notwithstanding the difference between non-Jewish DPs and Jewish survivors (who enjoyed the special treatment given by the Jewish welfare agencies), conditions remained unsatisfactory. Many reports testify concerning poor health and malnutrition among mothers and children due to the wartime and postwar supply shortages and crowded camp living, conditions that could not easily be overcome. All in all, the consequences of the Holocaust and the war in general, combined with postwar conditions, prevented full rehabilitation of health, and growing families placed an additional burden on achieving full physical recovery.[39]

Nevertheless, family life in itself proved to be a vital asset for mental and social rehabilitation. Indeed, it was not a one-track process. Psychological breakdowns and mental illness tortured many, even among those who outwardly appeared to have overcome the nightmares of the past. The lack of immediate professional psychological and mental therapy also contributed to this.[40] One must also take into account the norms of the period regarding psychological treatment. It was then generally believed that the best way to overcome an unbearable burden was to ignore it. Rather than speaking and getting it out of one's system, it was thought best to put it aside and concentrate on building a better future. Showing sympathy and offering compassion were not considered the correct path to rehabilitation. Thus, immediately establishing families (without considering mutual compatibility too deeply) was in itself a manifestation of the will to overcome the burden of the past simply by ignoring it. Unfortunately, mental problems that were thus repressed did not disappear. Many manifested themselves frequently in later years, occupying even the second and third generations. This has also placed a burden on current psychological research and treatment.[41] Be that as it may, it seems that the establishment of families was an indispensable framework for the creation of a semi-normal socio-cultural life.

Communication and the Media

Postal Service and Transportation

Contact between survivors, between the camps and the communities, and with the outside world represented a basic need and was essential for reintegration into society and for creating social and cultural programs. However, the availability of transportation and postal contacts was very limited in the immediate postwar period. To overcome this the military authorities created a special DP postal service for official correspondence. For their personal correspondence the DPs unofficially used the private services of the welfare personnel. German civil post service was unavailable. As for transportation, most civilians had to rely on public transportation, which was established quite late in 1946 and was limited to an infrequent bus route between Belsen and Hanover. At that time, use of private cars was very limited, and in the camps only welfare personnel, officials, and the newly rich had cars. During the summer of 1947 the JDC reported using thirty cars for their work in the British Zone. The German railway system was slowly returning to prewar activity, but camp inmates did not have freedom of movement in Germany. Furthermore, they usually could not afford it. Visitors to the British Zone also required official permits, which entailed complicated bureaucratic procedures.[42]

The constraints imposed by the military administration and general postwar difficulties necessitated the doubling of efforts in other directions. There was a concentrated effort by the survivors, which

New Beginnings

provided the basis for the manifold initiatives in the social, cultural, and political fields.

PUBLICATIONS

Periodicals

In July 1945, shortly after liberation, the first Yiddish publication appeared. This was *Unzer Sztyme*, which would in time become the official organ of the CC. It was initiated by David Rosenthal, Paul Trepman, and Rafael Olevsky, who had already planned its publication even before liberation. These men were all Zionists, and they had known each other previously and struggled together to survive in the concentration camps. Due to the strict British rule prohibiting publications in the camps, as well as the shortage of paper and printing equipment, they were only able to produce the first issue on July 12, 1945, during their stay in Celle, near Belsen. Handwritten in calligraphy copied by hectograph, it appeared in 150 copies. The following three issues appeared monthly, also handwritten. From November 1945, after receiving donations of three typewriters, the issues were typed, duplicated by stencil, and issued biweekly. However, because of the paper shortage the paper was not issued regularly. From its sixth issue, in January 1946, it appeared as the "Organ of *She'erit Hapletah* in the British Zone." In August 1946 it finally began to appear in print, thanks to the press donated by the New York Association of Jewish Writers. Hebrew fonts were later purchased through the efforts of others.[43] *Unzer Sztyme* was published for more than two years. The October 1947 issue, its twenty-fourth, was its last.

Unzer Sztyme was published in Yiddish with Hebrew fonts, but its title appeared also in Latin fonts, and later issues printed the name in English. Occasionally, leading articles appeared in English. It was meant to serve as the main tool for expressing the concerns and the wishes of the survivors; to become the central voice of the Belsen leadership inwardly and outwardly; to encourage the Jewish discourse with worldwide participation; and to become the channel for bringing the best of Jewish culture and national aspirations to the attention of the survivors. Over the years *Unzer Sztyme* grew in size and diversity and was read by most of the survivors in the British Zone and by many outside. Rosenthal, Trepman, and Olevsky served as editors throughout its publication and gave the paper its clear Zionist stance. A large portion of each issue was always dedicated to Palestine and Zionist information and news, both in articles and pictures. The paper was also open to many other themes, accepting articles from contributors both in Germany and abroad. Among the many participants—men and women—one could find Jewish authors and poets such as Melech Rawitch from Montreal, H. Leiwick from New York, and Ya'akov Zerubavel from Tel Aviv, as well as Jewish and Zionist leaders from different countries and of different views.[44]

Unzer Sztyme was replaced by the *Wochenblatt*, which started as a weekly Yiddish publication initiated by the editors of *Unzer Sztyme*. Its first issue appeared on December 5, 1947. In February 1949 it became a biweekly, and it continued to appear until the closing of Belsen. In the course of its existence it was edited by Rosenthal, Trepman, Olevsky, Lubliner, Kossowsky, and others. As a newspaper, *Wochenblatt* was concise and to the point. Mainly informative, it aimed at accompanying the process of the dissolution of the *She'erit Hapletah*. Issued at the time of the UN resolution to partition Palestine, it appeared until after the declaration of the State of Israel, the War of Independence, the accelerated Jewish emigration from Germany, the closing of Belsen, and the transfer of the remaining DPs to the transit camp in Upjever. There, in Upjever, its last issue was published.

Unzer Sztyme and *Wochenblatt* were the official organs of the CC. Besides them, the CC and its Cultural Department also regularly published bulletins, at first in Yiddish and later also in German. However, political parties initiated most of the publications that appeared from time to time in Belsen. Most prominent among them were those published by the Revisionists: *Unzer Front* (Our Front) appeared from 1947 to 1949 with eleven issues. *Revisionistisher Gedank* (Revisionist Thought), *Zum Sieg* (For Victory), and *Der Emeth* (The Truth) each appeared only once, at different times. The Revisionists also regularly issued a bulletin—*Informatsie* (Information).

The Socialist party Poale Zion Z.S.-Hitahdut published *Yedi'ot* (Information) (twenty-one issues) and *Zoiten* (Times) (three issues) during 1948 and 1949. Hashomer Hatza'ir also published their own periodicals, mostly in Yiddish but sometimes in German, and rarely in Hebrew. The various periodicals of the parties were printed at their own presses, located and run in the party headquarters. However, the main Zionist parties' newspapers were issued and published in the American Zone—in Munich—where the main Zionist and political party headquarters for Germany were located. These newspapers were also distributed in the British Zone, and because of this, most publications issued in the British Zone failed to appear regularly.[45]

Another popular medium of communication was the live newspaper, occasionally staged and voiced by groups of people who read loudly from newspapers. In addition, wall newspapers were posted in central locations. The different organizations used this medium for announcements, expressions of opinions, and even for feuilletons, photographs, and the like.[46] In late 1946 a live newspaper was established and performed by journalists at the cinema hall.[47]

Nonperiodical Publications

Both the rabbinical authority and individual rabbis devoted themselves to publishing religious material. This was mainly in the realm of Jewish law on issues concerning the survivors, such as missing spouses (*Kuntress Takanat Agunot; Osef Takanot Agunim ve-Agunot*), the law of Sabbath (*Sefer Siduro shel Shabbat*), keeping family ritual purity (*Sefer Tohorat Mishpakha*), and basic religious texts such as the Bible.

Another major area of publishing was initiated by the CC Cultural Department and was devoted to the Holocaust itself. Among them were *Sammlung fun Kazet Lider* (Anthology of Concentration Camp Poems) and *Tzurrik fun Gehinom* (Back from Hell). The Historical Committee, whose seat was in Göttingen, also published material in this field. In addition, individuals initiated publications to commemorate their shtetels and families.[48] Belsen excelled in literary activity. Some fifteen Yiddish authors lived and created there, publishing their works individually or in collections. Eventually they even formed the Association of Jewish Journalists and Writers in the British Zone of Germany—Bergen-Belsen.[49]

Most of the publishing activity designed for the DPs (beside that initiated by and designed specifically for German Jews) was focused in Belsen, and the main language was Yiddish. However, many of these publications mentioned above were not only meant for the whole British Zone and beyond but were also intended for German Jews. This was especially true concerning the official publications of the CC and its departments.[50]

OTHER COMMUNICATION MEDIA

One would have thought that in Belsen—which was, as previously noted, electrified, and where people were gradually acquiring electrical devices—radio would have been the simplest form of communication. However, this was not the case. There were, of course, a few radios, some owned by the authorities and others by camp residents, but the use of radio as a tool of communication for the DPs was limited, since local broadcasts were in German and those from abroad were in English. Since the common language among the survivors was Yiddish and there were no Yiddish broadcasts, there was almost no need to own a radio. The mass of printed media is therefore understandable. Nevertheless, over the course of time a public loudspeaker was placed in the central square, and the CC regularly translated the main news, especially from Palestine. People would gather in the square to listen to the latest news in Yiddish. For patients in the hospital, who were not able to do so, a special service of loudspeaker-visit was offered.[51]

In lieu of radio broadcast, there were mass gatherings in public areas. People would frequently convene in these places and there was no shortage of occasions. Films were regularly screened. Visitors from abroad—writers, poets, and musicians—came there to perform.[52] Lectures and performances by DPs or emissaries were regularly held.[53] This form of communication substituted for radio but also contributed an aspect the radio would have lacked: it encouraged people to gather publicly and thus promoted social interaction, along with maintaining connections between the DPs themselves and the world at large.

Arts and Leisure

Cultural activity substituted for regular work and also served as what we would call today adult education, continuing education, or supplemental education. Moreover, having too much free time was not the outcome of well-being, and could not be matched by a great choice of leisure activities such as clubs, coffee shops, and restaurants. Thus, cultural activity was very much encouraged, influenced, and financed by the various welfare agencies. However, many of the initiatives came from the survivors themselves, among whom there were numerous artists and professionals. The most common language in which these activities were held was Yiddish, but Hebrew was also used, especially within the Zionist kibbutzim.

The cultural activity in the camp can be divided into two levels: public, performed in central locations; and private, addressed to and performed within closed circles (clubs and kibbutzim). The camp leaders and the educational institutions initiated part of this activity at both levels, but most of it was at the initiative of political groups in accordance with their national, political, and religious views.

Public Activity

The public areas in Bergen-Belsen in many ways resembled a small town, with streets and plazas and one "City Center." And as in typical Eastern European small towns, cleanliness and quiet were not a matter of course. The Jewish police force as well as the Sanitary Department of the CC put much effort toward educating the public in developing the quality and aesthetics of the camp environment. They regulated shop hours and the forms of advertisement, kept the shops and streets clean, and prevented open black-marketing and other public nuisances.[54]

A large square constituted the center of the camp: the Liberty Square, which was surrounded by public buildings; the Roundhouse, which was the main administration building; the theater tent, with some 1,000 seats; and the cinema hall.[55] Here public cultural events took place, particularly on national and religious holidays such as Simhath Torah, Hanukkah, Purim, Shavuot, Israel Independence Day, and memorial days on which grand parades were organized.[56] These buildings also housed occasional art exhibitions, concerts, and public lectures delivered by teachers, emissaries, and visitors from abroad.[57] A major effort was made to establish a People's University, which offered seminars and lecture series.[58] The most popular attraction for the camp inmates was the cinema, where, thanks to the joint efforts of the JDC and UNRRA, films were regularly screened. Many of the films were Jewish, and some were even produced by the JDC with the cooperation of the camp inmates.[59]

A major feature open to the public was the dramatic activity, which was initiated by the survivors and attracted much interest. The earliest theatrical program was that of Sami Feder. Feder was born in Germany but deported to Poland in the 1930s. During the war he was again deported to many concentration camps, ending up in Belsen. An experienced Yiddish actor and director from Warsaw, he established in the summer of 1945, with a group of Polish DP actors, his Katzet Theater and the drama studio. The theater's premiere performance was held during the First Congress of the *She'erit Hapletah*, in September 1945. Despite the scarcity of printed plays and the fact that actors had to reconstruct and rehearse plays from memory, many productions were prepared and presented to the public. For two years the group staged in Belsen a variety of Yiddish plays before packed audiences. In the summer of 1947 they also performed in Belgium, Sweden, England, and Paris and were very well received. Unfortunately, some of the actors never returned from Paris, and Feder himself, though returning to Belsen, very quickly followed suit (and in 1962 he immigrated to Israel), and the theater had to close down.[60]

The Katzet Theater, however, was not the only one in Belsen. Another major initiative was that of the Yiddisher Arbeter Biene (Jewish Workers' Theater) of Poale Zion. This theater began its performances in 1947 and produced a variety of Yiddish plays with a clear social message.[61] Agudath Israel and Hamizrahi also established a drama group, Amatoren Gruppe (Amateur Group).[62] And, as already mentioned, a great variety of artistic visitors performed in the theater tent before the DPs.

A scene of the play *The Partisans* performed by the Kazet Theater (Yad Vashem Photo-Archives [FA 185 174])

New Beginnings

It seems that musical performances played a lesser role in the public domain. Music was more of a companion to public festivals and was central only in the smaller groups' activities. There may have been two reasons for this. First, organizing an orchestra required the availability of many different and expensive musical instruments. Second, theater could serve as a major therapeutic tool for both the performers and the audience. In general, theater, much more than concerts, is accessible to a wider public, since listening to concerts demands greater understanding and concentration. Be that as it may, classic concerts were rare, consisting mainly of recitals by famous visitors. A few small orchestras were eventually established, two of them by political groups—Poale Zion and the Revisionists—but apparently, besides these smaller groups, music did not attract much attention.[63]

PRIVATE ACTIVITY

Beyond the public area, many cultural activities were addressed to and performed in particular groups. These activities included initiatives by the camp leadership, among which the most important was the library, which was established in the summer of 1946. The main library, which opened with some 5,000 volumes and many newspapers, was located in a large reading room at the Roundhouse. Over time it grew into a whole system of mobile libraries and local reading rooms for the entire British Zone. The library services provided a solid basis for a diversity of cultural activities in small circles—public reading evenings, discussion groups, lectures, seminars, and the like.[64] Another form of cultural activity offered through the CC was occasional trips and picnics, or visits to the opera house in Hanover. Various parties and kibbutzim, however, also offered trips.[65]

Group activities were concentrated mainly within the various kibbutzim and organized along political lines. The kibbutzim frequently organized balls and parties, with music, dancing, and singing. Every event—a wedding, a holiday, a birthday—was an occasion for party. Friday evening was always, in all the kibbutzim, a special evening—Oneg Shabbat (The Pleasure of Saturday)—with singing, reading, and dancing, sometimes with a lecture and discussion. It seems that the kibbutzim competed with each other as to who attracted more people to Oneg Shabbat and parties.[66]

160

Sporting events attracted much attention and were very much encouraged by the camp leadership and the welfare agencies. The various kibbutzim established their own sport clubs, and over time seven clubs were active in Belsen and the British Zone. Public games and races were held regularly—mostly on Saturdays—in boxing, soccer, and other sports, and were popular events for the public.[67] Sports presented a major opportunity in the process of rehabilitation, and was considered the definite proof of the Jews' ability to overcome not only the degenerating impacts of the Holocaust but also the traditional stigma of Jewish weakness.

The Role of Zionism, Tradition, and Politics in Sociocultural Life

The variety of Jewish cultural and recreational activities in the camp carried a clear and outspoken message of national spirit and pride, both in the traditional religious meaning and in the secular Zionist meaning. Jewish traditional holidays were celebrated in public with accentuated Zionist overtones. For example, for the first Seder evening (eve of Passover), which happened to coincide with the first anniversary of Belsen's liberation, a special Hagadah (read at the Seder) was composed that compared the exodus from Egypt with the hopes for exodus from Europe and a Jewish state in Palestine.[68] Traditional holidays with national messages, such as Hanukkah and Purim, were celebrated with the help of schoolteachers who prepared and constructed the events to symbolize the current national struggle. A mass public event was made of the Eleventh of Adar—the commemoration of the heroes of Tel-Hai, who fell in the struggle on the northern border of Palestine in 1920 and symbolized the Zionist struggle for independence. And, of course, from 1948 on the Israel Independence Day became the most exciting and important festival.[69]

Side by side with an accentuated Zionist spirit, a marked traditional character was lent to social and cultural activities, and religious rituals were in focus in many public and private events. One could feel the Sabbath spirit, even though most of the camp inmates were not religious. On Friday night one could see candles in almost every window; Oneg Shabbat was celebrated with traditional meals, kiddush, traditional songs, and reading from the weekly Torah portion, even among the secular kibbutzim. On Sabbath mornings the camp's streets

New Beginnings

Sport groups with their various banners marching in the camp's streets (Yad Vashem Photo-Archives [176CO3])

were filled with people walking to the many synagogues scattered in the camp. This was not a matter of being Orthodox but simply a need to follow—after the enormous gap of the Holocaust—Jewish tradition and to reunite in a way with the memory of the family that perished.[70]

Nationalism and traditionalism were motivated and pursued by two factors that filled a central role in the sociocultural arena: Zionist political parties and Orthodox rabbinical authorities.

The Role of Political Parties

The role of party politics within the camps and among the survivors is an issue much discussed by both historians and the survivors themselves. In fact, almost everything in the lives of the *She'erit Hapletah* was run and organized by political parties, both Zionist and non-Zionist. This was true even in Belsen, despite the relatively great measure of cooperation and unity among the parties within the CC and the Belsen Committee.

The trend to run social life along party lines emerged as the outcome of basic historical traditions and current needs, and it was strengthened within the context of the Zionist struggle for a Jewish state. On the one hand was the political-cultural tradition of the Jewish community in pre-Holocaust Poland. Politics and party rivalries strongly shaped Jewish social life in Poland—the origin of most of the survivors. The Zionist arena was a battlefield between Zionist-Socialist, Zionist-Revisionist, and Zionist-Orthodox, but the main battle front was against the anti-Zionists, with the socialist Bund on the one hand and the extreme Orthodox Agudath Israel on the other. This tradition was carried through the tiny groups of survivors into the camps.

On the other hand, carrying on old political rivalries was not a matter of a deliberate program. On the contrary, the experience of the Holocaust and its consequences created a genuine will to forget the disputes of the past, which no longer seemed relevant, and to cooperate in the struggle for the future. The journey to survival, however, was led—in the concentration camps and thereafter—by the organized groups of youth movements, mainly Zionist. They were the ones that initiated the organization of the survivors.[71] Youth movements were by definition affiliated with political parties, and disputes and rivalries naturally arose very quickly.

However, the fact that pro-Zionism became a basic consensus among the survivors, as well as across the Jewish world, enabled the Zionist groups to keep the upper hand and place others—especially the Bundists—in the shadow, particularly in the British Zone. As much as the path of the Bund survivors can be traced, they either went back to Poland or eventually immigrated to America. No trace of them has been found in the camp life of Belsen. Moreover, during the immediate postwar years even the Bund abandoned the previous anti-Zionist approach and supported the Zionist struggle for aliyah.[72]

Particular for Belsen, however, was the strong presence of Agudath Israel, which composed a quarter of the camp population. It was organized as a *Kehillah* that ran some ten institutions within the camp. Nevertheless, political antagonism between Zionists and the Agudah almost disappeared after the war. Agudath Israel World Union declared in 1945 its agreement and support for the Zionist struggle and entered into agreement with the JA. A new, Zionist offshoot of Agudath Israel was founded during the war—Poale Agudath Israel (PAI)— which attracted many followers in Belsen. Orthodox thinkers such as Rabbi Yehudah Leb Gerst in Belsen developed the new Orthodox post-Holocaust thinking, explaining the Holocaust as a metaphysical struggle, yet with historical consequences, leading Judaism up the ladder of renewal and strengthening the Jewish legacy for the future. Aliyah and Jewish homeland in *Eretz Yisrael* were now considered as the consequence of the Holocaust and were translated politically and practically. It was adopted as part and parcel of the Agudah program, and the Agudah youth movement was organized in kibbutzim, preparing themselves for aliyah. In Belsen, Gerst organized the Olim movement of Orthodox youngsters preparing themselves for the "ascent" of Jewish existence through the ascent to Palestine.[73] The disputes between Agudah and Zionists centered on matters of keeping the Jewish law in the camps. As a consequence of Zionist domination, the heat of political rivalry and struggles became an internal Zionist affair.[74]

Social life along party politics was also shaped by two other factors. First, the survivors—and in particular the younger ones—looked for substitutes for their lost families. Being a part of a social group—and especially a communal group, the kibbutz—met a deep psychological need and offered an opening for rehabilitation. Such groups were led by party activists and organized along party lines. These groups created a sociocultural atmosphere shaped by their diversified ideologies, and soon they began to quarrel over recruiting members. Sometimes even young children, who had no idea of political ideology, became "members" of a political group, such as Hashomer Hatza'ir.[75]

And last but not least was the role of the Palestine emissaries, who were officially under the roof of the JA but were actually sent by—and represented—political kibbutz movements. The HaKibbutz Hame'uhad movement had, for various reasons, the strongest presence in the camps, and this fact even intensified interparty rivalries. While there is some dispute as to whether Palestine emissaries were the origin of party politics in the camps, there is agreement as to their contribution to it.[76] Within the context of the Zionist struggle, and due to emissaries' main target of preparing the survivors for immigration to Palestine, it is no wonder that every movement tried to attract as many followers as it could as potential members in Palestine. The fact that in Belsen party politics by emissaries was relatively mild has not diminished the fact that social life was strongly shaped by party politics.[77] Indeed, at first an effort was made to build a united Zionist front—Histadrut Zionit Ahida—established in February 1946. Soon enough, however, this organization was identified as the main Zionist Labor Party, Mapai, so that PAI and Betar, among others, created their own organizations.[78] After a year, the Histadrut Zionit Ahidah pulled off its mask of unity and officially became the Poale Zion Hitahdut Party—Mapai.[79]

Sociocultural life in Belsen was focused around politics. Most of the group activities were carried within or affiliated with kibbutzim. Beside many kibbutzim and *hachsharah* groups of the socialist Zionist kibbutz movements, there were four Orthodox PAI kibbutzim and a large kibbutz with many branches and clubs affiliated with the Revisionist Betar movement.[80] The activity within these groups touched every aspect of social, economic, and cultural life and education, which covered Hebrew, Palestine, and Jewish history, publications, sports, workshops or farming, drama and music, balls and parties, celebrations of holidays and commemorations, and even synagogues. Propaganda and political activity through meetings, conventions, and rallies made up a major part in these groups' activities. Many DPs filled the roles of party workers as their main or part-time jobs, and party business became their main social occupation.[81] Everything in the camp life thus became a matter of politics, and every misunderstanding or dispute became an issue for political struggle.[82]

The role of politics in everyday life had its impact on Belsen's participation in World Zionist Organization politics. For the Twenty-second Zionist Congress in Basel in December 1946, two delegates represented the British Zone, one of Histadrut Zionit Ahidah (Mapai) and one of leftist Poale Zion and Hashomer Hatza'ir. They were accompanied, however, by an impressive delegation of thirteen persons who represented the leadership of Belsen, there to attend the congress as observers.[83] Belsen's role in Zionist politics in general is not the issue here, but it is clear that the role of politics in its social life led to its political role.

Religion and Politics

The demand for religious services and supplies was great in Belsen. They made up a large part of the activities rendered by the CRREC, by the camp leadership, and by the British Zone's chief rabbinate. Kosher slaughter, ritual baths, and Hevra Kadisha (burial societies) operated in and outside of Belsen, and rabbis and *mohalim* conducted weddings and circumcisions.[84] Supplies of prayer books and Bibles, Torah scrolls and furniture for the synagogues, candles, *thalitim* and *tefillin*, Kosher food, *matzot* for Passover, specific foods and fruits for ritual needs—all these were of chief concern for the responsible authorities, as they were demanded not only by Orthodox. Some 2,000 people in the British Zone—of whom 1,200 were in Belsen alone (20 percent of the camp population)—were regular recipients of the CRREC supplies.[85]

Orthodox rabbis also tried to propagate religion by advertising, publishing, and preaching.[86] The chief rabbinate did not confine itself to religious welfare or propaganda, but sought to conduct public life accordingly. The major issue was the Sabbath, and the CC completely cooperated in trying to enforce it in public life—for example, by closing shops and stopping bus connection from inside the camp. This issue aroused a heated debate and bitterness.[87] It is not clear to what measure the rabbinate succeeded, but it seems that religion, despite some controversies, was a matter of consensus, going hand in hand with Zionist consensus. National spirit in both its meanings characterized the social and political culture of Belsen and lent it a sort of vibrant community life.

10

LOOKING TO THE FUTURE: THE EDUCATIONAL PROGRAM

The Children

When Bergen-Belsen was liberated, among the survivors were approximately five hundred children—quite a unique phenomenon. Some of them were babies born to the many pregnant women who were transferred to Belsen during the last phase of the Nazi regime. The majority of the children were deported from Buchenwald and Theresienstadt and arrived in Belsen shortly before liberation. Most of them were orphans or had been separated from their parents and had no information concerning their whereabouts. Some fifty were Dutch which the Nazis in December 1944 had placed in the women's camps after their parents had been deported from Belsen. They were of all ages, between eight months and fifteen years, and had survived the last months prior to liberation thanks both to the motherly care of the female prisoners and to supplies smuggled by male prisoners into the women's block. Most of the Dutch and Czech children were repatriated to Holland and Czechoslovakia. In the fall of 1945, another group of children was sent from Germany to England. Later, in the spring of 1946, approximately one hundred children, with special certificates, were sent to Palestine.[1]

In 1946, however, the number of children in Belsen increased due to the influx of Jewish refugees from Poland and Hungary. By the end of 1946 there were some 880 children in Belsen between the ages of three and eighteen who were in need of schooling. An additional few hundreds were in other camps and children's homes (these orphans numbered about 460). By the beginning of 1948, mainly due to the high birthrate, the total number of Jewish children in the British Zone was about 3,000, of whom 1,300 were under three years of age. In Belsen alone the number of children grew to some 2,300, of whom approximately 1,000 were under three years of age. From then on the number of children, in particular the older ones, began to drop gradually, due to the "Grand National Junior" operation for immigration of children to Palestine.[2]

The children survivors came from a variety of backgrounds. They had been deprived of a normal childhood, their lives and education interrupted by the war, but there was a clear distinction between those who had directly experienced the horrors of the death camps or hiding and those who had found some refuge in Soviet Russia during the war. The first group had shared the experience of the inferno of the Holocaust, had witnessed death and suffering, and each carried within a burden of despair, fear, and horror. For their survival they had to fight and to adopt the twisted norms of evil. They suffered from the trauma of what they had gone through. They had no trust or confidence in humanity and became cynical and suspicious toward the surrounding world. Children, young though they were, became old due to their experience. Six years of war had deprived them of any form of education and learning save the knowledge of brutality and evil. With the loss of their parents, they had to face their present and future alone in the world. The second group was of children who later arrived with the wave from Eastern Europe, and many of these were accompanied by their families. Although their childhood had also been shattered through wandering, hunger, and the lack of a normal home life and social atmosphere or systematic education, they were better balanced and had some foundation for education and learning.[3]

Challenge and Response: The Founding of Educational Institutions

The large number of children presented a serious challenge for any educational program. On the one hand, here was a mission to help children who needed understanding, compassion, and knowledge to develop normally. On the other hand, remaining in the camps in Germany seemed to be a temporary arrangement, and there were neither incentives nor resources available to invest in an educational program. The adult survivors had to cope with their own terrible loss and had their own burden to carry. They had to mobilize all their own strength to struggle for their rehabilitation. There was also a total lack of even minimal conditions necessary for teaching, namely, equipment, books, or trained teachers. Poor health and living conditions created a situation that placed children's other needs before schooling and education.

However, the instinctive immediate response of the adult survivors to the challenge was remarkable. Ignoring difficulties, they acted as if the children were their own, representing their own future as Jewish survivors. Willingly, they took upon themselves responsibility for the young generation.[4]

Initial responses were manifested even before liberation. Upon the children's arrival at Belsen, adults saw it as their obligation to take care of them. When the British liberated the camp, they too placed a special emphasis on the children, who were the first to be treated. They arranged for the children to be housed in children's homes and provided them with clothing, medical care, and even toys confiscated from the neighboring German population. This was the beginning.[5]

Shortly after liberation, a handful of teachers, doctors, nurses, and other professionals began to organize schools for the children. In

Children after the liberation near the barbed wire of the camp (Yad Vashem Photo-Archives [FA 181 80])

Germany, the British Zone pioneered this project. A kindergarten and primary school were first established in Celle in June 1945. During the following months, soldiers of the Jewish Brigade and emissaries from the JRU, ORT, JDC, and the Jewish Agency joined in and helped to develop the educational system initiated by the survivors.[6] By March 1946 there was a network of educational institutions in Belsen, including the kindergarten and primary school and two Beth Jacob Talmud Torah schools, one Polish and the other Hungarian. In November 1945, a yeshiva *She'erit Israel* and an orphanage were established. A month later, the Hebrew high school opened. In January 1946 a vocational school opened, teaching a variety of trades with the help of the local ORT organization and a popular university.[7] The Beth Jacob girls' school and teachers' seminar opened a little later.[8] In addition to the formal institutions, a great variety of informal education operated through the various youth movements and kibbutzim.

Children's homes and vocational schools also operated outside Belsen. However, most of the other camps and communities were too small, and the number of children was too negligible to enable regular schools to function.[9] Hanover, with some one thousand DPs, was an exception, and there a school was opened on a regular basis.[10] Another exception was Celle with its Orthodox community, where a Beth Jacob seminar opened in 1946.[11] The educational network of the British Zone is shown in Table 2 (the passengers from the ship *Exodus*[12] are not included).

Initiators and Teachers

Most institutions were established and operated by camp inmates, either professional teachers or people with some academic training. This was the case with the elementary school, founded by Rabbi Israel Moshe Olevsky and the teacher Paul Trepman, both of whom were also active in the CC. The headmistress was Sela Lefkowitch, a camp inmate. Some of the teachers were also survivors. The case of the Hebrew high school was outstanding. The initiator, Dr. Helen Wrubel, who was an experienced teacher and geographer in her native Poland, established the high school against many odds and became its headmistress until the closing of Belsen and her immigration to Israel. Most of the teachers of the high school were survivors—during the first year, fourteen out of nineteen and later all of them save one, David Littman.[13] The popular university, the vocational school, and

Table 2: Educational Institutions in the British Zone

BELSEN

NURSERY
  no information available

CHILDREN'S HOME
  Opened November 1945
  Supervisor: Sadi Rurka of JRU
  Children: 70 orphans and semi-orphans ages 3–13

KINDERGARTEN
  Opened in Celle, June 1945, and moved to Belsen
  Operated by JDC
  Children: 60–80 ages 2–6

JACOB EDELSTEIN ELEMENTARY SCHOOL
  Opened in Celle, June 1945, and moved to Belsen
  Initiators: Rabbi Israel Moshe Olevsky and Paul Trepman
  Headmistress: Sela Lefkowitch
  Teachers: T. Gunzman, T. Drucke, S. Wittenberg, Hana Weiner, Meir Markowitch, sisters D. and P. Zimmermann, Hava Kimmelman-Singer, Rivka Rosenthal
  Students: 100–300 ages 6–15

TWO BETH JACOB GIRLS SCHOOLS, POLISH AND HUNGARIAN, BELSEN
  Students: 200

YESHIVA "SHE'ERIT ISRAEL" IN BELSEN
  Opened November 1945
  Headmaster: Rabbi Zvi Meisels
  Teachers: Rabbis Gershon Liebman, Joel Fotaschevitch, Israel Aryeh Zalmanovitch
  Students: 80–100

HEBREW HIGH SCHOOL NAMING THE JEWISH BRIGADE
  Opened December 1945
  Initiators: Dr. Helen Wrubel and David Littman
  Headmistress: Dr. Helen Wrubel; from April 1947, Dr. Michael Lubliner
  Teachers: Menahem Ehrlic, Miriam Gold, Rabbi Avraham Greenbaum, Haim Kagan, Dr. Helen Wrubel, Moshe Kaganowitch, Sela Lefkowitch, Dr. Michael Lubliner, David Littman, Dr. Leon Friedman
  Students: 120–130 ages 15–22 from Belsen and outside

BETH JACOB SEMINAR
  Opened summer 1946
  Initiator: Mordechai Breuer
  Headmaster: Rabbi Yehudah Leb Gerst
  Students: 40

New Beginnings

ORT Vocational School
    Opened January 1946
    Headmaster: Josef Mack
    Teachers: Fischer and Moskowitch
    Students: 250 (in rotation) ages 13–35

Popular University
    Opened January 1946
    Initiator: Rafael Olevsky

Workshops in Kibbutzim of various youth movements
    Students: 1,500 in Belsen

Youth movements:
    Noham, Bethar, Hashomer Hatza'ir, Bene Akiva, Noar Agudathi, Ezra

Three Halutz Houses
    no information available

OUTSIDE BELSEN

Children's home in Neustadt
    Opened January 1946

Children's home in Villa Warburg, Blankenese near Hamburg
    Operated by JDC and JRU until summer 1947 and became a convalescent home
        for children in the British Zone
    Supervisor: Sylvia Markowich
    Teachers: Reuma Schwartz, Genia Schwadron, Hava Isick
    Children: 120 (in rotation) ages 3–14

Children's home in Lüneburg for Orthodox children
    Children: 30 (in rotation) ages 5–14

Elementary School in Hanover
    Opened spring 1946
    Initiators/teachers: Nizan Tykoshinsky, Jehuda Merin
    Students: 30 ages 6–20

Beth Jacob girls seminar in Celle
    Students: 25

Vocational school in Hanover
    Opened 1946
    Initiator/Headmaster: Dr. Oswald Dutch; from 1948, Mark Lister
    Students: 100

Fishery school in Blankenese near Hamburg
    Opened March 1946, operated until October 1946
    Initiator: *Poale Zion* Left and the Hamburg community

Looking to the Future

Supervisor: a Polish survivor
Students: 70–100 ages 20–30; organized as a kibbutz

MARITIME AND VOCATIONAL SCHOOL IN NEUSTADT
Opened May–June 1947
Initiator: ORT
Director: David Krawitz

AHLEM AGRICULTURAL SCHOOL
Operated by ORT from June 1946
Instructors: Lifschitz, Menuha Yaffeh

AGRICULTURAL TRAINING FARMS
Alleheim, Katzberg, Olsheim, Schloss Laach (for Orthodox)
Students: Kibbutzim in rotation

KIBBUTZIM
Brunswick, Celle, Hanover, Lüneburg

ASSOCIATION OF UNIVERSITY STUDENTS, HANOVER
Assistance of CC, JRU, Jewish students UK
Students: 80

Note to table 2: Based on the sources listed in the various notes above and hereafter, plus the following: Program for the opening ceremony of the popular university (n.d.), YV, JM/10.374; circular by Rafael Olevsky (n.d.), YV, 0–70/28; Sir Raphael Cilento to the British Zone Director, May 7, 1946, WLL, Henriques/Jewish Training Farms; JRU's report on Brunswick, May 25, 1946, WLL, Henriques/Braunschweig Reports; JDC report, June 19, 1946, PRO, FO/1052/349; report by Mary Wise, Aug. 6, 1946, WLL, Henriques/Düsseldorf; Wodlinger to JRU, and report by Ruth Ring, Aug. 7, 1946, WLL, Henriques/Jewish Training Farm Ollesheim; Warburg to Wodlinger, Aug. 29, 1946, GJA, Geneva 1/7A/C-48.403; Weingreen's report, Oct. 15, 1946, WLL, Henriques/LV NRW; Leo Kempe to JRU, Oct. 21, 1946, WLL, Henriques/Schloss Laach Training Centre; Wollheim's report, Oct. 28, 1946, YV, 0–70/63; Henriques interview with Dr. Holzer, Oct. 31, 1946, HL, Schonfeld/130/2; plan for ORT maritime training school, Nov. 11, 1946, PRO, FO/1049/368; report on Schloss Laach training center, Mar., 13, 1947, WLL, Henriques/Schloss Laach Training Center; Sylvia Markowitz to Eric Warburg, Apr. 8, and 30, 1947, GJA, Geneva 1/7A/C-48.403; *Central Committee*: ORT report; reports by David Umansky, Jan. 10, 1948, CZA, L58/370, and with no dates, CZA, L58/378, CZA, S32/204; JDC report on children attending schools in Belsen, Mar. 1948, YV, 0–70/17; folder on Noham in Germany; reports of emissaries, 1947–1949, CZA, S86/343; GJA folder Geneva 1/7A/C-48.403; *Unzer Sztyme*, Sept. 15, 1946, article by Izakov on Blankenese; *Unzer Sztyme*, July 12, 1947, article by Lubliner on education in Belsen, and Sept. 14, 1947: 48, on Noham youth movement; *Zum Sieg*; *Unzer Front*; Warschawsky's article in *Belsen Book*; Enreich, "From Bergen Belsen."

the yeshivas were also established through the initiative of camp inmates, particularly the activists of the Provisional Committee and the later CC.

In many cases, however, even though the first initiative was independent, emissaries soon joined in, in some cases paving the way and playing a central role in running the school. The clearest case was that of the vocational school. It began to operate on a regular basis only after the arrival of Professor Weingreen from England, who served as supervisor of the educational system in the British Zone on behalf of the JRU and took special interest in vocational training, and Joseph Mack of ORT, who organized the school. The Hebrew high school, too, greatly benefited from the soldiers of the Jewish Brigade, from David Littman, who helped Dr. Wrubel in her initiative, and from other soldiers and emissaries from Palestine, who at first made up a decisive portion of the high school teaching staff. The presence of teacher soldiers at the elementary school was also remarkable: five out of the eight teachers were soldiers of the Jewish Brigade.[14]

Religious education was also a joint initiative. A Talmud Torah and a yeshiva were founded by Polish and Hungarian rabbis from

School children marching in the camp (Yad Vashem Photo-Archives [FA 135 A190])

174

among the survivors. Emissaries from the CRREC helped materially, but teaching was done almost exclusively by local personnel. The seminar Beth Jacob, however, was initiated by the Palestine Poale Agudath Israel (PAI) emissary Mordechi Breuer, who directed the school and taught both there and at the Hebrew high school.[15]

Agricultural training was dependent on the welfare agencies and the Palestinian emissaries. Agricultural farms were not available without being allocated by UNRRA and the military authorities, and only the JDC, JRU, and Jewish Agency could negotiate with UNRRA in this matter and secure places for training.[16] Emissaries from Palestine were also in charge of organizing the groups of students, usually from among the kibbutzim of the various Zionist youth movements. Illustrating the complicated case of agricultural training is Ahlem, which had been a Jewish gardening school (Israelitische Gartenbauschule Ahlem) in the Weimar Republic. Under the Nazi regime it first became a Jewish ghetto, then a Gestapo prison from which Jews were deported to the death camps. Later on it also served as a forced labor camp—an extension of Neuengamme—to serve the ammunition factories in the Hanover area. Upon liberation the surviving prisoners were evacuated from it, but it was still occupied by former German/Nazi residents. Nevertheless, in late 1945 a group of Hashomer Hatza'ir, led by a young refugee from Poland, Nizan Tykoshinsky, settled there. However, the process of securing it for training purposes, and indeed retrieving it to Jewish ownership, was complicated, in particular as matters of restitution were not settled (the Ahlem school in the past had been the property of the Hanover Jewish community). After lengthy negotiations in which the JRU, ORT, and JDC offered to finance the running of the farm, they were able to obtain it through UNRRA. Only in August 1946 were groups of trainees absorbed there on a regular basis.[17] A few other farms were available, but in many cases negotiations fell through, thus reducing the possibility of agricultural training.

Children's homes were also dependent on the JDC, the JRU, and the Jewish Agency. The JDC provided the main material basis, while the JRU and the Jewish Agency provided mainly the personnel.[18]

In addition to their main assignment to prepare and organize aliyah, many of the Palestinian emissaries were largely occupied with education. This is not surprising, given the Zionist-political aspect of their mission on the one hand and their inferiority regarding general welfare on the other. The Jewish Agency did not act as a welfare agency but sent them as Zionist missioners. A list of emissaries from May 1946 (about two months after the arrival of the Jewish Agency emissaries to the British Zone) illustrates this: six emissaries were specifically assigned to work in educational institutions: Genia Schwadron and Hava Isick to the children's home in Bergen-Belsen, Menahem Ehrlich and Mordechai Breuer to the high school in Bergen-Belsen, Menuha Yaffeh to the *hachsharah* in Ahlem, and Rivka Weber to the youth in Bergen-Belsen. Another emissary, Reuma Schwartz, who came from London to join the Jewish Agency mission, fulfilled the educational role in the children's home of Blankenese. Only three people had more general assignments: Kurt Lewin, the head of the commission; Yitzhak Kaminsky, who was in charge of Hanover; and Meir Caspi in Neustadt. For all of them, education was an integral part of their assignment.[19] The Youth Aliyah, on the other hand, started to operate in Germany only later, in 1947. David Umansky, the head of the Youth Aliyah for the British Zone, was occupied mainly with preparing the children in the children's homes for aliyah.[20]

Conditions and Constraints of Educational Activity

Operating a school system depended mainly on the availability of professional teachers. However, despite their goodwill and devotion, many of those who volunteered to start the school system were not trained, professional educators. Moreover, those who had been teachers during the war had no connection with any academic environment. Furthermore, some of them had either never been familiar with Jewish culture or had nothing to teach but Jewish tradition. Besides, very few had a Zionist background and/or Hebrew proficiency.

Teaching also requires appropriate facilities, furniture, essential materials such as notebooks, pens, and pencils, tools for vocational training, and above all, books for both teachers and students. In this respect the limitations were crucial. That the schools began to operate without the proper facilities and equipment must be seen as a miracle. Classes were held in residential blocks, without any appropriate furniture, which was only finally obtained due to the efforts of the JRU and JDC emissaries many months after the beginning of teaching. Initially there were allocations of neither paper nor notebooks. Students had to memorize or somehow write on scraps of paper they found. Later on things improved. The high school, for instance, which started in two rooms with broken windows and benches serving for tables, moved to block no. 41 with five furnished rooms. Pencils, pens, and drawing materials became regular components in the JDC and JRU shipments from abroad.

The main problem was the scarcity of books. At first, teachers tried to obtain books on their own initiative, asking relatives to send them from Palestine or purchasing them in bookstores in Hanover in exchange for cigarettes. However, the need was mainly for books from Palestine, and it was a long time before regular shipments of books started to arrive. Since books were needed not only by teachers (who needed them to revive their memory) but also by students, the lack was difficult to overcome. As late as July 1946, classes were conducted practically without books for the students. Every textbook for students had to be duplicated many times, and this meant either special printing of entire editions before shipping or getting permission to make photocopies of the book in Germany. Moreover, teaching and learning are based on the availability of a library with a variety of books, journals, and other publications not directly used in the classroom. Libraries were only gradually developed, and they were dependent on moving the limited book resources from place to place. Even the drive to secure

A children's performance for the camp's community (Yad Vashem Photo-Archives [FA 135 A185])

thousands of books through the campaign Sefer la-golah (books for the Diaspora) did not satisfy this need. The situation worsened with the growing student population coming from Poland. Indeed, this need not have affected the British Zone, which absorbed only a small portion of the refugees. However, the books were always sent to Munich, the seat of the Jewish Agency headquarters. The growing needs of the American Zone, with its greater Jewish population, often delayed or even prevented the transfer of books to the British Zone. As late as October 1947—namely, with the beginning of the third school year in the camps—there was still a shortage of books, even for teachers. The problem seems to have been solved only during 1948, by the printing or copying of books in Germany. Thus in June 1948 an order for Hebrew dictionaries and 2,800 textbooks in mathematics, history, Hebrew, and Palestinian geography was instantly filled.[21]

These material conditions were exceptionally crucial due to the abnormal educational background of both teachers and students, who were suffering from their trials and tribulation during six years of war. The psychological burden was even more crucial. Many of the children were haunted by traumas, deprived of any moral sociopsychological upbringing in the past or a normal family atmosphere in the present, which prevented them from adjusting to their present situation. The teachers, suffering from similar problems, had to combat the vast psychological challenge with practically no professional assistance. The welfare agencies were able to provide only very few expert psychologists, who mainly were occupied with mapping the problems and unable to provide individual assistance. The Palestinian emissaries lacked any preparation or training with regard to psychological and social problems caused by the Holocaust, and the use of compassion and intuition could not replace professional treatment. As Selma Selby and Lily Holt of JRU, who were active in Kaunitz, wrote to their superiors:"The main tragedy, of course, is the fact that there is absolutely nothing to occupy their minds—their past is uppermost in their minds, the future is almost without hope as far as they are concerned. . . . We will try and commence classes and sports, but the lack of equipment hampers our efforts."[22]

In addition, there were two other obstacles on the road to educational programming. On the one hand was the problem of forming classes in accordance with age. Since many of the children had been absent from schooling for longer or shorter periods, it was difficult to organize classes according to age. On the other hand, it was also impossible to place together in one class young children and adolescents who were far apart in terms of life experience and maturity, particularly because of experiences during the war that caused many youngsters to develop prematurely.[23]

The other problem was that of a common language. Yiddish, the language most Eastern European Jewish adults knew regardless of which country they came from, was not a language spoken by most of the children. They grew up during the war lacking a Jewish framework and thus spoke the languages of the areas in which they lived—in or outside camps. As in the tale of the tower of Babel, a mixture of many languages reigned, with many children lacking of a proper knowledge of any language. Teachers mainly spoke Yiddish, and a few of them also knew Hebrew. It was necessary, then, to first select which of the two languages to use as the common language, and second, to acquire, as quickly as possible, the basics of that language as a precondition of any teaching. Since most of the teachers were more familiar with Yiddish, it soon became the main teaching language and the common language in the camps in general, regardless of Zionist aspirations that favored Hebrew. This was not only a matter of practicality. David Rosenthal, editor of *Unzer Sztyme*, believed that both languages—Hebrew and Yiddish—should be taught as the basis for Jewish culture.[24]

Hanukkah celebration at the children's home in Blankenese (private collection)

The supremacy of Yiddish, however, gradually began to give way to Hebrew through the help of Palestinian teachers and the growing supply of textbooks from Palestine. In the second half of 1946, teaching in Hebrew became the norm in the three Zionist-secular institutions in Belsen: the kindergarten, the elementary school, and the Hebrew high school. The teaching of Hebrew in all the other schools bore fruit as well.[25]

Ideology, Organization, and the Politics of Education

The story of Jewish education in the British Zone can be characterized without hesitation as a Zionist story. Organization, curricula, and the role of the schools in daily social life and culture manifest this.

ORGANIZATION

A unique phenomenon in the British Zone was that despite dependence on the welfare agencies, the educational system was fully subordinated to the CC. This may well have been the result of several factors that distinguished the British Zone from the American Zone: first, the concentration of the greater part of the DP population in one camp; second, the presence of such persons as Trepman, Olevsky, and Wrubel, who started the educational operation without any help; third, the militant attitude of the CC and its unequivocal Zionist stance; fourth, the fact that the JRU was mainly interested in education, and many of the JRU emissaries—who took an active part in educational work—were Zionists; and finally, the relative disinterest of the Palestinian emissaries in party politics (as compared with the emissaries in the populous American Zone). This also related to their devotion to their teaching activities in the formal system of the schools. Thus, a strong basis was laid for cooperation between all parties—the CC, the Jewish Agency, and the JRU—in the field of education.[26]

This had its positive consequences in terms of organization. Education became part and parcel of the CC agenda. An education committee was operating beside the CC. The members were Rafael Olevsky of the CC's Cultural Department; Bertha Weingreen on behalf of the JRU; Sela Lefkowitch, the elementary school's headmistress; Helena Wrubel, headmistress of the Hebrew high school; Josef Mack, the director of the ORT school; and the soldiers representing the Jewish Brigade. The committee regularly held meetings to consider educational issues. Now that both the teachers and the parents had a forum in which they could address their problems, they no longer had to act in a vacuum, as was the case in the American Zone. The CC also set the standards and supervised the system by collecting reports, organizing registration, and issuing diplomas for studies completed in all schools. Even the announcements for a youth guides' seminar were issued by the CC.[27]

It was therefore unnecessary for an external organization to form an additional educational system. The Board of Education, established in 1947 by the Jewish Agency and the JDC, was earmarked only for the American Zone in Germany. This was not because the JDC and the Jewish Agency were less interested in the British Zone, with its relatively small population, or because the CC in the British Zone would reject such intervention. The reason was that in the British Zone there was no need for such an external initiative. While in the American Zone the system was greatly hampered by strikes, the British Zone was quiet. The relationships among the teachers, the CC, and the welfare agencies were generally untroubled.[28]

The teachers' mission from Palestine, which arrived in Germany in September 1947, had little impact on the British Zone. Five teachers had been allocated to the British Zone, but there is no record as to which of the various emissaries were active in the school year 1947–48 as teachers, and it seems that nothing changed with their arrival.[29]

The Orthodox educational system, although separate, was integrated with the general system. Indeed, rivalries between the CC and the Agudah originating in issues relating to supplies also affected cooperation within the educational system, but these were eventually solved. Rabbis of the CRREC who taught were officially under the JRU. The CC education committee represented and supervised the Orthodox institutions along with the others. Orthodox emissaries from Palestine operated in both secular and Orthodox institutions.[30]

CURRICULA

Developing school curricula presented the most difficult challenge due to the constraints of books and language. It seems, however, that the dominance of a Zionist orientation among the teachers, together with the influence of Palestinian emissaries, enabled the development of teaching programs that very much resembled the curricula in Palestine.

On the other hand, objective constraints and the survivors' specific needs also played a role in shaping the curricula.

Pedagogic aims may be illustrated through the Hebrew high school case. Wrubel and Littman defined its aims as follows: spiritual and mental rehabilitation, shaping of Jewish cultural identity, and preparing for life in *Eretz Yisrael*. Accordingly, the curriculum was composed of humanities (English, literature), sciences (mathematics, physics, chemistry, geography, anatomy, natural sciences), Jewish culture (history of the Jewish people, Agadah, and eventually Bible), *Eretz Yisrael* and Zionism (Hebrew, *Palästinographie*, archeology), and recreation (handwork and drawing, singing, gymnastics).

The program closely followed the curriculum used by the *Yishuv*'s educational system. However, there were differences. First, greater emphasis was placed on the general sciences and humanities. Second, English lessons were more intensive. The reasons are obvious: language constraints and the availability of books and professional teachers determined the curriculum. Teaching the Bible had to wait for Hebrew proficiency. On the other hand, Wrubel was a professional

High school students in a gymnastics lesson (Yad Vashem Photo-Archives [178AO9])

geographer, Professor Jacob Weingreen was an expert on the archeology of Palestine, and finally, English teachers were provided by the JRU.[31]

The language issue was crucial. As already mentioned, Hebrew became the common language in the secular institutions, and it was taught systematically in all the other institutions. While the Palestinian emissaries were indispensable for teaching Hebrew, JRU emissaries filled the role for English. There were ideological and practical considerations for teaching both languages. Ideologically, Hebrew was the key for Jewish culture and national awareness. English, on the other hand, could pave the way to sciences and broad human enlightenment. Practically, both languages were essential for preparing the students for immigration and absorption in their chosen destinations.[32]

Zionist- and *Eretz Yisrael*-oriented education was largely created by extracurricular activities. These played a central role in the schools and fulfilled the desire to link the *Galuth* (Exile, Diaspora) to *Eretz Yisrael*. Materials for holiday celebrations were provided by the Jewish National Fund (Keren Kayemet Le'israel). Preparations for events such as the Fifteenth of Shevat occupied teachers and students well beyond the class hours and created a sociocultural atmosphere that made the school a "Palestinian island" in the midst of the *Galuth*. Soldiers from the Jewish Brigade and other Palestinian emissaries played a crucial role in organizing and creating an authentic atmosphere.[33]

Indeed, there were many problems, and teaching programs may not reveal the shortcomings in implementation. Mordechai Breuer sharply criticized the low standard of the high school, even as compared with the worst schools in Palestine. Lady Henriques criticized the poor management of the Ahlem agricultural school. The British authorities found fault with the vocational schools, arguing that the survivors declined to participate in productive rehabilitation and preferred black-marketing instead. They particularly suspected the maritime school in Hamburg for smuggling and illegal immigration, which caused the early closure of this school.[34] It should also be kept in mind, though, that implementation could not be immediately achieved due to the lack of personnel and books.

The case of the Hebrew high school, used above for illustration, may be unique. Different problems troubled those involved with vocational training, where the needs differed. General instruction was essential for technical training, and English was much more important than Hebrew. Thus less time and opportunity were left for Jewish or Zionist education. Shortage of time and a clear mind was a basic problem. Indeed, students were eager to learn and to make up for the lost years, but they had already lost the will of young adolescents to devote themselves or to be enthusiastic about general knowledge without a practical goal. They had to face, with their teachers, the question regarding priorities: how to allocate their time and energy between general education, preparing for normal life, specific preparation for immigration, and national education, namely, preparing for the Zionist struggle and endeavor. The answer was diversified, as reflected in the teaching programs. While the Hebrew high school focused on Hebrew-Zionist education, following the educational system of the *Yishuv*, the ORT vocational school emphasized the English language. The Orthodox institutions, while focusing on Jewish religious education, taught both Hebrew and English and included a minimum of general sciences on the one hand and *Eretz Yisrael* studies on the other. While a few institutions like the high school aimed at preparing the students for aliyah, others aimed at a preparation for either aliyah or immigration to other countries. Adult education in the form of evening classes and lecture series provided a partial solution, but it failed to provide a good source of Jewish education for the adult survivors.[35]

However, examining the general picture reveals the common denominator: all the schools provided essentials for a national solidarity, either in Palestine or abroad. All of them—including vocational and Orthodox schools—taught Hebrew and Jewish national culture. The pro-Zionist consensus, which reigned in those years in the Jewish international arena, met with the yearning of the survivors for freedom and self-respect as Jews and provided the basis for cooperation in the sphere of education.

THE ROLE OF INFORMAL EDUCATION

Informal education was found in two areas. The first was in the schools' extracurricular activities in the cultural life of the camp. Indeed, the extracurricular activity in the school was practically taken over by the camp leaders to serve the needs of public events. The schools' celebrations of Jewish religious and national holidays indeed became relevant for the camp population at large and were attended by large audiences with enthusiastic coverage in *Unzer Sztyme*. In these events, special emphasis was placed on *Eretz Yisrael*—Fifteenth of Shevat, Eleventh of

Adar, Shavuot, and later Yom Ha'atzmaut (Israel Independence Day). The schools' exhibitions of students' work were a time for the general public to share the joy and satisfaction of the students' achievements.[36]

The second place where informal education was found was in adult education in general, and also within the activities of the kibbutzim and youth movements. The interaction was created because the same persons worked in both the formal and informal frameworks. It could have led to politicization of the schools, but within a short time after the arrival of the Jewish Agency emissaries—and due to the example set by the Jewish Brigade on the one hand and the CC's determination on the other—this was avoided. Political activity was prohibited within schools, and lines between formal and informal education were crossed only in the terms of Zionist education in general. Even the children's homes were not divided along political parties, as was the case in the American Zone. For example, Breuer served as a teacher providing Zionist and religious education in both secular and Orthodox schools, and at the same time he helped organize the Ezra youth movement and PAI kibbutzim. Kaminsky, with great effort, devotedly taught Hebrew, Jewish, and *Eretz Yisrael* history, both in the school and in the various kibbutzim. On the other hand, seminars for youth leaders on Zionist issues were organized for all the youth movements together, under the auspices of the CC. Weingreen devoted his public lectures mainly to *Eretz Yisrael*, past and present.[37]

Indeed, the common denominator for serving in both frameworks was Zionism. Thus Zionist education within the formal system gained from the inputs in informal education, and vice versa. If any issue caused disharmony within the system, formal and informal, it was the matter of religion, which sooner or later caused a schism between the Orthodox subdivision of schools, children's homes, and youth movements and the secular system. This was not, however, a division between Zionists and non-Zionists. The Orthodox Zionists shared the concerns of Agudah leaders in matters of religion, while the Agudah leaders shared the sympathy for *Eretz Yisrael* propagated by the Hamizrahi.[38]

An excellent illustration for how everything was coordinated within a clear national-Zionist system is the CC *pekudat hayom* (Announcement of the Day) for the second Liberation Day. Like many other events, this was run and organized by the CC using mainly youth groups and educational institutions to march in a parade that ended up in a public rally at the memorial.[39]

The educational programs in the camps, despite many obstacles, and although it may have not reached the highest academic levels, fulfilled a major role in rehabilitating the young survivors of the Holocaust. Students were eager to study. The social environment within the school was a substitute for the family that was no longer. The knowledge acquired and, even more so, the acquaintances and bonds created with the free world were decisive for future absorption in the countries of immigration, mainly Palestine and the United States. Educational institutions created an oasis in the desert of camp lives, an escape from the bitter past and grim present, and a safe path toward the future of those involved, both as individuals and as members of a Jewish people.[40]

Jewish Education in the Communities

In the Jewish communities, the picture was much less positive, since they had actually no basis upon which to develop Jewish education. The problem was not only that there were very few children, but also that there was practically no one with a basic knowledge of Jewish culture who could teach Jewish children. Rabbis and JRU emissaries were barely able to provide for their ritual needs. The few children and youth thus attended German schools or, in some cases, joined the DP schools, as was the case in Hanover.

However, there were some 150–200 youngsters scattered in the larger communities. Cologne had 36, and Düsseldorf and Hamburg had 60 in each community. As for their general education, they may have joined a vocational school or enrolled in a German university, but this was no substitute for an elementary Jewish education. The communities could not provide for their spiritual needs. Thus, with the help of the JRU, the Palestinian emissaries, and the CC they formed, in the summer of 1947, an informal framework for Jewish education, namely, a youth organization. Certainly, for the Jewish Agency emissaries the main purpose was recruiting the youngsters for *hachsharah* and eventual aliyah. As the DP camps and assembly centers were closing down, helping the local children became one of the main goals for both the JRU and the communities' leadership for many years to come.[41]

An important phenomenon that had its impact on Jewish education in the communities was the students' organization. As already mentioned, there were some youngsters enrolled in German universities. Though mostly of German Jewish origin, they also included a few DPs who were in the quotas set for DPs (according to nationality) and managed to overcome the language barriers. The Verband der jüdischen Studenten in der britischen Zone (Union of Jewish Students in the British Zone) was founded in Hanover in the summer of 1947. The representatives of the welfare organizations and the CC were present. The JRU's chief representative, E. G. Lowenthal, showed particular interest in the union's development and helped to establish connections with the Jewish Students Federation in England, which sent books and other equipment. The JDC provided a monthly allocation of 250 DM for each of the twenty-seven students (the number grew to fifty with the decision to include the students of technical schools). The basic cause for organizing, however, was to create a Jewish cultural framework with discussions, lectures, a reading room, and so forth. Moreover, the students took part in educational activities. They lectured and taught to the best of their ability in many circles, such as the Ahlem agricultural school, the DP school in Hanover, and the youth organizations and the kibbutzim in and around Hanover. They also helped to establish a library with a reading room in one of the assembly centers in Hanover. Beginning in 1948, the union published its own supplement issue in the *Gemeindeblatt*. The title was *Berg Scopus*, alluding to Mount Scopus and the Hebrew University of Jerusalem.[42]

It is not clear if this intensive Jewish educational activity of the university students was a unique phenomenon for Hanover, due to the organization's headquarters being there and the fact that most of the students were enrolled in the University of Hanover and the technical school there. It is also not clear if the union had any enduring impact. For the Jewish students in the immediate post-Holocaust period, studying in Germany was a temporary arrangement, a path to rehabilitation and to later establishing a new life in America or Palestine. In any event, in 1949 the union transferred its headquarters to Bonn, the seat of the government of the newly established German Federal Republic.[43]

Toward the closing of the DP camps, educational enterprises eventually became a matter for the local communities' leadership. The JRU and ORT especially aimed at helping the communities develop educational systems of their own. Vocational schools were opened in Hamburg and Cologne, and the children's home in Blankenese became a convalescent home for the communities' children. At that time, in 1949, there were already 500 children, of whom 300 were infants under the age of three. At the convention on the future of the Jews in Germany held in Heidelberg in September 1949, special emphasis was placed on the duty of the Jewish welfare organizations to help with vocational, as well as with Jewish, education in the communities. The issue of education became indeed a central issue for the Central Council of Jews in Germany, founded in 1950.[44]

11

ZIONIST PARTY POLITICS

As we have seen, nationalist spirit dominated the organizational and cultural-educational spheres, both in the camps and in the communities. In the political arena, moreover, Zionism was the name of the game and was manifested through the survivors' active participation in the struggle for aliyah and an independent state.

The Political Front

Political activity on behalf of the Zionist cause transcended the division between Zionists and non-Zionists, as is illustrated by both the Anglo-American Committee of Inquiry and the *Exodus* affair. In both events, the focus was the issue of aliyah.

THE ANGLO-AMERICAN COMMITTEE OF INQUIRY

The Zionist manifesto that was declared in the September 1945 congress held in Belsen was put to test when the DPs there were called to testify before the Anglo-American Committee. The British Mandatory immigration policy was based on the White Paper of 1939, which allowed within five years the entrance of only 75,000 Jews to Palestine. Due to World War II, even this limited number was not filled. The British Labor government, elected shortly after the war ended, decided to continue the White Paper policy and to permit, temporarily, the entrance of 1,500 immigrants monthly until a long-term policy would be decided upon.[1]

There was, however, continuous American pressure placed on the British to be more flexible in their immigration policy in Palestine in order to enable the DP problem in Europe to be solved. There is no doubt that the Americans had their own interests at heart in pressing the British to open Palestine for Jewish immigration. Such a step would take the burden off American shoulders and ease their conscience. A first step in this direction was President Truman's proposal—based on Earl G. Harrison's report of August 1945—to allow the immigration to Palestine of 100,000 Jewish survivors.[2] British refusal to accept Truman's proposal was followed by the initiative to establish a joint Anglo-American Committee of Inquiry, which was to investigate the DP problem and the Palestinian question and see to what extent immigration to Palestine could help provide a solution. The announcement concerning the Anglo-American Committee was made by British foreign secretary Ernest Bevin on November 13, 1945. At the same time, Bevin declared an extension of the White Paper until a decision on a long-term policy was reached. His announcement left no doubt regarding his belief that the DP problem should be solved elsewhere, not in Palestine.[3] The immediate response to Bevin's speech was a protest by the DPs in the British Zone. A mass demonstration took place in Hanover on November 16, and this was followed by arrests, and later a trial.[4]

    The Anglo-American Committee, composed of six American and six British members, began its investigations with hearings during January 1946 in Washington and then in London. The committee was then divided into subcommittees which, before going to Palestine, visited the various centers of the survivors in Germany, Austria, and Poland, and in particular the DP camps. The subcommittee that visited Bergen-Belsen was composed of the American chairman, Judge Hutchinson, and three British members—Lord Morrison, Sir John Singleton, and Mr. Vincent, who served as a secretary. They arrived in Belsen on February 10, 1946. At a meeting with eight representatives of the Central Committee, who were chosen very carefully by the military commander of the camp to represent all segments of the DP population, the message was very clear: after Auschwitz there was only one solution—Palestine. Yossele Rosensaft emphasized the Jews' disappointment at being denied the only assistance they needed—the opportunity to rebuild their lives: "After these years, in which the Jewish people had sacrificed six million Jews we have the right to build a new life in the land which is our only homeland: Palestine." Norbert Wollheim accentuated the fact that he was a German Jew and had been far from Zionism before being deported to Auschwitz. His Zionism, for him as for any Jew, he said, emerged as the only possible response to

Auschwitz. He explained that there were only two small groups of Jews who might say "no" to Palestine: German Jews who were old and sick, or partners in a mixed marriage, and those who had relatives overseas with whom they wished to reunite. Both groups together, he stated, made up no more than 15 percent of the Jews in the British Zone.

Other witnesses, among them Rabbi Halpern representing the non-Zionist Orthodox, testified similarly. Particularly impressive was the testimony of Sela Kleinmann-Lefkowitch, the headmistress of Bergen-Belsen's Jewish school, who told the committee that although she had refrained from teaching or disseminating Zionist ideology in her school, Zionism had spontaneously been introduced in the educational context. Hebrew was the only common language, and Palestine was the only hope shared by all.

The committee was not content with the formal meetings in which many officials—among them the camp commander, Major Murphy, UNRRA directors, and the JRU field director, Henry Lunzer—were present, and went out to visit the camp to obtain firsthand impressions. Random encounters with camp inmates elicited the same response. The answer to all questions was unanimous: if we can't go to Palestine, our only alternative is to return to Auschwitz.[5]

Was this a genuine Zionist stance or perhaps only a well-orchestrated manipulation enacted by JA emissaries, as is claimed with reference to the American Zone?[6] It seems well beyond doubt that at least in the British Zone, the Zionist response to the committee was a view genuinely shared by most camp inmates and had little or nothing to do with any JA manipulation. As we have noted already, strong support for Zionism had been manifested in the process of self-organization. Moreover, there was no official Zionist presence in Belsen except for the Jewish Brigade. David Ben-Gurion, who paid a short visit to Belsen in late October 1945 while visiting the DP camps in Germany, was deeply impressed by the strong Zionist mood he encountered there.[7] As for the Palestine-JA mission that arrived in Germany in December, it so happened that the first emissary to the British Zone, Kurt Lewin, only arrived in March 1946.[8] Indeed, there was some uncertainty among Zionist leaders as to the DPs' attitude toward Zionism, and there was an effort to prepare them for the committee's visit, although that effort focused on the much larger population of the American Zone. The details of the committee's visit to Belsen may indicate that there was no need for any Zionist indoctrination. At least

New Beginnings

in the British Zone, a Zionist stance was a natural response to conditions there.[9]

There is no doubt as to the deep impression that the direct encounter with the survivors had on the committee members, British and American alike.[10] Be that as it may, and notwithstanding the considerable political obstacles facing the British Mandate that were manifested in the hearings held in Palestine, the Anglo-American Committee reported to the two governments on April 22, 1946, and recommended the adoption of Harrison's original proposal—the immediate immigration of 100,000 DPs to Palestine.

In a few weeks it became obvious that the British would not abide by the recommendation, and the survivors in the British Zone were left with little hope for the future. About a week before the committee submitted its recommendations, on the first anniversary of the liberation of Belsen, April 15, 1946, which that year fell on the first day of the Passover holiday, the CC issued a circular. It called upon all the DPs to voice their demands for free aliyah and to express their unanimous support for the *Yishuv* and its struggle against British Mandatory policy. The circular—in Yiddish—clearly called for the support of the United Resistance Movement in Palestine (Tenu'at HaMeri), which, despite their mutual antagonism, was founded by all three underground movements—Haganah, Irgun, and Lehi—as a response to the British immigration policy and the plight of the survivors: "Long live the Jewish people! Long live the Jewish State in *Eretz Yisrael*! Long live the free aliyah!"[11]

Indeed, the ceremony that took place at Bergen-Belsen on that day to unveil the Jewish monument to the victims turned into a protest against the British liberators. About seven thousand Jews marched from the DP camp to the former concentration camp. Rosensaft opened the ceremony by unveiling the monument. After various speeches in Hebrew and Yiddish, Wollheim addressed the audience in English. Denouncing the British not only for their present policy but also for the lack of assistance and compassion for the Jews in their desperate struggle to survive, he blamed the British for their share as perpetrators of the Holocaust.[12]

The DPs' frustration in all of Germany was deeply felt, but the survivors did not give up the struggle. Even in the British Zone, which from the beginning of 1947 enjoyed a special allocation of 350 certificates per month,[13] the struggle for aliyah as a political cause did not weaken, as may be indicated by the *Exodus* affair.

The *Exodus* Affair

The well-known *Exodus* affair was part and parcel of the Zionist struggle and soon became a focus for political struggle in the British Zone. The large number of illegal ships caught by the British on their arrival in the territorial waters of Palestine brought about the British decision in August 1946 to expel the illegal passengers aboard these vessels to detention camps in Cyprus. After a year, with the detention camps holding some 50,000 *ma'apilim* (illegal immigrants), the British realized that this was not stopping the flow of illegal immigrants and decided to adopt an alternative policy—to return the ships back to their ports of departure. The first—and only—implementation of this policy involved the *Exodus 1947* and resulted in an international scandal.

On July 11, 1947, *Exodus 1947* (formerly the SS *President Warfield*) departed from the port of Sète in southern France with some 4,500 *ma'apilim* on board. Upon its arrival at the coast of Palestine, the *Exodus* was caught by the British navy. After a fierce struggle with the British sailors and marines who boarded the vessel (which resulted in many casualties and even a fatality), the *ma'apilim* were forced into three British ships to return them to France. They arrived on July 29 at Port de Bouc in France, but the passengers on board refused to disembark. The whole affair had by now become an international issue. The United Nations Special Committee on Palestine (UNSCOP) had been just then visiting Palestine and was shocked when witnessing the survivors being dragged ashore. The French government, while willing to help the exhausted passengers and ready to accept them as refugees, refused to support the British by forcing them to disembark. After more than a month, during which time the passengers were subjected to severe physical and psychological stress, the British decided to send the ships to the British Zone in Germany, hoping that they would then be able to force the *ma'apilim* to transfer to France. But this was a miscalculation on their part.[14]

The three ships arrived at the port of Hamburg on September 6 and 7. By now the *Exodus* affair was a political issue for the Jews in the British Zone and the various Jewish organizations active there. Anticipating the arrival of the ships in Hamburg, on August 25 a general strike was held and a fast was declared by all the Jews of the British Zone. Tempers were running high, and the demonstrations were on the verge of deteriorating into violence. This, however, at the last moment was avoided by Rosensaft and Wollheim, who were consulted by the representatives of the World Jewish Congress—Marc Jarblum from Paris and Noah Barou from London.[15] Another mass demonstration took place upon the arrival of the first ship in Hamburg, and again the situation was very tense. Not only the DPs but also the Jewish communities, in particular that of Hamburg, joined the protest. A third round of violent clashes between the *ma'apilim* and the British was anticipated, but this was eventually avoided. The CC and the heads of the JA (Lewin and Chomsky), JDC (Dallob), and JRU (Bloomberg) joined forces with Noah Barou of the WJC and took charge to calm down the situation.[16]

The *ma'apilim* were convinced then to disembark and were interned in two camps near Lübeck—Poppendorf and Am Stau—selected for them by the British. These were army camps, very poorly equipped and lacking the most basic facilities, surrounded with barbed wire and soldiers. They were intentionally separated from the DP camps and their organizations, and were identified by the British, ironically, with the code name "Oasis." The reasoning behind the British policy was quite obvious. They hoped that the poor conditions would induce the *ma'apilim* to leave for France or apply for refugee status under the auspices of the International Refugee Organization in order to get a better treatment. Both alternatives aimed at removing the burden from the British. However, the *ma'apilim* refused to surrender, claiming to be citizens of Palestine who were illegally deported and were entitled to return. At this point the British had to recognize that the *Exodus* passengers would stay in Germany, and in November they transferred them to more suitable camps to enable them to survive during the winter months.

At the same time, the JA's efforts to persuade the British to give priority to the *ma'apilim* when allocating certificates (in the same manner that they gave preference to the inmates of the Cyprus detention camps and the DPs in the British Zone) were rejected. The Mandatory government was anxious to close the camps in Cyprus, while the occupation authorities in Germany were anxious to relieve themselves of the DPs under their responsibility.[17]

Jewish efforts were now directed toward two parallel goals: first, to ameliorate the material conditions of the *Exodus* passengers, which was mainly the responsibility of the JDC, and second, to enable them to reach Palestine despite the British, which was mainly to be dealt with by the DPs in Germany. The CC adopted a resolution that the DPs of Belsen waive their DP priority for certificates.[18] This was a manifestation of solidarity, since it meant a sacrifice by people who were waiting for their own aliyah.[19] Facing the British refusal to accept their waivers, the Belsen residents actively joined forces to smuggle *Exodus* passengers into Belsen and to give them the certificates as if they were local DPs. Similarly, a great number were smuggled into the American Zone to join illegal immigration from there.[20] Thus, by March 1948 some 1,000 of the *Exodus* passengers were already in Palestine.

The great majority of the *Exodus* passengers had, however, to wait much longer, and indeed the CC and its leaders became the chief and at times almost only link between them and world Jewry, while the JA was busy with the political situation in Palestine. Finally the day arrived when the United Nations voted on partition—November 29, 1947. The *ma'apilim* left in Germany were the concern of the CC and the various agencies there. If there was any hope, on either side, that after the UN decision the problem would be resolved through emigration, it was wishful thinking. The British refused to relinquish their control over immigration, and following the UN decision they became even more adamant about closing down the Cyprus detention camps before their withdrawal from Palestine. This was in order to avoid the possibility that the camps would become a burden on the British taxpayer.

An anti-British demonstration of Jewish survivors on the occasion of the *Exodus* affair (Yad Vashem Photo-Archives [FA 186 311])

Hence the potential immigrants in Cyprus received priority over others, including the *Exodus* passengers. After the British withdrawal from Palestine, in May 1948, the newly established Israeli government gave preference to those immigrants who were most suitable to join the armed forces in the war effort. Thus, as late as July 1948 the *Exodus* passengers were still the responsibility of the CC. Rosensaft then negotiated with the British authorities that they be transferred to Belsen.[21] Only in September 1948, a year after their arrival in Germany, were the *Exodus* passengers at last brought to the newly established State of Israel and their wandering came to an end.

Cooperation and Solidarity with the *Yishuv*

Besides the forceful and independent Zionist stand in relation to matters directly affecting themselves, the survivors continuously supported the *Yishuv* and the Zionist cause. The pages of *Unzer Sztyme* gave priority to matters concerning Zionism at large and the situation in Palestine. An emphasis on Zionist-Palestinian affairs also characterized every public event, particularly the anniversary of April 15, the Liberation Day.[22] On the whole, no major event passed without political comment. This concerned not only British policy and the struggle for aliyah, but Zionist policy as well. Most illustrative were the CC's protests against terrorist acts by the Jewish extremists in Palestine after the bombing of the King David Hotel in Jerusalem in June 1946 and following the hanging of the two British sergeants in July 1947. In these protests the survivors expressed their concern and their right to influence Zionist policy, based both on their Holocaust experience and on their being the focus of the Zionist struggle:

> We, the liberated Jews in camps and communities of the British Zone, Germany, learned with horror of the murder of two British sergeants in Palestine. We are thankful to the *Yishuv* in Palestine for its efforts to help liberate us from our hopeless situation. However, we know that such irresponsible actions cannot help us and we declare with conviction that we dissociate ourselves from them. In German concentration camps our hearts were filled with deep contempt against any form of terrorism. Today we also oppose all terrorist actions whose pretext is to help us toward our Land of Promise. We appeal to all groups whose influence will affect our fate to facilitate our entry into Palestine. Never will we permit ourselves to be identified with un-Jewish actions which draw the contempt of the *Yishuv* in Palestine and all humanity.[23]

Zionist Party Politics

The wish to be involved with Zionist politics reached a climax with the convening of the first postwar World Zionist Congress, the twenty-second, in Basle in December 1946. Frustration was great after the failure of the Anglo-American Committee, and the sense of bitterness had dominated public mood for several months. Now it gave way to new hopes and expectations that the Zionist movement would put aside disagreements and disputes for determined struggle for the common Zionist cause, above and beyond party politics. For weeks before the congress the election campaign dominated the public scene in Belsen and other camps.[24] Two delegates were elected to represent the British Zone, one representing Histadrut Zionit Ahidah (United Zionist Organization) and one representing both the leftist Poale Zion and Hashomer Hatza'ir. The congress was also attended by members of the CC who came as guests. Thus, the representation of the British Zone was comprised of twelve leaders of all sections and parties: Hadassa Bimko, Szmayahu Bloch, Dov Laufer, Chaim Poslushny, Rafael Olevsky, Josef Rosensaft, Yehezkel Rosinger, Moshe Sanek, Yerahmiel Singer, Heinz Solomon, Anshel Szesarik, and Shmuel Weintraub.[25]

The congress, however, created great anger because of the dichotomy between party politics, which were heightened during the congress, and the survivors' deep belief that the Zionist goal could only be achieved through a united Zionist front. Already the campaign preceding the congress had deteriorated into mutual offensive agitation between the parties, in particular between the Revisionists and the Histadrut Zionit Ahidah.[26] It seems that at this stage the desire for involvement in political Zionism reached a point of crisis. From the beginning of 1947 this involvement diminished tremendously, and the leaders of the British Zone concentrated on rebuilding a united front based on the survivors' national agenda, which was shaped—besides the struggle for recognition—by the struggle for aliyah.[27]

Aliyah: The Focus of Zionist Activity

The struggle for aliyah dominated Zionist activity in the British Zone as a matter of course. A distinction must, however, be drawn between the political struggle for that cause and the actual efforts in this sphere. The activity on behalf of aliyah may be divided into various areas: helping the *Briha* into the British Zone, smuggling refugees from the British Zone, and preparing for legal and illegal aliyah.

Actively helping the *Briha* became a major task after the British closed their borders at the end of 1945 and refused to accept any more DPs. From that time on they allowed only the entrance of "Refugees"—namely, Germans who returned from Poland in "Operation Swallow." While the Americans allowed Jewish refugees from Poland and Eastern Europe to enter their zone and facilitated their absorption as DPs in the camps, the Jews in the British Zone had to use quite an effort and join forces with the *Briha* to undermine the British control. Smuggling Jewish refugees into the British Zone was essential for two reasons: first, because the British Zone was accessible to one of the main *Briha* routes and served as a pass to the American Zone or the Dutch, Belgian, and French borders;[28] and second, because from the British Zone there was a constant trickle of legal emigration due to the British efforts to lighten their obligations. This trickle by the beginning of 1947 transformed into a stream due to operation "Grand National," in which the British allocated 350 certificates monthly for aliyah.[29] Certainly the possibility of entering the program was incentive enough, and thus the British Zone attracted many refugees and became an important locality for preparing them for aliyah.[30]

While the actual organization of *Briha* and illegal aliyah was the concern of the Haganah, the Jewish Brigade, and the *Yishuv* emissaries, the techniques of accepting and absorbing the refugees for a temporary stay in the British Zone were mainly the responsibility of Rosensaft and his colleagues. They were the main entrepreneurs in absorbing the infiltrees (who generally arrived with forged papers as German refugees, in the framework of "Operation Swallow") as DPs in the camps—mainly in Belsen—by giving falsified numbers, supplying forged papers, and dealing with the welfare organizations and the British authorities. In all stages of this enterprise the JDC and the JRU were—at least passively—of great help, but Rosensaft was the central figure, and was so described by the British officials:

> The so-called "Jewish Central Committee" which is officially unrecognized, are solely responsible for the presence in Hohne of the 2,000 illegal inmates.
>
> The long-term situation cannot be said to be very satisfactory so long as there is a large number of illegal infiltrees at Hohne. We understand that the Jewish Relief Unit may have proposals to make for dispersing these and C.C.G. are also considering the problem. The former cannot, however, say anything definite until the Basle Congress is over and Rosensaft is back in Hohne since any plan which

the J.R.U. might put up would not be effective unless it had been agreed with the Belsen Committee.[31]

Indeed, the constant flight of refugees from the East became a major concern to the British, and one of their main reasons for refusing to recognize Rosensaft's leadership. They quite correctly understood that there was a close connection between the illegal activity of absorbing the refugees in their zone—especially the false registration—and the fight on the shores of Palestine, and they tried desperately to combat the whole activity in various ways and on many fronts.[32] When the illegal traffic intensified in the summer of 1946, the British decided to open the detention camps in Cyprus, emphasizing the connection between the intensified illegal aliyah and the illegal movement of refugees into Germany.[33]

Preparing and organizing the candidates for illegal aliyah took place mainly in the various *hachsharah* farms, and in particular in the maritime school in Hamburg, and later—after its closure by the British—in Neustadt. These farms and schools were organized by the JA together with the JDC, JRU, and ORT and were—like every enterprise, including the illegal operations in the British Zone—functioning under the auspices of the CC.[34]

Emphasizing the survivors' leadership in activities on behalf of illegal immigration should not deter us from examining the centrality of the JA representatives in this field. This was actually their main purpose and interest—to prepare the DPs for aliyah. When Kurt Lewin arrived in the British Zone in the spring of 1946, his first act was to open the Palestine Office (this was the title of the offices abroad of the JA Immigration Department) to start to register candidates for immigration.[35] From then on, almost all the JA reports from the British Zone have only one theme—immigration.[36]

The survivors' desire for aliyah was strong and genuine, and they were prepared for illegal and dangerous activities so long as this was the only option.[37] However, after a period of accelerated legal immigration in the framework of operation "Grand National," this urge diminished and the focus of Zionist activity shifted once again to the struggle of party politics.

The Zionist Organization

From the very beginning, organized Zionists were found in Bergen-Belsen. These were the people who had been members of various

New Beginnings

Zionist movements—for example, Hashomer Hatza'ir—well before the war, and as we have already seen, they were the mainstays in organizing the community of survivors.[38] However, from the point of view of the survivors, the party model by which the existing groups were being organized was unsatisfactory. As was the case in the American Zone, the survivors' tendency was to overcome differences between the parties and to establish a united Zionist organization. In the British Zone, however, this tendency was much stronger than elsewhere. Against the obstacles raised by British policy, the will to cooperate transcended the borders between Zionists and non-Zionists and counterbalanced party rivalries.[39]

The beginning of 1946 saw the establishment of the British Zone's branch of Noham (Noar Halutzi Meuhad: United Pioneer Youth)[40] and the Histadrut Zionit Ahidah, the purpose of which was to establish a central Zionist Committee for the British Zone. A general meeting was held, attended by large number of registered members, and a central Zionist committee was elected for the British Zone, composed of fifteen representatives of all the Zionist organizations, all of whom were prewar veteran Zionists.[41]

The Zionist Committee established various departments, and its first initiative was the distribution of the Zionist shekel (buying the shekel granted both membership and the right to vote). This illustrated the politics of unity. It was not a party shekel but a federal shekel for the British Zone, distributed not only among the DPs but also in the Jewish communities. Even the Revisionists, who at that time were still outside the World Zionist Organization, but would soon return, applied for participation in the shekel committee.[42]

Shortly afterward, the basis was established for a constitutional assembly and the election of a permanent committee and executive for the British Zone. Members in the executive were Rafael Olevsky, Nahum Gittler, Jacob Glanz, Sarah Levkovich (Sela Lefkovitch?), Avraham Manela, Yehiel Kurnitz, and David Rosenthal. In May 1946 there were already forty-five local Zionist chapters in the British Zone.[43]

In the meantime the *Yishuv* emissaries had arrived, and some of them were acting primarily on behalf of their respective parties or kibbutz movements.[44] The results were manifested in the violent election campaign preceding the Twenty-second Zionist Congress, in particular between the Revisionists (list no. 4) and the Histadrut Zionit Ahidah (list no. 1). The central leaders of the survivors—Rosensaft, Wollheim, Karl (Moritz?) Goldschmidt of Cologne, and David Rosenthal—

Zionist Party Politics

appeared as candidates of list no. 1, identified with the ruling Zionist party Mapai, headed by David Ben-Gurion, the JA's chairman.[45]

The party politics of the emissaries, however, could not combat the will for cooperation. The attitude of Kurt Lewin, head of the JA in the British Zone, illustrated this. Lewin, a member of Kibbutz Kfar Hamakkabi (of Mapai), was accused by another emissary of not attending to party politics. Lewin, he complained, permitted the PAI emissary, Mordechai Breuer, and the Hamizrahi emissary, Menahem Ehrlich, to have positions in the elementary school and the high school despite the fact that they were not Histadrut members.[46] This illustrates the deep gap between the common understanding of the *Yishuv* emissaries, who could only see the world through the glasses of party politics, and the situation in Belsen, which Lewin understood and acted in accord with. Moreover, unlike in the American Zone, where party politics brought by the emissaries won the upper hand, in the British Zone the survivors had their way. The very fact that Lewin acted as he did was no doubt a response to the prevalent view; furthermore, he was not the only emissary in the British Zone to act in this fashion.[47]

As already indicated, the election campaign and the following Zionist congress brought about a crisis among the survivors. The result was that they sought to gain strength by reestablishing the united front on a more solid basis—not only between the various Zionist parties, but also between Zionists and non-Zionists. The background for reunification on a pro-Zionist basis was further strengthened through the anticipation of steady aliyah schedules following the British announcement of operation "Grand National."[48]

In March 1947 a new Allgemeine Koordinatzie Block (General United Bloc) was formed to elect a new committee for Belsen. The bloc explicitly and formally represented the following parties: Agudath Israel, the Revisionists, Hashomer Hatza'ir, Hitahdut Hazionim Haklaliim (Association of General Zionists), Hamizrahi, Poale Zion (Z.S.-) Hitahdut, and Poale Zion (Left). The bloc's platform focused on *Eretz Yisrael* and called on the Jews in the camps to unite for the sake of immigration as the only possible solution. Indeed, a committee was elected, and without party quarrels, with the full cooperation of all concerned (even the Revisionists) and the active support of Kurt Lewin, it began to function smoothly in the British Zone.[49] Even the registration, in March 1947, of the first group for immigration in the "Grand National" operation, under the auspices of the JA Palestine Office, was handled without party politics, in full accord with the nonpartisan tendencies of the survivors. So, too, Lewin stood fast against any pressure from Palestine.[50]

The Shift from a Zionist to a General Nationalist Agenda

In the framework of a united national organization that was established at the Second Congress of the *She'erit Hapletah* in Bad Harzburg, the Zionist organization was a centrist group, acting mainly on behalf of aliyah. As already indicated, this was also the main—almost the only—concern of the JA representatives. Indeed, at first the general response and desire for aliyah was strong and enthusiastic.[51] Aliyah and general Zionist issues remained, as before, an integral part of the national agenda of the survivors' community at large. However, toward the end of 1947 exclusive devotion to Zionism was replaced by a more general viewpoint, and the CC increased its efforts to act on behalf of the Jews in Germany—regardless of whether they intended to remain in Germany or emigrate elsewhere. The British Zone's Second Congress (July 1947) marked a turning point in this direction and greatly influenced the active participation of the CC in furthering the Jewish communities' organization and its insistence on representing them. Moreover, the CC at this stage decided to accept the invitation to join the WJC, symbolizing its claim to represent the Jews in Germany without reference to their intentions or attitudes—similar to other branches of the WJC.[52] Even the desire for aliyah, which at the beginning of 1947 had been strengthened in view of the projected "Grand National" operation, deteriorated over the course of time.[53]

This shift was due to several factors that had a cumulative effect on the survivors: the previously mentioned party politics brought by the *Yishuv* emissaries; legal aliyah, which simplified the process of immigration;[54] recent immigrants' encounter with the problems of absorption and the resulting negative reports;[55] and the fact that in November 1947, the Zionist aim, with which all the survivors had always identified themselves as a matter of principle, was at last achieved. The survivors' loyalty and identification with the developments regarding Palestine was undivided and reached a second climax in the summer and fall of 1947, in the testimonies before UNSCOP, which paved the way for the UN partition resolution,[56] the *Exodus* affair, and the celebration of November 29, 1947.[57]

Of course, during the months that preceded the foundation of the State of Israel the CC called for enrollment in the Jewish armed forces in Palestine. It raised money to help the *Yishuv* and transformed the third anniversary of the Liberation Day, April 15, 1948, into a day of protest on behalf of the struggling *Yishuv*.[58] However, there were many expressions of bitterness on both sides, from both the survivors and the Zionist emissaries.[59] Moreover, one cannot avoid the fact that almost all the leaders—Rosensaft, Bimko, Wollheim, Rosenthal, Trepman, Laufer, and others—did not find their way to Israel.

12

END AND NEW BEGINNINGS

Emigration and Aliyah

Throughout the occupation years, the emigration of German Jews and DPs from Germany persisted on a small scale. After the UN decision of November 29, 1947, on the partition of Palestine, which was followed a few months later by new immigration regulations in the United States, the pace of emigration changed dramatically.[1] However, in the British Zone the situation was quite different.

OPERATION "GRAND NATIONAL"

Following their rejection of the Anglo-American Committee's recommendation, the British decided nevertheless to gradually get rid of their own DP problem. Toward the end of 1946 the government drafted a new plan for the immigration of Jewish DPs to Palestine, titled "Grand National." According to the plan, 375 of the 1,500 certificates allocated monthly were to be allocated for the British Zone. As for establishing which DPs were eligible to immigrate, the British authorities adopted the scale and categories recommended by the Anglo-American Committee. Only those who had received their DP status by June 1946 were eligible for registration, and the first priority was given to those who had already been in the camps by October 1945. Eligibility was classified as follows: Belsen inmates, with agricultural workers, construction workers and their relatives of first degree (spouses and children), and unaccompanied children (orphans) up to the age of twelve, received first priority. Youth and the elderly would be considered next, and the elderly only if they could prove that they had relatives able to support them.[2]

The decision was made in January 1947, to be implemented retroactively as of November 1946. A Selection Board representing the British DP department, the Jewish Agency, and the Jewish Relief Unit and chaired by the British representative conducted the selection process. The submission of candidates' lists for approval lay mainly in the hands of the JA. Every emigrant was allowed to take along personal property weighing up to 250 kilograms, provided it was for personal use and not for sale or exchange. A transit camp was established in Bocholt, close to the railway and the French border, and the selected candidates were transferred there, where the final formalities were dealt with. From there they would travel by train to the port of Marseilles in southern France.[3]

German Jews were not included in this program. Moreover, the Jews who in the course of time had left the camps to settle in German towns and did not return prior to the deadline of July 1, 1946, were also excluded. Apart from these conditions, there still remained the problem concerning children and youth above the age of twelve and that of the many single and in many cases ailing elderly survivors. On the other hand, the JA in the British Zone, having the responsibility of preparing the list of candidates, and as a member of the Selection Board, had quite a broad range of options. They could exercise their own scale of preferences within the formal regulations, and they could try to persuade the British to be more flexible in certain cases. The burden of organization, from the very first instance of registering through the actual transportation to the port, with shipping space secured on regular dates—all this was the responsibility of the JA. This may be illustrated in the case of the first transport.

In February 1947, having received the first allocation of certificates, the Palestine Office at Bergen-Belsen established an Aliyah Committee to represent the various Zionist "pioneer movements," namely, the political parties. Representation in the committee was to reflect the results of the elections at the Twenty-second Zionist Congress of December 1946. However, after protests and arguments it was agreed to slightly modify the key actually reached in the congress election and adjust it to match the percentage existing in the British Zone. Thus the Revisionists, who were quite numerous in Belsen, got their actual share, and the Agudah, which was not a member of the Zionist organization but maintained training facilities for potential immigrants among its members, was also represented. Kurt Lewin, who headed the JA in the British Zone, also limited the role of the political parties in another way. They could submit candidates for 75 percent of the workers' quota, but the other 25 percent were to be reserved for workers not belonging to any party. All other categories were also not handled by the Aliyah Committee.

The schedule for the months from December 1946 to March 1947 included 640 certificates, but for the first transport only 402 were actually processed. The committee completed the list, which included mainly those who were defined as agricultural and construction workers, many of them young singles, mostly members of kibbutzim, some 40 orphans from the Blankenese children's home, and a few invalids and elderly persons. This list was actually approved en bloc by the Selection Board. By the middle of March all the candidates were transferred to the Bocholt transit camp. On April 1, after hasty negotiations between the British and French authorities concerning the crossing of the border and passing through French territory, the train with 395 DPs on board left Bocholt. Escorted by UNRRA personnel and a British officer, the train headed to Forbach, in France. There all the passengers changed to a French train which the JA hired and which was financed by the Hebrew Immigrant Aid Society (HIAS). The Red Cross and HIAS also supplied the meals for the passengers. On the long journey to Marseilles the train stopped twice, in Metz and Lyons, where the passengers were honored by the local Jewish communities. Early on the morning of Friday, April 4, the train arrived in Marseilles and was received by the representatives of the JA, HIAS, and the Red Cross. Four hundred fourth-class berths had been secured by the JDC on the American Lloyd ship *Providence*, and the passengers immediately embarked after having their documents checked once again by French officials and by the British officer who had escorted the train.

April 4 was also the Passover eve, and the passengers, with the help of the welfare agencies, organized a Seder celebration. Originally it had been hoped that by then they would be celebrating their freedom in *Eretz Yisrael*, but due to initial difficulties in implementing the project there had been many delays. Nevertheless, the symbolism was there. Passover, commemorating the exodus of Israel from Egypt, was the day on which Belsen was liberated in 1945, and now—two years later—the first group of legal immigrants could celebrate their exodus from Germany. Spirits ran very high that night, and on the following day in the late afternoon the ship sailed for Haifa. The JA Absorption Division, headed by Giora Josephtal, planned to distribute the

End and New Beginnings

Farewell to immigrants departing for Palestine in the "Grand National" operation (Yad Vashem Photo-Archives [FA 187 356])

new immigrants to central reception facilities according to their affiliation with the various settlement movements. For other, unaffiliated immigrants, central reception houses were prepared for the transitional period in Bat-Galim (near Haifa), Hadera, and Tel-Aviv.[4]

By the time the first transport had left Belsen, the British, under pressure from the JA, relented concerning various requirements. The age limit for unaccompanied children was raised to fourteen, and later the ban was lifted on children aged fourteen to eighteen. The British also agreed to include people who lived outside the camps but had first-degree relatives in Palestine to join in emigration. Later, as the third transport was being organized, they permitted it to include immigrants from camps other then Belsen.[5]

Operation "Grand National" proceeded as scheduled from then on, with transports departing monthly from Bocholt. Until May 1948 some six thousand immigrants left the British Zone for Palestine.[6] However, behind these statistics the reality was much more complicated.

"Grand National" and Zionist Immigration Policy

During the spring and summer of 1947, the Palestine Office was working under pressure as hundreds of people sought to immigrate as soon as possible. The number of those who were considered appropriate under British regulations was, however, much smaller. Moreover, unofficially, and consistent with the traditional Zionist attitude regarding aliyah, the preferences of the JA placed additional limits on who could be considered a potential immigrant. First priority was allotted to those organized in the kibbutzim who had been trained in agriculture. However, not only were there few such candidates, but they were considered less prepared for the hardships awaiting them in Palestine than those who had risked themselves in illegal immigration. Over the course of time, complaints and acrimony arose between Belsen and Jerusalem regarding the poor profile of the arrivals, their state of health, and their nonconformity with basic absorption plans. The immigrants themselves were also very disappointed with their initial experiences in Palestine.[7]

In addition, shortly after the beginning of operation "Grand National," other countries—Canada and Norway, for example—came forward with offers to absorb Jewish DPs, and many then rushed to JDC and HIAS offices to register for emigration rather than aliyah.[8] This state of affairs had its repercussions on Zionist policy. Outwardly, JA officials continued to expand the range of potential immigrants from the British Zone. They persistently demanded from the British authorities the inclusion of town dwellers and German Jews in the schedule of emigrants, and eventually received such approval.[9] Confronted with the eager response of Jews who faced the possibility of immigration to Sweden or Canada, the JA tried (with no success) to secure the cooperation of the JDC and HIAS to mutually exclude applicants who double-registered.[10] Privately, however, JA officials had great doubts concerning the moral standards of these Jews, many of whom were black marketers and had little or no devotion to Zionism.[11] The JA officials also demanded that the American Zone be included in the schedules, but this was refused.[12] Thus they encouraged suitable candidates in the American Zone to smuggle themselves into the British Zone and then included them in their lists. This was possible due to the many DP identification cards left behind in Belsen by those who had earlier emigrated illegally.

This course of action was carried out with ever greater intensity following the UN partition plan of November 29, 1947. With the intensification of the armed conflict in Palestine and anticipation of full-scale war, greater efforts were made to include the maximum number of potential soldiers. Since the supply of young men in the British Zone was already long exhausted, recruits from the American Zone were sought. Despite the strict British prohibition against including potential soldiers in the immigration quotas, the Zionist authorities nonetheless managed to smuggle them in. As a result, only about half of the immigrants to Palestine in operation "Grand National"—some three thousand—were originally residents of the British Zone.[13]

"Journey's End"

Operation "Grand National" was maintained until the foundation of the State of Israel. With the end of the British Mandate in May 1948 and the establishment of Israel, sole authority concerning immigration was in the hands of the Israeli government. The British government, which at first did not recognize the new state, refused to permit the distribution of Israeli immigration certificates and barred aliyah from the British Zone. This policy, however, suited the aims of the JA and the new state, which preferred immigration from the American Zone because of its greater supply of young pioneers and soldiers.[14]

In November 1948 the British government finally recognized the State of Israel and as a consequence removed the ban on aliyah, except for young and healthy single males, namely, potential soldiers. The reasoning behind this was the ongoing state of war in Israel. The British also continued to give priority to the DPs, this time including the *Exodus* passengers who were still in their zone (some 1,500 out of the original 4,000, the rest having managed to infiltrate into the American Zone). Early in 1949, aliyah from the British Zone was resumed and some 2,500 DPs, including the remaining *Exodus* passengers, immigrated to Israel. The British named this operation "Journey's End."[15]

Immigration to Other Countries

Due to limited possibilities of aliyah, and contrary to the JA's political view, emigration from the British Zone to countries other than Palestine existed throughout this period, even parallel to operation "Grand

National." Following President Truman's directive on Christmas Eve 1945 regarding immigration of DPs who had been persecuted by the Nazis, approximately 9,700 Jewish DPs emigrated from Germany to the United States between May 1946 and December 1947 through the port of Bremen.[16] Apart from this, there was a constant movement of Jews entering other countries. For example, 100 DPs left during November 1947 for Sweden, England, Rhodesia, Australia, the United States, and France.[17]

With the end of operation "Grand National," the Jewish DP population of the British Zone consisted of some 7,000 living in camps and 4,500 in towns.[18] A few months later the gates to the United States were opened wider for the DPs through the Immigration Act of 1948. By now immigration to the United States competed fiercely with aliyah. This reflected both the DPs' reluctance to enter a country at war and the Israeli authorities' decision to withhold immigration permits from those unsuited for participation in the war effort. Thousands of DPs and German Jews applied to immigrate to the United States, as well as England and many other countries.[19] In May 1949 only 4,500 DPs were left in the British Zone, including 500 of the *Exodus* passengers.[20] In any event, the feeling that there was an end in sight reigned throughout the British Zone after the fall of 1948.

Closing the Bergen-Belsen DP Camp

Rumors regarding the British intention to close Bergen-Belsen due to the rapid departure of its inhabitants spread, and by June 1948 they were already a source of great concern. The rumors suggested that the British were quickly transferring the remaining Jews to a smaller camp in order to use Hohne (as the British continued to refer to Belsen) either for military needs or to accommodate Polish DPs there.[21] However, the alleged plan was postponed, and in anticipation of a wave of emigration to Israel in the fall of 1948 the British decided to use Belsen as a transit camp and to concentrate there all the prospective immigrants, including the *Exodus* passengers.[22]

Belsen once again served as a Jewish center, this time to accommodate all the candidates for emigration through the process of registration and preparing for the journey. Accordingly, despite the ongoing diminishing of tasks for the CC and its membership due to the emigration of its members, the CC not only did not cease to function, but adapted to its new role by concentrating on organizing aliyah. Indeed, it was anticipated that most the DPs would immigrate to Israel. However, Rosensaft, in line with his traditional claim to represent all the Jews in the Zone, insisted that the CC would control the entire process of emigration without discriminating against immigrants to countries other than Israel.[23]

Was it possible that Rosensaft already knew by then that he himself, as well as many of his colleagues, would not immigrate to Israel, thereby refuting their own long-conducted campaign for aliyah? It is a difficult question to answer. Just recently a close friend and member of the CC, Paul Trepman, was almost banned because rather than registering for aliyah and military service, he announced that he was going to America (this was because his fiancée's eye illness could receive the proper treatment only in America).[24] It might, however, be that Rosensaft acted purely out of a sense of responsibility. He and Wollheim still had work to carry out, and it would be almost an additional two years before both of them would leave Germany—this despite the fact that most other members of the CC left either for Israel (like Dov Laufer and Rafael Olevsky) or for the United States (like David Rosenthal and Israel Moshe Olevsky).[25]

Along with the departure of most of the DPs, toward the middle of 1949 the JDC gradually liquidated most of its activities in the British Zone, leaving the issue of emigration to the HIAS. On the other hand, the JRU regarded caring for the communities as an important task to be pursued further.[26] The JA also began to close down its activities. In July 1949 it announced that organized immigration would cease by August 1949, warning those who still hesitated to act. The official closing of the JA offices in Germany was to follow in September 1950.[27]

From May 1949 the British authorities renewed their efforts to clear Bergen-Belsen, transferring the rest of its Jewish residents to a smaller camp. However, more than half a year elapsed before this was realized, mainly due to the fear of Jewish resistance. In May 1950 the remaining Jews, including Rosensaft, were transferred to Jever (Upjever), in Friesland, close to the Dutch border. Jever continued to function as the last remaining camp in the British Zone. In April 1951 there were still seven hundred Jews living there. In August 1951 it was at last closed after the emigration of most of them and the hospitalization of the sick who could not emigrate.[28]

New Beginnings

Jews in Germany after Liquidation

German Jews also immigrated, mainly to America. This process was accelerated after the American Immigration Act of 1948 and continued on a small scale throughout 1950. Nevertheless, the membership of the Jewish communities was not reduced, since German Jews were replaced by the DPs who joined the communities. It should be noted, however, that even then the average percent of DPs who were now members did not exceed 32 percent, and in some of the communities (for example, Hanover) the membership was still exclusively German Jews. The number of Jews living in the main communities was about 14,000: 7,000 in Berlin and 3,500 each in the British and the American Zones.[29] It now became evident to all that the Jewish community in Germany would continue into the future.[30]

The founding of the German Federal Republic in May 1949 was the turning point that evoked negotiations concerning the future of the Jewish community. On September 1, 1949, Harry Greenstein, the adviser on Jewish affairs in the American Zone, called a conference on "The Future of the Jews in Germany." He had two primary objectives: first, to bring together the representatives of the Jewish communities and of the major local and international Jewish organizations in Germany; and second, to lay the foundation for coordinating the work of all the interested parties and organizations concerned with the welfare of the Jews in Germany. Greenstein emphasized the need to concentrate on the practical issues rather than on the complicated ideological or moral questions regarding the future relations between Germans and Jews, and he announced that the most important outcome of the conference would be to establish an overall Jewish organization that "will make it possible for us to plan together for all of the Jews in Germany." Planning together became vital in anticipation for the future solutions regarding restitution and the role of the Jewish communities vis-à-vis the German government on the one hand and the Jewish world community on the other.[31]

The participants at the conference included representatives of the provisional central organization of the Jews in Germany in Stuttgart and some of the Jewish communities and regional organizations in all three zones of occupation. In addition, the Central Committees of the British and American Zones were represented. The major world Jewish organizations also participated: the World Jewish Congress, B'nai B'rith, the Jewish Restitution Successor Organization, ORT, and the

Jewish Agency for Palestine. American Jewish organizations in attendance included the American Jewish Committee, the JDC, the Central Orthodox Committee, and HIAS, as well as the adviser on Jewish affairs. British Jewish organizations were represented only by the Jewish Committee for Relief Abroad and the JRU. The non-Jewish representatives included the American OMGUS (Official Military Government of the United States) Education and Religious Affairs Section and a few German newspapers.[32] As can be noted, in comparison with the American Zone the British representation was small. However, the communities of the British Zone were considered more stabilized in terms of integration within the German economy and were a model for the future because they, unlike the Jewish communities in the American Zone, were all affiliated with the CC.[33]

The discussions at the conference reflected how crucial the Jewish presence in Germany was considered by all the participants.[34] Those who supported the future development of the Jewish community in Germany included the American high commissioner in Germany, John J. McCloy, German Jews, and some of the representatives of world Jewish organizations. Among them were Rabbi Isaac Klein of the Synagogue Council of America, who acted as liaison representative for education and religious matters in OMGUS, and Rabbi Dr. Joachim Prinz, who had escaped from Germany to America before the war and spoke on behalf of the WJC. They noted that the Jewish community of Germany was now a reality and as such had to be supported. The very continuity of a Jewish community would symbolize the ultimate victory over Hitler and his vicious program to exterminate the Jews of Germany. It was therefore essential to assist the Jews in Germany, who would be unable to develop a strong Jewish cultural and religious community on their own. The development of such a community would reflect and testify to the survival of Jewish will and honor. Through its relations with German society and the process of its integration in the new Germany, it would also "be one of the real touchstones and the test of Germany's progress towards the light."[35]

Those who were skeptical concerning the future of Jews in Germany or who rejected it altogether on a matter of principle included mainly the representatives of the Central Committees (Rosensaft and Wollheim of the British Zone and Piekatsch of the American Zone) and the JA and Israeli representatives. They argued that there was no place for Jews in Germany, that Jews should live in Israel and thus demonstrate the victory over anti-Semitism and Nazism, that there was no hope for an immediate improvement in the German attitude toward the Jews, and that the initiative for Germany's opening a new page in history lay entirely with the Germans.

There was, however, one crucial practical issue that demanded an immediate response and action: restitution and compensation. Now that the Federal Republic had to take responsibility for this matter, the question of Jewish representation and negotiation vis-à-vis the German government demanded the settlement of differences between the Jewish organizations and bodies. Thus the common interest shared by all the participants was to lay a basis for an overall organization of the Jews in Germany that would participate in the Jewish-German negotiations and future arrangements. Accordingly, the conference elected a committee that would prepare the overall organization. The committee included not only representatives of the communities of Berlin and the three Western Zones but also members of the Central Committees of the American and British Zones. It was chaired by Dr. Eliyahu Livneh, the Israeli consul. Jewish presence in Germany was now officially legitimized, and the way was opened for the establishment of the Central Council of the Jews in Germany.[36]

Conclusion: The *She'erit Hapletah* and Jewish Nationalism in the Post-Holocaust Era

The years of the mid–twentieth century were a dramatic turning points in Jewish history, encompassing both the horrific destruction of European Jewry on the one hand and the establishment of the State of Israel on the other. Discerning the extent to which these dramatic events were related has fed many historiography discussions. Still, the deep transitions in Jewish history after the Holocaust were much more complex and multifaceted than the argument regarding the ostensibly direct relationship between the Holocaust and the establishment of the State of Israel seems to imply.

The concept of the *She'erit Hapletah* refers to Holocaust survivors in general, but it focuses specifically on those survivors who, having been forced by postwar conditions to stay in DP camps, became an ex-territorial immigrant population. It is not only what they had experienced in the Holocaust. It also relates to the postwar conditions they were living in—lacking any control over their fate and destiny, living in difficult conditions, in a deadlocked trap, a small enclave cut off to a large extent from the external world in detested Germany, exposed to anti-Semitic taunts by German and other nationalities so that they were deeply vulnerable and easily demoralized.

The study of the *She'erit Hapletah* has attracted the attention of historians in Israel and elsewhere, both because of its unique location at the crossroads between the Holocaust and the establishment of the State of Israel and because of the role Holocaust survivors played in the political struggle of the Zionist movement and in the international arena.

It seems that current research literature contains two contradictory arguments: first, that the survivors were a group of people who were caught up in an impossible situation, wishing to emigrate and leave the camps, but in fact trapped and used or manipulated as an instrument in the Zionist struggle; or second, that the survivors were a group of people who learned the "Holocaust lesson," developed accordingly a Zionist ideology, and actively joined the Zionist struggle, thus seeing themselves as living symbols of the miraculous transition "from Holocaust to revival."[1] Studying individuals and public life in the DP camps themselves provides an alternative thesis: that the national leanings of the *She'erit Hapletah* were neither a manipulative effort by external forces nor a constructed ideology, but rather a spontaneous creation born in, and in the context of, the issues, experiences, and struggles within and in relation to the camps themselves. This national leaning might be termed a "functional Zionism" that the survivors used, discovered, interpreted, and implemented as a renewed kind of Zionism in the context of their own experiences and struggles.

Life in the camps became a greenhouse for a new Jewish national identity. As a result of the living conditions in the camps, the survivors' lives were highly cohesive. These conditions called for the formation of a shared public life while providing a unique setting for a new discourse. Lacking any previously accepted organization styles, agreed-upon norms, codes, or behavioral habits, they had to create and negotiate these among themselves. The survivors' sole common ground was their past and present difficult experiences and their deep desire to achieve, once again, a free, normal life. Here, then, developed a unique paradigm of public Jewish life, one that had to dictate to itself new or renewed norms and values, and which struggled to crystallize and achieve a common goal.

The detailed analysis of the survivors' activities unveils the various mechanisms involved in the formation of such a "community in transition." Through their mutual experiences—and not only in relation to their Holocaust experience, or as a direct outcome of a deliberate efforts made by the Zionist movement—they began a process of shaping and experimenting with a new complex, post-Holocaust, Jewish national identity. Hence, exploring everyday life and examining the *She'erit Hapletah* from "within," from the "bottom," in the DP camps themselves and in the developing communities in Germany after the war enables us to evaluate from a different perspective the role and position the survivors occupied in shaping a new or renewed Jewish national identity. We can then understand how, following the Holocaust, despite the terrifying experiences and despite the harsh conditions of the camps, the survivors' rehabilitation and integration was generally a success story.

Conclusion

Our study is a case study, and indeed Bergen-Belsen was one of a kind due to its size, its socio-demographic composition, and its centrality within the British Zone, which differed radically from the American Zone, where most of the DPs were concentrated. Still, the processes generated in this camp exemplify the unique situation of the Jewish survivors-DPs-immigrants after the Holocaust. While they lived without an inviting absorbing society, their personal rehabilitation processes were inseparably combined with the formation of a new society—struggling both for its collective identity and for its members' rehabilitation. The various activities, institutions, and organizations and the formation of economical, political, social, educational, religious, and cultural systems and of a "culture of memory" were inseparably interwoven with many conflicts and struggles that accompanied the development of new internal and external, Jewish and non-Jewish, channels of communication.

We should note that it was precisely the difficult conditions of life in the barracks that produced various initiatives and improvisations. In contrast to the widely accepted stereotypical images of the devastating consequences of the Holocaust, and of the welfare-dependent life with its forced or willful idleness and black market, there were also other aspects to life in the camp. In time people succeeded in making their dwellings look more like normal residential flats, and many of them succeeded in obtaining a profitable employment and accumulating some property. In addition, much vocational training was carried out, which served as a basis for future employment.

The most important incentive to emerge out of the despair and deep depression and loss was establishing new families—compensation for the loss of relatives and families in the Holocaust. Family life became a vital basis for physical and mental rehabilitation. Struggling with Holocaust traumas was postponed for days to come, as we later learned. There was neither the time nor the human resources for dealing directly with the terrible traumatic experiences of the Holocaust. Moreover, according to the social norms of the time—though not necessarily the effective one—the best way to open a new page in life was covering up, ignoring, and hiding difficulties.

Specifically, I would like to point to the centrality of the children—children who came as some consolation, some replacement for the million and half Jewish children murdered in the Holocaust. Raising children reflects the combination of individual and collective aspects of life in the camp. These children were not only a source of personal joy for their parents, but also became the center of the camp's social and public life. Around them and their families the whole social and cultural system was built.

Every day's life in its public expressions, the intensive literary and theatrical activities, reveals the will to commemorate and preserve the Holocaust memory, along with the desire to revive the former vital Jewish culture and tradition, combined with the aspiration to establish a new Jewish national sovereignty in Palestine. Among the many DPs there were a number of outstanding thinkers, both Orthodox and liberal, occupied with the attempt to explain the disaster that had befallen the Jewish people and to draw conclusions as to the meaning and mission of being Jewish thereafter. These people took an active part in the leadership, and they also wrote intensively, created, and expressed their thinking in many forms—in newspapers, in the realm of education, and in their cultural performance and political activity. Their lessons found a fertile ground among their fellow survivors, who longed for some form of self-respect, meaning, and a sense of belonging within their empty and meaningless existence as DPs.

Much emphasis in cultural and social life was put on the Zionist-nationalistic aspects, but this was not as an antithesis to traditional Jewish culture. It was carried out in a unique new version that tried to integrate them. Hence, in contrast to common images that relate the "Holocaust lesson" with antagonistic attitudes toward religion, religious life in the camp had a prestigious status. Rabbis actively participated in the leadership of the camp and of the British Zone at large, and throughout the camp could be felt spontaneous yearning for Jewish religious traditions, which could be seen as a link in a long Jewish chain. Thus, in spite of disagreements, many possibilities were found and played out in the course of time, as most residents wished for a public life that would have a "Jewish" character. On the other hand, previously anti-Zionist ultra-Orthodox inhabitants wished in the context of the new special circumstances to become an integral part of the national body. This was manifested in their active participation in both the organizing committee and in cultural and educational life. This does not mean that everything was smooth and agreed-upon, for there were many antagonisms and difficulties. However, the shared desire to construct some form of Jewish respectful existence in the present and for the future overcame to a certain degree these difficulties.

Political orientations and affiliations served as a social cohesive glue bringing people together who formed groups that debated and

Conclusion

struggled with each other. Recent historiography often deals with the question of the politicization among the *She'erit Hapletah* and emphasizes its radical, even grotesque aspects. The evaluation of these aspects of life in the camp is basically negative. The only question usually asked regards who is to be blamed. Was it the political tradition of Polish Jewry, or the import of the *Briha* groups and of the children's homes organized according to differing political orientations, or perhaps the emissaries from Palestine who came to the camp on behalf of diverse political movements?

It seems that we can analyze this matter from a totally different perspective, essentially positive. The political activities in the camp served as an important vehicle for creating an intimate and defining framework, separated and contrasted with other such frameworks. These political settings were a crucial sociocultural space for nourishing an active involvement in public life, for building genuine motivation in the survivors to hold to an important cause, and thus for acquiring a renewed sense of belonging, of feeling they were once again, despite everything, masters of their destiny and heading forward, toward the future.

Hence this civil society grew from the bottom up. It started with individuals who were developing their families. But these individuals were searching to become involved in something that would go beyond a basic personal identification. In this sense they yearned to belong to a wider worldview, and the political parties could supply this. The enthusiastic political activities, with their separatist inclinations, were in this context a positive factor in the process of developing a new shared public life. It was precisely the clear and salient identity given by the political activities and debates that gave some color and meaning to the individuals, each in his or her group, and which deeply fermented public life in the camp. This intensive schismatic activity created a form of national consensus in the camps and pushed to the margins the "non-belonging" groups (such as the Bund), excluding them from the *She'erit Hapletah* as an exclusive group. Alternatively, this same process pulled toward the inside whoever stood in the past at a certain distance, such as Agudath Israel. Inside this evolving national consensus—Jewish and Zionist alike—the excluding, separatist system served as a life elixir.

All these processes had a direct impact on the shaping of life and leadership in the camp. The vast political activity could take place and become a permanent part of the camp's public life, thanks to a leadership that took the initiative at the beginning and then continued it throughout the existence of the camp community.

The rehabilitation mechanisms, combined with a tough British policy, formed the centralized organization of the DP community. The paradoxical outcome of the British policy was that Jews had no choice but to become organized in a national and militant fashion, assisted and backed by world Jewish organizations. The Jews related their struggle to improve their living conditions (and their demand to be released from their new trap) to a more general Jewish struggle for national recognition. This linkage was ipso facto tied up with the struggle with the British on the other front—the British Mandate in Palestine. The organizational constellation in the camp, which made Zionism the center of political activity, was based on the obvious functional advantages of Zionism at that time. Zionism was the only political agent that could supply an operational, ready-made organizational and ideological paradigm, some hope for the future, and a cause worth fighting for. No wonder, then, that the leadership which emerged right at the beginning and persisted throughout the camp period consisted mainly of young Holocaust survivors who were former political activists, mostly in Zionist organizations. The personal and functional makeup of the committee can be characterized by three aspects: a Zionist bent open to collaboration with non-Zionists; pluralism, which meant participation of all ethnic, political, and religious groups, including German Jews; and a broad concept of both its roles and representational scope, including Jewish groups and communities outside the camp.

The educational system in Bergen-Belsen illustrates the dynamics of shaping national consensus. The atmosphere in most of the educational institutions was nationalistic. The most dominant and determining factor in its operation was the survivors themselves, led by the Central Committee and enjoying the cooperation of external organizations in fostering a Zionist atmosphere. The group of emissaries from Palestine arrived in Belsen only after most institutions were already at the peak of their activities. Representatives of the JDC provided basic equipment and agents of JRU provided professional and organizational skills, alongside much active support in the Zionist mode of the educational system. This Zionist bent of the external organizations was the outcome not only of the fact that even the emissaries of non-Zionist organizations happened to personally be Zionists, but also from the fact that these organizations recognized the functional importance of

Conclusion

the national spirit as a mechanism for elevating the DPs' morale and preparing them for the future.

An overall Jewish collaboration in the Zionist struggle became inseparably mixed up with participation in the struggle for British recognition of the Central Committee as the representative political leadership of the DPs, a struggle that was greatly supported by Colonel Solomon, the special adviser for Jewish matters of the British occupation headquarters. It seems, then, that the *She'erit Hapletah* had an active role in the creation of a pro-Zionist cooperation among the entire Jewish public in the free world in these years.

One of the most interesting phenomena in the organizational processes of the camp community in the British Zone was the reciprocation and collaboration that took place between the DPs and the local Jewish communities organizations. We have already pointed at some of the special circumstances of this zone that stimulated this cooperation and helped to establish it on a national, even militant basis: the British policy, the funneling power of the Central Committee in Bergen-Belsen, its stable population, and its living together in comparison to the scattering, mobility, and multiplicity that characterized the American Zone.

These circumstances were relevant not only for the camp community but also to the renewing local Jewish communities, in spite of the fact that in many respects there were many differences between them and the DPs. The relatively large Jewish communities in the British Zone—Hamburg, Cologne, Düsseldorf, and Hanover—were all established by Jews of German origin who had been hidden or returned from the concentration camps. This fact left its special mark on their character. They were an aging and ill population of people who had married Gentiles and had been in their past remote from Judaism. They could hardly think of the possibility of emigrating and building a Jewish life elsewhere. Nevertheless—and perhaps as a consequence—in building these communities they were wishing for some sort of a new Jewish identity that would relate to their vanished, extinct Jewish past and give them some continuity with that past. Their leaders understood that their ability to provide an answer to the complex needs involved in building a new Jewish life in Germany was dependent to a large extent on their integration with the overall national Jewish organizations, both in the local and international contexts. Thus, at the beginning of 1946 the Jews of the British Zone started to organize on the basis of regional states, which soon after turned into the parent organization of the entire British Zone, in cooperation with the Central Committee. At the same time, they acted under the banner of a Zionist-nationalistic struggle alongside their struggle for international recognition of the local Jewish community in Germany. The issue of the future of Jews in Germany turned thus into an integral part of the Central Committee's agenda. The process of organizing the communities became interwoven with the Zionist organization, and even with protests aimed at expressing solidarity with the struggle to open the gates of Palestine.

It is thus no coincidence that the Jewish communities of the British Zone were the ones that created the foundations for the establishment of the Central Council of the Jews in Germany, established in 1950; that their leaders became the leaders of this council; and that the periodical founded in Düsseldorf in 1946 became the journal of German Jewry, the *Allgemeine Wochenzeitung der Juden in Deutschland*. The founding editor, Karl Marx, who served as an editor for many years, struggled with the question of the essence of his Judaism. German Jews and DPs, local leaders and thinkers from abroad, German Jews living outside of Germany and German spiritual figures—all participated in a Jewish national discourse and in lively ongoing discussions carried out on the pages of his journal. The new concept of Jewish nationalism in Germany struggling for its existence and participating in the post-Holocaust Jewish entity began to be discussed in this journal.

It is possible to define as "nationalistic" the various active responses of these Holocaust survivors to the situation in which they found themselves, a condition they described as "liberated—but not free." Their heritage as Holocaust survivors was indeed a starting point, but their Zionistic moves were a spontaneous response to the new circumstances, not imposed and manipulated from the outside. This response developed into a major axis point while they confronted and struggled with myriad obstacles on their road to freedom. It grew from the inside and received much encouragement and collaborations by many Jewish organizations sharing a pro-Zionist consensus in the wake of the Holocaust. The struggle for freedom was identified and closely combined with the Zionist struggle for Jewish sovereignty in Palestine.

This was true to a large extent of all Jewish DP communities in central Europe. However, it is reasonable to assume that in the British

Conclusion

Zone in Germany it was particularly noticeable due to the special circumstances and because Britain stood as an obstacle to the Jewish cause on all fronts at once. It is thus possible that in the British Zone, more than in the American Zone, there was much collaboration between the various Zionist parties, between Zionists and non-Zionists, and between the DPs and the communities of German Jews.

Our study pinpoints the development of a new or renewed Jewish sociopolitical life. It is precisely there, in the DP camps, lacking an absorption society, that the rehabilitation process of the survivors as individuals was interwoven with the formation of a new society struggling over its national existence. It shows that the educational system served as a meeting point for discussing and crystallizing a new Jewish national discourse implicitly and explicitly radiated by the *She'erit Hapletah*. It reveals the formation of a Jewish nationalistic culture tied both with the Holocaust memory and with nationalistic lessons, and at that hour it conjoined with the struggle of all Jews for a national independent state.

The Zionism of the *She'erit Hapletah* was shaped, then, by continuous restriction on the survivors. It was strengthened in reaction to the many hindrances placed in their way to freedom, and it found much encouragement in the pro-Zionist consensus in the Jewish world in the post-Holocaust era. The distress of the *She'erit Hapletah* stood at the center of this affinity, and the *She'erit Hapletah* stood at the center of the formation of a new Jewish national identity—with its main focal point embodied in itself, its fate and struggle. The *She'erit Hapletah* embodied both the horrors of the Holocaust and the challenges toward which the discourse concerning the future of the Jewish people was directed. It became a nerve center, and through it and in relation to it the new contours of Jewish identity were defined—with the active input and participation of the Holocaust survivors themselves in this evolving process. In this sense the DP camps served as an active meeting place of national solidarity despite many differences—a unprecedented phenomenon in Jewish history.

When the gates were opened and the DPs were released, many found their way to Palestine. Many others—among them Bergen-Belsen's leaders, including Rosensaft, Wollheim, Rosenthal, Laufer, Trepman, and Bloch—built their future in North America. This does not change the fact that as long as the DP community was living in Bergen-Belsen it existed as a national Zionist community, and that

Conclusion

in and through its existence new meanings and mechanisms of Jewish national identity were formed. As time went by it also became apparent that after the Zionist struggle was over, after the establishment of the State of Israel, the new Jewish nationalism would be shaped so that its boundaries stretched well beyond living within or identifying with the new Jewish state.

Notes

Abbreviations

AGH	Archiv der jüdischen Gemeinde Hannover, Hanover
BD	Board of Deputies of British Jews
BDA	Board of Deputies of British Jews Archives, London
CBF	Central British Fund for Jewish Relief and Rehabilitation
CZA	Central Zionist Archives
GJA	Givat Joint Archives, Jerusalem
Henriques	Rose Henriques Collection
HL	Hartley Library at the University of Southampton, Special Collection Division
IWM	Imperial War Museum, London
JC	*Jewish Chronicle*
JTA	Jewish Telegraphic Agency
OHD	Oral History Division, Institute of Contemporary Jewry, The Hebrew University of Jerusalem
PALCOR	Palestine Correspondence
PRO, FO	Public Record Office, London, Foreign Office files
WLTA	Wiener Library Tel Aviv
WLL	Wiener Library London
YV	Yad Vashem Archives, Jerusalem
ZAH	Zentralarchiv zur Erforschung der Geschichte der Juden in Deutschland, Heidelberg

Preface

1. Leonard Dinnerstein, *America and the Survivors of the Holocaust* (New

York, 1982); Wolfgang Jacobmeyer, "Jüdische Überlebende als Displaced Persons. Untersuchungen zur Besatzungspolitik in den deutschen Westzonen und zur Zuwanderung osteuropäischer Juden 1945–1947," *Geschichte und Gesellschaft* 9, no. 3 (1983): 421–52; Arieh J. Kochavi, *Displaced Persons and International Politics: Britain and the Jewish Displaced Persons after the Second World War* (Tel Aviv, 1992) [Hebrew]; Angelika Königseder, *Flucht nach Berlin. Jüdische Displaced Persons 1945–1948* (Berlin, 1998); Michael Marrus, *The Unwanted. European Refugees in the Twentieth Century* (New York and Oxford, 1985).

2. Yehuda Bauer, *Out of the Ashes* (Oxford, 1989); Julius Carlebach, "Flight into action as a method of repression. American military rabbis and the problem of Jewish DPs," *Jewish Studies Quarterly* 2, no. 1 (1995): 59–76; Alex Grobman, *Rekindling the Flame. American Jewish Chaplains and the Survivors of the European Jewry 1944–1948* (Detroit, 1993); Irit Keynan, *Holocaust Survivors and the Emissaries from Eretz-Israel: Germany 1945–1948* (Tel Aviv, 1996) [Hebrew]; Roland Webster, "American Relief and Jews in Germany, 1945–1960. Diverging Perspectives," *Leo Baeck Institute Year Book* 38 (1993): 293–321.

3. Angelika Eder, "Jüdische Displaced Persons im deutschen Alltag," in *Überlebt und Unterwegs. Jüdische Displaced Persons in Nachkriegsdeutschland*, ed. Jacqueline Giere (Frankfurt a.M., 1997), 163–87; Atina Grossmann, "Trauma, Memory and Motherhood: Germans and Jewish Displaced Persons in Post-Nazi Germany, 1945–1949," *Archiv für Sozialgeschichte* (1998): 215–41; Rodney Livingstone, "Germans and Jews since 1945," *Patterns of Prejudice* 19, no. 2–3 (1995): 45–59; Edith Raim, "1946: der "Aufruhr" von Landsberg. US-Besatzungsmacht und deutsche Bevölkerung gemeinsam gegen jüdische DPs," *Tribüne* 128 (1993): 153–62; Frank Stern, *The Whitewashing of the Yellow Badge: Antisemitism and Philosemitism in Postwar Germany* (Oxford, 1992); idem, "The Historic Triangle: Occupiers, Germans and Jews in Postwar Germany," *Tel Aviver Jahrbuch* 19 (1990): 47–76; idem, "Im Anfang war Auschwitz. Besatzer, Deutsche und Juden in der Nachkriegszeit," *Dachauer Hefte* 6 (1990): 25–42; idem, "Wider Antisemitismus—für christlich-jüdische Zusammenarbeit. Aus der Entstehungszeit der Gesellschaften und des Koordinierungsrats," *Menora* 3 (1992): 182–209; idem, "Antisemitismus und Philosemitismus in der politischen Kultur der entstehenden Bundesrepublik Deutschland," in *Aufbau nach dem Untergang. Deutsch-jüdische Geschichte nach 1945. In Memoriam Heinz Galinski*, ed. Andreas Nachama and Julius H. Schoeps (Berlin, 1992), 150–63; idem, "German-Jewish Relations in the Postwar Period: the Ambiguities of Antisemitic and Philosemitic Discourse," in *Jews, Germans, Memory: Reconstruction of Jewish Life in Germany*, ed. Y. Michal Bodemann (Ann Arbor, 1996), 77–98.

4. Thomas Albrich, *Exodus Durch Österreich - jüdische Flüchtlinge 1945–1948* (Innsbruck, 1987); idem, "Way Station of Exodus: Jewish Dis-

placed Persons and refugees in Postwar Austria," in *The Holocaust and History. The Known, the Unknown, the Disputed, and the Reexamined*, ed. Michael Berenbaum and Abraham J. Peck (Bloomington, 1998), 716–32; David Engel, *Between Liberation and Flight. Holocaust Survivors in Poland and the Struggle for Leadership, 1944–1946* (Tel Aviv, 1996) [Hebrew]; William B. Helmreich, *Against All Odds* (New York, 1992); Hanna Yablonka, *Foreign Brethren: Holocaust Survivors in the State of Israel, 1948–1952* (Jerusalem, 1994) [Hebrew]; Idith Zertal, *From Catastrophe to Power: Holocaust Survivors and the Emergence of Israel* (Berkeley, 1998).

5. Toby Blum-Dobkin, "Rituals of Transition: An Ethnographic Approach to Life in a Displaced Persons Camp," in *The Netherlands and Nazi Genocide, Papers of the 21st Annual Scholars' Conference*, ed. G. Jan Colijn and Marcia S. Littell (Lewiston/Queenston/Lampeter, 1992), 489–500; Michael Brenner, *After the Holocaust. Rebuilding Jewish Lives in Postwar Germany* (Princeton, 1997); Jacqueline D. Giere, "'Wir sind unterwegs, aber nicht in der Wüste.' Erziehung und Kultur in den jüdischen Displaced Persons Lagern der amerikanischen Zone im Nachkriegsdeutschland 1945–1949" (Ph.D. thesis, Frankfurt a.M., 1993); idem, "Kulturelles Vermächtnis und kulturelle Selbstverständigung. Die Lager der jüdischen Displaced Persons im besetzten Deutschland," in *Im Schatten des Holocaust. Jüdisches Leben in Niedersachsen nach 1945*, ed. Herbert Obenaus (Hanover, 1997), 119–30; idem, "We're on Our Way, but Not in the Wilderness," in *The Holocaust and History*, 699–715; Wolfgang Jacobmeyer, "Die Lager der jüdischen Displaced Persons in den deutschen Westzonen 1946/47 als Ort jüdischer Selbstvergewisserung," in *Jüdisches Leben in Deutschland nach 1945*, ed. Micha Brumlik (Frankfurt a.M., 1986), 31–48; Königseder, *Flucht nach Berlin*; Angelika Königseder and Juliane Wetzel, *Lebensmut im Wartesaal. Die jüdischen DPs (Displaced Persons) im Nachkriegsdeutschland* (Frankfurt a.M., 1994); Cilly Kugelmann, "The identity and Ideology of Jewish Displaced Persons," in *Jews, Germans, Memory*, 65–76; Ze'ev Mankowitz, "The Politics and Ideology of Survivors of the Holocaust in the American Zone of Occupied Germany 1945–1946" (Ph.D. thesis, The Hebrew University of Jerusalem, 1987) [Hebrew]; idem, "The Formation of *She'erit Hapleita*: November 1944–July 1945," *Yad Vashem Studies* 20 (1990): 337–70; idem, "The Affirmation of Life in the She'erith Hapletah," *Holocaust and Genocide Studies* 5, No. 1 (1990: 13–22; Abraham J. Peck, "Jewish Survivors of the Holocaust in Germany: Revolutionary Vanguard or Remnants of a Destroyed People?" *Tel Aviver Jahrbuch* 19 (1990): 33–45; idem, "'Unsere Augen haben die Ewigkeit gesehen.' Erinnerung und Identität der *She'erit Hapletah*," in *Überlebt und Unterwegs*, 27–49; Angelika Schardt, "'Der Rest der Geretteten.' Jüdische Überlebende im DP-Lager Föhrenwald 1945–1957," *Dachauer Hefte* 8 (1992): 53–68; Judith Tydor Baumel, "The Politics of Spiritual Rehabilitation in the DP Camps," *Simon Wiesen-*

tal Center Annual 6 (1989): 57–79; idem, "Kibbutz Buchenwald: The establishment of the first *Hachsharah*," *YIVO Annual of Jewish Social Science* 23 (1996): 445–73; idem, "Kibbutz Buchenwald and Kibbutz Hafetz Hayyim: Two Experiments in the Rehabilitation of Jewish Survivors in Germany," *Holocaust and Genocide Studies* 9, no. 2 (1995): 231–249; Nicholas Yantian, "Studien zum Selbstverständnis der jüdischen 'Displaced Persons' in Deutschland nach dem Zweiten Weltkrieg" (M.A. thesis, Berlin, 1994); idem, "'Aus der Versteinerung heraustreten'— Das 'Kazet-Theater' im jüdischen 'Displaced Persons'-Lager Bergen-Belsen, 1945–1947," in *Im Schatten des Holocaust*, 131–63.

6. Hagit Lavsky, "'She'erit Hapletah' - Object or Subject of History? New Directions in Historical Research," *Yahadut Zemanenu*, 6 (1990): 25–43 [Hebrew]; Dan Diner, "Elemente der Subjektwerdung. Jüdische DPs in historischem Kontext," in *Überlebt und Unterwegs*, 229–48.
7. Y. Michal Bodemann, "Staat und Ethnizität: Der Aufbau der jüdischen Gemeinden im Kalten Krieg," in *Jüdisches Leben in Deutschland seit 1945*, 49–69; Brenner, *After the Holocaust*.
8. Sander L. Gilman, *Jews in Today's German Culture* (Bloomington, 1995), 1.
9. *Jüdisches Leben in Deutschland seit 1945*.
10. Monika Richarz, "Juden in der Bundesrepublik Deutschland und in der Deutschen Demokratischen Republik seit 1945," in *Jüdisches Leben in Deutschland seit 1945*, 13–30.
11. Along with his book appeared two collection of essays dealing with Jewish life in today's Germany: *Jewish Voices, German Words: Growing Up Jewish in Post-war Germany and Austria*, ed. Elena Lappin (North Haven, CT, 1994); *Speaking Out - Jewish Voices from United Germany*, ed. Susan Stern (Chicago, Berlin, Tokyo and Moscow, 1995).
12. *Zwischen Antisemitismus und Philosemitismus. Juden in der Bundesrepublik*, ed. Wolfgang Benz, (Berlin, 1991); Wolfgang Benz, "Sitzen auf gepackten Koffern," *Der Spiegel Spezial Juden und Deutsche* 2 (1992): 47–53; idem, "Germans, Jews and Antisemitism in Germany after 1945," *Australian Journal of Politics and History* 41, no. 1 (1995): 118–29; *Jews, Germans, Memory*; Frank Stern, see note 3, above.
13. Neima Barzel, "The Attitude of Jews of German Origin in Israel to Germany and Germans after the Holocaust, 1945–1952," *Leo Baeck Institute Year Book* 39 (1994): 271–301; Y. Michal Bodemann, "'Ich verlasse dieses Land mit Verbitterung, doch vor keinen Volk darf man die Fensterläden zuschlagen . . .' Zur Abschiedspredigt von Rabbiner Dr. Wilhelm Weinberg (1901–1976) in Frankfurt/Main am 11. November 1951," *Menora* 6 (1995): 345–57; Michael Brenner, "East European and German Jews in Postwar Germany, 1945–50," in *Jews, Germans, Memory*, 49–63; idem, "Wider den Mythos 'Stunde Null:' Kontinuitäten im innerjüdischen Bewusstsein und deutsch-jüdischen Verhältnis nach 1945," *Menora* 3 (1992): 155–81; Josef Foschepoth,

"'Helfen Sie uns, und Sie helfen Deutschland...' Die Anfänge der Gesellschaften für Christlich-Jüdische Zusammenarbeit," in *Zwischen Antisemitismus und Philosemitismus*, 63–70; Yeshayahu M. Jelinek, *Zwischen Moral und Realpolitik. Deutsch-israelische Beziehungen 1945–1965* (Gerlingen, 1997); Arno Mohr, "Das Auschwitz-Syndrom—Geschichte der Juden in Deutschland nach 1945," *Neue Politische Literatur* 10, no. 1 (1995): 62–94; works by Frank Stern, see note 3, above.
14. For example: *Jüdische Geschichte in Berlin. Essays und Studien*, ed. Reinhard Rürup (Berlin, 1995), therein especially: Andreas Nachama, "Nach der Befreiung: Jüdisches Leben in Berlin 1945–1953," 267–85.
15. Doris Kushner, "Die jüdische Minderheit in der Bundesrepublik Deutschland" (Ph.D. thesis, Cologne, 1977); Lynn Rapaport, *Jews in Germany after the Holocaust. Memory, Identity, and Jewish-German Relations* (Cambridge, 1997); Richard Chaim Schneider, *Wir sind da! Die Geschichte der Juden in Deutschland von 1945 bis heute* (Berlin, 2000).
16. Brenner, "East European and German Jews;" idem, *After the Holocaust*.

Introduction

1. Michael Balfour and John Mair, *Survey of International Affairs, 1939–1946: Four-Power Control in Germany and Austria, 1945–1946* (London, 1956); Christoph Klessmann, *Die doppelte Staatsgrüdung—deutsche Geschichte, 1945–1955* (Göttingen, 1982); Henry Ashby Turner, *The Two Germanys since 1945* (New Haven and London, 1987).
2. Margaret Bourke-White, *Deutschland, April 1945* (Munich, 1979); Robert W. Carden, "Before Bizonia: Britain's Economic Dilemma in Germany, 1945–1946," *Journal of Contemporary History* 14 (1979): 535–55; Victor Gollanz, *In Darkest Germany* (London, 1947); Alfred Grosser, *Deutschland Bilanz: Geschichte Deutschlands seit 1945* (Munich, 1970); Klessman, *Die doppelte Staatsgründung*; Rolf Steininger, *Deutsche Geschichte seit 1945: Darstellung und Dokumente in vier Bänden* (Frankfurt a.M., 1996); Lothar Kettenacker. *Germany Since 1945.* (Oxford, 1997); *West Germany Under Construction. Politics, Society, and Culture in the Adenauer Era*, ed. Robert G. Moeller (Ann Arbor, 1997).
3. For details of the British Zone see chapter 3.
4. For the Jewish population see chapter 1.
5. Balfour and Mair, *Survey of International Affairs, 1939–1946; Flüchtlinge und Vertriebene in der westdeutschen Nachkriegsgeschichte*, ed. Rainer Schulze et al. (Hildesheim, 1987); Klessmann, *Die doppelte Staatsgründung*.
6. Werner Abelshauser, *Wirtschaft in Westdeutschland, 1945–1948: Reconstruktion und Wachstumsbedingungen in der amerikanischen und britischen Zone* (Schriftenreihe der Vierteljahreshefte für Zeitgeschichte, no. 30) (Stuttgart, 1975); idem, "Die Rekonstruktion der westdeutschen Wirtschaft und die Rolle der Besatzungspolitik," in *Politische und ökonomische*

Stabilisierung Westdeutschlands, 1945–1949, ed. Claus Scharf, Hans J. Schröder, and Hans Jürgen (Wiesbaden, 1977), 1–17; Nicholas Balabkins, *Germany under Direct Control: Economic Aspects of Disarmament, 1945–1948* (New Brunswick, N.J., 1964); Carden, "Before Bizonia"; John E. Farquharson, *The Western Allies and the Politics of Food: Agrarian Management in Postwar Germany* (Leamington Spa, Warwickshire and Dover, New Hampshire, 1985); Karl Hardach, *The Political Economy of Germany in the Twentieth Century* (Berkeley, 1980); Alan Kramer, "Demontagepolitik in Hamburg," in *Britische Deutschland- und Besatzungspolitik, 1945–1949*, ed. Josef Foschepoth and Rolf Steininger (Paderborn, 1985), 265–80; Rainer Klump, "Diskussionsschwerpunkte und Ergebnisse der Währungsreformforschung," in *40 Jahre Deutsche Mark: Die politische und ökonomische Bedeutung der westdeutschen Währungsreform von 1948 (Beiträge zur Wirtschafts- und Sozialgeschichte* 39), ed. Rainer Klump (Wiesbaden, 1989), 51–66; Koppel Pinson, *Modern Germany: Its History and Civilization* (New York, 1954); Wilhelm Treue, *Die Demontagepolitik der Westmächte nach dem Zweiten Weltkrieg (unter besonderer Berücksichtigung ihrer Wirkung auf die Wirtschaft in Niedersachsen)* (Göttingen and Hanover, 1967); Rolf Steininger, "Die Sozialisierung fand nicht statt," in *Britische Deutschland- und Besatzungspolitik 1945–1949*, ed. Josef Foschepoth and Rolf Steininger (Paderborn, 1985), 135–51; Günter J. Trittel, "Das Scheitern der Bodenreform im 'Schatten des Hungers,'" ibid., 153–70; D. Cameron Watt, "Grossbritannien, die Vereinigten Staaten und Deutschland," ibid., 15–25; Harald Winkel, *Die Wirtschaft im geteilten Deutschland, 1945–1970* (Wiesbaden, 1974).

7. Carden, "Before Bizonia"; Grosser, *Deutschland Billanz;* Pinson, *Modern Germany;* Steininger, *Deutsche Geschichte;* Turner, *The Two Germanys.*
8. Based mainly on the following sources: Nicolas Balabkins, *West German Reparations to Israel* (New Brunswick, N.J., 1971); Norman Bentwich, *They Found Refuge: An Account of British Jewry's Work for Victims of Nazi Oppression* (London, 1956), chap. 11; idem, *The United Restitution Organization, 1948–1968* (London, n. d.); Jelinek, *Zwischen Moral; Jewish Restitution Successor Organization: Report on the Operations, 1947–1972;* Herbert Obenaus, "Die widerwillige Wiedergutmachung," in *Im Schatten des Holocaust: Jüdisches Leben in Niedersachsen nach 1945*, ed. Herbert Obenaus (Hanover, 1997), 83–116; Nana Sagi, *German Reparations: A History of the Negotiations* (Jerusalem, 1980); Ayaka Takei, "Question of '*Rechtsnachfolge:*' The Jewish Restitution Successor Organization and the Postwar Jewish *Gemeinden* in Germany" (unpublished draft authorized by the author); "Die Wiedergutmachung in Deutschland," *Jewish Travel Guide, 1952/3*, 78–90; Ronald Zweig, "Restitution and the Problem of Jewish Displaced Persons in Anglo-American Relations, 1944–1948," *American Jewish History* 78 (1988): 54–78.
9. For further details see chapters 5, 8, and 12.
10. For additional details see chapter 12.

Chapter 1

1. Yehuda Bauer, "The Death Marches—January–May 1945," *Yahadut Zemanenu—Contemporary Jewry* 1 (1983): 199–221 [Hebrew].
2. Memoranda of Shalom Adler-Rudel: June 7, 1945, CZA, A140/75; June 11, 1945, CZA, A140/154; June 28, 1945, CZA, A140/272.
3. Proudfoot's estimate is 75,000: Malcolm Proudfoot, *European Refugees* (London, 1957), 306. Yehuda Bauer sets the figure at 70,000: "The Jewish Displaced Persons from the Concentration Camps and the Problems of the She'erit Hapletah," in *The Nazi Concentration Camps: Proceedings of the Fourth Yad Vashem International Historical Conference, Jerusalem, January 20–24, 1980* (Jerusalem, 1984), 385–95 [Hebrew]. Vernant goes even higher—80,000 in Germany and Austria—but he deals only with the second half of 1945: Jacques Vernant, *The Refugees in the Post-war World* (London, 1953), 62.
4. Albrich, *Exodus*, 12. On page 20 he cites a maximum of 30,000. For the total number of DPs in Austria he relies on Y. Von Stedingk, *Die Organisation des Flüchtlingswesen in Österreich seit dem Zweiten Weltkrieg*, 6 (Wien, 1970), 29. See also Vernant, *Refugees*, 62, 109.
5. Albrich, *Exodus*, 20–26.
6. See also Yehuda Bauer, *Out of the Ashes* (Oxford, 1989), 36; Wolfgang Jacobmeyer, "Jüdische Überlebende als Displaced Persons," *Geschichte und Gesellschaft* 99, no. 3 (1983): 421–52.
7. *Encyclopedia of the Holocaust*, entry on Germany and the statistical summaries (by O. D. Kulka and E. Hildesheimer).
8. Based on Kulka and Hildesheimer's data (ibid.) and on Harry Maor, "Über den Wiederaufbau der jüdischen Gemeinden in Deutschland seit 1945" (Ph.D. thesis, Mainz, 1961).
9. Maor, "Über den Wiederaufbau," 2–4.
10. Haim S. Halevi, "The Influence of World War II on the Demographic Characteristics of the Jewish People" (Ph.D. thesis, The Hebrew University of Jerusalem, 1973) [Hebrew].
11. Maor, "Über den Wiederaufbau," 2–4.
12. Ibid. See also Doris Kuschner, "Die jüdische Minderheit in der BRD" (Ph.D. thesis, Cologne, 1977); Norbert Muhlen, *The Survivors: A Report on the Jews in Germany Today* (New York, 1962).
13. Adler-Rudel memorandum, June 11, 1945, CZA, A140/154.
14. Ibid. Adler-Rudel notes that Hungarian, Czechoslovakian, and Romanian Jews were initially reluctant to return to their countries, but in his memorandum of June 28, 1945 (CZA, A140/272), he writes that the repatriation of the Czech Jews had begun.
15. The first survey appears in Zorah Warhaftig, *Uprooted* (New York, 1946), 53. The second appears in Leo Srole, "Why the DP's Can't Wait," *Commentary*, January 1947, 13–24.

Notes to Chapter 1

16. According to the Jewish Organization for Child Care, Oeuvre Secours pour Enfants Juifs (OSE), in *JC*, July 13, 1945, 1.
17. Srole, "Why the DP's Can't Wait"; Koppel Pinson, "Jewish Life in Liberated Germany: A Study of the Jewish DP's," *Jewish Social Studies* 9, no. 2 (1947): 101–26.
18. Srole, "Why the DP's Can't Wait."
19. In Pinson, "Jewish Life," based on his impressions of the American Zone, especially the Landsberg camp. See also Irving Heymont, *Among the Survivors of the Holocaust 1945: The Landsberg DP Camp Letters of Major Irving Heymont, United States Army* (Cincinnati, 1982).
20. Yehuda Bauer, *Flight and Rescue: Brichah* (New York, 1970); Yisrael Gutman, *The Jews in Poland after the Second World War* (Jerusalem, 1985) [Hebrew]; Engel, *Between Liberation and Flight*; *She'erit Hapletah, 1944–1948: Rehabilitation and Political Struggle, Proceedings of the Sixth Yad Vashem International Historical Conference*, ed. Yisrael Gutman and Adina Drechsler (Jerusalem, 1990) [Hebrew], especially the articles by Nathaniel Katzburg: "Between Liberation and Revolution: The Jews of Hungary Confronting a Changing Regime, 1945–1949," 103–26; and Jean Anchel: "The Remnants in Romania during the Time of Transition to the Communist Regime, August 1944–December 1947," 127–48. See also Bauer, *Out of the Ashes*, 57–8, 71–82, 133–58.
21. Gutman, *Jews in Poland*.
22. Dinnerstein, *America and the Survivors of the Holocaust* (New York, 1982).
23. Estimates for the DP population in central Europe vary widely. The above estimates are based on the following sources: Proudfoot, *European Refugees*; *Report of the Anglo-American Committee of Inquiry Regarding the Problems of European Jewry and Palestine*, (Lausanne, 1946); *American Jewish Year Books*, 1949, 1950; Warhaftig, *Uprooted*; Srole, "Why the DP's Can't Wait"; and various reports issued by the World Jewish Congress, the Central Committee of Liberated Jews in Germany, and UNRRA. See also Bauer, *Out of the Ashes*; Jacobmeyer, "Jüdische Überlebende."
24. Ze'ev Mankowitz, "The Affirmation of Life in *She'erit Hapleitah*," *Holocaust and Genocide Studies* 5, no. 1 (1990): 13–21; idem, "The Politics and Ideology of Survivors of the Holocaust in the American Zone of Occupied Germany, 1945–1946" (Ph.D. thesis, The Hebrew University of Jerusalem, 1987) [Hebrew]; Marc Dvorjetski, "Adjustment of Detainees to Camp and Ghetto Life and Their Subsequent Re-adjustment to Normal Society," *Yad Vashem Studies* 5 (1963): 193–220; idem, "Demographic and Biological Problems of Immigrant Holocaust Survivors, 1946–1956," *Niv Harofeh* 34, no. 1 (1963): 3–29 [Hebrew]; Srole, "Why the DP's Can't Wait"; interviews with Zvi Asaria-Helfgott (1964) and Josef Rosensaft (1964), OHD; my interviews with Norbert Wollheim (Jerusalem, 1990), OHD; Bauer, *Out of the Ashes*, 207; Jacobmeyer, "Jüdische Überlebende," 437.
25. Bauer, *Out of the Ashes*.

26. On the British Zone, see details and analysis in chapter 3.
27. Dinnerstein, *America*; Bauer, *Out of the Ashes*, especially 39–61; Haim Genizi, *The Adviser on Jewish Affairs to the American Army and the Displaced Persons, 1945–1949* (Moreshet, 1987) [Hebrew].
28. Based on Dinnerstein, *America*; Amitzur Ilan, *America, Britain, and Palestine* (Jerusalem, 1979) [Hebrew]; Bauer, *Out of the Ashes*.
29. Nahum Bogner, *The Resistance Boats: The Jewish Illegal Immigration, 1945–1948* (Tel Aviv, 1993) [Hebrew]; Bauer, *Flight and Rescue*; Ze'ev Venia Hadari, *Refugees Win against the Empire* (Tel Aviv, 1985) [Hebrew].
30. See chapter 12; Dinnerstein, *America*, 287.
31. See chapter 12. Legal immigration to Palestine from all over Europe from 1946 to 1948 totaled approximately 48,500 persons—1,440 from Germany. See Moshe Sicron, *The Immigration to Israel, 1948–1952* (Jerusalem, 1957), vol. 2, table A8.
32. Sicron (ibid.) mentions 1,440 immigrants from Germany, but it is impossible to determine how many of them were DPs; Dinnerstein, *America*, 288, does not cite any figures for German Jewish immigration to the United States until 1949. According to the *American Jewish Year Book* for 1947–48, however, 4,500 Germans immigrated to the United States during that period, and most of them were presumably Jews.
33. See sources in note 23 above. Also see *Encyclopedia of the Holocaust*, "Displaced Persons, Jewish."

Chapter 2

1. Belsen exhibition at the IWM; Eberhard Kolb, *Bergen-Belsen: Geschichte des "Aufenthaltslager," 1943–1945* (Hanover, 1962), 157; also idem, *Bergen-Belsen: Vom "Aufenthaltslager" zum Konzentrationslager, 1943–1945* (Göttingen, 1996); interview with Josef Rosensaft, July 1962, OHD; Derrick Sington, *Belsen Uncovered* (London, 1946), 9–21.
2. The following survey is based mainly on Kolb, *Bergen-Belsen (1962)*; *Bergen-Belsen: Texts and Pictures of the Exhibition in the Central Memorial of the Land Lower Saxony on the Site of the former Concentration- and Prisoner of War Camp Bergen-Belsen*, ed. Niedersächsische Landeszentrale für Politische Bildung (Hanover, 1990); *Konzentrationslager Bergen-Belsen Berichte und Dokumente*, ed. Monika Gödecke et al. (Hanover, 1995).
3. See Arnold Jürgens and Thomas Rahe, "Zur Statistik des Konzentrationslagers Bergen-Belsen: Quellengrundlagen, methodische Probleme und neue statistische Daten," *Die frühen Nachkriegsprozesse: Beiträge zur Geschichte der Nazionalsozialistischen Verfolgung in Norddeutschland* 3 (1997): 128–48.
4. Kolb, *Bergen-Belsen (1962)*, 136 (author's translation from the German).
5. See also Yona Immanuel, *Yessupar Lador: Memories* (Jerusalem, 1994) [Hebrew]; Abel J. Herzberg, *Between Two Streams: A Diary from Bergen-*

Belsen, translated from the Dutch by Jack Santcross (London and New York, 1997); Renata Laqueur, *Bergen-Belsen-Tagebuch* (Hanover, 1983); Hanna Levy-Hass, *Inside Belsen*, translated by Ronald L. Taylor, with an introduction by Jane Caplan (Brighton, 1962); *Belsen in History and Memory*, ed. Jo Reilly et al. (London and Portland, 1997).

6. Joanne Reilly, *Belsen: The Liberation of a Concentration Camp* (London and New York, 1998), 19–49; Bernard Wasserstein, *Britain and the Jews of Europe, 1939–1945* (Oxford, 1979), 169–80, 343; Tony Kushner, *The Persistence of Prejudice: Antisemitism in British Society during the Second World War* (Manchester, 1989); idem, "The Impact of the Holocaust on British Society and Culture," *Contemporary Record* 5, no. 2 (1991): 349–75.
7. RAF aerial photograph of Sept. 19, 1944, in the Belsen exhibition, IWM.
8. My interview with Rabbi Isaac Levy in March 1991, OHD; Sington, *Belsen Uncovered*, chap. 1; Foreign Office file, PRO, FO/1030/381; Belsen exhibition, IWM; also see Kolb, *Bergen-Belsen (1962)*, 171–85.
9. Sington, *Belsen Uncovered*, chap. 2; *British Zone Review*, Supplement, Oct. 13, 1945 [hereafter cited as *BZR*]; G. Raperport, "Expedition to Belsen," *Middlesex Hospital Journal*, July 1945, YV, 0–70/24; Kolb, *Bergen-Belsen (1962)*, 164–66.
10. Kolb, *Bergen-Belsen (1962)*, 164–66; Sington, *Belsen Uncovered*, chap. 1; Josef Rosensaft, "Our Belsen," in *Belsen*, published by Irgun She'erit Hapleita Meha'ezor Habriti, Israel [The Organization of the Surviving Remnant in the British Zone, Israel] (Tel Aviv, 1957) [hereafter cited as *Belsen Book*], 24–26.
11. Kolb, *Bergen-Belsen (1962)*, 67; *BZR*; W. R. F. Collis, "Belsen Camp, a Preliminary Report," *British Medical Journal*, June 6, 1945, YV, 0–70/24; Raperport, "Expedition"; Sington, *Belsen Uncovered*, chap. 1.
12. *BZR*; Belsen exhibition, IWM.
13. Raperport, "Expedition"; *BZR*.
14. Raperport, "Expedition"; *BZR*; Meiklejohn at a London press conference, as reported by JTA, June 7, 1945, YV, 0–37/19/1 [hereafter cited as Meiklejohn]; Leslie H. Hardman, *The Survivors: The Story of the Belsen Remnant* (London, 1958), 48–9; Isaac Levy, *Witness to Evil: Bergen-Belsen, 1945* (London, 1995), 19. See also Shmuel Immanuel, *Zichronot umahshavot: Memories* (Sha'albim, 1996) [Hebrew], on the failure of the British to live up to the challenge of rescuing starved people, despite their goodwill.
15. *BZR*.
16. S. Immanuel, *Zichronot*.
17. *BZR*.
18. Ibid.; Kolb, *Bergen-Belsen (1962)*, 168–69. The number 23,000 appears in the Belsen exhibition, IWM. For descriptions of burial ceremonies, see Hardman, *The Survivors*, and Zvi Asaria (Helfgott), *We Are the Witnesses* (Tel Aviv, 1970) [Hebrew]. See also Levy, *Witness to Evil*, 11–12.

19. Collis, "Belsen Camp"; Raperport, "Expedition"; *BZR*; Kolb, *Bergen-Belsen (1962)*, 170–71; Levy, *Witness to Evil*; Eryl Hall Williams, *A Page of History in Relief* (York, 1993), 20–38, on the work of the Friend Relief Service in Belsen.
20. *BZR*.
21. The British *Daily Express*, May 4, 1945, YV, 0–37/19/1; Collis, "Belsen Camp"; Raperport, "Expedition"; *BZR*; Williams, *A Page of History*, ibid. In rare cases, a German POW doctor did develop close ties with his Jewish patient. See S. Immanuel, *Zichronot*. On the special relationship between Brigadier Glyn Hughes and his Jewish patients, see Levy, *Witness to Evil*, 19, 134–36; *Belsen Book*.
22. Meiklejohn; Roger A. Ritvo and Diane M. Plotkin, *Sisters in Sorrow: Voices of Care in the Holocaust* (College Station, Tex., 1998), 187–93.
23. Hardman, *The Survivors*; Levy, *Witness to Evil*; *BZR*; Anton Gill, *The Journey Back from Hell: Conversations with Concentration Camp Survivors* (London, 1988); Ritvo and Plotkin, *Sisters in Sorrow*, 187–234. The role of the Jewish chaplains and rabbis will be dealt with in chapter 6.
24. Ralph Segalman, "The Psychology of Jewish Displaced Persons," *Jewish Social Service Quarterly* 23, no. 1 (1946): 361–69; Irit Keynan, *Holocaust Survivors*, 19–41.
25. Levy, *Witness to Evil*; Asaria, *We Are the Witnesses*; Raperport, "Expedition."
26. Hardman, *The Survivors*, 46–47; Raperport, "Expedition"; report by Glyn Hughes, *BZR*.
27. The British *Daily Express*, May 4, 1945; *BZR*.
28. Kolb, *Bergen-Belsen (1962)*, 170–71; *BZR*'s numbers apply to the repatriation and deaths in Camp One only; Belsen exhibition, IWM.
29. Raperport, "Expedition"; Asaria, *We Are the Witnesses*.
30. Meiklejohn; Kolb, *Bergen-Belsen (1996)*, 84–85; *BZR*.
31. Meiklejohn; Raperport, "Expedition."
32. Quotation in Sington, *Belsen Uncovered*, 48. See also Kolb, *Bergen-Belsen (1962)*, 171; Raperport, "Expedition."

Chapter 3

1. Gollanz, *In Darkest Germany*; *Volks- und Berufszählung vom 29. October 1946 in den vier Besatzungszonen und Gross-Berlin* (Berlin and Munich); Abelshauser, *Wirtschaft*; idem, "Die Rekonstruktion"; Farquharson, *The Western Allies*; Kochavi, *Displaced Persons*, 15–220.
2. Ration scale for DPs, June 16, 1945, PRO, FO/1030/369: including the following items: meat, bread, potatoes, butter, sugar, jam, rye flour, pulses, coffee, salt, and skim milk, total of 2,224 calories; memoranda by Adler-Rudel on the Jews in Germany, June 28, 1945, CZA, A140/272, and July 23, 1945, CZA, A140/650; report on the hunger strike in Belsen, in the British *Observer*, Oct. 14, 1945, YV, 0–37/19/1; survey on

conditions of Jews in the British Zone, March 1946 undertaken at request of UNRRA, signed by Brotman and Viteles on Mar. 29, 1946, YV, 0–70/6; circular by the CRREC and JCRA, March 1947, WLL, Henriques/Bad Harzburg.
3. Ursula Büttner, "Not nach der Befreiung—die Situation der deutschen Juden in der britischen Besatzungszone 1945–1948," in *Das Unrechtsregime—Internationale Forschung über den Nationalsozialismus, Band 2: Verfolgung—Exil—Belasteter Neubeginn*, ed. Ursula Büttner et al. (Hamburg, 1986), 373–406; see also Instruction no. 20, Dec. 4, 1946, PRO, FO/1049/1770.
4. Büttner, "Not nach der Befreiung."
5. Collis, "Belsen Camp"; Raperport, "Expedition; *BZR*; Foreign Office file, PRO, FO/1030/381; Belsen exhibition, IWM; see also John Bridgman, *The End of the Holocaust: The Liberation of the Camps* (London, 1990). The one exception was Captain Sington; see Sington, *Belsen Uncovered*. See also Reilly, *Belsen*, elaborating on the British attitude, 50–117.
6. Memorandum by S. Adler-Rudel, June 11, 1945, CZA, A140/154.
7. Büttner, "Not nach der Befreiung."
8. Report by S. Rurka, September 1945, WLL, Henriques/Belsen Reports. See also Bentwich, *They Found Refuge*, 176–77.
9. Conference on the position of Displaced and Stateless Jews in Germany, May 23, 1945, BDA, C11/13/17/2; emergency resolutions by the BD, July 15, 1945, BDA, C11/13/16/3; notes on an interview with Prof. S. Brodetsky and Mr. A. G. Brotman, July 25, 1945, and P. Mason on Jews in Germany, July 25, 1945, PRO, FO/1049/81; Chief of Staff Control Commission for Germany [CCG] British Element [BE] to Lord Reading, July 26, 1945, PRO, FO/1030/300; Chief of Staff CCG BE to the War Office, August 1945, F. Bovenschen (War Office) to Lt. Gen. Sir Brian Robertson, Aug. 20, 1945, and Robertson to Sir Eric B. B. Speed (Permanent Under Secretary of State for War), Oct. 6, 1945, PRO, FO/1049/81; A. G. Brotman, BD, to the Secretary of State for Foreign Affairs, Oct. 9, 1945, and L. Easterman, World Jewish Congress [WJC] to I. L. Henderson, Refugee Dept., Oct. 12, 1945, PRO, FO/1049/195; from the Foreign Office to T. J. Kash (The War Office), Oct. 24, 1945, PRO, FO/1049/195; CRREC, report of activities for the period ending Nov. 1, 1945, HL, Schonfeld/576/1; directions by the HQ Prisoners of War & Displaced Persons Division CCG BE, Nov. 19, 1945, PRO, FO/1049/81. As for the American policy, see Dinnerstein, *America*.
10. Sagi, *German Reparations*, chap. 3; Bentwich, *They Found Refuge*, chap. 11; Zweig, "Restitution."
11. Kochavi, *Displaced Persons*; Büttner, "Not nach der Befreiung"; Zweig, "Restitution."
12. Kochavi, *Displaced Persons*, 27–35.
13. See British sources in note 9 above, and also notes on letter from Lord Reading, August 1945, PRO, FO/1049/195; Chief of Staff, CCG BE to

Under Secretary of State for War, Aug. 18, 1945, PRO, FO/1030/300; idem to Directory of Civil Affairs, the War Office, Sept. 6, 1945, PRO, FO/1049/81.
14. Wasserstein, *Britain and the Jews of Europe*; Louise London, "British Government Policy and Jewish Refugees, 1933–1945," *Patterns of Prejudice* 23, no. 4 (1989–90): 26–43; Kushner, *Persistence of Prejudice*.
15. Adler-Rudel, memorandum of June 28, 1945, CZA, A140/272; Tsemach Tsamriyon, *The Press of the Jewish Holocaust Survivors in Germany as an Expression of Their Problems* (Tel Aviv, 1970) [Hebrew], 32–36; Jacobmeyer, "Jüdische Überlebende."
16. Kolb, *Bergen-Belsen (1962)*, 170–71; *BZR*; Belsen exhibition, IWM.
17. Kolb, *Bergen-Belsen (1962)*, 106–14; Kolb does not estimate the number of Jews; Jürgens and Rahe, "Zür Statistik."
18. Kolb, *Bergen-Belsen (1962)*, 134.
19. Ibid., 186–200.
20. *BZR*; Hardman, *The Survivors*; Levy interview.
21. Sington, *Belsen Uncovered*, 47, 76. Sington estimates that there were 40,000 people in Camp One. The official British estimate in *BZR* is 45,000.
22. Letter in CZA, S25/5233, appeared in *JC*, May 4, 1945, 1.
23. Hardman, *The Survivors*, 1.
24. Sington, *Belsen Uncovered*, 162–68.
25. Hardman in *Yorkshire Post*, June 16, 1945, YV, 0–37/19/1; Levy interview.
26. Sington, *Belsen Uncovered*, 202; *BZR*.
27. Sington, *Belsen Uncovered*, 202.
28. Kudish letter to Hashomer Hatzair in Eretz Israel, May 16, 1945, YV, 0–37/19.
29. *JC*, June 8, 1945, 1.
30. Sington, *Belsen Uncovered*, 190ff.; Belsen exhibition, IWM.
31. Kolb, *Bergen-Belsen 1962*, 308–16, cites the total number of deaths until June 20, 1945.
32. *JC*, June 8, 1945. Kolb (see note) says there were 27,000 inmates on May 21, 1945, the day Camp One was evacuated.
33. The *JC* complains about this on June 8, 1945. The book listing the survivors' names is in the Belsen exhibition, IWM.
34. Sington, *Belsen Uncovered*; Hardman, *The Survivors*; Levy, *Witness to Evil*; letters of Rabbi Isaac Levy, *JC*, May 4, 1945, 1, and June 8, 1945, 1; Rosensaft interview; Hadassa Bimko Rosensaft, "Children in Belsen," *Belsen Book*, 88–97; *Unzer Sztyme*, Nov. 29, 1945, 7; Williams, *A Page of History*, 28–29, quotes estimates for the number of orphaned children ranging from 237 to 700; Thomas Rahe, "Jüdische Waisenkinder im Konzentrationslager Bergen-Belsen," *Dachauer Hefte* 14 (1998): 31–49.
35. Letter by Rabbi Klein (of the Hungarian Orthodox community in Belsen), *JC*, June 22, 1945, 14; letter by Rabbi Levy, *JC*, 4 May,

Notes to Chapter 3

1945; Sington, *Belsen Uncovered*, 202; Zvi Asaria, "Eine Chassidische Gemeinde in Celle (1945–1950)," *Zur Geschichte der Juden in Celle* (Celle, 1974), 103–7; *Celle '45—Aspekte einer Zeitenwende*, ed. Mijndert Bertram (Bomann-Museum) (Celle, 1995).

36. Asaria interview; Wollheim interview; Bimko Rosensaft, "Children in Belsen," *Belsen Book*; *Wochenblatt*, Jan. 16, 1948, 3; *Jerusalem Post*, article published July 23, 1965, in CZA, A140/130.
37. *Konzentrationslager in Hannover—KZ-Arbeit und Rüstungsindustrie in der Spätphase des Zweiten Weltkriegs*, ed. Rainer Fröbe et al. (Hildesheim, 1985), 2:285, 331–69, 407–564; *Konzentrationslager in Hannover, 1943–1945* (Ausstellungskatalog) (Hanover, 1983); Klaus Mlynek et al., "Deutsche und Juden nach 1945," in *Reichskristallnacht in Hannover*, ed. Marlis Buchholz et al. (Hanover, 1978), 97–104; Detlef Garbe and Sabine Homann, "Jüdische Gefangene in Hamburger Konzentrationslagern," in *Die Juden in Hamburg, 1590–1990*, ed. Arno Herzig and Saskia Rohde (Hamburg, 1991), 545–59; *Konzentrationslager in Hamburg—Ansichten 1990*, ed. Max Andree et al. (*Hamburg Porträt: Museum für hamburgische Geschichte 26–27*) (Hamburg, 1990); Werner Johe, *Neuengamme: Zur Geschichte der Konzentrationslager in Hamburg* (Hamburg, 1984).
38. CBF, *Annual Report, 1945*; *Unzer Sztyme*, July 12, 1945, 33–35; *JC*, July 6, 1945, 1.
39. *Unzer Sztyme*, Aug. 15, 1945, 33–35; PALCOR item, Sept. 24, 1945, YV, 0–37/19/1.
40. Bulletin of the Rescue Committee of the Jewish Agency, August 1945, and JTA item, Sept. 16, 1945, YV, 0–37/19/1; *JC*, Oct. 19, 1945, 1.
41. *JC*, Nov. 23, 1945, 9; HQ Military Government, North Rhine Province to Control Commission (BE) Main HQ, Oct. 11, 1945, PRO, FO/1050/1491.
42. Information on the Jews in the British Zone, January 1946, PRO, FO/945/655; statistics on Jews in the British Zone in Germany living outside DP camps, Jan. 31, 1946, BDA, C11/13/16/4.
43. Jacobmeyer, "Jüdische Überlebende," 444, according to UNRRA statistics for June 1946.
44. Memorandum on resettlement of Jews, by Col. Solomon, May 1946, PRO, FO/945/384; report submitted by the Central Jewish Committee, British Zone, to the director-general of UNRRA, Aug. 23, 1946, YV, 0–70/6; *Volks- und Berufszählung*.
45. Lt. Col. Sir Brian Robertson (CCG Berlin) to Sir Arthur Street (War Office), May 7, 1946, PRO, FO/945/384; CBF, *Annual Report, 1947*, 2–9; internal memo of the Foreign Office, Aug. 13, 1947, PRO, FO/371/61821; Foreign Office to Paris Embassy, Sept. 11, 1947, PRO, FO/371/61826. See also Jacobmeyer, "Jüdische Überlebende." See also chapter 12.

Notes to Chapter 4

Chapter 4

1. Sington, *Belsen Uncovered*, 76.
2. Article by Rafael Olevsky, one of the committee members, in *Unzer Sztyme*, Aug. 15, 1945. This is the most reliable version of the facts, closest in time to the actual events, and much closer to the time than Rosensaft's recollections in the late 1950s, which appear in the *Belsen Book*, and his July 1964 interview, OHD. See also Rafael Olevsky, *The Tear* (Tel Aviv, 1983) [Hebrew], which is based on this article.
3. Interview with Rosensaft, translated from the Yiddish, July 1964, OHD.
4. Rabbi Levy's letter to the *JC*, dated April 26, shows that the committee was active well before the transfer to the military camp, which took place from April 24 to May 19 (see chapter 2). In the above interview Rosensaft refers to an even earlier date. The first entry in the committee's protocol book is June 24, 1945, YV, 0–70/1.
5. Levy's letter to the *JC*, CZA, S25/5233. The letter was published in *JC*, May 4, 1945, 1. Levy quotes this letter in his book (*Witness to Evil*, 16–17), but this paragraph is not included.
6. Kudish to friends, May 16, 1945, YV, 0–37/19/1.
7. Quote from Deutsch's letter of June 19, 1945, in Knopfelmacher's letter to Beilin, July 2, 1945, CZA, S25/5233.
8. Olevsky, in *Unzer Sztyme*, Aug. 15, 1945, and *The Tear*, says the committee members were Yossele Rosensaft of Bedzin, Poland (chairman); Mottl Spiegler, Felix Bleich, Rabbi Israel Moshe Olevsky and his brother Rafael, Aaron Joseph Russak, Berl Laufer, and Isaac Eisenberg—all from Poland; Naftali Rosenberg and Anjy Alter from Hungary. Russak, I. M. Olevsky, Rosenberg, Alter, Spiegler, and Bleich do not appear on the list in the *Belsen Book*, but several new names are added: Dr. Tybor Hirsch, Dr. Halina Grzesz, Dr. A. Klein, Dr. Hadassa Bimko, Paul Trepman, and Dr. Zvi Helfgott. The protocol of the congress in September 1945—*Yiddisher Heftlings-congress in Bergen-Belsen, 25–27 September 1945*—does not offer a separate listing of Provisional Committee members, but the report on its activities contains names that are not on the original list. Some of the persons mentioned in the committee protocol book (YV, 0–70/1) are from other camps and welfare organizations.
9. Asaria interview; Wollheim interview; interview with Yitzhak Kerbel, February 1993, OHD; A. S. Stein, "Portraits," 1967 [Hebrew], in Kressel Collection, Oxford; essays by Norbert Wollheim and Leo Easterman, in *Belsen Book*; M. Zanin, *This Is How It Happened: Testimonies by Bergen-Belsen Survivors* (Tel Aviv, 1987) [Hebrew], preface; Lucy S. Dawidowicz, "Belsen Remembered," in *The Jewish Presence: Essays on Identity and History*, ed. Lucy S. Dawidowicz (New York, 1977), 289–97; Samuel Joseph Goldsmith, "Yossl Rosensaft," in *20th Century Jews* (New

Notes to Chapter 4

York, 1962), 86–92. I thank Mr. Menachem Rosensaft for information about his father, given to me in March 2000.
10. Asaria, "Eine Chassidische"; Angelica Hack, "Vom Zwang befreit: 'Displaced Persons' in Stadt und Landkreis Celle," in *Celle '45—Aspekte einer Zeitenwende*, ed. Mijndert Bertram (Bomann-Museum) (Celle, 1995), 89–124, esp. 112–16; Olevsky, *The Tear*.
11. *Belsen Book*; Olevsky, *The Tear*.
12. Bimko Rosensaft's article "Children in Belsen," in *Belsen Book*, 88–97; Bimko's memoirs in *Unzer Sztyme*, Oct. 15, 1945, 25; Stein, "Portraits"; Wollheim interview; Samuel Joseph Goldsmith, "Hadassa Bimko Rosensaft," in *Jews in Transition* (New York, 1969), 107–11; Ritvo and Plotkin, *Sisters in Sorrow*, 187–96.
13. Asaria, *We Are the Witnesses*; Asaria interview.
14. Wollheim interview; also Wollheim's talks with Y. Jelinek, 1988, and A. Margaliyot, 1981, OHD; L. Cohen's letter from Lübeck, July 2, 1945, WLL, Henriques/Cohen reports; protocol of a meeting in Belsen, July 16, 1945, YV, 0–70/25; *Yiddisher Heftlings-congress*.
15. Tsamriyon, *The Press*, 46–47; Kerbel interview; Wollheim interview; *Unzer Sztyme*, July 12, 1945, 10.
16. *Belsen Book*; *Unzer Sztyme*, July 12, 1945; *Memorandum*, a documentary produced in 1965 by the National Film Board of Canada, about the visit of a group of survivors, including Laufer, to Bergen-Belsen (thanks to Prof. L. D. Stokes of Dalhousie University, Halifax, Nova Scotia, Canada, who provided the video cassette of *Memorandum*); Wollheim interview.
17. *Belsen Book*; Tsamriyon, *The Press*, 46–54; Wollheim interview.
18. The only previous acquaintance we know of for sure was between Rosenthal and Rafael Olevsky, who met in a slave labor camp near Auschwitz and spoke about how they would commemorate the Holocaust if they survived. See Olevsky's article in *Unzer Sztyme*, July 12, 1946; Tsamriyon, *The Press*, 54. Olevsky and Rosensaft (in Rosensaft interview) also testified that the group from Bedzin knew Rosensaft, which helped him to be elected chairman.
19. Kudish to friends, May 17 and 22, 1945, YV, 0–37/19/1 (English). Emphasis in the original.
20. Report on the conference, YV, 0–70/25.
21. See protocols of both conferences in YV, 0–70/25. A report on the first meeting appears in *Unzer Sztyme*, Aug. 15, 1945, 7. See also protocols of Belsen committee's meetings on July 1 and 22, 1945, YV, 0–70/1.
22. For further details about the educational system, see chapter 10.
23. It was preceded by *Tehiat Hametim* ("The Resurrection of the Dead"), first published in Buchenwald on May 14, 1945. See Ze'ev Mankowitz, "Formation of *She'erit Hapleita*": 337–70.
24. Which was founded in Palestine in 1944 as a framework for Jewish

soldiers in the British army and took part in the battles of north Italy. More details in chapter 6.
25. On the Jewish Brigade soldiers see *Unzer Sztyme*, July 12, Aug. 15, 1945; Olevsky, *The Tear*. See also chapter 6.
26. Resolutions of Agudath Israel convention in London, May 21, 1945, PRO, FO/1050/1491; protocol of the conference of British Jewish organizations held in London, on the Jewish DPs problem, May 23, 1945, BDA, C11/13/17/2; draft decision by the BD, July 15, 1945, BDA, C11/13/16/3; Levy interview; personal interviews with Sara Eckstein-Grebenau (July 1992), Arieh Handler (April 1993), Asher Leo Kempe (August 1992), Hanna Landau (May 1993), Henry Lunzer (March 1993), Shalom Maagan-Markovitz (May 1992), and Bertha and Jacob Weingreen (March 1993), all in OHD. For more details see chapter 6.
27. Report by Sadi Rurka, September 1945, WLL, Henriques/Belsen Reports.
28. See, for instance, report on "Jewish Congress" at Hohne Camp, Sept. 25/27 by Major Rickford, PRO, FO/1049/81.
29. JTA report on the Munich congress, July 31, 1945, YV, 0–37/19/1; Yehuda Bauer, "The Initial Organization of the Holocaust Survivors in Bavaria," *Yad Vashem Studies* 8 (1971): 127–57; Mankowitz, "Formation of *She'erit Hapleita*."
30. *Yiddishe Heftligs-congress*, quoted from page 13, my translation from the Yiddish. See also Levy, *Witness to Evil*, 98; PALCOR report, Sept. 27, 1945, JTA Bulletin, Sept. 28, 1945, YV, 0–37/19/1; report on "Jewish Congress" at Hohne Camp, Sept. 25/27 by Major Rickford, PRO, FO/1049/81; "Behind the Scenes at Belsen," by Norman Lurie, War Correspondent, Jewish Brigade Group, Brussels, CZA, WJC/A9; *Unzer Sztyme*, Oct. 15, 1945, 15–16, 62–67.
31. The congress protocol and the *Belsen Book* differ with regard to many of these appointments. See also the protocol of the first meeting of the committee, Oct. 3, 1945, YV, 0–70/1.
32. The Zionist leadership under Ben-Gurion and Weizmann still hoped for a change in the Mandatory immigration policy (the 1939 White Paper policy; see introduction). In her book on Belsen, Joanne Reilly, while presenting her arguments against "Zionist" historiography, is misled by the false assumption that Zionism in 1945 meant exclusively the struggle for a Jewish state. See Reilly, *Belsen*, 145–91.
33. Ben-Gurion's report on his visit to the camps at a meeting in London, Nov. 6, 1945, CZA, S25/5231.

Chapter 5

1. For more details and a demographic profile see chapter 1.
2. *Jüdisches Schicksal in Köln, 1918–1945*, ed. Horst Matzer, Hannelore

Notes to Chapter 5

Brabender, et al. Ausstellung des historischen Archiv der Stadt Köln (Cologne, 1989); Adolf Klein, *Köln im Dritten Reich: Stadtgeschichte der Jahre 1933–1945* (Cologne, 1983); Horst Matzerath and Brigitte Holzhauser, *"Vergessen kann man die Zeit nicht, das ist nicht möglich . . .": Kölner erinnern sich an die Jahre 1929–1945* (Cologne, 1985); Bruno Reicher, *Jüdische Geschichte und Kultur in NRW—Ein Handbuch* (Essen, 1993), 151–72; *Widerstand und Verfolgung in Köln, 1933–1945*, ed. Franz Irsfeld and Bernd Wittschier (Cologne, 1974).

3. *JC*, Nov. 3 and 9, 1945; statistics on Jews in the British Zone in Germany living outside DP camps, Jan. 31, 1946, BDA, C11/13/16/4; report on the Jews in Cologne, Jan. 31, 1946, WLL, Henriques/Synagoge Gemeinde Köln; *Conference on the Future of the Jews in Germany* (Heidelberg, Sept. 1, 1949, mimeograph, GJA), 11; Günther B. Ginzel, "Phasen der Etablierung einer Jüdischen Gemeinde in der Kölner Trümmerlandschaft, 1945–1949," in *Köln und das rheinische Judentum*, ed. Jutta Bohnke-Kollwitz (Festschrift Germania Judaica 1959–1984) (Cologne, 1984), 445–61, here 457; Monika Grübel, "Nach der Katastrophe. Jüdisches Leben in Köln, 1945–1949," in *Zuhause in Köln. Jüdisches Leben 1945 bis heute*, ed. Günther B. Ginzel and Sonja Güntner (Cologne-Weimar-Wienna, 1998), 42–56.

4. *Encyclopedia Judaica*, 6:262–63; Hans P. Görgen, *Düsseldorf und der Nationalsozialismus* (Düsseldorf, 1969); Reicher, *Jüdische Geschichte*, 88–89; Angelika Voigt, *Juden in Düsseldorf: Die Zerstörung der Jüdischen Gemeinde während der Nationalsozialistischen Herrschaft* (Aschendorf, 1983); *1933 1945 Einzelschicksale und Erlebnisse von Bürger die im Bereich des heutigen Stadtbezirkes 3 wohnen*, ed. Landeshauptstadt Düsseldorf, 3 vols. (Düsseldorf, 1986).

5. *JC*, Nov. 3 and 9, 1945; statistics on Jews in the British Zone in Germany living outside DP camps, Jan. 31, 1946, BDA, C11/13/16/4; interviews with Eugenie Brecher, H. Israel, and H. Rubinstein, Düsseldorf, September 1992, OHD; *Conference on the Future of the Jews in Germany*, 11; *Die Neue Synagoge in Düsseldorf—Zur Einweihung am 7. September 1958* (Düsseldorf, 1958); Barbara Suchy, "Zwischen den Zeiten: Die jüdische Gemeinde Düsseldorf von 1945–1948," in *Neuanfang: Leben in Düsseldorf*, ed. Stadtmuseum Düsseldorf (Düsseldorf, 1986), 330–40.

6. *Encyclopedia of the Holocaust*: "Hamburg"; *Encyclopedia Judaica*, 7:1228; *Geschichte der Juden in Hamburg, Altona, und Wandsbeck*, ed. Günter Marwedel (*Historischer Verein für Hamburgische Geschichte* 25) (Hamburg, 1982); Ina S. Lorenz, "Die Jüdische Gemeinde Hamburg, 1860–1943: Kaiserreich—Weimarer Republik—NS-Staat," in *Die Juden in Hamburg, 1590–1990*, ed. Arno Herzig and Saskia Rohde (Hamburg, 1991), 77–100; Baruch Z. Ophir, "Zur Geschichte der Hamburger Juden, 1919–1939," in *Juden in Preussen—Juden in Hamburg*, ed. Peter Freimark (Hamburg, 1985), 81–97; *"Wo Wurzeln waren . . .": Juden in*

Hamburg-Eimsbüttel 1933 bis 1945, ed. Sybille Baumbach et al. (Hamburg, 1993).
7. Garbe and Homann, "Jüdische Gefangene"; Johe, *Neuengamme*.
8. JTA item of June 13, 1945, YV, 0–37/19/1; report on the position in Hamburg by Leonard Cohen, July 6, 1945, WLL, Henriques/L. Cohen Reports; report on Polish Jewish DPs in Hamburg by Shalom Markovitz, July 7, 1945, WLL, Henriques/Markovitz Reports; Bulletin of the Rescue Committee of August 1945, YV, 0–37/19/1; *JC*, Oct. 10, 1945, 1; statistics on Jews in the British Zone in Germany living outside DP camps, Jan. 31, 1946, BDA, C11/13/16/4; Bruno Blau, "Jewish Population in Nazi Germany," *Jewish Social Studies* 12, no. 1 (1950): 161–72; Ursula Büttner, "Rückkehr in ein normales Leben? Die Lage der Juden in Hamburg in den ersten Nachkriegsjahren," in *Die Juden in Hamburg, 1590–1990*, ed. Arno Herzig and Saskia Rohde (Hamburg, 1991), 613–32, see 614; Ina S. Lorenz and Jörg Berkemann, "Kriegsende und Neubeginn: Zur Entstehung der neuen Jüdischen Gemeinde in Hamburg, 1945–1948," ibid., 633–55; Hans Lamm, "Der Wiederaufbau der Hamburger jüdischen Gemeinde nach 1945," in *Die Drei-Gemeinde: Aus der Geschichte der jüdischen Gemeinden Altona-Hamburg-Wandsbeck*, ed. Oskar Wolfsberg-Aviad (Munich, 1960), 134–36; Raoul W. Michalski, "Die jüdische Gemeinde Hamburg seit den 50er Jahren," in *Die Juden in Hamburg, 1590–1990*, ed. Arno Herzig and Saskia Rohde (Hamburg, 1991), 101–12.
9. Zvi Asaria, *Die Juden in Niedersachsen* (Leer, 1979), 564; Marlis Buchholz, *Die hannoverschen Judenhäuser: Zur Situation der Juden in der Zeit der Ghettoisierung und Verfolgung, 1941–1945* (Hildesheim, 1987); Friedel Homeyer, *100 Jahre Israelitische Erziehungsan Anstalt. Israelitische Gartenbauschule, 1893–1993: Mahn- und Gedenkstätte des Landkreises Hannover in Ahlem* (Hanover, 1993); Otto D. Kulka and Baruch Z. Ophir, "Leben und Schicksal in sechseinhalb Jahrhunderten," in *Leben und Schicksal: Zur Einweihung der Synagoge in Hannover* (Hanover, 1963), 15–40. See also Herbert Obenaus, *"Sei Stille, sonst kommst Du nach Ahlem!" Zur Funktion der Gestapostelle in der ehemalige Israelitischen Gartenbauschule von Ahlem (1943–1945)*. Hannoversche Geschichtsblätter 41 (Hanover, 1987); Peter Schulze, *Juden in Hannover: Beiträge zur Geschichte und Kultur einer Minderheit* (Hanover, 1989).
10. *Konzentrationslager in Hannover—KZ-Arbeit*, 2:285, 331–39, 407–564; *Konzentrationslager in Hannover, 1943–1945*; Mlynek et al., "Deutsche und Juden."
11. Statistics on Jews in the British Zone in Germany living outside DP camps, Jan. 31, 1946, BDA, C11/13/16/4; Asaria, *Die Juden in Niedersachsen*, 564; Blau, "Jewish Population"; Kulka and Ophir, "Leben und Schicksal"; Mlynek et al., "Deutsche und Juden," 97.
12. Avraham Seligman, "An Illegal Way of Life in Nazi Germany," *Leo Baeck Institute Year Book* 37 (1992): 327–61; Rivka Elkin, *The Survival*

of the Jewish Hospital in Berlin, 1938–1945 (Berlin, 1993); interview with Helmut Fürst in Hanover, September 1992, OHD. For more on the characteristics of the German Jewish remnant, see chapter 1.

13. Daniel Fraenkel, *On the Edge of the Abyss* (Jerusalem, 1994) [Hebrew]; Hagit Lavsky, *Before Catastrophe: The Distinctive Path of German Zionism* (Jerusalem and Detroit, 1996); Doron Niederland, *German Jews: Emigrants or Refugees? Emigration Patterns between the Two World Wars* (Jerusalem, 1996) [Hebrew]; Ruth Zariz, *Flight before Catastrophe: Emigration from Germany, 1938–1945* (Tel Aviv, 1990) [Hebrew].
14. Dr. Alfred Philippson (emerit. ordentl. Professor der Geographie an der Universität Bonn), Denkschrift über die Lage der jetzt in Deutschland wohnenden Juden, Oct. 4, 1945, Stadtsarchiv Bonn, N10/177.
15. See chapter 1.
16. See chapter 3.
17. See chapter 3.
18. Eckstein-Grebenau interview; Handler interview; Landau interview; Lunzer interview; Maagan-Markovitz interview; Weingreen interview; Wollheim interview. See also chapter 6.
19. Notes on the memorandum of the Reichsvereinigung der Juden in Deutschland, June 6, 1945, by Dr. Walter Lustig, BDA, C11/13/16/2; memorandum by Shalom Adler-Rudel, June 11,1945, CZA, A140/134; Bulletin of the Rescue Committee of the Jewish Agency for Palestine, August 1945, YV, 0–37/19/1; Rev. Avraham Greenbaum to Leonard Cohen, Aug. 5, 1945, and report on work in Hamburg by Rev. A. Greenbaum, Aug. 29, 1945, WLL, Henriques/Hamburg Reports; Denkschrift by Prof. A. Philippson, Oct. 4, 1945, Stadtsarchiv Bonn, N10/177; Robert Weltsch, "Berliner Tagebuch," *Mitteilungsblatt*, Jan. 9, 1946; Gershom Scholem, "Besuch bei der Juden in Deutschland," *Mitteilungsblatt*, Nov. 22, 1946; Julius Posner, *In Deutschland, 1945–1946* (Jerusalem, 1947), 109–17; Harry Goldstein, "Die heutigen Jüdischen Gemeinden in Deutschland," *Jewish Travel Guide 1952/3*, 96–98; Büttner, "Not nach der Befreiung"; idem, "Rückkehr"; Ginzel, "Phasen"; Maor, "Über den Wiederaufbau," 1–14; Suchy, "Zwischen den Zeiten."
20. *JC*, Nov. 9, 1945, 1; Zvi Asaria, *Die Juden in Köln von den ältesten Zeiten bis zur Gegenwart* (Cologne, 1959), 404–22; Ginzel, "Phasen"; Grübel, "Nach der Katastrophe"; Maor, "Über den Wiederaufbau," 1–14; Antje Clara Naujoks, "Die Funktion des Zionismus in den jüdischen Gemeinden in Deutschland nach 1945," in *Im Schatten des Holocaust: Jüdisches Leben in Niedersachsen nach 1945*, ed. Herbert Obenaus (Hanover, 1997), 165–96; *Jewish Travel Guide 1952/3*, 36.
21. Philipp Auerbach, Düsseldorf—Former Chief Administrator of the Camp of Buchenwald, Memorandum, Aug. 15, 1945, PRO, FO/1013/2104; Constantin Goschler, "Der Fall Philipp Auerbach: Wiedergutmachung in Bayern," in *Wiedergutmachung in der Bundesrepublik Deutschland*, ed. Ludolf Herbst and Constantin Goschler (Munich, 1989),

Notes to Chapter 5

77–98; *Die neue Synagoge in Düsseldorf*, 7–8; Voigt, *Juden in Düsseldorf*, 11; Elke Fröhlich, "Philipp Auerbach (1906–1952) 'Generalanwalt für Wiedergutmachung,'" in *Geschichte und Kultur der Juden in Bayern, II: Lebensläufe*, ed. Manfred Treml, Josef Kirmeier, et al. (*Veröffentlichungen zur bayerischen Geschichte und Kultur*, 17–18) (Munich, 1988), 315–20. On the regional organization see chapter 8.

22. JTA item, June 13, 1945, YV, 0–37/19/1; report on position in Hamburg by Leonard Cohen, July 6, 1945, WLL, Henriques/L. Cohen Reports; report on Polish Jewish DPs in Hamburg by Shalom Markovitz, July 7, 1945, WLL, Henriques/Markovitz Reports; Protocol of Belsen Conference, July 16, 1945, YV, 0–70/25; Bulletin of the Rescue Committee of the JAP, August 1945, YV, 0–37/19/1; *JC*, Oct. 10, 1945, 1; Büttner, "Rückkehr"; Lamm, "Der Wiederaufbau"; Lorenz and Berkemann, "Kriegsende und Neubeginn"; Maor, "Über den Wiederaufbau," 1–14.

23. Mlynek et al., "Deutsche und Juden," 97–99. For more details see below on the DP communities.

24. Asaria, *Die Juden in Niedersachsen*, 563; Norbert Prager, "Wiederaufbau," in *Leben und Schicksal: zur Erweihung der Synagoge in Hannover* (Hanover, 1963), 41–44; Fürst interview; Anke Quast, "Jewish Committee und Jüdische Gemeinde Hannover: Der schwierige Anfang einer Gemeinschaft," in *Im Schatten des Holocaust: Jüdisches Leben in Niedersachsen nach 1945*, ed. Herbert Obenaus (Hanover, 1997), 55–74.

25. JTA item, June 13, 1945, YV, 0–37/19/1; report on position in Hamburg by L. Cohen, July 6, 1945, WLL, Henriques/L. Cohen Reports; report by Markovitz, July 13, 1945, WLL, Henriques/Markovitz Reports; report by Jane Leverson, July 31, 1945, WLL, Henriques/Leverson Reports; Greenbaum to Cohen, Aug. 5, 1945, WLL, Henriques/Hamburg Reports.

26. See chapter 1.

27. Report on position in Hamburg, July 6, 1945, by Leonard Cohen, WLL, Henriques/L. Cohen Reports; report on Polish Jewish DPs in Hamburg, July 7, 1945, WLL, Henriques/Markovitz Reports.

28. Interview with Selig Brodetsky, *JC*, Oct. 5, 1945, 5; Mlynek et al., "Deutsche und Juden," 97; Quast, "Jewish Committee."

29. *Brunsvicensia Judaica: Gedenkbuch für die jüdischen Mitbürger Braunschweig, 1933–1945* (Brunswick, 1966); Buchholz, *Die hannoverschen Judenhäuser*; *Encyclopedia Judaica*, 4:1928–1933; Asaria, *Die Juden in Niedersachsen*, 491–539, 598.

30. Minutes of a conference held in Belsen, July 16, 1945, YV 70/25; Leverson, notes about the Jews in Braunschweig, Aug. 31, 1945, WLL, Henriques/Leverson Reports; Leverson on Braunschweig, Nov. 30, 1945, WLL, Henriques/Braunschweig; statistical-demographical report by Rabbi Goldfinger on behalf of the JCRA on the Jewish population in Braunschweig, Dec. 20, 1945, WLL, Henriques/Braunschweig; Asaria, *Die Juden in Niedersachsen*, 598.

31. "Celle," in *Historisches Handbuch der Jüdischen Gemeinden in Niedersachsen und Bremen* (Yad Vashem and the Hebrew University, Jerusalem, and the University of Hanover, available on the internet).
32. About Olevsky, who served also as a member of the Central Committee, see chapter 4.
33. Kudish's letter of May 16, 1945, YV, 0–37/19/1; report by J. Leverson on Celle, May 22, 1945, WLL, Henriques/Leverson Reports; letter of R. L. Henriques, Celle, 3 Aug., 1945, WLL, CBF/23/124; CBF, *Annual Report, 1945*; Angelica Hack, "Displaced Persons in Stadt und Landkreis Celle," in *Celle '45*, ed. Mijndert Bertram (Bomann-Museum) (Celle, 1995), 89–123; Asaria, "Eine Chassidische"; Olevsky, *The Tear*. Today there are no Jews in Celle, but the synagogue was turned into a museum documenting the history of the community, and a group of Hanover Jews has been holding religious services there since 1997. I thank Prof. Herbert Obenaus and Dr. Sibylle Obenaus of Hanover for worthy information about Celle and its Jews, past and present.
34. *Encyclopedia Judaica*, 11:555–6; Albert Schreiber, *Zwischen Davidstern und Doppeladler, Chronik der Juden* (Lübeck, 1983); *Die Juden in Schleswig-Holstein*, ed. Wolfgang Hubrich and Rüdiger Wenzel (Kiel, 1988).
35. PALCOR item, Sept. 24, 1945, YV, 0–37/19/1; *Unzer Sztyme*, July 12, 1945, 33–5; Bertha Weingreen to Leonard Cohen, Aug. 14, 1945, WLL, Henriques/Lübeck DPs; *Jüdische Gemeindeblatt*, Dec. 20, 1948, statistical table; Wollheim Interview.
36. About Wollheim, see chapter 4.
37. Interview with L. Cohen, July 7, 1945, WLL, Henriques/Cohen Reports; minutes of a conference on July 16, 1945, in Belsen, YV, 0–70/251; Bertha Weingreen to Leonard Cohen, Aug. 14, 1945, WLL, Henriques/Lübeck DPs; *Yiddischer Heftlings-congress*.
38. See chapter 8.

Chapter 6

1. Bauer, *Out of the Ashes*, 23–30, 41–42.
2. Williams, *A Page of History*; Levy, *Witness to Evil*, 27. See below about Jane Leverson.
3. Report by Jane Leverson on Diepholz DP Center, June 25, 1945, WLL, Henriques/Diepholz. Emphasis in the original.
4. Report by Leverson on Brunswick, Nov. 30, 1945, WLL, Henriques/Leverson.
5. Levy's letter to the *JC*, Apr. 26, 1945, CZA, S25/5233, appeared in the *JC*, May 4, 1945; interview with Rev. L. Hardman in *Yorkshire Post*, June 6, 1945, YV, 0–37/19/1; Levy interview; Levy, *Witness to Evil*; Hardman, *The Survivors*; Asaria, *We Are the Witnesses*; oral account by

Notes to Chapter 6

Arnold Horwell, April 1995 in London, a British officer who arrived at the camp with Levy and others.
6. Hardman, *The Survivors*; Levy, *Witness to Evil*.
7. Levy, *Witness to Evil*, 7–32; see also chapter 4 for more details on Helfgott; Greenbaum interview in Jerusalem, August 1992, OHD.
8. Greenbaum to L. Cohen, Aug. 5, 1945, WLL, Henriques/Hamburg; Greenbaum's report on Hamburg, Aug. 29, 1945, WLL, Henriques/Hamburg Reports; report by Goldfinger on Brunswick, Dec. 20, 1945, WLL, Henriques/Brunswick; CRREC general meetings, Aug. 8, 1945, Oct. 21, 1945, Feb. 24, 1946, and notes on the agreement between the CRREC and the JCRA, Nov. 28, 1945, HL, Schonfeld/576/1; CBF, *Annual Report, 1945*; Greenbaum interview. See chapter 5.
9. JCRA's Department for Religious Reconstruction appointed by the CRREC: Draft Explanatory Memorandum on Post-War Religious Reconstruction, n.d., HL, Schonfeld/81/2; CRREC, report of activities for the period ending Nov. 1, 1945, HL, Schonfeld/576/1. For details on religious life see chapter 9. For the communities' scene, see chapters 5 and 8.
10. On the problems with Rabbi Vilensky: The CRREC's report of Aug. 8, 1945, HL, Schonfeld/576/1; Jack Brass to the JA's Immigration Department, Sept. 5, 1945, CZA, S6/4644; a letter from Adath She'erith Yisrael to Rabbi Schonfeld, Nov. 14, 1945, HL, Schonfeld/144; Levy, *Witness to Evil*, 31–32, 81–84.
11. The CRREC Executive meeting, Oct. 21, 1945, and notes on the agreement between the CRREC and the JCRA, Nov. 28, 1945, HL, Schonfeld/576/1.
12. See chapters 7 and 9.
13. CBF, *Report for 1933–1943*; idem, *Annual Report, 1944*, 5–6; idem, *Annual Report, 1945*, 3.
14. Bentwich, *They Found Refuge*, 130–32; Handler interview.
15. Leverson reports to JCRA, May 6 and 22, June 6 and 25, 1945, WLL, Henriques/Leverson Reports; Levy, *Witness to Evil*, 27; Williams, *A Page of History*, 33, 116–22, quote on 116.
16. Reports by Shalom Markovitz, June 1 and July 7, 1945, WLL, Henriques/Markovitz Reports; reports by S. Rurka, August 1945 and September 1945, WLL, Henriques/Diepholz; *JC*, Apr. 27, 1945, on the team sent to Holland; CBF, *Annual Report, 1945*, 7–8; Maagan-Markovitz interview; Weingreen interview; Levy, *Witness to Evil*, 25–29; Bentwich, *They Found Refuge*, 138–40.
17. Kochavi, *Displaced Persons*, 18; Levy, *Witness to Evil*, 103.
18. List of field-workers of JCRA, May 10, 1946, HL, Schonfeld/130/1; CBF, *Annual Report, 1946*, 3.
19. Eckstein-Grebenau, Handler, Kempe, Landau, Lunzer, Markovitz, and Weingreen interviews.

Notes to Chapter 6

20. See note 11 above.
21. Handler, Landau, and Lunzer interviews.
22. See below, on the JDC.
23. On the cultural activities and education, see chapters 9 and 10.
24. CBF, *Annual Reports*, 1945, 1946, and 1947.
25. Reports by Rabbi Goldfinger, January and March 1946, and by Reverend Carlebach, Oct. 20, 1946, Dec. 7, 20, and 31, 1946, WLL, Henriques/Brunswick, Hamburg, and Lübeck. See also sources in note 8 above.
26. B. Weingreen, report on Jews in the North Rhine Region, Oct. 15, 1945, WLL, Henriques/LV North Rhine–Westphalia [hereafter LV NRW]; memorandum on the German Jews in Germany, Dec. 4, 1945, PRO, FO/945/384; memorandum from Henriques to Solomon, Aug. 10, 1946, PRO, FO/1049/368; CBF, *Annual Report, 1946*, 5. On the legal advisers and the Lawyers' Conference on Restitution organized by JRU, see chapter 8.
27. CBF, *Annual Report, 1948*, 5–9. For the JRU welfare enterprise in the communities, see Bentwich, *They Found Refuge*, 176–82.
28. D. S. Norman, Mil. Gov. Berlin, to HQ CCG BE, Dec. 11, 1945, PRO, FO/1050/1491; a meeting of British Military authorities, May 20, 1946, PRO, FO/1049/418; report by Lily Holt, July 8, 1946, WLL, Henriques/Kaunitz Reports; Lowenthal, Field Director, Germany, to Germany Dept., JCRA, June 14, 1947, WLL, Henriques/Reorganization of Communal Life.
29. For more details regarding communal activities and the persons involved, see chapter 8.
30. Lunzer interview and private papers given to author; Eckstein to Brodetsky, Mar. 4, 1947, BDA, C11/13/17/1.
31. Bovenshen to Grasett, May 19, 1945, PRO, FO/1049/81; note of conference on the position of Displaced and Stateless Jews in Germany, May 23, 1945, BDA, C11/13/17/2; Anglo-Jewish Association's memorandum to the Foreign Office, June 18, 1945, and Brodetsky to Anthony de Rothschild, June 29, 1945, WLL, CBF/12/64; Eva Reading to Field Marshal Montgomery, Sept. 20, 1945, PRO, FO/1052/284; WJC [Easterman and Silverman] to Henderson of the FO (Refugee Dept.), Oct. 12, 1945, PRO, FO/1049/195; Major General Templer, Deputy Military Governor of the British Zone, to Lady Reading, Oct. 29, 1945, PRO, FO/1049/81.
32. FO to Washington, Oct. 5, 1945, and Lt. Col. Sir Brian Robertson (Chief of Staff British Zone) to Sir Eric Speed (P.U.S., WO), Oct. 6, 1945, about a conference with Brodetsky et al., PRO, FO/1049/81; Brotman (BD) to the Secretary of State for Foreign Affairs, Oct. 9, 1945, PRO, FO/1049/195; on British policy see also chapter 3.
33. CCG BE Germany to all Military District HQs, Nov. 19, 1945, on segregation of Jews, PRO, FO/1049/81; Zone Policy instruction no. 20,

Dec. 4, 1945, YV, 0–70/6; report on a visit of the Parliamentary Committee headed by Sec. Hynd to Bergen-Belsen, Jan. 21, 1946, YV, 0–70/5; N. Barou of WJC to A. Skeffington (Control Office for Germany and Austria, London), Mar. 8, 1946, YV, 0–70/16; Robertson, CCG Berlin, to Street, War Office, May 7, 1946, PRO, FO/945/384. See also chapter 3.

34. A letter of introduction for Brotman and Viteles, from Sir Raphael Cilento (UNRRA Zone Director), Mar. 8, 1946, PRO, FO/1013/1948; A. G. Brotman (JCRA) and Harry Viteles (AJDC): survey on conditions of Jews in the British Zone of Germany in March 1946, Mar. 29, 1946, YV, 0–70/6; Jewish Survey meetings, Apr. 1 and 2, 1946, PRO, FO/1050/1491; Viteles to Schwartz, Apr. 2, 1946, GJA, Geneva 1, 7A/C-48.0099, and see below on JDC.
35. See, for example, Major Murphy to DP HQ, Apr. 15, 1946, PRO, FO/1030/307; Robertson to Solomon, May 2, 1946, and notes on a proposal for the resettlement of Jews, by the Adviser Col. Solomon, May 8, 1946, PRO, FO/945/384. For more on this subject, see chapters 7 and 8.
36. CBF, *Annual Report, 1947*, 2–9, and see chapter 12.
37. Examples may be found in other chapters, especially 7 and 8.
38. Rosensaft and Wollheim to Kubowitzky, [July 1947], CZA, WJC/9A; Shlomo Shafir, "Der Jüdische Weltkongress und sein Verhältnis zu Nachkriegsdeutschland, 1945–1967," *Menora* 3 (1992): 210–37; *Belsen Book*, see the articles by Rosensaft, 35–36, Wollheim, 62–63, Barou, 73–79, and Easterman, 80–84; see also chapters 7 and 11.
39. Nadich stayed from August to November 1945, Rifkind from October 1945 to March 1946, Bernstein from May 1946 to August 1947, Levinthal from June to December 1947, etc.; finding a replacement was always difficult. See Genizi, *Adviser on Jewish Affairs*.
40. See chapter 7.
41. On the high JDC employee turnover, see Bauer, *Out of the Ashes*, and below in this chapter.
42. Gideon Shimoni, "Selig Brodetsky and the Ascendancy of Zionism in Anglo-Jewry (1939–1945)," *The Jewish Journal of Sociology* 12, no. 2 (1980): 125–61; BD resolution on British Jewry and Jews in Germany, July 15, 1945, BDA, C11/13/16/3; Kochavi, *Displaced Persons*, 25. See also chapter 4.
43. Resolutions accepted by the conference of the Agudath Israel Organization of Great Britain on May 21, 1945, PRO, FO/1050/1491.
44. See chapters 5 and 8. Also see Bentwich, *They Found Refuge*, 164–82.
45. Lunzer interview and private papers.
46. See chapter 8.
47. Bauer, *Out of the Ashes*, 25, 42–44.
48. Such a soldier was Kudish, whose letters from Celle were sent to his Hashomer Hatza'ir comrades in May 16, 17, and 22, 1945, YV, 0–37/19/1.

Notes to Chapter 6

49. Knopfelmacher to Beilin, July 2, 1945, CZA, S25/5233; *Unzer Sztyme*, July 12, 1945, 10; Jack Brass to JA's Immigration Dept., Sept. 5, 1945, CZA, S6/4644; Shimon Enreich, "From Bergen-Belsen," in *Sefer Hahitnadvut* [Hebrew: *The Book of the Volunteers*], ed. Ze'ev Shefer (Jerusalem, 1949), 786–87.
50. Knopfelmacher to Beilin (July 2, 1945, CZA, S25/5233) on Captain Deutsch's complaints regarding the absence of any connection with *Eretz Yisrael*, the lack of Hebrew books and newspapers, etc.; Ben Appelbaum (Jewish Brigade soldier in Belsen) to Berl Locker of the JA, Sept. 11, 1945, and Adler-Rudel to Berl Locker, Oct. 3, 1945, CZA, A140/366; Yoav Gelber, *Jewish Palestinian Volunteering in the British Army during the Second World War*, vol. 3, *The Standard Bearers: Rescue Mission to the Jewish People* (Jerusalem, 1983) [Hebrew], 324–529, esp. 487–90; Bauer, *Out of the Ashes*, 44.
51. This contradicts somewhat the description by Gelber, *The Standard Bearers*, 479–87. See chapter 4.
52. Edna Elazary, "The Hebrew Gymnasium in Bergen-Belsen, December 1945–March 1947" (M.A. thesis, The Hebrew University of Jerusalem, 1988) [Hebrew]. See more in chapter 10.
53. Keynan, *Holocaust Survivors*, 84–100, 117–31.
54. Lily Holt, report from Kaunitz Camp, Aug, 9, 1946, WLL, Henriques/Kaunitz Reports; Gelber, *The Standard Bearers*, 512–29; Elazary, "The Hebrew Gymnasium."
55. Haim Yahil, "The Activities of the Palestine Mission for *She'erit Hapletah*, 1945–1949," *Yalkut Moreshet* 30 (November 1980): 7–40, 31 (April 1981): 133–76 [Hebrew].
56. Ibid.; Histadrut Zionit Ahida in Bergen-Belsen to the JA, Paris, Apr. 2, 1946, CZA, L10/232I.
57. Report on emissaries, May 26, 1946, CZA, S86/343; JA mission diary no. 3, Feb. 9, 1947, CZA, S25/5231; Keynan, *Holocaust Survivors*, 197–205.
58. Keynan, *Holocaust Survivors*.
59. Bichler to comrades, [December 1946], CZA, S6/1911; Lewin to Behar, July 2, 1947, CZA, S6/3658; *Belsen Book*, Tsamriyon's article, 159–63. Tsamriyon, *The Press*; Mordechai Breuer interview and personal letters, OHD.
60. Many letters of complaint testify to the absence of regular contact with either the Jewish Agency's headquarters in Jerusalem or the mission's center in the American Zone. See, for example, Chomsky to Behar, Aug. 20, 1947, CZA, S6/1627, and many others in CZA, S86/284. JA correspondence with the British Zone occupies only a very small section of the Emissaries Division archive (S86). See also Yahil, "The Activities," 147–51. On the united organization see chapter 4. On the Zionist Organization, see chapter 11.
61. For their general roles in postwar Germany, see Bauer, *Out of the Ashes*; for their specific roles in the British Zone, see chapters 9, 10, and 12.

Notes to Chapter 7

62. Bauer, *Out of the Ashes*, xiv–xxi. On Warburg's properties see discussions of the JRU's work.
63. Bauer, *Out of the Ashes*, 30, 41–42. On the arrival and activities of the first JDC team in Belsen, see Rosensaft to E. Warburg, Nov. 11, 1945, YV, 0-70/17. On JDC participation in the July conference, see chapter 4.
64. Bauer, *Out of the Ashes*, 61–62, 99–100, 228, 279–80.
65. On the problem of supplies from America and the conditions in the British Zone, see ibid., 122–30; Brotman-Viteles report, Mar. 29, 1946, and meetings thereafter, Apr. 1, 1946, in note 34 above; Bauer, *Out of the Ashes*, 100. On the improvements, see chapters 3 and 9.
66. Bauer, *Out of the Ashes*, 130, 228; *Belsen Book*, Rosensaft's article, 37, and note by Kaufman, 136–38. On specific JDC contributions see also chapters 7, 9, and 10.
67. As will be shown in chapter 7.
68. Bauer, *Out of the Ashes*, 62.
69. Summaries of roles and activities of the various welfare organizations: Kurt R. Grossmann, "Die jüdischen Auslandsorganisationen und ihre Arbeit in Deutschland," in *Die Juden in Deutschland, 1951/52: Ein Almanach*, ed. Heinz Gänther (Frankfurt a.M. and Munich), 91–120.

Chapter 7

1. See chapter 4; *Belsen Book*, 183.
2. In his memorandum of May 1946 (PRO, FO/1049/367), Colonel Solomon, the Jewish adviser, writes about an official subcommittee for the Belsen camp, although in practice the CC and the Belsen Committee were the one and the same. On the Belsen Committee, see *Belsen Book*, 183–84. The establishment of a subcommittee seems to have been connected with the struggle for the British recognition.
3. B. Laufer on the need for unity: *Unzer Sztyme*, Nov. 29, 1945, 29.
4. Rosensaft in a meeting with British Parliament Commission in Belsen on Jan. 20, 1946 (report dated Jan. 21), YV, 0-70/5; Viteles and Nurock on the CC, in a Jewish survey meeting, Apr. 1, 1946, PRO, FO/1050/1491; protocol of a meeting of all the committees and the communities, May 9, 1946, Community of Hanover Archives, now at ZAH, B1/6; Rosensaft to La Guardia—Director General of UNRRA, Aug. 23, 1946, YV, 0-70/6.
5. On the first transport of children from the British Zone, October 1945, HL, Schonfeld/142/123; meeting on question of Jewish children from camps in Germany, Nov. 6, 1945, BDA, C11/13/16/3; Landauer to Rosensaft, Nov. 12, 1945, CZA, L58/637; Brodetsky to Rosensaft, Nov. 12, 1945, BDA, C11/13/16/3; Adler-Rudel (Jewish Refugee Comm. London) to UNRRA HQ in Germany, Dec. 21, 1945, CZA, A140/713; Adler-Rudel to the JA Executive, Dec. 31, 1945, CZA, A140/546; *Belsen*

Notes to Chapter 7

    Book, articles by Rosensaft, 34–35, Bimko Rosensaft, 91–93, and Adler-Rudel, 110–13; Bentwich, *They Found Refuge*, 74–77.
6. Report by Wollheim, Mar. 10, 1946, YV, 0–70/63.
7. See chapter 6.
8. Wollheim interview.
9. A letter from the Hungarian Jewish committee at Bergen-Belsen, *JC*, June 22, 1945, 14; the rabbis of Adath She'erith Yisrael to Rabbi Hertz, [October 1945], HL, Schonfeld/144; official document with the letterhead "Adath Sche'erith Yisrael" and a list of officials, signed by Rabbi H. Meisels and Jacob Bornstein [November 1945], and a letter from Meisels to Baumgarten, Nov. 14, 1945, HL, Schonfeld/144; Rabbi Meisels [posing as the Chief Rabbi of the British Zone], to Mil. Gov., Jan. 23, 1946, PRO, FO/1050/149.
10. Minutes of Extra-ordinary Executive Meeting of the CRREC, Feb. 24, 1946, HL, Schonfeld/576/1.
11. See Adath She'erith Yisrael budget for April 1946, listing affiliated groups and institutions, HL, Schonfeld/144; Mil. Gov. Main HQ to War Office, Apr. 16, 1946, PRO, FO/945/731.
12. See chapter 6.
13. Minutes of the CRREC, Feb. 24, 1946, above, note 10; Meisels to Schonfeld, 9 of Nissan (April) 1946, HL, Schonfeld/144.
14. Rabbi Rosen's report on his recent visit to Germany, June 20, 1946, HL, Schonfeld/576/1; Silberstein to CRREC, 26 Marheshvan (October or November) 1946, HL, Schonfeld/292.
15. Adath She'erith Yisrael to the CRREC, Jan. 20, 1947, and the CRREC reply, Feb. 3, 1947, HL, Schonfeld/292.
16. Wollheim and Helfgott to Brodetsky, Feb. 12, 1947, CZA, WJC/9A.
17. Unsigned letter [Solomon?] to Brodetsky, Feb. 27, 1947, BDA, C11/13/17/1; Sarah Eckstein to Brodetsky (with copies to L. Cohen, Chairman of JCRA, and D. Osborne, Deputy Field Director of JRU in Germany), Mar. 4, 1947, ibid.; Wollheim to Adler-Rudel, Apr. 3, 1947, CZA, WJC/9A; report of Mr. L. Cohen on his visit to Germany, Apr. 10, 1947, BDA, C11/13/19/1; minutes of a meeting of the CRREC executive, July 22, 1947, HL, Schonfeld/576/1.
18. *Central Committee of Liberated Jews in the British Zone Germany 1945–1947* (activity report submitted to the Second Congress of the *She'erit Hapletah*, July 1947, Bad Harzburg), YV, 0–70/40 (available also at Yad Vashem Library and at Wiener Library in Tel Aviv), 13, 20; Bauer, *Out of the Ashes*, 100. It is now up to the historian to compare the conflicting accounts of JDC officials and the CC and establish who was really in charge.
19. Beckleman of JDC Paris to JDC Belsen, June 25, 1947, GJA, Geneva 1, 7A/C-48.007; Kassa-Bericht of the CC, for 1/1/46–30/6/46, YV, 0–70/30.
20. Circular by the CC and Auerbach to all the communities and commit-

Notes to Chapter 7

tees, Aug. 6, 1946, YV, 0–70/13; circular by the chairman of the LV North Rhine-Westphalia, Oct. 5, 1946, WLL, Henriques/LV NRW.
21. *Central Committee*, 20.
22. See chapter 8.
23. Report of Mr. L. Cohen on his visit to Germany, Apr. 10, 1947, BDA, C11/13/19/1; see also *Central Committee* above. On the rescue operation see chapter 2.
24. *Central Committee*, 9, 16, 21–23; an undated circular sent to mothers regarding the importance of cod-liver oil (vitamins A and D) for children, YV, JM/10.374/1577; Bimko Rosensaft's account in *Belsen Book*, 88–97.
25. Report forms distributed by the CC Kultur Abteilung to various cultural institutions and schools, YV, 0–70/30; certificates for various schools, issued and signed by the CC, YV, 0–70/28; CC Bulletin no. 8, March 1946 (Yiddish), YV, JM/10/374/1573; reports of the CC Kultur Abteilung, July 2 and Nov. 4, 1946 (Yiddish), YV, JM/10.374/1578. Not all cultural initiatives, however, were under the auspices of the CC. For more details, see chapter 10.
26. *Central Committee*, 24–26; minutes of CRREC Executive meetings, Feb. 24 and 28, 1946, HL, Schonfeld/576/1; Prager and Nussbaum of Hanover to the Rabbinate of Belsen, seeking advice regarding conversion, Oct. 28, 1946, ZAH, B1/6.
27. *Unzer Sztyme*, July 12, 1947, 59.
28. *Central Committee*, 24–26; Announcements by the Chief Rabbinate, one undated and one from July 1947, YV, JM/10.374/1575; circular of January 1946, mentioned in the Resolutions of the Chief Rabbinate, July 22, 1947, WLL, Henriques/Reorg. Communal Life; form for appeals to the *Bet Din* (judicial court) for *Aguna* (a married woman who cannot be considered a widow and is ineligible to remarry because there is no evidence of her husband's death. This situation was a widespread and unprecedented outcome of the Holocaust, and was particularly problematic for women from the halakic point of view. The problem challenged the rabbinical establishment to invent creative solutions, enabling widows to remarry while keeping conformity with the halakah), n.d., YV, 0–70/29.
29. On the Belsen Committee, see below; resolutions of the CRREC, July 22, 1947, HL, Schonfeld/132/3.
30. Resolution of the Chief Rabbinate, July 22, 1947, WLL, Henriques/Reorg. Communal Life; Chief Rabbinate of all Communities in the British Zone to the JA, Mar. 7, 1948, CZA, S6/3659.
31. *Unzer Sztyme*, Jan. 1, 1946, p. 22 on the attack and demonstration, p. 11 on the protest of Dov Laufer; report of the Hohne Jewish Civil Police, April 1946, BDA, C11/13/17/1; *Central Committee*, 29–30.
32. "Notes on interview with Mr. Rosensaft and Dr. Barou at the House of Commons on 13th March, 1946," PRO, FO/945/378; *Unzer Sztyme*, Mar. 17, 1946, 23; report by Wollheim, May 6, 1946, YV, 0–70/7; report

Notes to Chapter 7

by Brigadier Kenchington (PW & DP Division), May 31, 1946, PRO, FO/1049/626.
33. Report of the Jewish police, April 1946, BDA, C11/13/17/1; from CONFOLK to CONCOMB, May 29, 1946, PRO, FO/1050/720; report by Brigadier Kenchington, and Parliamentary Question, May 31, 1946, PRO, FO/1049/626; *Central Committee* 29–30; Dallob to Katzki on the Feb. 18 raid of British police on Belsen, Mar. 3, 1948, GJA, Geneva 1, 7A/C-48.416.
34. Announcement by the Jewish police, Aug. 29, 1946, YV, JM/10.374/1576; police report, May 3, 1947, PRO, FO/945/723; *Central Committee* 29–30. See also chapter 9.
35. Report by JRU on Belsen, Apr. 24, 1946, WLA, Henriques/Belsen Reports; announcement by the "Yiddisher Gericht" (Yiddish), May 16, 1946, YV, 0–70/30; *Unzer Sztyme*, Aug. 20, 1946, 22. The court is not mentioned in the *Central Committee*.
36. Alex Kraut to Leonard Cohen, Feb. 24, 1946, WLL, Henriques/Neustadt Reports; report by Wollheim, Mar. 10, 1946, YV, 0–70/63.
37. Announcement by the Kultur Abteilung of the CC, on the establishment of Holocaust Archive, Nov. 1, 1945, YV, 0–70/30.
38. *Central Committee*, 18.
39. Ibid., 28.
40. Ibid., 27; CC circular, Jan. 20, 1947, YV, 0–70/13.
41. Jewish Survey meeting, Apr. 1, 1946, PRO, FO/1050/1491.
42. Announcement of the CC, Apr. 14, 1946 (Yiddish), YV, JM/10.375/1608; Major Murphy to DO HQ 30 Corps, on unveiling of memorial at Camp One in Belsen, Apr. 15, 1946, PRO, FO/1030/307; circular published by the CC about the memorial day, Apr. 15, 1947 (Yiddish), YV, JM/10.3714/1572; resolutions of the CC, Apr. 15, 1947, YV, 0–70/4; circular of the CC to all committees and Jewish communities, Apr. 15, 1947, ZAH, B1/6. For more details see chapters 9 and 11.
43. Hanover Jewish Committee to CC, July 15, 1946, and Nov. 17, 1946, WLL, Henriques/Hanover.
44. Circular on CC handling of affairs in various communities, Dec. 16, 1945, YV 0–70/64; report by Wollheim, Jan. 21, 1946, YV, 0–70/5; reports by Wollheim, Mar. 14 and Apr. 8, 1946, YV, 0–70/63; protocol of a meeting of Jewish committees and communities in Bremen, May 9, 1946, ZAH, B1/6; CC circular, July 31, 1946, YV, 0–70/13; *Unzer Sztyme*, Oct. 2, 1946, 28, on a German newspaper put out by the Cultural Department for the communities. For more details see chapter 8.
45. Jewish Survey meeting on German Jewish welfare, Apr. 1, 1946, PRO, FO/1050/1491 (the term in quotation marks was used by Nurock, and Viteles of the JDC strongly supported it); PW & DP Division, May 2, 1946, PRO, FO/1049/367.
46. Rosensaft to Edward Warburg, Nov. 11, 1945, YV, 0–70/17; Landauer to Rosensaft, Nov. 12, 1945, CZA, L58/637; Rosensaft to Mayor of

Hanover, Nov. 17, 1945, CZA, L10/232I; telegram from FO to Lübeck, Dec. 7, 1945, PRO, FO/1049/81; report by Adler-Rudel to the CBF on the evacuation of Jewish children from Germany, Dec. 21, 1945, A140/713; Bulletin of the CC, Mar. 4, 1946, YV, JM/10.374/1573; Barou to Cleffington, Mar. 8, 1946, YV, 0–70/16; circular of the CC, Sept. 17, 1946, YV, 0–70/13; report by Wollheim, Sept. 21, 1946, YV, 0–70/1; from Control Commission Berlin (CONCOMB) to Control Office London on a visit of Rosensaft to the UK, Nov. 1, 1946, PRO, FO/945/399; JTA Bulletin, Nov. 26, 1946, about representatives of Jews in Germany received by the War Secretary and Chancellor of the Duchy of Lancaster, YV, 0–70/37; "Jewish DP Leaders Received at W.J.C. Headquarters," January 1947, and Barou to the CC on outcome of Wollheim's visit to London, Dec. 2, 1947, CZA, WJC/9A; *Unzer Sztyme*, Nov. 15, 1946, and July 12, 1947, on the travels of Rosensaft and Wollheim. See also *Central Committee* 9–19.

47. "Jewish DP Leaders Received at W.J.C. Headquarters," January 1947, CZA, WJC/9A; Wollheim on negotiations with the WJC executive in New York, Feb. 4, 1947, YV, 0–70/16; Rosensaft and Wollheim to Kubowitzky, July 1947, CZA, WJC/9A; Rosensaft and Wollheim to Kalman Stein, WJC, on the affiliation, Aug. 14, 1947, YV, 0–70/16.

48. Election of the delegation, Apr. 14, 1948, YV, 0–70/4; minutes on the meeting in Montreux, July 4, 1948, and Wollheim to Jacoby (WJC), July 14, 1948, ZAH, B1/10.

49. Briefing for the Chancellor's meeting with Solomon, July 29, 1947, and Brodetsky and Solomon meeting with Lord Packenham, July 30, 1947, PRO, FO/945/384; Wollheim to Brodetsky, Sept. 29, 1947, BDA, C11/13/18/4; Wollheim's report on discussions with Solomon, Oct. 30, 1947, YV, 0–70/63; Solomon's report to Lord Packenham, November 1947, PRO, FO/938/287. See also chapter 8.

50. Wollheim to Bakstansky (UJA), Mar. 20, 1947, and Wollheim to Roth (WJC), May 26, 1947, CZA, WJC/9A; documents above regarding the economic dispute.

51. Meeting of CC Executive, Aug. 11, 1947, YV, 0–70/4. See more details in chapter 8.

52. Circular by Laufer of the CC to all committees and Jewish communities in the British Zone, Jan. 20, 1947, YV, 0–70/13; CC on the Belsen Committee, Feb. 10, 1947, and on the elections to the Belsen Committee, Mar. 10, 1947, YV, 0–70/32;; Wollheim to Adler-Rudel, Apr. 3, 1947, CZA, WJC/9A.

53. On negotiations up until recognition: Sir Brian Robertson to Gilmore Jenkins, Jan. 9, 1947, PRO, FO/945/399; Jenkins to Robertson, Feb. 14, 1947, PRO, FO/1049/890; Wollheim to Barou, May 30, 1947, CZA, WJC/9A; Barou to Rosensaft, Aug. 1, 1947, CZA, WJC/9A; Dallob to Katzki, Jan. 21, 1948, on the British authorities finally recognizing the CC as representative of the camps, GJA, Geneva 1, 7A/C-48.009;

summary by Rosensaft in *Unzer Sztyme*, Aug. 20, 1947, 15–16; protocol of the CC Executive, planning for liquidation, Nov. 28, 1948, YV, 0-70/4. See also chapter 3 on British policy, and chapter 8 on the process of communal organization.

Chapter 8

1. *Conference on the Future of the Jews in Germany.*
2. See Naujoks, "Die Funktion." And see below in this chapter.
3. CRREC executive meeting, July 22, 1947, HL, Schonfeld/576/1; CRREC resolutions, July 22, 1947, WLL, Henriques/Reorganization of Communal Life. See also note 18 below; Naujoks, "Die Funktion"; Ginzel, "Phasen," 447; Lorenz and Berkemann, "Kriegsende und Neubeginn," 641–45.
4. Ginzel, "Phasen"; *Jüdisches Schicksal in Köln*, 200; *Wegweiser durch das jüdische Rheinland*, ed. Ludger Heid and Julius H. Schoeps (Salomon Ludwig Steinheim Institut, [n.p.] 1992), 160–68.
5. Rev. A. Greenbaum to Leonard Cohen, Aug. 5, 1945, and report on work in Hamburg by Rev. A. Greenbaum, Aug. 29, 1945, WLL, Henriques/Hamburg Reports.
6. Lunzer and Wodlinger to Cilento, Jan. 3, 1946, YV, 0–70/6; LV to Mary Wise, Feb. 15, 1946, WLL, Henriques/LV NRW; Willmot on Jewish equipment in Hamburg, Feb. 27, 1946, PRO, FO/1050/1491; Brotman-Viteles report, Mar. 29, 1946, YV, 0–70/6; Solomon's memorandum, Apr. 24, 1946, WLL, Henriques/LV NRW; Auerbach, on behalf of the Jewish communities to the *Länder* governments, May 19, 1946, YV, 0–70/62.
7. Meeting of the Council of the Jewish Communities in the British Zone, Jan. 9, 1947, AGH.
8. Auerbach's circular, July 12, 46, YV, 0–70/62; report of the LV NRW, July 17, 1946, WLL, Henriques/LV NRW.
9. Rev. A. Greenbaum to Leonard Cohen, Aug. 5, 1945, and report on work in Hamburg by Rev. A. Greenbaum, Aug. 29, 1945, WLL, Henriques/Hamburg Reports; *Jüdisches Schicksal in Köln*, 200; Hugo Nothmann, "Die religiöse Situation des Judentums im Nachkriegsdeutschland," in *Die Juden in Deutschland, 1951/2 (5712): Ein Almanach*, ed. Heinz Ganther (Frankfurt a.M. and Munich, 1953), 185–87. Nothmann argues that the religion did not function as a basis or backbone of the communities but rather the struggle for *Wiedergutmachung*, and against anti-Semitism. This argument is not verified by the evidence of the sources. See also Mlynek et al., "Deutsche und Juden," 97–99; Prager, "Wiederaufbau," 43; *Wegweiser durch das jüdische Rheinland*, 160–68. For more details regarding the rabbis' work, see chapter 6.
10. CCG BE Berlin to Control Commission London, Oct. 29, 1946, PRO,

FO/1050/720; Rev. Carlebach to L. Cohen, Dec. 31, 1946, WLL, Henriques/Hamburg Reports.
11. Carlebach to Cohen, Dec. 31, 1946, WLL, Henriques/Hamburg Reports; Lowenthal to JCRA, Aug. 7, 1947, WLL, Henriques/Osnabrück Reports. See also chapter 6.
12. Jewish Survey meeting, Apr. 1, 1946, PRO, FO/1050/1491; CCG BE Berlin to Control Commission London, Oct. 29, 1946, PRO, FO/1050/720.
13. Rev. A. Greenbaum to L. Cohen, Aug. 5, 1945, and Report by Greenbaum, Aug. 29, 1945, WLL, Henriques/Hamburg Reports; Brotman-Viteles report, Mar. 19, 1946, YV, 0–70/6; Rev. Carlebach to L. Cohen, Dec. 31, 1946, WLL, Henriques/Hamburg Reports; Barker to Dreifuss, Jan. 13, 1947, WLL, Henriques/Düsseldorf; Lowenthal to JCRA, Feb. 16, 1948, WLL, Henriques/Oldenburg Reports.
14. Mitteilung aus Lübeck, Dec. 16, 1945, YV, 0–70/64; Brotman-Viteles report, Mar. 19, 1946, YV, 0–70/6; Wollheim, report on the damaging of Jewish cemeteries in Lübeck/Schleswig-Holstein, Apr. 8, 1947, YV, 0–70/63, list of twenty-six incidents of cemetery desecration in the British Zone during the year 1947, Jan. 3, 1948, ZAH, B1/10.
15. Protocol of the meeting of the LV, Jan. 9, 1946, PRO, FO/1013/1948; Auerbach to Mary Wise, Feb. 15, 1946, WLL, Henriques/LV NRW; survey on the conditions in the British Zone (Brotman-Viteles report), Mar. 29, 1946, YV, 0–70/6; *Jüdisches Gemeindeblatt*, May 24, 1946, 3–4.
16. See sources in note 15 above.
17. Speeches of Auerbach and Wollheim at the LV meeting of Jan. 9, 1946, PRO, FO/1013/1948.
18. Constitution of the *Landesgemeinde* of Schleswig-Holstein, February 1946, YV, 0–70/63.
19. Comparative figures of the Jewish Population of towns with more than 100,000 inhabitants within the British Zone, July 1946, Bundesarchiv Koblenz, Z40/486; list of members of the Jewish community in Göttingen, July 1, 1946, YV, 0–70/63; L. Cohen to Brotman, Jan. 17, 1946, BDA, C11/13/16/4; the Jewish DP situation, Jan. 22, 1946, PRO, FO/1049/625; Brotman-Viteles report, Mar. 29, 1946, YV, 0–70/6.
20. Protocol of the assembly, May 9, 1946, AGH; *Jüdisches Gemeindeblatt*, May 24, 1946, 3–4.
21. LV North Rhine Province to W. Asbury, HQ Military Government, June 21, 1946, PRO, FO/1013/1948; Auerbach to HQ CC, June 27, 1946, WLL, Henriques/LV NRW; *Jüdisches Gemeindeblatt*, July 10, 1946, 40; circulars by the Zonenausschuss (zone committee), July 12, Aug. 14 and 19, 1946, YV, 0–70/62.
22. Circular by the Zonenausschuss, Aug. 28, 1946, and circular by the LV NRW, Sept. 9, 1946, YV, 0–70/62; circular by the LV NRW, Oct. 3, 1946, WLL, Henriques/LV NRW; protocol of the Zonenausschuss

Notes to Chapter 8

meeting on Oct. 30, 1946, YV, 0–70/63; *Jüdisches Gemeindeblatt*, Sept. 26, 1946, 8–10, and Nov. 9, 1946, 10–11.
23. "Interessenvertretung der jüdischen Gemeinden und Kultusvereinigungen der drei westlichen Zonen Deutschlands," May 19, 1946, and circular of the Arbeitsgemeinschaft der jüdischen Gemeinden Nordwestdeutschland, May 21, 1946, YV, 0–70/62; protocol of the meeting of the Interessenvertretung (Interests-Representation of the Jewish Communities, abbreviated in the text as I-RJC), Jan. 26, 1947, CZA, C7/268/1; *Jüdisches Gemeindeblatt*, July 10, 1946, 40–44.
24. Meeting of the Council of the British Zone, Feb. 25, 1947, and a letter to the Interessenvertretung from the assembly in Eilshausen, Apr. 20, 1947, YV, 0–70/62; protocol of the I-RJC, and report, and a letter from the Council to the I-RJC, all of Mar. 2, 1947, CZA, C7/268/1; Lowenthal to Addi Bernd, Mar. 25, 1947, and to Henriques, Apr. 24, 1947, and protocol of the assembly in Eilshausen, Apr. 20, 1947, WLL, Henriques/Reorganization of Communal life; protocol of the I-RJC, Apr. 13, 1947, ZAH, B1/6; *Jüdisches Gemeindeblatt*, Mar. 19, 1947, 1–2.
25. Meeting of the Council of the British Zone, June 1, 1947, YV, 0–70/62; a statement by Hans Lamm, June 9, 1947, CZA, C7/268/1; JTA Daily News Bulletin no. 6, June 24, 1947, YV, 0–70/37; *Jüdisches Gemeindeblatt*, July 9, 1947, 1–2.
26. Protocols of the Council of the British Zone, of the Interest-Representation, and of the Work Association, note 24 above.
27. B. Kossowsky, *Bibliography of the Jewish Publications in the British Zone of Germany, 1945–1950* (Bergen-Belsen, 1950) [Yiddish]; *Israel und Wir, Keren Hajessod Jahrbuch der jüdischen Gemeinschaft in Deutschland, 1955–1965* (Frankfurt a.M., 1966), 368.
28. *Jüdisches Gemeindeblatt*, June 11, 1947, 1–2.
29. Meeting of the Council of the Jewish Communities in the British Zone, June 1, 1947, YV, 0–70/62; Lowenthal to JRU London, June 6, 1947, WLL, Henriques/Reorganization of Communal Life; Solomon to Henriques, June 10, 1947, WLL, Henriques/Lowenthal Reports; *Jüdisches Gemeindeblatt*, June 11, 1947, 2; report of the representative of the Jewish Welfare, June 18, 1947, ZAH, B1/6; Henriques to Lowenthal, July 2, 1947, WLL, Henriques/Central Committee; Bentwich to Cohen, July 22, 1947, WLL, Henriques/Lowenthal Reports.
30. Press release of the Second Congress, July 20, 1947, YV, JM/10.3714, 1572; Bulletin no. 167 of the congress, July 20, 1947, YV, 0–70/37; resolution of the Chief Rabbinate to the Second Congress, July 22, 1947, WLL, Henriques/Reorganization of Communal Life; agenda for the Second Congress, July 22, 1947, Wiener Library Tel Aviv, W1F/CEN; resolution of the Chief Rabbinate, July 23, 1947, YV, 0–70/29; Lowenthal to JCRA, July 29, 1947, WLL, Henriques/Reorganization of Communal Life; *Jüdisches Gemeindeblatt*, July 29, 1947, 1–5.
31. Citation of Wollheim's speech in Lowenthal to JCRA, July 29, 1947,

Notes to Chapter 8

WLL, Henriques/Reorganization of Communal Life; *Jüdisches Gemeindeblatt*, July 29, 1947, 1–5.
32. The *Exodus* affair is dealt with in chapter 11.
33. Solomon to Henriques, June 10, 1947, report on a visit of Silverman to the Chancellor of the Duchy of Lancaster, June 16, 1947; minutes of a meeting held on June 18, to discuss Jewish problems in the British Zone of Germany; German Refugee Dept. to the Chancellor, June 23, 1947, Brownjohn to Dean, Aug. 22, 1947, all in PRO FO/945/399. Lowenthal to Germany Dept. JCRA, June 14, 1947, WLL, Henriques/Reorganization of Communal Life; Henriques to Lowenthal, on central representative body in the British Zone, July 2, 1947, WLL, Henriques/6/Central Committee; Wollheim to Brodetsky, July 25, 1947, BDA, C11/13/17/2; paper for the Chancellor meeting with Solomon, July 29, 1947. Report on the meeting of Brodetsky and Solomon with Lord Pakenham, July 30, 1947; Freeman to Solomon, Oct. 4, 1947; Ivimy on appointment of deputy, Representation of German Jews, Neustadt Fishery School and Solomon's Resignation, Oct. 10, 1947; Control Office London to Freeman, German Section on Representation of German Jews, Oct. 16 all in PRO, FO/945/384; Brownjohn to Bishop, Sept. 13, 1947, PRO, FO/1049/891.
34. CBF, *Annual Report, 1947*, 2–9; Hagit Lavsky, "British Jewry and the Jews in Post-Holocaust Germany: The Jewish Relief Unit, 1945–1950," *Journal of Holocaust Education* 4, no. 1 (1995): 29–40, here 35–36. See also in chapter 12.
35. Protocol of the CC Presidency meeting, Aug. 20, 1947, YV, 0–70/4; letter of the Rat der Gemeinden beim Zentralkomitee der befreiten Juden der britischen Zone Deutschlands to members of the Council, Aug. 29, 1947, ZAH, B1/6; extract from JTA Bulletin, Sept. 10, 1947, WLL, Henriques/Reorganization of communal Life.
36. See chapter 11.
37. Wollheim to Jacoby of the WJC in New York, July 14, 1948, and to Breslauer, London, July 16, 1948, ZAH, B1/10; report of Wollheim on his trip to London, July 21–28, 1948, YV, 0–70/4; Shafir, "Der Jüdische Weltkongress."
38. *American Jewish Year Book*, 51/1950, p. 327, and see in chapter 12.
39. Lowenthal to JCRA, Sept. 17, 1948, WLL, Henriques/Cologne Reports; statistics on Germany, Austria, and Italy, JDC, Oct. 6, 1948, GJA, Geneva 1, 6AC-45.068A; Protocols of the CC Presidency meetings, Nov. 11, 1948, Nov. 2, 1948, Feb. 15, 1949, and of the CC Executive meeting, Feb. 2, 1949, YV, 0–70/4; Lowenthal to Henriques, Feb. 10, 1949, WLL, Henriques/6/Central Committee; Laufer to the Jewish Community in Hanover, Mar. 8, 1949, and Olevsky to the Jewish Communities and Committees in the British Zone, Mar. 14, 1949, ZAH, B1/6.
40. Hans Lamm regarding the second convention of the Arbeitsgemein-

schaft, October 1947, CZA, C7/268/1; summary of the resolutions and suggestions of the second meeting of the Arbeitsgemeinschaft of the Jewish Communities in Germany, Oct. 19–22, 1947, PRO, FO/1049/316 (also in WLL, Henrique/Reorganization of Communal Life); *Der Weg* (Berlin), Oct. 24, 1947; *Jüdisches Gemeindeblatt*, Oct. 24, 1947, 1–2; Lowenthal to JCRA, June 14, 1948, WLL, Henriques/Reorganization of Communal Life; circular by Wollheim to all members of the communities members, Sept. 2, 1948, YV, 0–70/63; circular by Warsher on behalf of the Interessenvertretung, Nov. 4, 1948, ZAH, B1/6; Wollheim to the Interessenvertretung Stuttgart, June 20, 1949, AGH; *Conference on the Future of the Jews in Germany*.
41. H. van Dam to R. Henriques, Oct. 10, 1948, WLL, Henriques/Reorganization of Communal Life; Regional Governmental Office, HQ Land Niedersachsen to Office of the Political Adviser, Oct. 28, 1948, PRO, FO/1049/1316; *Jüdisches Gemeindeblatt*, Dec. 10, 1948, 1; van Dam to L. Cohen, Mar. 3, 1949, WLL, Henriques/6/Belsen 4b.
42. M. Fischer to Henriques, May 17, 1949, WLL, Henriques/Harzburg 1949.
43. M. Karger, KKL (Keren Kayemet Leyisrael) delegate in Germany, to the KKL head-office in Jerusalem, Sept. 22, Nov. 14, Dec. 19, Dec. 15, 1949, Jan. 29, July 4, 1950, and to M. Goldschmidt of the KKL office in Munich, June 13, 1950, and Goldschmidt to Karger, June 23, 1950, CZA, KKL/5–17451; *Jüdisches Gemeindeblatt*, July 28, 1950, 4–5; Neima Barzel, "Israel and Germany, 1945–1956: Development of the Attitude of Israeli Society and State to Germany Following the Holocaust" (Ph.D. thesis, Haifa University, 1990) [Hebrew], 79; *Die Juden in Deutschland, 1951/52: Ein Almanach*, ed. Heinz Ganther (Frankfurt a.M. and Munich, 1953), 144–45.
44. Protocol of the convention in Hamburg, Nov. 21, 1949, YV, 0–70/63, 6, translation from the German by the author.
45. Protocol of a meeting of the communities' representatives in the British Zone, Sept. 9, 1949, YV, 0–70/63; Heymann to Fischer, Dec. 2, 1949, WLL, Henriques/LV NRW; meeting of the executive of the Central Committee, Dec. 22, 1949, WLL, Henriques/Reorganization of Communal Life; Statuten des Verbandes, October 1950, ZAH, B1/10.

Chapter 9

1. Title of an article by Rafael Olevsky, *Unzer Sztyme*, Feb. 20, 1946.
2. For details see chapters 2, 3, 4, and 6.
3. Declaration of the Jewish Workers Committee against taxes on pensions of refugees, Aug. 23, 1947, YV, 0–70/32; Dallob to Katzki, Mar. 3, 1948, on the British police raid on Belsen on Feb. 18, GJA, Geneva 1, 7A/C-48.416.
4. Report by Rosensaft to Kenchington, Aug. 10, 1947, YV, 0–70/7; cir-

cular of the CC, August 1947, YV, 0–70/13; statistics for the year 1947, January 1948, ZAH, B1/310.
5. As for the black market, see below in this chapter. On hiring German workers, see Brotman-Viteles report, Mar. 29, 1946, YV, 0–70/6.
6. Report of attack by Polish hooligans on Belsen synagogue, December 1945, YV, JM/10.374/1575; report by Wollheim, May 6, 1946, on Polish attacks and shootings against Jews, YV, 0–70/7; Paul Trepman, "*Arum Uns*" (Around Us), *Unzer Sztyme*, Aug. 20, 1946, 7–8; Greenbaum interview.
7. Dallob to Katzki, note 3 above; E. M. Tobin (Senior Control Officer, Niedersachsen) to Dallob (JDC), July 15, 1948, GJA, Geneva 1, 7A/C-48.410.
8. Trepman, "*Arum Uns*," note 6 above; report by Bloomberg on the Jewish Police, May 3, 1947, PRO, FO/945/723; Dallob to Katzki, note 3 above.
9. JRU Newsletter no. 6, January 1947, WLL, CBF 126/149; Breuer's letters to his wife, January 1947 and Mar. 2, 1947 (personal letters attached to Breuer interview).
10. Report by Lady Henriques on her tour in Germany from Jan. 21 to Feb. 5, 1947, CZA, WJC/A9; Bauer, *Out of the Ashes*, 228.
11. Brotman-Viteles report, note 5 above; report by Jack Weingreen, Apr. 24, 1946, WLL, Henriques/Belsen Reports; my interviews with Mordechai Breuer, Sara Eckstein-Grebenau, Arieh and Sonia Havkin, Michael Klodovsky, and Yitzhak Kerbel, OHD; a lecture by Bertha Weingreen, in her private papers attached to her interview, OHD.
12. Announcements by the Sanitary Department of Belsen Committee and the police, YV, JM/10.374/1573.
13. Brotman-Viteles report, note 5 above.
14. Announcement by Belsen Committee regarding the use of electricity, YV, JM/10.374/1573.
15. Interviews with Fischler, Greenbaum, Havkin, Klodowsky, and Kerbel.
16. *Unzer Sztyme*, Oct. 15, 1945.
17. Brotman-Viteles report, note 5 above; Jack Weingreen's report, note 11 above; Breuer to his wife, June 11, 1946, private letters; lecture by Bertha Weingreen, note 11 above.
18. Breuer to his wife, July 9, 1946, private letters; announcement by JRU and CRREC, March 1947, WLL, Henriques/Bad Harzburg; list of supplies by JRU for the period June 15–July 1, 1947, WLL, Henriques/6/CC; reports by JRU, JDC, and HIAS in the *Central Committee*; report by Rabbi Carlebach, July 11, 1947, BDA, C11/13/17/1; announcement by the JDC on special allocation, July 7, 1947, GJA, Geneva 1, 7A/C-48.412; list of adopting and adopted communities, Oct. 27, 1947, WLL, Henriques/Adoption Scheme; lecture to Palestine emissaries in Germany and Austria, November 1947, CZA, S86/284.
19. Adath She'erit Yisrael to the Chief Rabbinate, November 1946 (26th Mar heshvan), and CRREC to Adath She'erit Yisrael, Feb. 3, 1947,

HL, Schonfeld/292; Breuer to his wife, July 9, 1947, private letters; Carlebach's report, July 11, 1947, BDA, C11/13/17/1; interviews with Havkin, Kerbel, Klodowsky.
20. Lecture to Palestine emissaries, note 18 above; Fischler interview.
21. Report of the Jewish Police, Apr. 2, 1946, YV, JM/10/374; Dallob to Katzki, Mar. 3, 1948, note 3 above; CID to Niedersachsen authorities, July 8, 1948, and Control Officer Niedersachsen to CID, July 15, 1948, GJA, Geneva 1, 7A/C-48.414.
22. Report by Jack Weingreen, note 11 above; ORT report, *Central Committee*, 40–42; lecture by Bertha Weingreen, note 11 above.
23. Report of Rose Henriques on her visit in Germany between Aug. 9–26, 1947, BDA, C11/13/17/1; Bulletin of JCRA, Jan. 1, 1948, HL, Schonfeld/130/1; Eva Kahn in a letter to Sara Eckstein-Grebenau, September 1981, attached to Grebenau interview.
24. Report of the Health Department, *Central Committee*.
25. Report by Jack Weingreen, note 11 above; dictation by UNRRA Chief Officer for the British Zone, Rafael Cilentio, May 7, 1946, WLL, Henriques/Jewish Training Farms; *Zum Sig* (For Victory), published by the Revisionist-Zionist movement in Bergen-Belsen (material attached to Kerbel interview).
26. JDC report, *Central Committee*; Henriques report, note 23 above. Many details on Ahlem's former and later history can be studied at the permanent exhibition in Ahlem, now a memorial of the Holocaust and the Jews of Hanover. See also Anke Quast, "Jüdische Gemeinden in Niedersachsen nach 1945: Das Beispiel Hannover" (Ph.D. thesis, University of Hanover, 1999), 166–68. More details in chapter 11.
27. Kraut to Blumberg (JRU), June 9, 1947, WLL, Henriques/Neustadt Reports; JDC report, *Central Committee*.
28. JDC report, *Central Committee*; Dutch (ORT) to Dallob (JDC), Apr. 29, 1948, YV, 0–70/17.
29. JDC report.
30. JDC report, note 27 above.
31. Klodowsky interview.
32. For some of these fortunate events see Asaria, *We Are the Witnesses*.
33. Report of the department for searching relatives *Central Committee*: during the period from September 1946 to June 1947, 950 cases for search were submitted, of which 380 ended successfully.
34. Brotman-Viteles report, note 5 above; *Unzer Sztyme*, Dec. 15, 1946, 32 (report of the Chief Rabbinate).
35. Even Rosensaft, who was considered leftist and secular and who was even accused of being anti-religious, had kept Jewish religious customs such as holding a "*Sholem Zachar*" ritual on the occasion of the birth of his son; see invitation, YV, 0–70/29.
36. As for the search for relatives, see the following section in this chapter.
37. Congratulatory announcements on the occasion of the engagement of

Rafael Olevsky and Rachel Zalmanowich, *Unzer Sztyme*, Oct. 15, 1945; for weddings within the Bar Kochva Revisionist kibbutz, see *Der Emeth*, December 1946; many invitation cards in YV, JM/10.374/1575 and 0-70/29; Havkin, Kerbel, Schmuelewitz, Wollheim interviews; Asaria, *We Are the Witnesses*; Olevsky, *The Tear*.

38. JDC report, *Central Committee*, 31–35; JDC report, Sept. 29, 1947, YV, 0–70/35; JDC statistics for the British Zone, Jan. 1, 1948, YV, 0–70/17.
39. Brotman-Viteles report, note 5 above; circular of the CC, Sept. 17, 1946, announcing the opening of Bad Harzburg convalescent home, YV, 0-70/13; JRU Volunteers Newsletter no. 25, October 1946, HL, Schonfeld/440/2, and Newsletter of January 1947, WLL, CBF/126/149; report by Naomi Cohen, report on health conditions and care, and the JDC report, 31–35, and the JRU report, 35–38, all in *Central Committee*; circular of the CC, August 1947, YV, 0–70/13, on children to Switzerland; Henriques report for Aug. 9–26, 1947, BDA, C11/13/17/1; JDC report, Sept. 29, 1947, YV, 0–70/35. On health care see also chapters 4 and 6.
40. The JDC and JRU initiated professional mental treatment at the Glyn Hughes Hospital only at the end of 1947: JCRA Bulletin, Jan. 12, 1948, HL, Schonfeld/130/1.
41. Keynan, *Holocaust Survivors*; Pinson, "Jewish Life"; Segalman, "Psychology of Jewish Displaced Persons."
42. Report by Jack Weingreen, note 11 above; JRU London to the Military Secretary for North Rhine, July 17, 1946, PRO, FO/1013/8; *Unzer Sztyme*, Aug. 20, 1946, 3–5, on the difficulties of visiting poets to move freely between the camps; JDC report, *Central Committee*, 31–35. As car ownership or use by persons in office, see above in this chapter.
43. Report by the Culture Department of the CC to YIVO, New York, July 2, 1946, YV, JM/10.374/1578; Olevsky in *Unzer Sztyme*, July 12, 1946, 4–5.
44. Kossowsky, *Bibliography*; Tsamriyon, *The Press*, 41–47; a complete series of *Unzer Sztyme* can be found in YV, 0–70. There are no reliable data concerning its distribution.
45. Tsamriyon, *The Press*, 54. Many of the various newspapers are located at YV, 0–70/39, others are attached to various interviews at OHD, and some can be found in YIVO, New York (better known for its collections of the American Zone material), and the National and University Library at The Hebrew University of Jerusalem.
46. Breuer to his wife, Oct. 29, 1946, private collection, on live newspaper of Poale Agudath Israel; *Der Emeth*, December 1946, on the Revisionist wall newspapers published by their various groups.
47. *Unzer Sztyme*, Nov. 15, 1946, 34.
48. Kossowsky, *Bibliography*; various publications collected in YV, 0–70/41.
49. Announcement and invitations, YV, JM/10.375/1605; *Unzer Sztyme*, Aug. 20, 1947, 34; Tsamriyon, *The Press*, 52.

50. Kossowsky, *Bibliography*; Tsamriyon, *The Press*.
51. Klodowsky interview. Szmayahn (Sam) Bloch of the Belsen Committee was the initiator (information by Menachem Rosensaft).
52. *Unzer Sztyme*, Mar. 17, 1946, on the visits of the poets H. Leiwick and Israel Efrath and the singer Emma Scheiber; July 12, 1946, on the visit of the violinist Hayas and the pianist Michaelson, and the actors Dina Blumenfeld, Yona Turkov, and Yedidya Epstein; circular of the Culture Department on the visit of the famous Yiddish comedians Dzhigan and Schumacher (date not mentioned), YV, JM/10.375/1606.
53. See below in this chapter.
54. Police regulations, YV, 0–70/30; police circulars, YV, JM 10.374/1576; report by Bloomberg on the Jewish police, May 3, 1947, PRO, FO/945/723.
55. Breuer to his wife, Aug. 10, 1946, private collection; Bertha Weingreen in a lecture attached to Weingreen interview; *Unzer Sztyme*, June 15, 1947, 32; invitations and announcements on various events, YV, JM/10.375/1605, 1606, and 0–70/28, 0–70/30.
56. Breuer to his wife, Aug. 10, 1946, private collection; *Unzer Sztyme*, Mar. 17, 1946, 22; May 24, 1946, 31; May 15, 1947, 40, 44–45; Kerbel interview.
57. Tzamriyon, *The Press*, 38–40; Bertha Weingreen's lecture, note 55 above; announcements in YV, 0–70/30.
58. Tsamriyon, *The Press*; announcements, YV, 0–70/28; circular of the Cultural Department, Nov. 4, 1946, YV, JM/10.374/1578.
59. They may be viewed at the Spielberg Film Archives, The Hebrew University of Jerusalem, and at the National Jewish Film Archives at Brandeis University, Waltham, Massachusetts. See also *Unzer Sztyme*, Sept. 15, 1946, 12; Tsamriyon, *The Press*, 38–40; Klodowsky interview.
60. The Theater Diary, YV, 0–70/31; Bertha Weingreen lecture, note 55 above; *Unzer Sztyme*, Oct. 15, 1945, and May 24, 1946, 34, on a tour in the British Zone; Aug. 20, 1946, 15–17 (a review by Miriam Gold on a Shalom Aleichem's play); June 15, 1947, 33, on a new Shalom Aleichem play and on the forthcoming tour; report by the Cultural Committee, Sept. 17, 1946, and report of the CC, Feb. 5, 1947, YV, 0–70/13. See also: Nicholas Yantian, "'Aus der Versteinerung heraustreten'—Das 'Kazet-Theater' im jüdischen 'Displaced Persons'-Lager Bergen-Belsen, 1945–1947," in *Im Schatten des Holocaust. Jüdisches Leben in Niedersachsen nach 1945*, ed. Herbert Obenaus, 131–63 (Hanover, 1997); idem, "Studien zum Selbstverständnis der jüdischen 'Displaced Persons' in Deutschland nach dem Zweiten Weltkrieg," (M.A. thesis, Berlin, 1994).
61. *Unzer Sztyme*, May 15, 1947, 35; announcements on performances, YV, JM/10.375/1606.
62. Announcement, YV, JM/10.375/1606.

63. Tsamriyon, *The Press*, 38–40; Bertha Weingreen lecture, note 55 above; *Unzer Sztyme*, Dec. 15, 1946, 16, on the first concert; Kerbel interview.
64. CC circular, Sept. 17, 1946, YV, 0–70/13; *Unzer Sztyme*, Oct. 2, 1946, 28; circular of the Cultural Department, Nov. 4, 1946, YV, JM/10.374/1578; circular by Olevsky, June 1, 1947, YV, 0–70/30; report by Henriques, Aug. 9–26, 1947, BDA, C11/13/17/1; Bertha Weingreen lecture, note 55 above; Tsamriyon, *The Press*.
65. Announcements, YV, 0–70/30.
66. *Zum Sieg*, September 1946; circular of the Cultural Department, note 64 above; Kerbel and Havkin interviews; Tsamriyon, *The Press*, 38–40.
67. Report by Weingreen, Apr. 24, 1946, note 11 above; CC circular, July 31, 1946, YV, 0–70/13; *Zum Sieg*, September 1946; *Unzer Sztyme*, May 15, 1947, 40; announcements, YV, 0–70/30; Klodowsky interview; Tsamriyon, *The Press*; Bertha Weingreen lecture, note 55 above.
68. See a copy of the Hagadah in the Jewish Brigade archives, CZA.
69. Elazary, "The Hebrew Gymnasium"; Klodowsky interview.
70. Asaria, Greenbaum, and Kerbel interviews. See also Judith Tydor Baumel, "The Politics of Spiritual Rehabilitation in the DP Camps."
71. Mankowitz, "Politics and Ideology"; idem, "The Affirmation." See chapter 4.
72. Daniel Blatman, *For Our Freedom and Yours: The Jewish Labor Bund in Poland, 1939–1949* (Jerusalem, 1996) [Hebrew], 329–35; Engel, *Between Liberation and Flight*; Yosef Grodzinsky, *Good Human Material* (Jerusalem, 1998) [Hebrew].
73. Gershon Greenberg, "Yehudah Leb Gerst's 'Ascent' through the Holocaust," *Holocaust and Genocide Studies* 13, no. 1 (1999): 62–89. Also idem, "From *Hurban* to Redemption: Orthodox Jewish Thought in the Munich Area, 1945–1948," *Simon Wiesental Center Annual* 6 (1989): 81–112.
74. The Budget of Adath She'erith Yisrael, April 1946, HL, Schonfeld/144; Breuer interview; see also chapters 3, 6, 7.
75. In the American Zone even children's homes were affiliated with political parties. See Ada Schein, "Educational Systems in the Jewish DP Camps in Germany and Austria (1945–1951)" (Ph.D. thesis, The Hebrew University of Jerusalem, 2000) [Hebrew]; Mankowitz, "Politics and Ideology." This was not true for the British Zone, where the only division was between Orthodox and non-Orthodox children's homes; see chapter 11.
76. Keynan, *Holocaust Survivors*; Grodzinsky, *Good Human Material*; interview with Ze'ev and Rachel Fishler.
77. See chapter 6.
78. A circular letter by Histadrut Zionit Ahida in Belsen, Mar. 6, 1946, CZA, L10/232I; Breuer's letters of June 4 and June 19, 1946, private collection; article by Kerbel, *Zum Sieg*, September 1946.
79. The party circular of Mar. 7, 1947, YV, 0–70/32.

80. Breuer to his wife, June 4, 1946, private collection; article by Kerbel, note 78 above; reports on parties' meetings, etc., in *Unzer Sztyme*, July 12, Sept. 14, 1947; party advertisement in YV, 0–70/32.
81. Histadrut Zionit Ahidah to the JA, Apr. 2, Apr. 20, and May 28, 1946, CZA, L10/232/1; political propaganda, December 1946, YV, JM/10.375/1610; reports in *Zum Sieg*, September 1946, and *Unzer Front*, February–March 1947; Klodowsky interview; Kerbel interview.
82. *Unzer Front*, February–March 1947; Fishler interview; Kerbel interview.
83. *Unzer Sztyme*, Nov. 15, 1946, 32, and Dec. 15, 1946, 29. See also chapter 12.
84. Bulletin no. 3 of the CC, Mar. 4, 1946, YV, JM/10.374/1573; *Unzer Sztyme*, Sept. 15, 1946, 11, and Dec. 15, 1946, 32; announcements regarding wedding services and regulations, YV, JM/10.374/1575, and 0–70/29.
85. Jack Weingreen report, note 11 above; list of supplies, note 18 above; Rabbinate report, July 1947, *Central Committee*; report by Rabbi Karlebach, July 11, 1947, BDA, C11/13/17/1. See also Tydor Baumel, "Politics of Ritual Rehabilitation."
86. See above, under "Nonperiodical Publications."
87. Announcements and counter announcements, YV, 0–70/29, 0–70/30, JM/10.374/1575; announcement of the Rabbinate, July 22, 1947, WLL, Henriques/Reorganization of Communities Life; announcement of Agudath Israel and PAI, September 1947, YV, 0–70/13; Rabbi Broch to Wollheim, Nov. 9, 1948, YV, 0–70/63.

Chapter 10

1. Rabbi Levy's letters to JC, May 4 and June 8, 1945; Collis, "Belsen Camp"; *Unzer Sztyme*, May 24, 1946, 11; Bimko Rosensaft, "Children in Belsen," *Belsen Book*; Rosensaft interview; Gisella Perl, *I Was a Doctor in Auschwitz* (Tamarac, Fla., 1987), 161–75; *Frauen in Konzentrationslagern: Bergen-Belsen, Ravensbrück*, ed. Claus Füllberg-Stolberg et al. (Bremen, 1994), 147–55; Rahe, "Jüdische Waisenkinder"; Schein, "Educational Systems," chap. 2. See also chapter 7 and note 5 there.
2. Brotman-Viteles report, Mar. 29, 1946, YV, 0–70/6; Elazary, "The Hebrew Gymnasium," 52, based on JCRA reports; Kurt Lewin to Col. Solomon, Oct. 28, 1947, PRO, FO/945/469; statistics of JDC for Jan. 1, 1948, YV, 0–70/17; JCRA Bulletin of Mar. 3, 1948, HL, Schonfeld/130/1.
3. Elazary, "The Hebrew Gymnasium"; Schein, "Educational Systems"; Paul Trepman, "A lekzie pedagogic," *Unzer Sztyme*, Sept. 10, 1945, 15–20.
4. See chapter 6 regarding the refusal to send the children to England. See also Rosensaft interview; Rosensaft, "Our Belsen," *Belsen Book*; Bimko

Rosensaft, "Children in Belsen," *Belsen Book;* Dov Laufer's article in *Unzer Sztyme,* July 12, 1945; Trepman, "A lekzie pedagogic."
5. Bimko Rosensaft, "Children in Belsen," *Belsen Book;* Collis, "Belsen Camp"; Gill, *Journey Back from Hell,* 391–98; *Frauen in Konzentrationslagern,* 27–42, 147–55.
6. Aliyat Hanoar (Youth Aliyah) started to operate in Germany in September 1946; Meta Flanter to George Landauer, Sept. 9, 1946, CZA, L58/637. As for the other welfare agencies and their function, see chapter 6.
7. Reports by Jane Leverson, June 25, 1945, and by Shalom Markovitz, July 12, 1945, WLL, Henriques/Diepholz Reports; *Unzer Sztyme,* July 12, 1945, 10; Jack Brass to the JA, Sept. 5, 1945, CZA, S6/4644; report by Sadie Rurka, Sept. 18, 1945, WLL, Henriques/Belsen Reports; report of *Beth Jacob,* [September 1945], YV, 0–70/29; Liebman et al. to Rabbi Schonfeld, [December 1945], HL, Schonfeld/144; report by Rabbi Greenbaum, Feb. 22, 1946, WLL, Henriques/Belsen Reports; CC Bulletin, Mar. 4, 1946. YV, JM/10.374/1573; report of the CC Cultural Department, July 2, 1946; Brotman-Viteles report, note 2 above; Elazary, "The Hebrew Gymnasium"; Olevsky, *The Tear;* Tsamriyon, *The Press,* 38–39. As to the later initiatives in the American Zone, see Schein, "Educational Systems," chap. 2.
8. Breuer's letters of June 4, 11, 16, July 9, 22, 31, Aug. 3, 10, Oct. 27, 31, Nov. 6, 14, 1946, Jan. 22, 1947, private collection.
9. Weingreen's reports, Aug. 22, 1946, WLL, Henriques/Harzburg, and Aug. 25, 1946, WLL, Henriques/Schleswig Holstein.
10. Ibid.; Quast, "Jüdische Gemeinden," 80.
11. Breuer's letter, July 9, 1946, private collection.
12. See chapter 11.
13. Elazary, "The Hebrew Gymnasium," 115.
14. Ibid., 53.
15. Breuer's letters, note 8 above.
16. Solomon's notes on the proposal for the settlement of Jews, May 8, 1946, PRO, FO/945/384; Kempe to JRU, Dec. 14, 1946, WLL, Henriques/Schloss Laach Training Center.
17. CBF on Ahlem, HL, Schonfeld/440/2; Quast, "Jüdische Gemeinden," 21–23, 68–70.
18. See chapter 6.
19. Report of May 26, 1946, CZA, S86/343; Itzhak Kaminski, *The Mission of the Yishuv to the DP Camps in Germany, 1945–1947: Letters* (Haifa, 1985) [Hebrew]; Breuer interview; my interview with Reuma Weizmann (Schwartz), 1993, OHD; *Cherries on the Elba: The Story of the Children's Home at Blankenese, 1946–1948,* ed. Yizhak Tadmor ([n.p.] Yad Yaari, 1996) [Hebrew]; Yahil, "The Activities." See also Elazary, "The Hebrew Gymnasium," 53.

Notes to Chapter 10

20. Letter to headquarters in Paris, Sept. 17, 1946, CZA, L58/367; report by Umansky, May 17, 1948, CZA, L58/378.
21. Report by Rabbi Greenbaum, Feb. 22, 1946, WLL, Henriques/Belsen Reports; Brotman-Viteles report, note 2 above; report on Kaunitz by Selma Selby and Lily Holt, Apr. 9, 1946, WLL, Henriques/Kaunitz Reports; Weingreen's reports, Apr. 24, 1946, WLL, Henriques/Belsen Reports, and Sept. 10, 1946, YV, 0–70/28; meeting of the Jewish Communities Committee for Northwest Germany, May 9, 1946, AGH; report of the CC Cultural Department, July 2, 1946, YV, JM/10.374/1578; Katzki to JDC Munich, Oct. 13, 1947, YV, 0–70/17; correspondence between David Etstein and the JA Jerusalem during August and September 1947, CZA, S86/284; Etstein to Youth Aliyah, Oct. 30, 1947, CZA, S32/1479; Elazary, "The Hebrew Gymnasium," 58, 84–87; Schein, "Educational Systems," chap. 2. See also chapter 9.
22. Report on Kaunitz by Selma Selby and Lily Holt, Apr. 9, 1946, WLL, Henriques/Kaunitz Reports. See also Elazary, "The Hebrew Gymnasium"; Schein, "Educational Systems," chap. 2.
23. Elazary, "The Hebrew Gymnasium"; Schein, "Educational Systems," chap. 2.
24. *Unzer Sztyme*, Aug. 20, 1947.
25. Brotman-Viteles report, note 2 above; Elazary, "The Hebrew Gymnasium," 58–59.
26. See chapters 6, 7, and 11.
27. Files YV, 0–70/28 and 30; Weingreen's report Dec. 18, 1946, WLL, Henriques/Weingreen Reports; Elazary, "The Hebrew Gymnasium," 56. See also chapter 7.
28. JA Paris to JA Jerusalem, Oct. 16, 1946, CZA, S86/284; CBF, *Annual Report, 1946*; Schein, "Educational Systems," chap. 2; Elazary, "The Hebrew Gymnasium," 57.
29. JA report, October 1947, no. 30, CZA, A140/165; Elazary, "The Hebrew Gymnasium," 58.
30. Weingreen's reports, Apr. 24, 1946, WLL, Henriques/Belsen Reports, Sept. 10, 1946, YV, 0–70/28, and Dec. 18, 1946, WLL, Henriques/Weingreen Reports.
31. Weingreen report, Apr. 24, 1946, WLL, Henriques/Belsen Reports; *Central Committee:* JDC report; Zalman Slesinger, "Jewish Education in DP Camps," *Jewish Education* 19, no. 3 (1948): 64; Elazary, "The Hebrew Gymnasium," 90–93. The curriculum of the ORT school was discussed in chapter 9.
32. Elazary, "The Hebrew Gymnasium," 57.
33. Ibid., 95–96, 102.
34. Memorandum on Maritime Training School, Dec. 21, 1946, PRO, FO/1049/368; Kenchington on Jewish vocational training, Dec. 21, 1946, PRO, FO/945/723; Breuer letters; notes on Scarlett's phone call, July 23, 1947, PRO, FO/945/755; Henriques report, Sept. 11, 1947, BDA, C11/13/17/1.

35. Meeting of the Jewish Communities Committee for Northwest Germany, May 9, 1946, AGH; Weingreen's reports, Apr. 24, 1946, WLL, Henriques/Belsen Reports, and Sept. 10, 1946, YV, 0–70/28.
36. Program for performance of the elementary school children, October 1945, YV, JM/10.374/1579; *Unzer Sztyme*, Feb. 20, 1946, 26; Weingreen's report, Dec. 18, 1946, WLL, Henriques/Weingreen Reports; Elazary, "The Hebrew Gymnasium," 57.
37. Announcement on seminar, YV, 0–70/30; Weingreen's reports, Apr. 24, 1946, WLL, Henriques/Belsen Reports, and Sept. 10, 1946, YV, 0–70/28; Bigun's letter, [December 1946], CZA, S6/1911; Umansky's report, May 17, 1948, CZA, L58/378; Breuer's interview and letters; Kaminsky, *The Mission*; Elazary, "The Hebrew Gymnasium," 104. See also chapter 6.
38. Weingreen's reports, Apr. 24, 1946, WLL, Henriques/Belsen Reports, and Sept. 10, 1946, YV, 0–70/28.
39. *Eufen Freiheit Platz* (To the Liberation Square), Apr. 15, 1947, YV, JM/10.3714/1573.
40. Elazary, "The Hebrew Gymnasium"; Helmreich, *Against All Odds*; Yablonka, *Foreign Brethren*. See also chapter 12.
41. Jewish Survey meeting, Apr. 1, 1946, PRO, FO/1050/1491; reports of the CC Educational Department, Aug. 19, 1946, WLL, Henriques/LV NRW, and May 19, 1948, YV, 0–70/30; Weingreen's reports, Aug. 22, 1946, WLL, Henriques/Harzburg, and Aug. 25, 1946, WLL, Henriques/Schleswig Holstein; information of the Cultural Committee of LV NRW, June 8 and Oct. 19, 1947, WLTA, W1F/LAN; Etstein to JA, Oct. 13, 1947, CZA, S86/284; report on youth conference, Jan. 25, 1948, WLL, Henriques/Hamburg Gemeinde; JRU report, [January 1948], WLL, Henriques/Hamburg Reports; see chapters 5, 8, and 12.
42. CBF report on Jewish students in Europe, Nov. 11, 1946, HL, Schonfeld/440/2; lists of Jewish students, n.d., WLL, Henriques/Adoptions Lists; Henriques report, Sept. 11, 1947, BDA, C11/13/17/1; Lowenthal to JCRA, Oct. 3, 1947, WLL, Henriques/Hanover; Inter-University Jewish Federation of Great Britain and Ireland to JCRA, Germany, Nov. 24, 1947, WLL, Henriques/Adoptions schemes—students; conference of the Union of Jewish Students in the British Zone, Dec. 12, 1947, and statutes of the Union of Jewish Students, Jan. 26, 1948, YV, 0–70/64; Lipski's reports, Jan. 1, Apr. 15, and June 4, 1948, WLL, Henriques/Hanover.
43. Quast, "Jüdische Gemeinden," 126–28.
44. Henriques report Dec. 4, 1948, BDA, C11/13/18/3; Lowenthal report, Feb. 10, 1949, WLL, Henriques/Central Committee; Heymann to Henriques, July 22, 1949, WLL, Henriques/Cologne Reports; *Conference on the Future of the Jews in Germany*.

Notes to Chapter 11

Chapter 11

1. Kochavi, *Displaced Persons*, 42–45.
2. Dinnerstein, *America*. Dinnerstein deals systematically with the American immigration policy.
3. More detailed analyses may be found in a series of studies of both British and American policies, for example: Michael J. Cohen, *Palestine to Israel: From Mandate to Independence* (London, 1978); Dinnerstein, *America*; Kochavi, *Displaced Persons*; Amikam Nachmani, *Great Powers Discord in Palestine: The Anglo-American Committee of Inquiry into the Problems of European Jewry and Palestine, 1945–1946* (London, 1987).
4. Report on Jewish disturbances, Nov. 16, 1945, PRO, FO/1049/195; Rosensaft to the Town Mayor of Hanover, Nov. 17, 1945, CZA, L10/232I.
5. Report by Wollheim, Feb. 15, 1946, YV, 0–70/1 (from which the citations were taken); *Central Committee*, 11–12. See also Bauer, *Out of the Ashes*, 85–86.
6. See, for example, Bauer's reference to the same issue, *Out of the Ashes*, 85–86.
7. Report by Ben-Gurion on his visit to the camps, Nov. 6, 1945, CZA, S25/5231; *Unzer Sztyme*, Nov. 29, 1945, 12–14; Bauer, *Out of the Ashes*, 83–84.
8. See chapter 6.
9. A BD report on the problems of the Jews in Germany, Dec. 17, 1945, BDA, C11/13/16/2.
10. Bartley Cavanaugh Crum, *Behind the Silken Curtain: A Personal Account of Anglo-American Diplomacy in Palestine and the Middle East* (New York, 1947), 79–92.
11. Circular by the CC, Apr. 14, 1946, YV, JM/10.375/1608.
12. Report by Major Murphy, Apr. 15, 1946, PRO, FO/1030/307. Murphy could not of course report about the contents of the Hebrew and Yiddish addresses.
13. See chapter 12.
14. Aviva Halamish, *Exodus: The Real Story* (Tel Aviv, 1990) [Hebrew].
15. Barou to Brotman, Aug. 25, 1947, BDA, C11/13/17/1; *Unzer Sztyme*, Aug. 20, 1947, 34, announcing the strike.
16. *Unzer Sztyme*, Sep. 14, 1947; Wollheim to Barou, Aug. 26, 1947, CZA, WJC/9A; Dallob, Lewin and Bloomberg to the CC, Sep. 4, 1947, YV, 0–70/17; Adler-Rudel to the JA, Sep. 8, 1947, CZA, A140/75; Resolution by the Jewish community Hamburg, Sep. 9, 1947, PRO, FO/1014/640; Barou to Packenham, Sep. 13, 1947, BDA, C11/13/17/1; a meeting of the Work Association of the Jewish communities, Oct. 19, 1947, CZA, C7/268/1.
17. Halamish, *Exodus*; Kochavi, *Displaced Persons*.
18. Barou to Packenham, above, note 16; record of interview between

Notes to Chapter 11

German Refugee Department and M. Orbach of the WJC, Oct. 7, 1947, PRO, FO/945/384; Adler-Rudel to the JA, Oct. 14, 1947, CZA, A140/75; JTA item of Oct. 15, 1947, YV, 0–70/37.
19. Although the drive for aliyah in the British Zone diminished at that time, as most of those willing to immigrate had already immigrated through certificates.
20. Halamish, *Exodus*.
21. Meeting of the CC Executive, July 11, 1948, YV, 0–70/4; HQ PW & DP Division to Zonal Executive, Aug. 20, 1948, PRO, FO/1049/1402.
22. As for the first anniversary, see above. As for the second anniversary, see *Unzer Sztyme*, May 15, 1945, 19–24.
23. Circular by Auerbach, July 25, 1946, WLL, Henriques/LV NRW; copy of cable from Rosensaft and Wollheim received by the European secretariat of the WJC, [July 1947], CZA, WJC/9A, from which the citation; Rosensaft and Wollheim to Barou, July 31, 1947, YV, 0–70/16; report circulated by Rosensaft and Wollheim to the executive members, Aug. 26, 1947, YV, 0–70/62.
24. Report on the elections in Neustadt, [October 1946], WLL, Henriques/Neustadt; party election announcements, YV, 0–70/32.
25. *Unzer Sztyme*, Nov. 15, 1946, 32, and Dec. 15, 1946, 29; *Central Committee*, 16; Bimko Rosensaft in *Belsen Book*, 46.
26. See note 24; Bimko Rosensaft in *Belsen Book*, 46.
27. For further details on the struggle for recognition see chapter 7.
28. HQ PW & DP Division to Zonal Executive, Aug. 20, 1948, PRO, FO/1049/1402; CONCOM to CONFOLK, Dec. 12, 1946, PRO, FO/1049/418. See also Kochavi, *Displaced Persons*, and Bauer, *Out of the Ashes*.
29. See chapter 12.
30. HQ PW & DP Division to Zonal Executive, above, note 28; Hoffmann of the JA, Munich, to the JA Immigration Department, Jerusalem, Mar. 6, 1947, CZA, S6/3658; CC to Barou, Mar. 20, 1947, CZA, WJC/9A.
31. CONCOM to CONFOLK, above, note 28, from which the first citation was taken; Crawford to the Chancellor, Dec. 14, 1946, PRO, FO/945/723, from which the second citation was taken. For the activities of the JDC and the JRU see chapter 6, and also Bauer, *Flight and Rescue* and *Out of the Ashes*. Most illustrative in this connection was the case of Henry Lunzer, mentioned above, in chapter 6.
32. Meeting at the War Office on illegal immigration to Palestine, Apr. 27, 1946, PRO, FO/945/655; CCG Berlin to Control Office London, July 23, 1946, PRO, FO/1049/515; HQ PW & DP Division to Zonal Executive, above, note 28.
33. Cabinet Distribution from Foreign Office to Paris no. 859, Aug. 11, 1946, PRO, FO/1049/417.
34. See chapter 10.

Notes to Chapter 11

35. Histadrut Zionit Ahidah to the JA, Jerusalem, Apr. 2, 1946, CZA, L10/232I. See chapter 6.
36. Lewin to Shapiro, June 2, 1947, CZA, S6/3658; Kurt Goldmann to Ada Fishman, Oct. 3, 1946, CZA, S6/1911.
37. Lunzer to the *Daily Telegraph*, Mar. 27, 1947, BDA, C11/13/17/1.
38. See chapter 4.
39. See chapters 4 and 7.
40. Avraham Manela to the JA, Feb. 26, 1946, CZA, S6/1911.
41. The Center of the Zionist Org. in Bergen-Belsen (signed by Nahum Gittler and Gershon Katz) to the JA in Paris, Mar. 8, 1946, CZA, L10/232/2. The description above refers to January 1946.
42. Gittler and Katz to JA-Paris, Apr. 2 and Apr. 20, 1946, CZA, S6/232/I.
43. Rosenthal and Gittler to the Zionist Organization Department in Jerusalem, May 28, 1946, CZA, S6/232/I.
44. Letter from Belsen by the emissary Jehoshua B. to [Dobkin?], [December 1946; before the Zionist Congress], CZA, S6/1911.
45. Party election announcements, note 24 above.
46. Jehoshua B's letter, note 44 above.
47. Breuer interviews and letters.
48. CONFOLK to BERCOMB, Jan. 28, 1947, PRO, FO/1049/798; reports on Operation Grand National, Jan. 29, 1947, CZA, S6/3659.
49. CC circular, Mar. 14, 1947, YV, 0–70/32; Lewin to the JA Immigration Department, Apr. 9, 1947, CZA, S6/3658; the Revisionist secretary for the British Zone to Col. Solomon, Dec. 23, 1947, YV, 0–70/32.
50. Wollheim to Barou, Mar. 20, 1947, CZA, WJC/9A; CC circular, Mar. 24, 1947, YV, 0–70/13; Lewin to the JA, note 49 above; Chomsky to JA, Aug. 20, 1947, and Feb. 25, 1948, CZA, S6/1627.
51. See above in this chapter, and also Distribution of CONFOLK, Aug. 16, 1946, PRO, FO/945/729.
52. CC announcement for the press, July 20, 1947, YV, JM/10.3714/1572; Lowenthal to JCRA, July 29, 1947, WLL, Henriques/Reorg. Of Communal Life. As for joining the WJC, see chapter 7.
53. Brief for the Chancellor, Apr. 23, 1947, PRO, FO/945/384; Lewin to Shapiro, note 36 above; Lewin to Bechar, July 2, 1947, CZA, S6/3658; Lewin's memorandum to the PW & DP Division, Aug. 20, 1947, CZA, S6/3659.
54. Lewin to Bechar, July 2, 1947, CZA, S6/3658.
55. Ibid.
56. Meeting of the CC representatives with the JA in Geneva, July 15, 1947, CZA, S25/5215; meeting of the CC Executive, Aug. 11, 1947, and Wollheim's report on the UN Fact Finding Commission in Belsen, Aug. 14, 1947, YV, 0–70/4; CC bulletin, Aug. 17, 1947, YV, 0–70/37; CC distribution, Aug. 26, 1947, YV, 0–70?62.
57. *Exodus* affair—see above. November 29th: CC manifest, Nov. 29, 1947, YV, JM/10.375/1608.

58. Rosensaft's circular, Feb. 10, 1948, GJA, Geneva 1, 7A/C-48.003; CC call for "Haganah-Fond," Feb. 26, 1948, ZAH, B1/6, and April 1948, and CC call for demonstration on Apr. 15, 1947, YV, JM/10.375/1607; CC proclamation on the establishment of the State of Israel, May 1948, ZAH, B/10.
59. As for the survivors: Kahani to Adler-Rudel and attachments, Aug. 18, 1948, CZA, A140/490, about the Trepman case; Rosensaft interview; Wollheim interview. As for the emissaries, see Lewin's letters and JA reports above.

Chapter 12

1. See chapter 1.
2. Minutes of conference on emigration of Jewish DPs to Palestine, Jan. 28, 1947, PRO, FO/945/467; Operation Grand National, Jan. 29, 1947, CZA, S6/3659.
3. See note 2.
4. Kurt Lewin to the JA Immigration Dept. in Jerusalem, Mar. 6, 1947, and Chaim Hoffmann's report of Mar. 4, attached to Lewin, CZA, S6/3658; Hillel Chomsky of the JA in the British Zone, to the Palestine Offices in the Zone, Mar. 11, 1947, ibid.; Shalom Adler-Rudel's letters to Linton and to Lewin, Mar. 14, 1947, ibid.; letter to the Foreign Office representative in Paris, Mar. 21, 1947, PRO, FO/1049/798; Josephtal to Absorption Branches in Haifa and Tel Aviv, Apr. 2, 1947, CZA, S6/1466; report by Major A. K. Jones, Apr. 14, 1947, PRO, FO/945/467; report by Avraham Goldberg of the JA in Paris to the JA Immigration Dept., Apr. 21, 1947, CZA, S6/3568; Isaac Gittleson of the committee for the immigration of Orthodox youth to the Immigration Dept., Apr. 21, 1947, CZA, S6/3361.
5. Lewin on Mar. 6, 1947, and Hoffmann on Mar. 4, 1947 (above, note 4); Lewin to Shapira, Apr. 9, 1947, CZA, S6/3658.
6. Calculation of the reports on the various transports collected from the files in CZA, S6; see also Yahil, "The Activities."
7. Lewin to Bechar, July 2, 1947, CZA, S6/3658; letter by Josephtal, July 23, 1947, CZA, S6/1466.
8. Kalman Stein of the WJC to Rosensaft, Apr. 23, 1947, YV, 0–70/16; Lewin to Bechar, July 2, 1947, CZA, S6/3658.
9. N. Barou to Rosensaft, Aug. 1, 1947, CZA, WJC/9A; Lewin to DP & PW Division in the British Zone, Aug. 20, 1947, CZA, S6/3659; Lewin to Shapira, Nov. 11, 1947, CZA, S6/3569.
10. Lewin to Bechar, July 2, 1947, CZA, S6/3658; Herbert Katzki to Samuel Dallob, Feb. 10, 1948, GJA, Geneva 1, 7A/C-48.009.
11. Lewin to Bechar, July 2, 1947, CZA, S6/3658; JA Immigration Dept. to Lewin, Aug. 8, 1947, CZA, S6/3658; Chomsky to Bechar, Aug. 20, 1947, CZA, S6/1627; Lewin to Shapira, Dec. 31, 1947, CZA, S6/3659.

12. Colonial Office to the Palestine High Commissioner, General Sir Arthur Canningham, May 2 and Aug. 1, 1947, PRO, FO/945/468; Foreign Office (German Section) to BERCOMB, Berlin, May 16, 1947, PRO, FO/1049/2106; British Military Governor, Sir Brian H. Robertson, to the American Military Governor, General Lucius D. Clay, May 31, 1947, PRO, FO/1049/799.
13. Lewin to Shapira, Dec. 31, 1947, CZA, S6/3659; Yahil, "The Activities."
14. Lewin to Shapira, Dec. 31, 1947, CZA, S6/3659; Yahil, "The Activities." The mobilization for the war in Israel was apparently much more intensive in the American Zone. Archival sources for the British Zone indicate mainly financial mobilization; see, for example, the call on Apr. 13, 1948. See Grodzinsky, *Good Human Material*.
15. D. Logan-Gray, Director of the PW & DP Div., to the Central Secretariat of the British Zone, Oct. 8, 1948, PRO, FO/1049/1402; Wollheim to the Presidency of the CC, Oct. 20, 1948 and meeting of the presidency of the CC, Nov. 4, 1948, YV, 0–70/4; CCG BE PW & DP Div., Nov. 16, 1948: Technical Instruction no. 32—Emigration of Jewish DPs to Palestine, Operation "Journey's End," PRO, FO/1049/1383; protocol of the CC Executive, Nov. 28, 1947, YV, 0–70/4; Mia Fisher report, Mar. 3, 1949, WLL, Henriques/6/Central Comm.; Logan-Gray to Garren, May 19, 1949, PRO, FO/1049/1778.
16. J. Eisen, Emigrant Staging Area AJDC, Bremen, to Irwing Rosen and Herbert Katzki, Dec. 25, 1947, GJA, Geneva 1, 7A/C-47.101. Dinnerstein mentions a total number of 28,000 Jewish DPs who immigrated to the United States under the Truman Directive throughout the period May 1946–June 1948, including DPs from Austria, Italy, Shanghai, etc. (*America*, 252).
17. JDC report for the British Zone for November 1947, GJA, Geneva 1, 7A/C-48.009.
18. JDC report for Aug. 15, 1948, included in the general report of the Adviser William Haber, Oct. 6, 1948, GJA, Geneva 1, 6A/C-45–068.
19. Reports by E. G. Lowenthal, Senior Field Representative of JRU, Aug. 16, Sept. 21, WLL, Henriques/Düsseldorf Reports, and Nov. 11, 1948, WLL, Henriques/Lowenthal Reports; report of Dallob of the JDC to the presidency of the CC, July 11, 1948, YV, 0–70/4.
20. Chief Administration Officer of the British Zone to the Political Adviser in Berlin, May 5, 1949, and Logan-Grey to Garren, May 19, 1949, PRO, FO/1049/1778.
21. Report by Leonard Cohen, June 9, 1948, WLL, Henriques/L. Cohen Reports.
22. Logan-Gray to the Central Administration, Oct. 8, 1948 (above, note 15); protocol of the CC presidency meeting, Nov. 4, 1948, YV, 0–70/4.
23. Protocol of the CC presidency meeting, Nov. 4, 1948, and protocol of the CC Executive meeting, Nov. 28, 1948, YV, 0–70/4; CC meeting, Oct. 11, 1949, YV, 0–70/30.

24. Correspondence regarding Trepman's affair attached to a letter from Rosensaft to Adler-Rudel, June 14, 1948, CZA, A140/490.
25. Farewell letters of Berl Laufer, Mar. 8, and Rafael Olevsky, Mar. 14, 1949, ZAH, B1/6.
26. Report by Lady Henriques, Dec. 4, 1948, BDA, C11/13/18/3; monthly report of JRU, Mar. 17, 1949, WLL, Henriques/Lowenthal Reports; Dallob to M. W. Beckelman, Aug. 22, 1949, GJA, Geneva 1, 7A/C-48.403; E. Heymann, Senior Representative of JRU, to Mia Fisher, Aug. 22, 1949, BDA, C11/13/18/4; A. Kohane, JDC Supply Dept., to Samuel Haber, JDC Director for Germany, Dec. 2, 1949, GJA, Geneva 1, 7A/C-48.017.
27. *Jüdische Gemeindeblatt*, July 1, 1949, 1; announcement of the JA, July 31, 1950, correspondence of the JA toward final liquidation by the end of September 1950, CZA, L10/501.
28. Logan-Gray to Garren, May 19, 1949, PRO, FO/1049/1778; K. W. Matthews, Deputy Chief, DP Div., to Chief, DP. Div., July 14, 1949, PRO, FO/1049/1778; Chief Administration Officer in the British Zone to the Political Director, Berlin, Oct. 18, 1949, PRO, FO/1049/1778; *Jüdische Gemeindeblatt*, May 5, 1951, 16, and Apr. 27, 1951.
29. Survey presented to the *Conference on the Future of the Jews in Germany*, 9–12. The survey did not estimate the total number, which was still fluctuating due to in- and outmigrations.
30. Report by Henriques, Dec. 4, 1948, BDA, C11/13/18/3; Heymann to Mia Fisher, Aug. 22, 1949 (note 26 above); *Jüdisches Gemeindeblatt*, Nov. 17, 1950, 15; Harry Greenstein, Adviser on Jewish Affairs in the conference (note 29 above), 5.
31. *Conference*, preface, and 5, 8.
32. List of participants, ibid.
33. Ibid., 7, 12.
34. The discussion of the proceedings of the conference is based on the brochure mentioned in note 29.
35. Citation from McCloy, ibid., 21.
36. Decision by the Interests Representation in Stuttgart, Dec. 16, 1949, Bundesarchiv Koblenz, B136/5862. See also protest announcement by Rosensaft and Wollheim, Oct. 12, 1949, YV, 0–70/4, on Philipp Auerbach's initiatives to negotiate with the government on behalf of the Jews, without any authorization by the representative Jewish organizations in Germany.

Conclusion

1. Mankowitz, "Politics and Ideology."

Bibliography

Archives

Archiv der jüdischen Gemeinde Hannover, Hanover

Board of Deputies of British Jews Archives, London

Bundesarchiv Koblenz

Central Zionist Archives, Jerusalem

Givat Joint Archives, Jerusalem

Hartley Library at the University of Southampton, Special Collection Division, Schonfeld Archives

Imperial War Museum, London, Belsen Exhibition

Kressel Collection, Oxford

National Jewish Film Archives at Brandeis University, Waltham, Massachusetts

Oral History Division, Institute of Contemporary Jewry, The Hebrew University of Jerusalem, interviews with:
    Asaria-Helfgott, Zvi, 1964
    Brecher, Eugenie, 1992
    Breuer, Mordechai, 1992
    Eckstein-Grebenau, Sarah, 1992
    Fishler, Ze'ev and Rachel, 1994
    Fürst, Helmut, 1992
    Greenbaum, Avraham, 1992
    Handler, Arieh, 1993
    Havkin, Arieh and Sonia, 1993
    Israel, Helen, 1992
    Kempe, Asher Leo, 1992
    Kerbel, Yitzhak, 1993

Bibliography

    Klodovsky, Michael, 1997
    Landau, Hanna, 1993
    Levy, Rabbi Isaac, 1991
    Lunzer, Henry, 1993
    Maagan-Markovitz, Shalom, 1992
    Rosensaft, Josef, 1964
    Rubinstein, Hermann, 1992
    Weingreen, Bertha and Jacob, 1993
    Weizmann, Reumah (Schwarz), 1993
    Wollheim, Norbert, 1990
    Wollheim's talks with Y. Jelinek, 1988, and A. Margaliyot, 1981

Public Record Office, London, Foreign Office files

Spielberg Film Archives, The Hebrew University of Jerusalem

Stadtsarchiv Bonn

Wiener Library London

Wiener Library Tel Aviv

Yad Vashem Archives, Jerusalem

Zentralarchiv zur Erforschung der Geschichte der Juden in Deutschland, Heidelberg

Newspapers, Periodicals, and Reports

American Jewish Year Books, 1949, 1950

British Zone Review, Supplement, Oct. 13, 1945

Central British Fund for Jewish Relief and Rehabilitation: Annual Report, 1945; 1946; 1947

Conference on the Future of the Jews in Germany. Heidelberg, Sept. 1, 1949 [mimeograph]

Der Emeth. Published by the Zionist-Revisionist movement in Bergen-Belsen, 1946 [Yiddish]

Jewish Chronicle (Jewish weekly, London)

Jewish Restitution Successor Organization—Report on the Operations, 1947–1972

Jewish Travel Guide 1952/3

Jüdisches Gemeindeblatt. Düsseldorf, 1946

Mitteilungsblatt. Tel Aviv, 1946

Report of the Anglo-American Committee of Inquiry Regarding the Problems of European Jewry and Palestine. Lausanne, 1946

Bibliography

Central Committee of Liberated Jews in the British Zone Germany 1945–1947 (activity report submitted to the Second Congress of the *She'erit Hapletah*, July 1947, Bad Harzburg)

Unzer Front. Published by the Zionist-Revisionist movement in Bergen-Belsen, 1947 [Yiddish]

Unzer Sztyme. Published by the Central Committee, Bergen-Belsen [Yiddish]

Volks- und Berufszählung vom 29. October 1946 in den vier Besatzungszonen und Gross-Berlin. Berlin and Munich

Yiddisher Heftlings-Congress in Bergen-Belsen, 25–27 September 1945 [Yiddish]

Zum Sig. Published by the Revisionist-Zionist movement in Bergen-Belsen, 1946 [Yiddish]

Secondary Sources

Abelshauser, Werner. "Die Rekonstruktion der westdeutschen Wirtschaft und die Rolle der Besatzungspolitik." In *Politische und ökonomische Stabilisierung Westdeutschlands, 1945–1949,* ed. Claus Scharf, Hans Schröder, and Hans Jürgen, 1–17. Wiesbaden, 1977.

——. *Wirtschaft in Westdeutschland, 1945–1948: Reconstruktion und Wachstumsbedingungen in der amerikanischen und britischen Zone.* Schriftenreihe der Vierteljahreshefte für Zeitgeschichte, no. 30. Stuttgart, 1975.

Albrich, Thomas. *Exodus durch Österreich—jüdische Flüchtlinge, 1945–1948.* Innsbruck, 1987.

——. "Way Station of Exodus: Jewish Displaced Persons and refugees in Postwar Austria." in *The Holocaust and History. The Known, the Unknown, the Disputed, and the Reexamined,* ed. Michael Berenbaum and Abraham J. Peck, 716–32. Bloomington, 1998.

Asaria (Helfgott), Zvi. "Eine Chassidische Gemeinde in Celle (1945–1950)." *Zur Geschichte der Juden in Celle,* 103–7. Celle, 1974.

——. *Die Juden in Köln von den ältesten Zeiten bis zur Gegenwart.* Cologne, 1959.

——. *Die Juden in Niedersachsen.* Leer, 1979.

——. *We Are the Witnesses.* Tel Aviv, 1970 [Hebrew].

Balabkins, Nicholas. *Germany under Direct Control: Economic Aspects of Disarmanent, 1945–1948.* New Brunswick, N.J., 1964.

——. *West German Reparations to Israel.* New Brunswick, N.J., 1971.

Balfour, Michael, and John Mair. *Survey of International Affairs, 1939–1946: Four-Power Control in Germany and Austria, 1945–1946.* London, 1956.

Barzel, Neima. "Israel and Germany, 1945–1956: Development of the Attitude of Israeli Society and State to Germany Following the Holocaust." Ph.D. thesis, Haifa University, 1990 [Hebrew].

———. "The Attitude of Jews of German Origin in Israel to Germany and Germans after the Holocaust, 1945–1952." *Leo Baeck Institute Year Book* 39 (1994): 271–301.

Bauer, Yehuda. "The Death Marches—January–May 1945." *Yahadut Zemanenu—Contemporary Jewry* 1 (1983): 199–221 [Hebrew].

———. *Flight and Rescue: Brichah.* New York, 1970.

———. "The Initial Organization of the Holocaust Survivors in Bavaria." *Yad Vashem Studies* 8 (1971): 127–57.

———. "The Jewish Displaced Persons from the Concentration Camps and the Problems of the She'erit Hapletah." In *The Nazi Concentration Camps: Proceedings of the Fourth Yad Vashem International Historical Conference, Jerusalem, January 20–24, 1980,* 385–95. Jerusalem, 1984 [Hebrew].

———. *Out of the Ashes.* Oxford, 1989.

Belsen, published by Irgun She'erit Hapleita Meha'ezor Habriti, Israel [Organization of the Surviving Remnant in the British Zone, Israel]. Tel Aviv, 1957.

Belsen in History and Memory. Ed. Jo Reilly et al. London and Portland, 1997.

Bentwich, Norman. *They Found Refuge: An Account of British Jewry's Work for Victims of Nazi Opression.* London, 1956.

———. *The United Restitution Organization, 1948–1968.* London, n.d.

Benz, Wolfgang. "Sitzen auf gepackten Koffern." *Der Spiegel Spezial Juden und Deutsche* 2 (1992): 47–53.

———. "Germans, Jews and Antisemitism in Germany after 1945." *Australian Journal of Politics and History* 41, no. 1 (1995): 118–29.

Bergen-Belsen: Texts and Pictures of the Exhibition in the Central Memorial of the Land Lower Saxony on the Site of the Former Concentration- and Prisoner of War Camp Bergen-Belsen. Ed. Niedersächsische Landeszentrale für Politische Bildung. Hanover, 1990.

Bick Berkowitz, Sarah. *Where Are My Brothers?* New York, 1965.

Blatman, Daniel. *For Our Freedom and Yours: The Jewish Labor Bund in Poland, 1939–1949.* Jerusalem, 1996 [Hebrew].

Blau, Bruno. "Jewish Population in Nazi Germany." *Jewish Social Studies* 12, no. 1 (1950): 161–72.

Blum-Dobkin, Toby. "Rituals of Transition: An Ethnographic Approach to Life in a Displaced Persons camp." In *The Netherlands and Nazi Genocide, Papers of the 21st Annual Scholars' Conference,* ed. G. Jan Colijn and Marcia S. Littell, 489–500. Lewiston/Queenston/Lampeter, 1992.

Bibliography

Bodemann, Y. Michal. "Staat und Ethnizität: Der Aufbau der jüdischen Gemeinden im Kalten Krieg." in *Jüdisches Leben in Deutschland nach 1945*, ed. Micha Brumlik, 49–69. Frankfurt a.M., 1986.

———. "'Ich verlasse dieses Land mit Verbitterung, doch vor keinem Volk darf man die Fensterläden zuschlagen . . .' Zur Abschiedspredigt von Rabbiner Dr. Wilhelm Weinberg (1901–1976) in Frankfurt/Main am 11. November 1951." *Menora* 6 (1995): 345–57.

Bogner, Nahum. *The Resistance Boats: The Jewish Illegal Immigration, 1945–1948*. Tel Aviv, 1993 [Hebrew].

Bourke-White, Margaret. *Deutschland, April 1945*. Munich, 1979.

Brenner, Michael. *After the Holocaust*. Princeton, 1997.

———. "Wider den Mythos 'Stunde Null': Kontinuitäten im innerjüdischen Bewusstsein und deutsch-jüdischen Verhältnis nach 1945." *Menora* 3 (1992): 155–81.

———. "East European and German Jews in Postwar Germany, 1945–50." in *Jews, Germans, Memory. Reconstruction of Jewish Life in Germany*, 49–63. Ann Arbor, 1996.

Brewster, Chamberlin, and Marcia Feldman, eds. *The Liberation of the Nazi Concentration Camps: Eyewitness Accounts of the Liberators*. Washington, D.C., 1987.

Bridgman, John. *The End of the Holocaust: The Liberation of the Camps*. London, 1990.

Brunsvicensia Judaica: Gedenkbuch für die jüdischen Mitbürger Braunschweig, 1933–1945. Brunswick, 1966.

Buchholz, Marlis. *Die hannoverschen Judenhäuser: Zur Situation der Juden in der Zeit der Ghettoisierung und Verfolgung, 1941–1945*. Hildesheim, 1987.

Büttner, Ursula. "Not nach der Befreiung—die Situation der deutschen Juden in der britischen Besatzungszone, 1945–1948." In *Das Unrechtsregime—Internationale Forschung über den Nationalsozialismus, Band 2: Verfolgung—Exil—Belasteter Neubeginn*, ed. Ursula Büttner et al., 373–406. Hamburg, 1986.

———. "Rückkehr in ein normales Leben? Die Lage der Juden in Hamburg in den ersten Nachkriegsjahren." In *Die Juden in Hamburg, 1590–1990*, ed. Arno Herzig, 613–32. Hamburg, 1991.

Carden, Robert W. "Before Bizonia: Britain's Economic Dilemma in Germany, 1945–1946." *Journal of Contemporary History* 14 (1979): 535–55.

Carlebach, Julius. "Flight into action as a method of repression. American military rabbis and the problem of Jewish DPs." *Jewish Studies Quarterly* 2, no. 1 (1995): 59–76.

Celle '45—Aspekte einer Zeitenwende. Ed. Mijndert Bertram (Bomann-Museum). Celle, 1995.

Cherries on the Elba: The Story of the Children's Home at Blankenese, 1946–1948. Ed. Yizhak Tadmor. Yad Yaari, 1996 [Hebrew].

Cohen, Michael J. *Palestine to Israel: From Mandate to Independence.* London, 1978.

Crum, Bartley Cavanaugh. *Behind the Silken Curtain: A Personal Account of Anglo-American Diplomacy in Palestine and the Middle East.* New York, 1947.

Dawidowicz, Lucy S. "Belsen Remembered." In *The Jewish Presence: Essays on Identity and History,* 289–97. New York, 1976.

Diner, Dan. "Elemente der Subjektwerdung. Jüdische DPs in historischem Kontext." in *Überlebt und Unterwegs. Jüdische Displaced Persons in Nachkriegsdeutschland,* ed. Jacqueline Giere, 229–48. Frankfurt a.M., 1997.

Dinnerstein, Leonard. *America and the Survivors of the Holocaust.* New York, 1982.

Dvorjetski, Marc. "Adjustment of Detainees to Camp and Ghetto Life and Their Subsequent Re-adjustment to Normal Society." *Yad Vashem Studies* 5 (1963): 193–220.

———. "Demographic and Biological Problems of Immigrant Holocaust Survivors, 1946–1956." *Niv Harofeh* 34, no. 1 (1963): 3–29 [Hebrew].

Eder, Angelika. "Jüdische Displaced Persons im deutschen Alltag." in *Überlebt und Unterwegs. Jüdische Displaced Persons in Nachkriegsdeutschland,* ed. Jacqueline Giere, 163–87. Frankfurt a.M., 1997.

Eicher, Bruno. *Jüdische Geschichte und Kultur in NRW: Ein Handbuch.* Essen, 1993.

Elazary, Edna. "The Hebrew Gymnasium in Bergen-Belsen, December 1945–March 1947." M.A. thesis, The Hebrew University of Jerusalem, 1988 [Hebrew].

Elkin, Rivka. *The Survival of the Jewish Hospital in Berlin, 1938–1945.* Berlin, 1993.

Engel, David. *Between Liberation and Flight: Holocaust Survivors in Poland and the Struggle for Leadership, 1944–1946.* Tel Aviv, 1996 [Hebrew].

Enreich, Shimon. "From Bergen-Belsen." In *Sefer Hahitnadvut* [Hebrew: *The Book of the Volunteering*], ed. Ze'ev Shefer, 786–87. Jerusalem, 1949.

Farquharson, John E. *The Western Allies and the Politics of Food: Agrarian Management in Postwar Germany.* Warwickshire, U.K., 1985.

———. "Grossbritannien und die deutschen Reparationen nach 1945." *Vierteljahreshefte für Zeitgeschichte* 46, no. 1 (1998): 43–67.

Bibliography

Flüchtlinge und Vertriebene in der westdeutschen Nachkriegsgeschichte. Ed. Rainer Schulze et al. Hildesheim, 1987.

Foschepoth, Josef. "'Helfen Sie uns, und Sie helfen Deutschland...' Die Anfänge der Gesellschaften für Christlich-Jüdische Zusammenarbeit." in *Zwischen Antisemitismus und Philosemitismus: Juden in der Bundesrepublik.* ed. Wolfgang Benz, 63–70. Berlin, 1991.

Fraenkel, Daniel. *On the Edge of the Abyss.* Jerusalem, 1994 [Hebrew].

Frauen in Konzentrationslagern: Bergen-Belsen, Ravensbrück. Ed. Claus Füllberg-Stolberg et al. Bremen, 1994.

Fried, Hedi. *Fragments of Life: The Road to Auschwitz.* London, 1990.

Fröhlich, Elke. "Philipp Auerbach (1906–1952): 'Generalanwalt für Wiedergutmachung.'" In *Geschichte und Kultur der Juden in Bayern, II: Lebensläufe,* ed. Manfred Treml, Josef Kirmeier, et al., 315–20. Veröffentlichungen zur bayerischen Geschichte und Kultur, 17–18. Munich, 1988.

From Division to Unification: Germany 1945–1990, ed. Shulamit Volkov. Tel Aviv, 1994 [Hebrew].

Garbe, Detlef, and Sabine Homann. "Jüdische Gefangene in Hamburger Konzentrationslagern." In *Die Juden in Hamburg, 1590–1990,* ed. Arno Herzig and Saskia Rohde, 545–59. Hamburg, 1991.

Gelber, Yoav. *Jewish Palestinian Volunteering in the British Army during the Second World War.* Vol. 3, *The Standard Bearers: Rescue Mission to the Jewish People.* Jerusalem, 1983 [Hebrew].

Genizi, Haim. *The Adviser on Jewish Affairs to the American Army and the Displaced Persons, 1945–1949.* Moreshet, 1987 [Hebrew].

Geschichte der Juden in Celle: Festschrift zur Wiederherstellung der Synagoge. Celle, 1974.

Geschichte der Juden in Hamburg, Altona, und Wandsbeck. Ed. Günter Marwedel. Historischer Verein für Hamburgische Geschichte, 25. Hamburg, 1982.

Giere, Jacqueline D. "'Wir sind unterwegs, aber nicht in der Wüste.' Erziehung und Kultur in den jüdischen Displaced Persons Lagern der amerikanischen Zone im Nachkriegsdeutschland 1945–1949." Ph.D. thesis, Frankfurt a.M., 1993.

———. "Kulturelles Vermächtnis und kulturelle Selbstverständigung. Die Lager der jüdischen Displaced Persons im besetzten Deutschland." in *Im Schatten des Holocaust. Jüdisches Leben in Niedersachsen nach 1945,* ed. Herbert Obenaus, 119–30. Hanover, 1997.

———. "We're on Our Way, but Not in the Wilderness." in *The Holocaust and History. The Known, the Unknown, the Disputed, and the Reexamined,* ed. Michael Berenbaum and Abraham J. Peck, 699–715. Bloomington, 1998.

Bibliography

Gill, Anton. *The Journey Back from Hell: Conversations with Concentration Camp Survivors.* London, 1998.

Gilman, Sander L. *Jews in Today's German Culture.* Bloomington, 1995.

Ginzel, Günther. "Phasen der Etablierung einer Jüdischen Gemeinde in der Kölner Trümmerlandschaft, 1945–1949." In *Köln und das rheinische Judentum,* ed. Jutta Bohnke-Kollwitz, 445–61. Festschrift Germania Judaica, 1959–1984. Cologne, 1984.

Görgen, Hans P. *Düsseldorf und der Nationalsozialismus.* Düsseldorf, 1969.

Goldsmith, Samuel Joseph. "Hadassah Rosensaft." In *Jews in Transition*, 107–11. New York, 1969.

———. "Yossel Rosensaft." *20th Century Jews,* 86–92. New York, 1962.

Gollanz, Victor. *In Darkest Germany.* London, 1947.

Goschler, Constantin. "Der Fall Philipp Auerbach: Wiedergutmachung in Bayern." In *Wiedergutmachung in der Bundesrepublik Deutschland,* ed. Ludolf Herbst and Constantin Goschler, 77–98. Munich, 1989.

Greenberg, Gershon. "From *Hurban* to Redemption: Orthodox Jewish Thought in the Munich Area, 1945–1948." *Simon Wiesental Center Annual* 6 (1989): 81–112.

———. "Yehudah Leb Gerst's 'Ascent' through the Holocaust." *Holocaust and Genocide Studies* 13, no. 1 (1999): 62–89.

Grobman, Alex. *Rekindling the Flame. American Jewish Chaplains and the Survivors of the European Jewry 1944–1948.* Detroit, 1993.

Grodzinsky, Yosef. *Good Human Material.* Jerusalem, 1998 [Hebrew].

Grosser, Alfred. *Deutschland Bilanz: Geschichte Deutschlands seit 1945.* Munich, 1970.

Grossmann, Atina. "Trauma, Memory and Motherhood. Germans and Jewish Displaced Persons in Post-Nazi Germany, 1945–1949." *Archiv für Sozialgeschichte* (1998): 215–41.

Grossmann, Kurt R. "Die jüdischen Auslandsorganisationen und ihre Arbeit in Deutschland." In *Die Juden in Deutschland, 1951/52: Ein Almanach,* ed. Heinz Ganther, 91–120. Frankfurt a.M. and Munich.

Grübel, Monika. "Nach der Katastrophe. Jüdisches Leben in Köln, 1945–1949." in *Zuhause in Köln. Jüdisches Leben 1945 bis heute,* ed. Günther B. Ginzel and Sonja Güntner, 42–56. Cologne-Weimar-Wienna, 1998.

Gutman, Yisrael. *The Jews in Poland after the Second World War.* Jerusalem, 1985 [Hebrew].

Hack, Angelica. "Displaced Persons in Stadt und Landkreis Celle." In *Celle '45,* ed. Mijndert Bertram (Bomann-Museum), 89–123. Celle, 1995.

Hadari, Ze'ev Venia. *Refugees Win against the Empire.* Tel Aviv, 1985 [Hebrew].

Bibliography

Halamish, Aviva. *Exodus: The Real Story.* Tel Aviv, 1990 [Hebrew].

Halevi, Haim S. "The Influence of World War II on the Demographic Characteristics of the Jewish People." Ph.D. thesis, The Hebrew University of Jerusalem, 1973 [Hebrew].

Hardach, Karl. *The Political Economy of Germany in the Twentieth Century.* Berkeley, 1980.

Hardman, Leslie H. *The Survivors: The Story of the Belsen Remnant.* London, 1958.

Helmreich, William. *Against All Odds.* New York, 1992.

Herzberg, Abel J. *Between Two Streams: A Diary from Bergen-Belsen.* Translated from the Dutch by Jack Santcross. London and New York, 1997.

Heymont, Irving. *Among the Survivors of the Holocaust 1945: The Landsberg DP Camp Letters of Major Irving Heymont, United States Army.* Cincinnati, 1982.

Holocaust and Rebirth: Bergen-Belsen, 1945–1965. Ed. Sam E. Bloch. New York, 1965.

Homeyer, Friedel. *100 Jahre Israelitische Erziehungsan Anstalt. Israelitische Gartenbauschule, 1893–1993: Mahn- und Gedenkstätte des Landkreises Hannover in Ahlem.* Hanover, 1993.

Ilan, Amitzur. *America, Britain, and Palestine.* Jerusalem, 1979 [Hebrew].

Immanuel, Shmuel. *Zichronot umahshavot: Memories.* Sha'albim, 1996 [Hebrew].

Immanuel, Yona. *Yessupar Lador: Memories.* Jerusalem, 1994 [Hebrew].

Israel und Wir, Keren Hajessod Jahrbuch der jüdischen Gemeinschaft in Deutschland, 1955–1965. Frankfurt a.M., 1966.

Jacobmeyer, Wolfgang. "Jüdische Überlebende als Displaced Persons." *Geschichte und Gesellschaft* 99, no. 3 (1983): 421–52.

———. "Die Lager der jüdischen Displaced Persons in den deutschen Westzonen 1946/47 als Ort jüdischer Selbstvergewisserung." in *Jüdisches Leben in Deutschland nach 1945*, ed. Micha Brumlik, 31–48. Frankfurt a.M., 1986.

Jelinek, Yeshayahu M. *Zwischen Moral und Realpolitik. Deutsch-israelische Beziehungen 1945–1965.* Gerlingen, 1997.

Jewish Voices, German Words: Growing Up Jewish in Post-war Germany and Austria, ed. Elena Lappin. North Haven, CT, 1994.

Johe, Werner. *Neuengamme: Zur Geschichte der Konzentrationslager in Hamburg.* Hamburg, 1984.

Die Juden in Deutschland, 1951/52 (5712): Ein Almanach. Ed. Heinz Ganther. Frankfurt a.M. and Munich, 1953.

Bibliography

Die Juden in Schleswig-Holstein. Ed. Wolfgang Hubrich and Rüdiger Wenzel. *Gegenwartsfragen,* 58. Kiel, 1988.

Jüdisches Schicksal in Köln, 1918–1945. Ed. Horst Matzer, Hannelore Brabender, et al. Ausstellung des historischen Archiv der Stadt Köln. Cologne, 1989.

Jürgens, Arnold and Thomas Rahe. "Zur Statistik des Konzentrationslagers Bergen-Belsen: Quellengrundlagen, methodische Probleme und neue statistische Daten." *Beiträge zur Geschichte der nationalsozialistischen Verfolgung in Norddeutschland* 3 (1997): 128–48.

Kaminski, Itzhak. *The Mission of the Yishuv to the DP Camps in Germany, 1945–1947: Letters.* Haifa, 1985 [Hebrew].

Keynan, Irit. *Holocaust Survivors and the Emissaries from Eretz-Israel: Germany, 1945–1948.* Tel Aviv, 1996 [Hebrew].

Kettenacker, Lothar. *Germany Since 1945.* Oxford, 1997.

Klein, Adolf. *Köln im Dritten Reich: Stadtgeschichte der Jahre 1933–1945.* Cologne, 1983.

Klessmann, Christoph. *Die doppelte Staatsgründung—deutsche Geschichte, 1945–1955.* Göttingen, 1982.

Klump, Rainer. "Diskussionsschwerpunkte und Ergebnisse der Währungsreformforschung." In *40 Jahre Deutsche Mark: Die politische und ökonomische Bedeutung der westdeutschen Währungsreform von 1948* (Beiträge zur Wirtschafts- und Sozialgeschichte 39), ed. Rainer Klump, 51–66. Wiesbaden, 1989.

Kochavi, Arieh J. *Displaced Persons and International Politics: Britain and the Jewish Displaced Persons after the Second World War.* Tel Aviv, 1992 [Hebrew].

Kolb, Eberhard. *Bergen-Belsen: Geschichte des "Aufenthaltslagers," 1943–1945.* Hanover, 1962.

———. *Bergen-Belsen: Vom "Aufenthaltslager" zum Konzentrationslager, 1943–1945.* Göttingen, 1996.

Königseder, Angelika. *Flucht nach Berlin. Jüdische Displaced Persons 1945–1948.* Berlin, 1998.

Königseder, Angelika and Juliane Wetzel. *Lebensmut im Wartesaal. Die jüdischen DPs (Displaced Persons) im Nachkriegsdeutschland.* Frankfurt a.M., 1994.

Konzentrationslager Bergen-Belsen Berichte und Dokumente. Ed. Monika Gödecke et al. Hanover, 1995.

Konzentrationslager in Hamburg—Ansichten 1990. Ed. Max Andree et al. (*Hamburg Porträt: Museum für hamburgische Geschichte* 26–27). Hamburg, 1990.

Bibliography

Konzentrationslager in Hannover—KZ-Arbeit und Rüstungsindustrie in der Spätphase des Zweiten Weltkriegs. Ed. Rainer Fröbe et al. Hildesheim, 1985.

Konzentrationslager in Hannover, 1943–1945 (Ausstellungskatalog). Hanover, 1983.

Kossowsky, B. *Bibliography of the Jewish Publications in the British Zone of Germany, 1945–1950.* Bergen-Belsen, 1950 [Yiddish].

Kramer, Alan. "Demontagepolitik in Hamburg." In *Britische Deutschland- und Besatzungspolitik, 1945–1949,* ed. Josef Foschepoth and Rolf Steininger, 265–80. Paderborn, 1985.

Kugelmann, Cilly. "The identity and Ideology of Jewish Displaced Persons." In *Jews, Germans, Memory: Reconstruction of Jewish Life in Germany,* ed. Y. Michal Bodemann, 65–76. Ann Arbor, 1996.

Kulka, Otto D., and Baruch Z. Ophir. "Leben und Schicksal in sechseinhalb Jahrhunderten." In *Leben und Schicksal: Zur Einweihung der Synagoge in Hannover,* published by Presseamt der Landeshaupstadt, 15–40. Hanover, 1963.

Kushner, Doris. "Die jüdische Minderheit in der Bundesrepublik Deutschland." Ph.D. thesis, Cologne, 1977.

Kushner, Tony. "The Impact of the Holocaust on British Society and Culture." *Contemporary Record* 5, no. 2 (1991): 349–75.

———. *The Persistence of Prejudice: Antisemitism in British Society during the Second World War.* Manchester, 1989.

Lamm, Hans. "Der Wiederaufbau der Hamburger jüdischen Gemeinde nach 1945." In *Die Drei-Gemeinde: Aus der Geschichte der jüdischen Gemeinden Altona-Hamburg-Wandsbeck,* ed. Oskar Wolfsberg-Aviad, 134–36. Munich, 1960.

Laqueur, Renata. *Bergen-Belsen-Tagebuch.* Hanover, 1983.

Lavsky, Hagit. *Before Catastrophe: The Distinctive Path of German Zionism.* Jerusalem and Detroit, 1996.

———. "'She'erit Hapletah'- Object or Subject of History? New Directions in Historical Research." *Yahadut Zemanenu,* 6 (1990): 25–43 [Hebrew].

———. "British Jewry and the Jews in Post-Holocaust Germany: The Jewish Relief Unit, 1945–1950." *Journal of Holocaust Education* 4, no. 1 (1995): 29–40.

Levy, Isaac. *Witness to Evil: Bergen-Belsen, 1945.* London, 1995.

Levy-Hass, Hanna. *Inside Belsen.* Translated by Ronald L. Taylor, with an introduction by Jane Caplan. Brighton, 1962.

Livingstone, Rodney. "Germans and Jews since 1945." *Patterns of Prejudice* 19, no. 2–3 (1995): 45–59.

Bibliography

London, Louise. "British Government Policy and Jewish Refugees, 1933–1945." *Patterns of Prejudice* 23, no. 4 (1989–90): 26–43.

Lorenz, Ina S. "Die Jüdische Gemeinde Hamburg, 1860–1943: Kaiserreich—Weimarer Republik—NS-Staat." In *Die Juden in Hamburg, 1590–1990*, ed. Arno Herzig and Saskia Rohde, 77–100. Hamburg, 1991.

Lorenz, Ina S., and Jörg Berkemann. "Kriegsende und Neubeginn: Zur Entstehung der neuen Jüdischen Gemeinde in Hamburg, 1945–1948." In *Die Juden in Hamburg, 1590–1990*, ed. Arno Herzig and Saskia Rohde, 633–55. Hamburg, 1991.

Mankowitz, Ze'ev. "The Affirmation of Life in *She'erith Hapleita*." *Holocaust and Genocide Studies* 5, no. 1 (1990): 13–21.

———. "The Formation of *She'erit Hapleita:* November 1944–July 1945." *Yad Vashem Studies* 20 (1990): 337–70.

———. "The Politics and Ideology of Survivors of the Holocaust in the American Zone of Occupied Germany, 1945–1946." Ph.D. thesis, The Hebrew University of Jerusalem, 1987 [Hebrew].

Maor, Harry. "Über den Wiederaufbau der jüdischen Gemeinden in Deutschland seit 1945." Ph.D. thesis, Mainz, 1961.

Markovitzky, Jacob. *Fighting Ember: Gahal Forces in the War of Independence*. Tel Aviv, 1995.

Marrus, Michael. *The Unwanted. European Refugees in the Twentieth Century*. New York and Oxford, 1985.

Matzerath, Horst, and Brigitte Holzhauser. *"Vergessen kann man die Zeit nicht, das ist nicht möglich . . .": Kölner erinnern sich an die Jahre 1929–1945*. Cologne, 1985.

Memorandum. Documentary produced in 1991 by the National Film Board of Canada (thanks to Prof. L. D. Stokes of Dalhousie University, Halifax, Nova Scotia, Canada).

Michalski, Raoul W. "Die jüdische Gemeinde Hamburg seit den 50er Jahren." In *Die Juden in Hamburg, 1590–1990*, ed. Arno Herzig and Saskia Rohde, 101–12. Hamburg, 1991.

Mlynek, Klaus, et al. "Deutsche und Juden nach 1945." In *Reichskristallnacht in Hannover*, ed. Marlis Buchholz et al., 97–104. Hanover, 1978.

Mohr, Arno. "Das Auschwitz-Syndrom—Geschichte der Juden in Deutschland nach 1945." *Neue Politische Literatur* 10, no. 1 (1995): 62–94.

Muhlen, Norbert. *The Survivors: A Report on the Jews in Germany Today*. New York, 1962.

Nachama, Andreas. "Nach der Befreiung: Jüdisches Leben in Berlin 1945–1953." In *Jüdische Geschichte in Berlin. Essays und Studien*, ed. Reinhard Rürup, 267–85. Berlin, 1995.

Bibliography

Nachmani, Amikam. *Great Powers Discord in Palestine: The Anglo-American Committee of Inquiry into the Problems of European Jewry and Palestine, 1945–1946.* London, 1987.

Naujoks, Antje Clara. "Die Funktion des Zionismus in den jüdischen Gemeinden in Deutschland nach 1945." In *Im Schatten des Holocaust: Jüdisches Leben in Niedersachsen nach 1945*, ed. Herbert Obenaus, 165–96. Hanover, 1997.

Die Neue Synagoge in Düsseldorf—Zur Einweihung am 7. September 1958. Düsseldorf, 1958.

Niederland, Doron. *German Jews: Emigrants or Refugees? Emigration Patterns between the Two World Wars.* Jerusalem, 1996 [Hebrew].

1933–1945: Einzelschicksale und Erlebnisse von Bürgern, die im Bereich des heutigen Stadtbezirkes 3 wohnen. Ed. Landeshauptstadt Düsseldorf. 3 vols. Düsseldorf, 1986.

Nothmann, Hugo. "Die religiöse Situation des Judentums im Nachkriegsdeutschland." In *Die Juden in Deutschland, 1951/2 (5712)—Ein Almanach*, ed. Heinz Ganther, 185–87. Frankfurt a.M. and Munich.

Obenaus, Herbert. *"Sei Stille, sonst kommst Du nach Ahlem!" Zur Funktion der Gestapostelle in der ehemalige Israelitischen Gartenbauschule von Ahlem (1943–1945).* Hannoversche Geschichtsblätter 41 (Hanover, 1987).

——. "Die widerwillige Wiedergutmachung." In *Im Schatten des Holocaust: Jüdisches Leben in Niedersachsen nach 1945*, ed. Herbert Obenaus, 83–116. Hanover, 1997.

Olevsky, Rafael. *The Tear.* Tel Aviv, 1983 [Hebrew].

Ophir, Baruch Z. "Zur Geschichte der Hamburger Juden, 1919–1939." In *Juden in Preussen—Juden in Hamburg*, ed. Peter Freimark, 81–97. Hamburg, 1985.

Peck, Abraham J. "Jewish Survivors of the Holocaust in Germany: Revolutionary Vanguard or Remnants of a Destroyed People?" *Tel Aviver Jahrbuch* 19 (1990): 33–45.

——. "'Unsere Augen haben die Ewigkeit gesehen.' Erinnerung und Identität der *She'erit Hapletah*." in *Überlebt und Unterwegs. Jüdische Displaced Persons in Nachkriegsdeutschland*, ed. Jacqueline Giere, 27–49. Frankfurt a.M., 1997.

Perl, Gisella. *I Was a Doctor in Auschwitz.* Tamarac, Fla., 1987.

Pinson, Koppel. "Jewish Life in Liberated Germany: A Study of the Jewish DP's." *Jewish Social Studies* 9, no. 2 (1947): 101–26.

——. *Modern Germany: Its History and Civilization.* New York, 1954.

Posner, Julius. *In Deutschland, 1945–1946.* Jerusalem, 1947.

Bibliography

Prager, Norbert. "Wiederaufbau." In *Leben und Schicksal: Zur Einweihung der Synagoge in Hannover*, Presseamt der Landeshauptstadt, 41–44. Hanover, 1963.

Proudfoot, Malcolm. *European Refugees*. London, 1957.

Quast, Anke. "Jewish Committee und Jüdische Gemeinde Hannover: Der schwierige Anfang einer Gemeinschaft." In *Im Schatten des Holocaust, Jüdisches Leben in Niedersachsen nach 1945*, ed. Herbert Obenaus, 55–74. Hanover, 1997.

——. "Jüdische Gemeinden in Niedersachsen nach 1945: Das Beispiel Hannover." Ph.D. thesis, The University of Hanover, 1999.

Rahe, Thomas. "Jüdische Waisenkinder im Konzentrationslager Bergen-Belsen." *Dachauer Hefte* 14 (1998): 31–49.

Raim, Edith. "1946: der 'Aufruhr' von Landsberg. US-Besatzungsmacht und deutsche Bevölkerung gemeinsam gegen jüdische DPs." *Tribüne* 128 (1993): 153–62.

Rapaport, Lynn. *Jews in Germany after the Holocaust. Memory, Identity, and Jewish-German Relations*. Cambridge, 1997.

Reicher, Bruno. *Jüdische Geschichte und Kultur in NRW—Ein Handbuch*. Essen, 1993.

Reilly, Joanne. *Belsen: The Liberation of a Concentration Camp*. London and New York, 1998.

Richarz, Monika. "Juden in der Bundesrepublik Deutschland und in der Deutschen Demokratischen Republik seit 1945." In *Jüdisches Leben in Deutschland nach 1945*, ed. Micha Brumlik, 13–30. Frankfurt a.M., 1986.

Ritvo, Roger A., and Diane M. Plotkin. *Sisters in Sorrow: Voices of Care in the Holocaust*. College Station, Tex., 1998.

Rosensaft, Menachem Z. "My Father: A Model for Empowerment." In *Life Reborn: Jewish Displaced Persons 1945–1951*. Conference Proceedings, ed. Menachem Z. Rosensaft, 77–81. Washington, D.C., 2001.

Sagi, Nana. *German Reparations: A History of the Negotiations*. Jerusalem, 1980.

Schardt, Angelika. "'Der Rest der Geretteten.' Jüdische Überlebende im DP-Lager Föhrenwald 1945–1957." *Dachauer Hefte* 8 (1992): 53–68.

Schein, Ada. "Educational Systems in the Jewish DP Camps in Germany and Austria (1945–1951)." Ph.D. thesis, The Hebrew University of Jerusalem, 2000 [Hebrew].

Schneider, Richard Chaim. *Wir sind da! Die Geschichte der Juden in Deutschland von 1945 bis heute*. Berlin, 2000.

Bibliography

Schreiber, Albert. *Zwischen Davidstern und Doppeladler, Chronik der Juden.* Lübeck, 1983.

Schulze, Peter. *Juden in Hannover: Beiträge zur Geschichte und Kultur einer Minderheit.* Hanover, 1989.

Segalman, Ralph. "The Psychology of Jewish Displaced Persons." *Jewish Social Service Quarterly* 23, no. 1 (1946): 361–69.

Seligman, Avraham. "An Illegal Way of Life in Nazi Germany." *Leo Baeck Institute Year Book* 37 (1992): 327–61.

Shafir, Shlomo. "Der Jüdische Weltkongress und sein Verhältnis zu Nachkriegsdeutschland, 1945–1967." *Menora* 3 (1992): 210–37.

She'erit Hapletah, 1944–1948: Rehabilitation and Political Struggle, Proceedings of the Sixth Yad Vashem International Historical Conference. Ed. Yisrael Gutman and Adina Drechsler. Jerusalem, 1990 [Hebrew].

Shimoni, Gideon. "Selig Brodetsky and the Ascendancy of Zionism in Anglo-Jewry (1939–1945)." *The Jewish Journal of Sociology* 12, no. 2 (1980): 125–61.

Sicron, Moshe. *Immigration to Israel, 1948–1952.* Jerusalem, 1957.

Sington, Derrick. *Belsen Uncovered.* London, 1946.

Slesinger, Zalman. "Jewish Education in DP Camps." *Jewish Education* 19, no. 3 (1948): 64.

Speaking Out - Jewish Voices from United Germany, ed. Susan Stern. Chicago, Berlin, Tokyo and Moscow, 1995.

Srole, Leo. "Why the DP's Can't Wait." *Commentary*, January 1947, 13–24.

Steininger, Rolf. *Deutsche Geschichte seit 1945: Darstellung und Dokumente in vier Bänden.* Frankfurt a.M., 1996.

——. "Die Sozialisierung fand nicht statt." In *Britische Deutschland- und Besatzungspolitik, 1945–1949*, ed. Josef Foschepoth and Rolf Steininger, 135–51. Paderborn, 1985.

Stern, Frank. "Im Anfang war Auschwitz. Besatzer, Deutsche und Juden in der Nachkriegszeit." *Dachauer Hefte* 6 (1990): 25–42.

——. "The Historic Triangle: Occupiers, Germans and Jews in Postwar Germany." *Tel Aviver Jahrbuch* 19 (1990): 47–76.

——. "Antisemitismus und Philosemitismus in der politischen Kultur der entstehenden Bundesrepublik Deutschland." In *Aufbau nach dem Untergang. Deutsch-jüdische Geschichte nach 1945. In Memoriam Heinz Galinski*, ed. Andreas Nachama and Julius H. Schoeps, 50–163. Berlin, 1992.

——. "Wider Antisemitismus—für christlich-jüdische Zusammenarbeit. Aus

Bibliography

der Entstehungszeit der Gesellschaften und des Koordinierungsrats." *Menora* 3 (1992): 182–209.

———. *The Whitewashing of the Yellow Badge: Antisemitism and Philosemitism in Postwar Germany.* Oxford, 1992.

———. "German-Jewish Relations in the Postwar Period: the Ambiguities of Antisemitic and Philosemitic Discourse." In *Jews, Germans, Memory. Reconstruction of Jewish Life in Germany*, ed. Y. Michal Bodemann, 77–98. Ann Arbor, 1996.

Suchy, Barbara. "Zwischen den Zeiten: Die jüdische Gemeinde Düsseldorf von 1945–1948." In *Neuanfang: Leben in Düsseldorf*, ed. Stadtmuseum Düsseldorf, 330–40. Düsseldorf, 1986.

Takei, Ayaka. "Question of '*Rechtsnachfolge:*' The Jewish Restitution Successor Organization and the Postwar Jewish *Gemeinden* in Germany." unpublished draft authorized by the author.

Treue, Wilhelm. *Die Demontagepolitik der Westmächte nach dem Zweiten Weltkrieg (unter besonderer Berücksichtigung ihrer Wirkung auf die Wirtschaft in Niedersachsen).* Göttingen and Hanover, 1967.

Trittel, Günter J. "Das Scheitern der Bodenreform im 'Schatten des Hungers.'" In *Britische Deutschland- und Besatzungspolitik, 1945–1949*, ed. Josef Foschepoth and Rolf Steininger, 153–70. Paderborn, 1985.

Tsamriyon, Tsemach. *The Press of the Jewish Holocaust Survivors in Germany as an Expression of Their Problems.* Tel Aviv, 1970 [Hebrew].

Turner, Henry Ashby. *The Two Germanys since 1945.* New Haven and London, 1987.

Tydor Baumel, Judith. "The Politics of Spiritual Rehabilitation in the DP Camps." *Simon Wiesental Center Annual* 6 (1989): 57–79.

———. *Kibbutz Buchenwald.* Tel Aviv, 1994 [Hebrew].

———. "Kibbutz Buchenwald and Kibbutz Hafetz Hayyim: Two Experiments in the Rehabilitation of Jewish Survivors in Germany." *Holocaust and Genocide Studies* 9, no. 2 (1995): 231–49.

———. "Kibbutz Buchenwald: The establishment of the first *Hachsharah.*" *YIVO Annual of Jewish Social Science* 23 (1996): 445–73.

Vernant, Jacques. *The Refugees in the Post-war World.* London, 1953.

Voigt, Angelika. *Juden in Düsseldorf: Die Zerstörung der Jüdischen Gemeinde während der Nationalsozialistischen Herrschaft.* Aschendorf, 1983.

Warhaftig, Zorah. *Uprooted.* New York, 1946.

Wasserstein, Bernard. *Britain and the Jews of Europe, 1939–1945.* Oxford, 1979.

Watt, D. Cameron. "Grossbritannien, die Vereinigten Staaten und Deutschland," In *Britische Deutschland- und Besatzungspolitik 1945–1949*, ed. Josef Foschepoth and Rolf Steininger, 15–25. Padderborn, 1985.

Webster, Roland. "American Relief and Jews in Germany, 1945–1960. Diverging Perspectives." *Leo Baeck Institute Year Book* 38 (1993): 293–321.

Wegweiser durch das jüdische Rheinland. Ed. Ludger Heid and Julius H. Schoeps. Salomon Ludwig Steinheim Institut, 1992.

West Germany Under Construction. Politics, Society, and Culture in the Adenauer Era, ed. Robert G. Moeller. Ann Arbor, 1997.

Widerstand und Verfolgung in Köln, 1933–1945. Ed. Franz Irsfeld and Bernd Wittschier. Cologne, 1974.

Williams, Eryl Hall. *A Page of History in Relief*. York, 1993.

Winkel, Harald. *Die Wirtschaft im geteilten Deutschland, 1945–1970*. Wiesbaden, 1974.

"Wo Wurzeln waren...": Juden in Hamburg-Eimsbüttel 1933 bis 1945. Ed. Sybille Baumbach et al. Hamburg, 1993.

Yablonka, Hanna. *Foreign Brethren: Holocaust Survivors in the State of Israel, 1948–1952*. Jerusalem, 1994 [Hebrew].

Yahil, Haim. "The Activities of the Palestine Mission for *She'erit Hapletah*, 1945–1949." *Yalkut Moreshet* 30 (November 1980): 7–40; 31 (April 1981): 133–76 [Hebrew].

Yantian, Nicholas. "Studien zum Selbstverständnis der jüdischen 'Displaced Persons' in Deutschland nach dem Zweiten Weltkrieg." M.A. thesis. Berlin, 1994.

———. "'Aus der Versteinerung heraustreten'—Das 'Kazet-Theater' im jüdischen 'Displaced Persons'-Lager Bergen-Belsen, 1945–1947." In *Im Schatten des Holocaust. Jüdisches Leben in Niedersachsen nach 1945*, ed. Herbert Obenaus, 131–63. Hanover, 1997.

Zanin, M. *This Is How It Happened: Testimonies by Bergen-Belsen Survivors*. Tel Aviv, 1987 [Hebrew].

Zariz, Ruth. *Flight before Catastrophe: Emigration from Germany, 1938–1945*. Tel Aviv, 1990 [Hebrew].

Zertal, Idith. *From Catastrophe to Power. Holocaust Survivors and the Emergence of Israel*. Berkeley, 1998.

Zweig, Ronald. "Restitution and the Problem of Jewish Displaced Persons in Anglo-American Relations, 1944–1948." *American Jewish History* 78 (1988): 54–78.

Zwischen Antisemitismus und Philosemitismus. Juden in der Bundesrepublik, ed. Wolfgang Benz. Berlin, 1991.

Index

Adath She'erit Yisrael (Orthodox *Kehillah* in Bergen-Belsen), 114, 115, 118
Adenauer, Konrad, 22, 23
Adoption project, 145
Adult education. *See* Educational program in Bergen-Belsen
Agricultural training, 146, 147, 175
Agudath Israel, 117, 118, 219; in Allgemeine Koordinatzie Block (General United Bloc), 201; change in approach to Zionism, 74, 100–101, 163; drama group, 159; Agudath Israel World Union, 163; youth movement, 164
Ahlem, 82, 147, 175
Aid Committee for the Jews and Half-Jews of Hamburg, 86
Albrich, Thomas, 28
Aliyah (immigration to Palestine): Central Committee role in organizing, 211; as consequence of Holocaust, 164; illegal, in British Zone, 199; Jewish Agency efforts on behalf of, 202; Jewish Brigade goal of, 102; and Jewish survivors in postwar Germany, 204–11; legal, from British zone, 99; pressure for in American Zone, 54; struggle for as a political cause in British zone, 192, 197–202
Allgemeine Koordinatzie Block (General United Bloc), 201
Allgemeine Wochenzeitung der Juden in Deutschland, 134–35, 222
Allied Control Council for Germany, 15, 16
Altona, 80
Amatoren Gruppe (Amateur Group), 159
American-Jewish Conference, 133
American Jewish Joint Distribution Committee (JDC), 24, 25, 71, 91, 106–9, 213; agricultural school, 147; and Central Committee, 108, 115, 121–22; in "The Future of the Jews in Germany" conference, 213; help in search for relatives, 148; liquidation of activities in British Zone, 211; at Second Congress of the Liberated Jews in the British Zone, 136; support for educational system in Zionist mode, 220; vocational training, 146
American Jewish relief agencies, 106–7
American OMGUS (Official Military Government of the

Index

American OMGUS (*continued* United States), Education and Religious Affairs Section, 213

American Zone, occupied Germany: admission of Jewish refugees from Eastern Europe, 198; DP camps, 35; emissaries from Palestine to, 103; Jewish refugees in, 35; Military Rule No. 59, 26, 53; segregation between Jews and non-Jews, 53; size of, 15; smuggling in of *Exodus* passengers, 195; United Zionist organization, 200; Zionist party newspapers, 155

Am Stau camp for *Exodus* passengers, 194

Anglo-American Committee of Inquiry, 189–92, 197, 204

Anglo-Jewish Association (AJA), 95

Anti-Semitic attacks: on Jewish cemeteries and synagogues, 142; by non-Germans, 142; by non-Jewish DPs, 118–20

Arbeitsgemeinschaft der jüdischen Gemeinden Deutschlands (Work Association of the Jewish Communities of Germany), 133–34

Arbeitsgemeinschaft (Work Association) for the British Zone, 132

Arts and leisure, in Bergen-Belsen DP camp: private activity, 160; public activity, 158–60

Assembly Centers, 34, 35

Association of General Zionists. *See* Hitahdut Hazionim Haklaliim

Association of Jewish Journalists and Writers in the British Zone of Germany—Bergen-Belsen, 156

Auerbach, Philipp, 85, 86, 130, 131, 132, 133, 134

Auschwitz concentration camp, 42, 80

Austria, Jewish survivors in, 28

Babylon, 10

Bad Harzburg convalescent home, 97, 106, 116

Baeck, Rabbi Leo, 97

Bahad Poel Mizrahi (Associaton of Religious Zionist Pioneers), 96

Barou, Noah, 99–100, 111, 137, 138, 194

Baumgarten, Rabbi, 93

Beckelman, Moses W., 107

Bedzin, Ghetto, 66

Belsen Committee, 123

Bengal famine mixture, 43

Ben-Gurion, David, 35, 77, 104, 105, 191

Bentwich, Norman, 74, 95, 100, 134

Bergen-Belsen, as a concentration camp, 37–40; convalescent camp *(Erholungslager)*, 38, 40, 56–57; detention camp *(Aufenthaltslager)*, 37, 56; estimated number of deaths in, 39; Exchange Jews, in, 38, 56; Hungarians camp *(Ungarenlager)*, 38; Neutral camp *(Neutralenlager)*, 38; Special camp *(Sonderlager)*, 38; Star camp *(Sternlager)*, 38; starvation and disease, 40; women's camp, 38

Bergen-Belsen, as a DP camp, 11, 34; accommodations, 143–44; Aliyah Committee, 205; "American Zone," 143; arts and leisure, 157–61; Beth-Midrash, 119; births, 60, 150; British Army chaplains, 92–93; as center of Jewish life in British Zone, 56; Chief Rabbi's Religious Emergency Council for European Jews in, 93–94; children in, 167–68; closing of, 210–11; communication and

296

Index

the media, 153–57; educational program, 167–88, 220–21; establishment of a United National Front, 75–77; family formation, 148–53, 217; first wedding at, photo of, 151; food and other supplies, 144–45; JDC in, 107–8; Jewish Memorial, 121; Jewish organization efforts in, 63–70; Jewish population, 58–60; kibbutzim, 143, 160, 164–65; lack of proper nutrition for pregnant women, 150–51; Liberty Square, 158; library system, 160; literary activity, 156; national unification movement, 71–75, 217; nonperiodical publications, 156; nonprint communication media, 157; occupational and vocational training, 144–48; Palestine Office, 205–7; periodicals, 154–56; Polish Jews in, 59–60; postal service and transportation, 153; protest against British at unveiling of Jewish monument, 192; Provisional Committee, 66, 68–69, 70, 71, 73, 116, 117, 174; psychological breakdowns and mental illness, 152–53; publications, 154–56; religion and politics, 165–66; role of political parties, 162–65; smuggling in of *Exodus* passengers, 195; sociodemographic character, 59–60; sports events, 161; sports groups, photo of, 162; theatrical activity, 158–59; visit of Anglo-American Committee, 190–92; weddings, 149–50; Zionism, 161, 191–92, 220. *See also* Hohne camp

Bergen-Belsen, liberation of death camp, 37; aftermath of liberation, 41–43; British reaction to, 42; burying the dead, 44–45; food and water supply, 43–44; Jewish deaths in first weeks, 59; liquidation of, 47–48; manpower and supplies, 45–47; medical treatment and sanitation, 45

Berlin, Soviet blockade of, 22
Berlin Jews, 30–31
Berlin Wall, fall of, 10
Bernard-Rath, Hanna, 96–97
Beth Jacob Talmud Torah, 117, 170, 175
Bevin, Ernest, 190
Bimko (Rosensaft), Hadassa, 68, 150; Belsen survivor, 46, 68; escorting of children to Palestine, 112, 117; establishment of dental clinic and laboratory, 116, 146; at first postwar World Zionist Congress, 197; head of CC Health Department, 68, 77, 110, 116–17; marriage to Josef Rosensaft, 68, 150; photo of, 103

Births, in DP camps, 34, 60, 150
Bizonia (of American and British Zones in occupied Germany), 21, 22
Black market, 17, 118, 119, 142, 144, 145–46
Blankenese children's home, 116, 179, 206
Bloch, Szmayahu, 119, 197, 223
B'nai B'rith, 212
Board of Deputies of British Jews (BD), 74, 98, 100, 101
Board of Education, 181
Bocholt transit camp, 205, 206
Bodemann, Y. Michal, 11
Bonn, 61
Books, scarcity of, 177–78

297

Index

Bramson, Hermann, 85, 86
Brass, Jack, 96
Braunschweig, Rudolf, 85
Brenner, Michael, 11
Breuer, Mordechai, 105, 175, 176, 183, 185, 201
Briha, (flight enterprise from Europe to Palestine), 32, 101–2, 198
British Jewish Relief Unit (JRU), 74, 90, 94–98; agricultural school, 146; aid to German Jewish communities, 187, 211; friction with Rosensaft, 98; in "The Future of the Jews in Germany" conference, 213; pro-Zionism, 74, 106; at Second Congress of the Liberated Jews in the British Zone, 136; support for educational system in Zionist mode, 220; vocational training, 146
British Jewry: Army Chaplains, 92–93; emissaries to DP camps and Jewish community, 92–98; political intervention, 98–101. *See also* British Jewish Relief Unit (JRU); Chief Rabbi's Religious Emergency Council for European Jews (CRREC)
British Mandatory Government, Palestine, 11, 33, 189, 220
British Zone, occupied Germany, 11; central Zionist Committee, 200; conference of September 1945, 75–76; creation of *Länder*, 16; delegates to first postwar World Zionist Congress, 197; disruption of Jewish attempts to organize, 74–75; DP problem, 49–50; educational institutions in, 171–73; foundation of chief rabbinate, 135; German Jewish survivors in, 52, 61, 62, 78–82; JDC involvement in, 106–9; Jewish demonstrations in response to *Exodus* affair, 193–94; Jewish militantism as a result of policy in, 220; Jewish population of, 52, 55–62, 78–82; Jewish struggle for aliyah as a political cause, 192; Jewish survivors of Bergen-Belsen, 56–58; Jews in Bergen-Belsen DP camp, 58–60; latent anti-Semitism, 54–55; legal Aliyah from, 99; minor role of Palestine emissaries in, 106; number of children in, 167–68; number of DP camps in, 61; policy principles for restitution, 26, 53; policy regarding Jews, 51–55; population, economy, and occupation policy, 21, 49–51; recognition of Jewish communities under CC, 139; restrictions on DPs, 50, 54. *See also* Bergen-Belsen, as a DP camp; Central Committee (CC), British Zone; German Jewish communities, in the British Zone
British Zone Review, 52
Brodetsky, Selig, 74, 75, 76, 99, 100, 137
Brodie, Rabbi, 96
Brotman, Alexander, 108
Brumlik, Micha, 11
Brunswick, 61, 87–88
Buchenwald, 37, 59, 107–8
Bund (Jewish Workers Movement), 163, 219

Carlebach, Rabbi, 97
Caspi, Meir, 176
Celle, DP camp in, 46, 59, 60; Beth Jacob seminar, 170; DP Jewish community, 88–89; Hasidic community, 89
Central British Fund (CBF), 74, 95, 101

Index

Central Committee, American Zone: in "The Future of the Jews in Germany" conference, 212; issue of future of Jews in Germany, 222; struggle for British recognition, 221

Central Committee (CC), British Zone, 59, 67, 68, 69; authority for marriage licenses, 118; bulletins, 155; call for enrollment in Jewish armed forces, 202–3; call on DPs to demand free aliyah, 192; chief rabbinate, 165–66; conflict with Orthodox Jews, 113–16; Cultural Affairs Department activities, 117; economic control, 113–16; educational institutions, 174; educational program, 180–86; efforts to enforce Sabbath in public life, 166; election, 76–77; in "The Future of the Jews in Germany" conference, 212; goals and infrastructure, 110–13; Health Department, 116–17; Holocaust commemoration, 120; Holocaust publications, 156; and the JDC, 108, 115, 121–22; Jewish court, 119; Jewish police, 118–20; organization of aliyah, 211; organization of German Jewish communities, 132–33; organization of youth groups, 129; *pekudat hayom* (Announcement of the Day) for second liberation day, 185; protests against terrorist acts by Jewish extremists in Palestine, 196; Rabbinical Department, 117–18; resolution that DPs of Belsen waive their priority status, 194–95; responsibility for absorbing illegal refugees, 198–99; responsibility for *Exodus* passengers, 195, 196; shift to general nationalist agenda, 202–3; struggle for control of emigration without discrimination, 211; struggle for recognition, 120–23; supervision of Orthodox educational institutions, 181; *Wirtschaftsamt* (Economic Department), 115; and World Jewish Congress, 122, 202–3

Central Council of the Jews in Germany, 135, 140, 188, 214, 222

Central Orthodox Committee, 213

Chief Rabbi's Religious Emergency Council for European Jews (CRREC), 74, 90, 91; in Bergen-Belsen, 93–94; and CC Rabbinical Department, 117, 118; and JCRA, 94, 114; as major supplementary source of food, 144; religious services and supplies, 165–66

Children: centrality of in DP camps, 217–18; escorted to Palestine from British Zone, 112, 117; number of in British Zone, 167–68; trauma to, 178

Children's homes, 116, 175, 179. *See also* Blankenese children's home

Christian Democrats, 22

Clay, General, 16

Cohen, Leonard, 75, 95

Cold war, 22

Collis, W. R. F., 51, 52

Cologne: German Jewish community in, 78–79, 85, 127; Jewish population immediately after liberation, 61; Nazi persecution in, 78–79

Communication and the media, in Bergen-Belsen, 153–57; nonprint communication

Index

Communication and the media (*continued*)
   media, 157; postal service and transportation, 153; publications, 154–56
Compensation, 24, 25, 133, 214. *See also* Indemnification; Reparations; Restitution; *Wiedergutmachung*
Concentration camps, Jewish survivors of, demographic distribution, 31–32
Council for Welfare Groups for the Diaspora. *See* Jewish Agency for Palestine.
Council of the Jewish Communities in the British Zone (Rat der Jüdischen Gemeinden der britischen Zone), 132–33; at the Central Committee of the Liberated Jews in the British Zone of Germany (Rat der Gemeinden beim Zentralkomitee der Befreiten Juden der britischen Zone Deutschlands), 138, 139, 140
Council of States, 22
Cyprus detention camps, 194, 195, 199

Dallob, Samuel J., 108, 194
Decartelization, 19–20
Deggendorf, 29, 83
Deindustrialization, 19–20
Demilitarization, 19
Democratization, 19
De-Nazification, 19, 20, 23
Deutsch, Captain, 65, 66
Die aus Theresienstadt (Those from Theresienstadt), 86
Diepholz, 60, 96
Displaced Persons Act of 1948, 36
Displaced persons (DP) camps: baby boom in, 34; centrality of children in, 217–18; economic constraints, 142; as ex-territorial entities, 141; as greenhouse for new Jewish national identity, 216–24; intensive literary and theatrical activity, 218; liquidation, 36; political activities, 218–20; relations with German population, 141–42; religious life, 218; as a way out of Europe, 33; Zionism as center of activity in, 220. *See also* Bergen-Belsen, as a DP camp; Assembly Centers; Celle, DP camp; Diepholz; Feldafing DP camp; Föhrenwald DP camp
Displaced persons (DPs), 9, 34–35; anti-Semitic attacks by non-Jewish, 118–20; communities in postwar Germany, 87–90; defined, 17; emigration to Israel, 25, 36, 138; Jewish Committee, 87; and local German Jewish communities, 212, 221; migration and resettlement, 18; remaining in Western Zones of Occupation, 17–18; restitution and, 26; search for relatives, 148; threat to morale and rule of law, 18
Dobkin, Eliyahu, 104
Dora-Mittlebau camp, 39, 66
Dreifuss, Julius, 85, 86, 87, 132
Dreifuss, Meta, 85–86
Düsseldorf, 61; forced labor camps, 80; German Jewish community in, 79–80, 85–86, 127

Easterman, Alexander L., 75, 99
Eastern Europe, anti-Semitism, 33; Germans, deported from, 18
Educational institutions, in the British Zone, 168–70, 171–73, 174
Educational program, in Bergen-Belsen, 167–88; adult education,

INDEX

184, 185; agricultural training, 175; celebration of Jewish religious and national holidays, 184–85; conditions and constraints of, 176–80; curricula, 181–84; foundation of educational institutions, 168–70; initiators and teachers, 170–76; language issue, 183; lectures, 157; nationalistic atmosphere, 220–21; organization, 180–81; and Orthodox educational system, 181; pedagogic aims, 182; religious education, 174–75, 184; role of informal education, 184–86; Zionist- and *Eretz Yisrael*-oriented education, 183
Educational program, in German Jewish communities, 129, 186–88
Ehrlich, Menahem, 105, 176, 201
Eigen, Maurice, 107
Eleventh of Adar (commemoration of the heroes of Tel-Hai), 161, 184–85
Elton, Rabbi, 93
Der Emeth (The Truth), 155
Eretz Yisrael, 76, 182, 183, 184, 185, 192, 201, 206
Essen, German Jewish community in, 127
European Recovery Program, 21
Evian conference, 17
Exodus affair, 138, 192–96
Exodus passengers *(ma'apilim)*, 193–96, 209, 210
Ezra youth movement, 185

Family formation, in Bergen-Belsen, 148–53, 217
Feder, Sami, 77, 110, 158
Federal Republic of Germany (Bundesrepublik Deutschland), 22, 23, 212

Federal Supplementary Law, 53
Feldafing DP camp, 34
Fifteenth of Shevat, 184
Film screenings, in Bergen-Belsen, 157
Five Powers Conference on Reparations for Non-Repatriable Victims of Nazism, 25
Föhrenwald DP camp, 34, 36
Food and supplies, at Bergen-Belsen DP camp, 144–45
Foreign Secretaries Council, 16
Frankfurt, 22
French Zone, occupied Germany, 15, 22
Friends Relief Service, 45, 91, 92, 95
"The Future of the Jews in Germany" conference, 212–14

Galuth, 183
Gelsenkirchen, 61
German Democratic Republic (Deutsche Demokratische Republik), 23
German Jewish communities, in the British Zone, 78–82; after liquidation, 212–14; aid from JRU, 187, 211; beginnings of regional organizations, 130–32; from centralization to separatism, 137–40; demographic profile of, 29–31, 124–27; and displaced persons (DPs), 212, 221; educational program in, 129, 186–88; founders of, 85–87; immediate needs, 127–28; integration with national Jewish organizations, 221–22; motives for reestablishment of, 82–85; organization under CC, 132–33; population of immediately after liberation, 61, 62; question of status of

301

German Jewish communities (*continued*)
non-Jews, 126–27; shift from Zionist to non-Zionist attitude, 132; social and cultural roles, 128–30; status of under British policy, 52; welfare projects, 128; youth organization, 186. *See also specific communities*
German Jewish Work Association, 138–39
German universities, Jewish students in, 186–87
Germany, postwar: agricultural and industrial infrastructure, 19; economic conditions, 16–17; emigration from, 36; estimates of Jewish survivors in, 27–32; obstacles to economic recovery, 21–22; population growth, 17–19
Gerst, Rabbi Yehudah Leb, 163
Gilman, Sander L.: *Jews in Today's German Culture*, 10, 11
Gittler, Nahum, 200
Glanz, Jacob, 200
Glaubensjuden, 78, 79
Glyn Hughes Hospital, 97, 116, 146
Glyn Hughes, Brigadier H. L., 45, 75, 116
Goldfinger (Ben Jeshaya), Rabbi, 92, 97
Goldschmidt, Moritz, 85, 86
Goldstein, Harry, 86
Grabovsky-Argov, Meir, 75
"Grand National" operation, 138, 198, 199, 201, 202, 204–9; first transport, 205–7; "Grand National Junior," 168; and Zionist immigration policy, 208–9
Great Britain: repatriation policy, 25; recognition of Israel, 209; rejection of Anglo-American Committee recommendation, 204, 209. *See also* British Zone, occupied Germany
Greenbaum, Rev. Avraham, 90, 93, 97, 114, 150
Greenstein, Harry, 212
Grynzpan, Herschel, 81
Gur Hasidim, 66
Gutman, M. B., 110

Haber, Samuel L., 107
Habonim (Labor Zionists), 96
Hachsharah (pioneer training), 102, 186, 199
Haganah, 102, 192, 198
HaKibbutz Hame'uhad movement, 105, 164
Halakah, 117, 118, 126, 149
Halpern, Rabbi, 191
Hamburg, 15, 61, 194; Aid Committee, 127; concentration camps, 80; DP Jewish community, 87; German Jewish community, 80–81, 86; Hamburg Hebrew Congregation, 127
Hamizrahi, 77, 118, 185; in Allgemeine Koordinatzie Block (General United Bloc), 201; drama group, 159; representation in CC, 114, 115
Hanukkah, 119, 158, 179
Hanover: DP community, 87; forced labor camps, 81–82; German Jewish community in, 81–82, 86; Jewish population immediately after liberation, 61; school, 170; vocational school, 147
Hardman, Rabbi Leslie, 57–58, 92
Harrison, Earl G., 35, 53, 77, 190
Harrison Report, 190
Hashomer Hatza'ir, 96, 164, 165, 200; in Allgemeine Koordinatzie Block (General United Bloc), 201; delegates to first postwar World Zionist Congress,

Index

197; periodicals, 155; refugee settlement in Ahlem, 175
Hatikvah, 76
Hebrew, common language in secular institutions, 183
Hebrew high school, in Bergen-Belsen, 170, 182, 183–84
Hebrew Immigrant Aid Society (HIAS), 91, 106, 206
Hehalutz, 96
Heinemann, Max, 86
Helfgott (Asaria), Rabbi Hermann (Zvi), 68–69, 77, 92, 110, 117, 135
Henriques, Lady Rose, 96, 134, 183
Hertz, Chief Rabbi Joseph Herman, 74, 93–94, 100
Heuss, Theodore, 22–23
Hevra Kadisha, 165
Himmler, Heinrich, 57
Histadrut Zionit Ahidah (United Zionist Organization), 106, 164, 165, 197, 200–201
Hitahdut Hazionim Haklaliim (Association of General Zionists), 201
Hoffmann, Haim (Yahil), 103
Hohne camp, 75, 116. *See also* Bergen-Belsen, as a DP camp
Holland, 80
Holocaust publications, 156
Holocaust survivors. *See* Displaced persons (DPs); German Jewish communities, in the British Zone; Jewish survivors, in postwar Germany; *She'erit Hapletah*
Holt, Lily, 178
Hoover packages, 16
Hoter-Yishai, Aharon, 102
Hungarian Jews: in Bergen-Belsen, 60; establishment of separate *Kehillah* by orthodox, 114, 118

I. G. Farben factory, 69

Immigration Act of 1948, United States, 210, 212
Indemnification, 24, 26. *See also* Compensation; Reparations; Restitution; *Wiedergutmachung*
Informatsie (Information), 155
Interessenvertretung (Interests-Representation of the Jewish Communities [I-RJC]), 133, 134
Inter-Governmental Committee on Refugees (IGCR), 17
International Refugee Organization (IRO), 18, 25, 194
Irgun She'erit Hapletah Mehaezor Habriti, 68, 105, 192
Isick, Hava, 176
Israel: emigration of DPs to, 25, 36, 138, 203; foundation of, 202, 209; immigration restrictions, 210; Israeli government, 196
Israel Independence Day (Yom Ha'atzmaut), 158, 161, 185
Israelitische Asyl (Jewish Shelter), 127

Jarblum, Marc, 194
Ja-sagan zum Judentum, 128
Jever (Upjever), 211
Jewish Agency for Palestine (JA), 24, 25, 103; Absorption Division, 206–7; claims submitted to Allies, 53; Council of Welfare Groups for the Diaspora and Welfare Mission, 91, 103–6; efforts to persuade British to give priority to *Exodus ma'apilim*, 194; in "The Future of the Jews in Germany" conference, 213; and "Grand National," 205, 209; help in search for relatives, 148; illegal immigration efforts, 199; immigration efforts, 202, 208–9; liquidation of activities in British Zone, 211; resistance to Jewish future in Germany,

Index

Jewish Agency for Palestine (JA) (*continued*) 139; at Second Congress of the Liberated Jews in the British Zone, 136; vocational training, 146

Jewish Brigade: achievements in education, 102, 198; assistance in the *Briha*, 101–2; early representation in liberated camps, 73, 92, 96, 102; goals of rehabilitation and aliyah, 102; nonpartisan approach, 102–3; teacher soldiers, 174

Jewish cemeteries, restoration of, 130; attacks on, 142

Jewish Committee for Relief Abroad (JCRA), 74, 91, 94, 95, 101, 121–22, 213

Jewish communities. *See* German Jewish communities, in the British Zone

Jewish Diaspora, effect on post-Holocaust Jewish identity, 9

Jewish Memorial, in Bergen-Belsen, 121

Jewish National Fund. *See* Keren Kayemet Le'israel

Jewish Refugee Committee, 95

Jewish Relief Unit (JRU). *See* British Jewish Relief Unit (JRU)

Jewish Restitution Successor Organization (JRSO), 26, 53, 212

Jewish Students Federation, England, 187

Jewish survivors, in postwar Germany: in British Zone, 55–62; camp survivors, 28, 31–32, 58–60; cooperation and solidarity with the *Yishuv*, 196–97; demographic profile, 29–32; displaced persons, 34–35; emigration and aliyah, 204–11; in German Jewish communities, 29, 52, 61, 62, 78–82; intermarried couples, 30; population estimates, 27–32; population growth, 32–34; pro-Zionism, 163; refugees from Eastern Europe, 32–34; shift from Zionist to nationalist agenda, 202–3. *See also* Displaced persons (DPs); German Jewish communities, in the British Zone; *She'erit Hapletah*

Jewish students. *See* German universities, Jewish students in

Jewish Trust Corporation, 26, 53

Joint Distribution Committee (JDC). *See* American Jewish Joint Distribution Committee (JDC)

Joint Foreign Committee of the Board of Deputies of British Jews (BD) and the Anglo-Jewish Association (AJA), 95

Jonas, Alfred, 86

Josephtal, Giora, 206

"Journey's End" operation, 209

Judenhäuser, 81

Jüdisches Gemeindeblatt für die Nord-Rheinprovinz und Westfalen, 134

Kahan, Sydney, 119

Kalnitsky, David, 119

Kaminsky, Yitzhak, 176, 185

Kapos (KZ polizei), 42

Katz, Karl, 77, 111, 115, 132

Katzet Theater. *See* KZ Yiddish Theater

Katzki, Herbert, 107

Katznelson, Nissan, 103

Kaunitz, 60

Keren Kayemet Le'israel (Jewish National Fund), 67, 183

Kibbutz Kfar Hamakkabi, 105, 201

304

Index

Kibbutzim, in Bergen-Belsen, 143, 160; group activities affiliated with, 164–65; as opening for rehabilitation, 164
Kielce pogrom, 33
Kiel, 60, 125
King David Hotel, Jerusalem, 196
Klein, Rabbi Isaac, 213
Kleinmann-Lefkowitch, Sela. *See* Lefkowitch, Sela
Kolb, Eberhard, 39–40, 57
Költz, General, 16
Körperschaft des öffentlichen Rechts, 139
Kosher food, 144
Kosher slaughter, 118, 165
Kramer, Josef, 57
Krefeld, 79
Kristallnacht pogrom, 79, 81
Krupp plant, 20
Kudish, David, 65
Kurnitz, Yehiel, 200
KZ (Konzentrationslager), 82. *See also* Concentration camps, Jewish survivors of
KZ Yiddish Theater "Kazet Theater," 77, 158, photo of, 159

Lamm, Hans, 133
Landauer, Georg, 112
Länderrat (Lands' Council), 133
Landesverband (Land Association [LV]) of North Rhine region, 130–31
Landesverband (Land Association [LV]) of Schleswig-Holstein, 132
Landsberg, 34
Laufer, Berl (Dov Bernhard), 70, 150; member of the Central committee 77, 110, 119, 197; emigration to Israel, 211, 223
Lectures, 157
Lefkowitch, Sela, 170, 180, 191, 200
Lehi underground, 192
Leiwick, H., 155
Leverson, Jane, 92, 95
Levy, Rabbi Isaac, 57, 64–65, 92, 96
Lewin, Herbert, 85, 86
Lewin, Kurt, 176, 194, 201; and Aliyah Committee, 205–6; arrival in Belsen, 104, 191; avoidance of party politics, 105; opening of Palestine Office in British Zone, 199; support for Allgemeine Koordinatzie Block (General United Bloc), 201
Liberation Day, 120, 196
Libraries, 160, 177
Lingen, 59, 60
Literary and theatrical activity, in DP camps, 157, 158–59, 218
Littman, David, 102, 170, 182
Live newspapers, 156
Livneh, Eliyahu, 214
Łódź ghetto, 56, 79, 80, 82
Loeffler, Ludwig, 86
Loewenstein, Fritz, 85
Löwenthal, Alfred, 131
Lowenthal, E. G., 98, 133, 187
Lower Saxony, 15
Lübeck, 60, 61, 89–90, 133
Lüneburg, 60, 61
Lüneburg trials, 68
Lunzer, Erica, 96, 131
Lunzer, Henry, 114, 191
Lunzer, Judith, 96
Lurie, Norman, 76

Ma'apilim (illegal immigrants to Palestine), 193–96. *See also* Aliyah, illegal; *Exodus* passengers
Mack, Joseph, 174, 180
Manela, Avraham, 200
Markovitz, Shalom, 96
Marriage licenses, CC Rabbinical Department as authority for, 118
Marshall, George, 21
Marshall Plan, 21

Index

Marx, Karl, 134–35, 222
McCloy, John J., 213
Meiklejohn, Dr., 45
Meisels, Rabbi, 114, 144
Menora, 10
Merkaz Lagola (Center for the Diaspora), 101
Minden (Kahn), Eva, 146
Minsk ghetto, 79, 80
Mischlinge 1. Grades, 78
"Mobile Synagogue Ambulances," 93
Monetary reform, 21
Morgenthau, Henry, Jr., 19
Morgenthau Plan, 19–20
Mosad Le-Aliyah Bet (Haganah branch for illegal aliyah), 102. *See also Briha;* Aliyah, illegal
Mosberg, Karl, 87
Mühlenberg concentration camp, 82
München-Gladbach, German Jewish community in, 127, 131
Munk, Rabbi, 90, 93, 114, 131

Neuengamme, 80, 82
Neugraben am Falkenbergsweg, 80
Neustadt, 60, 61
Neustadt-Holstein, 147
Newspapers. *See* Periodicals in the British Zone
Nichtprivilegierte Sternträger (non-privileged Yellow Star bearers), 30
Noham (Noar Halutzi Meuhad), 70, 200
North Atlantic Treaty Organization, 23
North Rhine-Westphalia, 15
Notgemeinschaft der durch die Nürenberger Gesetze Betroffenen (Association of Victims of the Nuremberg Laws), 86
Nudnik, 10
Nussbaum, Adolf, 86

Nussbaum, Meinhold, 133

Oder-Neisse Line, 19
Oeuvre Secours pour Enfants Juifs (OSE), 91
Olevsky, Israel Moshe, 67, 150; on Central Committee, 77, 110; emigration to America, 211; founding of elementary school, 170; living conditions, 144; spiritual leader of Polish Hasidim, 89, 114
Olevsky, Rafael Gershon, 67–68, 150; CC Cultural Affairs Department, 110; CC Educational Committee, 180; emigration to Israel, 211; executive for the British Zone, 200; at first postwar World Zionist Congress, 197; and *Unzer Sztyme* (Our Voice), 73, 110, 154; and *Wochenblatt*, 155
Olim movement, 164
Oneg Shabbat (The Pleasure of Saturday), 160
"Operation Swallow," 198
ORT (Organization for Rehabilitation and Training), 91, 106, 147; aid to Jewish communities in developing educational systems, 187; dental laboratory, 116; in "The Future of the Jews in Germany" conference, 212; vocational training, 117, 146
Orphanage, in Bergen-Belsen, 170
Orthodox education. *See* Educational program, religious education
Orthodox *Kehillah*. *See* Adath She'erit Yisrael Orthodox *Kehillah*

Palestine: illegal immigration to, 36; official mission to British Zone, 103; partition of, 33, 123, 137–38, 195, 204; restrictions

Index

on Jewish immigration under Mandate, 33. *See also* Aliyah; British Mandatory Government, Palestine; Jewish Agency for Palestine
Palestine Mission (Welfare groups). *See* Jewish Agency for Palestine, Council of Welfare Groups; Palestine emissaries, in the British Zone
Palestine emissaries, in the British Zone, 101–6, 220–21; educational efforts, 175–76; party politics of, 200, 201; role of in Bergen-Belsen, 164; teachers' mission, 181
Passover, 206
Periodicals in the British Zone, 154–56
Plaut, Max, 86
Poale Agudath Israel (PAI), 105, 163, 175; kibbutzim, 164, 185
Poale Zion (Left), 66, 165; in Allgemeine Koordinatzie Block (General United Bloc), 201; delegates to first postwar World Zionist Congress, 197; Yiddisher Arbeter Biene (Jewish Workers' Theater), 159
Poale Zion Z. S.-Hitahduth, 155, 201
Poland: anti-Semitic violence, 18, 33; political-cultural tradition of Jewish community, 163
Polish DPs, anti-Semitic attacks, 119
Polish Jews: among camp survivors, 31; in Bergen-Belsen, 60; in Celle, 89; deported from Hanover, 81; Hasidim, 60, 114; refusal to return to Poland, 58–59
Politics and political parties, in DP camps, 162–65, 218–20
Poppendorf camp for *Exodus* passengers, 194
Population movements, postwar, 17–19
Poslushny, Chaim, 197
Potsdam conference, 15, 18, 19
Prager, Norbert, 86, 87
Prinz, Rabbi Joachim, 213
Privilegierte Mischehen (privileged mixed marriages), 29, 30, 81
Provisional Committee, Bergen-Belsen DP camp, 66, 68–69, 70, 71, 73, 116, 117, 174
Public loudspeaker newscasts, 157
Purim, 158

Raperport, G., 52
Rassejuden (Jews by race), 78
Rat der Gemeinden beim Zentralkomitee der befreiten Juden der britischen Zone Deutschlands (Council of Communities at the Central Committee of the Liberated Jews in the British Zone of Germany), 138
Rat der Jüdischen Gemeinden der britischen Zone (Council of the Jewish Communities in the British Zone), 132–33
Rath, Ernst vom, 79, 81
Ration cards, 144, 145
Rawitch, Melech, 155
Reading, Lady Eva, 99, 100
Red Cross, 45, 206
Regional organizations, 130–32
Regulation no. 59. *See* American Zone, occupied Germany, Military Rule No. 59
Reichsvereinigung der Juden in Deutschland (National Association of the Jews in Germany), 29
Religious publications, 156
Reparations, 19, 23; collective, 24; four components, 23–24; value of industries, 20.

Index

Reparations (*continued*)
See also Compensation; Indemnification; Restitution; *Wiedergutmachung*
Repatriation, 17, 24, 58
Restitution, 23–24, 214; Allied legislation of, 26; of communal and private property of German Jews, 127; of heirless or communal property, 26; and legal status, 127. See also Compensation; Indemnification; Reparations; *Wiedergutmachung*
Revisionistisher Gedank (Revisionist Thought), 155
Revisionists, 69, 70, 155, 164, 197, 200–201
Richards, Rabbi, 93
Richarz, Monika, 11
Riga ghetto, 79, 80
Ritual baths, 118, 165
Robertson, Brian, 16
Rosendorn, S., 110
Rosensaft, Hadassa. *See* Bimko (Rosensaft), Hadassa
Rosensaft, Josef (Yossele), 66–67, 107, 108; as chairman of Central Committee, 77, 110; close working relationship with Wollheim, 121; conflict with Orthodox, 114; dispute with JDC, 115; election to Belsen Jewish committee, 63–64; emigration to America, 223; and *Exodus* affair, 193–94, 196; at first postwar World Zionist Congress, 197; insistence on controlling emigration without discrimination, 211; and JRU, 98; living conditions at Belsen, 144; marriage, 68, 150; photograph of, 105, 111; relations with world Jewish leaders, 122–23; responsibility for absorbing illegal refugees, 198–99; skepticism about future of Jews in Germany, 213–14; testimony before Anglo-American Committee, 190; trips to London, 100; at unveiling of Jewish monument at Belsen, 76, 192
Rosensaft, Menachem, 68
Rosenthal, David: belief that both Hebrew and Yiddish should be taught in schools, 179; co-head of CC Cultural Affairs Department, 110; emigration to America, 70, 211, 223; executive for the British Zone, 200; and *Unzer Sztyme* (Our Voice), 70, 73, 77, 110, 154, 155; and *Wochenblatt*, 155
Rosinger, Yehezkel, 197
Ruhr Valley, 15, 19, 20, 21

Soviet Zone, occupied Germany, 15, 16
Saar Valley, 15, 19, 21
Sabbath, 161, 166. *See also* Oneg Shabbath
Sachsenhausen concentration camp, 80
Salaman, Redcliffe Nathan, 95
Sammlung fun Kazet Lider (Anthology of Concentration Camp Poems), 156
Sandbostel, 80
Sanek, Moshe, 197
Schleswig-Holstein, 15, 81
Schonfeld, Rabbi Solomon, 93, 114
Schumann, Robert, 21
Schumann Plan, 21
Schwadron, Genia, 176
Schwartz, Joseph J., 106–7
Schwartz, Reuma, 176
Second Congress of the Liberated Jews in the British Zone, 135–37

Index

Sefer la-golah (Books for the Diaspora), 178
Selby, Selma, 178
Semit-Times, 10
Sasel, 80
Shavuot, 158, 185
She'erit Hapletah (Surviving Remnant, Holocaust survivors), 74, 121, 162, 219; defined as ex-territorial immigrant population, 215; dissolution of, 155; First Congress of, 66, 72, 76, 100, 110, 158; and formation of new Jewish national identity, 9, 221, 223; functional Zionism, 216, 223; publication of *Unzer Sztyme*, 68; Second Congress of, 110, 113, 115, 117, 123, 202. *See also* Jewish survivors, in postwar Germany
Silverman, Samuel Sidney, 75, 76, 99, 137
Simhath Torah, 158
Singer, Yerahmiel, 197
Sington, Derrick A., 37, 38, 51, 57, 58
Sokolovsky, General, 16
Solomon, Heinz, 197
Solomon, Robert, 99, 100, 123, 134, 137, 138, 221
Sports events, Bergen-Belsen DP camp, 161
Sports groups, Bergen-Belsen DP camp, photo of, 162
Staatskommissar für die Opfer des Faschismus (State Commissioner for the Victims of Fascism), 85, 132
Stern, Frank, 11
Supplies for Overseas Survivors (SOS), 107
Synagogue Council of America, 213
Szesarik, Anshel, 197

Tachles, 10

Theatrical activity, in DP camps, 158–59, 218
Theresienstadt, 29, 30, 79, 80, 81, 82, 83
Trepman, Paul Pinhas, 69–70, 150; co-head of CC Cultural Affairs Department, 77, 110; emigration to America, 211, 223; founding of elementary school, 170; and *Unzer Sztyme* (Our Voice), 73, 77, 154–55; and *Wochenblatt*, 155
Tribüne, 10
Trizonia, 22
Trobe, Jacob L., 75, 107
Truman, Harry, 35, 190, 210
Truman Doctrine, 21
Tsamriyon, Tsemah, 105
Tuberculosis, 40
Twenty-second Zionist Congress, 73, 165, 205
Tykoshinsky, Nizan, 175
Typhoid, 40, 45
Tzurrik fun Gehinom (Back from Hell), 156

Umansky, David, 176
Union of Orthodox Hebrew Congregations in England, 93
United Jewish Appeal, 107, 123
United Nations Relief and Rehabilitation Administration (UNRRA), 17, 18, 24, 91, 148
United Nations Special Committee on Palestine (UNSCOP), 193
United Resistance Movement in Palestine (Tenu'at HaMeri), 192
United States: immigration regulations, 33, 36, 204, 210, 212; immigration to, 210; resettlement policy, 25
United States Holocaust Memorial Museum, 68

Index

United Zionist Organization (Histadrut Zionit Ahidah), 106, 164, 165, 197, 200–201
Untergrundler, 30, 85
Unzer Front (Our Front), 155
Unzer Sztyme (Our Voice), 68, 69, 70, 77, 110, 154–55; coverage of news of Jewish communities, 121; coverage of religious and national holidays, 184; first issues, 73; priority to matters concerning Zionism, 196

Vaad Leumi (National Council), 103
Van Dam, Hendrik, 97, 133, 135, 139
Verband der Jüdischen Gemeinden Nordwestdeutschland (Association of the Jewish Communities of North-West Germany), 140
Verband der jüdischen Studenten in der britischen Zone (Union of Jewish Students in the British Zone), 187
Vereinigung der Verfolgten des Naziregimes (Association of Those Persecuted by the Nazi Regime) (VVN), 124
Vereinigung der von Nürnberger Gesetzen Bertoffenen (Association of Those Affected by the Nuremberg Laws), 124, 126
Vernant, Jacques, 28
Vilensky, Rabbi, 93
Viteles, Harry, 108, 120
Vocational training, 144–48. *See also* Agricultural training; *Hachsharah*

Wall newspapers, 156
Wandsbeck, 80
Warburg, Edward, 106
Warburg, Felix M., 106
Warburg, Max, 86
Weber, Rivka, 176
Weddings, at Bergen-Belsen DP camp, 149–50
Weingreen, Bertha, 96, 174, 180
Weingreen, Jack Jacob, 146, 183, 185
Weintraub, Shmuel (Samuel), 77, 110, 114, 197
Weizmann, Chaim, 24
Welfare agencies: employment of camp inmates, 148; limited psychological help, 178; mother and child care, 151. *See also* American Jewish Joint Distribution Committee; British Jewish Relief Unit; Chief Rabbi's Religious Emergency Council; Jewish Agency for Palestine, Council of Welfare Groups for the Diaspora; United Nations Relief and Rehabilitation Association
Welfare projects, role of German Jewish communities, 128
White Paper of 1939, 33, 189, 190
Wiedergutmachung (compensation), 133; agreement, 26. *See also* Compensation; Indemnification; Reparations; Restitution
Williams, Eryl Hall, 45
Winnik, Simcha, 119
Wodlinger, David B., 108
Wohlfahrtsstelle (welfare station), 138–39
Wollheim, Norbert, 69, 111, 137, 150; aim of unifying Council of Jewish Communities and CC, 134, 135; and *Arbeitsgemeinschaft* (Work Association), 132, 133, 134; attempt to subordinate German Jewish community to world Jewish representation, 139; avoidance of violence in

response to *Exodus* affair, 193–94; close working relationship with Rosensaft, 121; emigration to America, 223; founding of Lübeck Jewish community, 89–90; head of Council of the Jewish Communities in the British Zone, 133; living conditions, 144; photograph of, 112; relations with world Jewish leaders, 122–23; at Second Congress of the Liberated Jews in the British Zone, 136–37; skepticism about future of Jews in Germany, 213–14; testimony before Anglo-American Committee, 190–91; trips to London, 100; at unveiling of Jewish monument at Belsen, 76, 192; Vice-Chairman of CC, 77, 110; view of the LV, 131–32

World Jewish Congress (WJC), 24, 98, 121; and CC, 122; claims submitted to Allies, 53; 1948 convention, 138; efforts to change British policy, 74; in "The Future of the Jews in Germany" conference, 212; at Second Congress of the Liberated Jews in the British Zone, 136

World Zionist Congress, Twenty-second, 73, 165, 197, 205

World Zionist Executive, 74

World Zionist Organization, 24, 77, 165

Wrubel, Helen, 102, 170, 180, 182

WVHA (Wirtschafts-Verwaltungshauptamt), 37

Yaffeh, Menuha, 176

Yedi'ot (Information), 155

Yeshiva *She'erit Israel* in Bergen-Belsen, 170

Yiddish, as common language in camps, 179

Yiddisher Arbeter Biene (Jewish Workers' Theater), 159

Yom Ha'atzmaut (Israel Independence Day), 161, 185

Youth Aliyah, 112, 176

Youth movements, 129, 163, 185, 186

Yugoslavian Anti-Fascist Committee, 68–69

Zerubavel, Ya'akov, 155

Zionism: as center of activity in the DP camps, 220; effect on post-Holocaust Jewish identity, 9; immigration policy and "Grand National," 208–9; and struggle for aliyah against British immigration policy in Palestine, 137

Zionist activity, in the British Zone: assistance to *Briha*, 198; kibbutz movements in Belsen, 164; organization in Belsen, 199–202; struggle for aliyah, 197–202; Zionist education within the formal and informal system, 185

Zionist Committee, British Zone, 200

Zionist Revisionist movement. *See* Revisionists

Zionist shekel, 200

Zoiten (Times), 155

Zonenausschuss (Zone Committee), 132

Zum Sieg (For Victory), 155